HIPPOCRENE STANDARD DICTIONARY
YOEME-ENGLISH
ENGLISH-YOEME

With a Comprehensive Grammar of Yoeme Language

HIPPOCRENE STANDARD DICTIONARY YOEME-ENGLISH ENGLISH-YOEME

With a Comprehensive Grammar of Yoeme Language

FELIPE S. MOLINA

HERMINIA VALENZUELA

DAVID LEEDOM SHAUL

HIPPOCRENE BOOKS
New York

For information, address:
HIPPOCRENE BOOKS, INC.
171 Madison Avenue
New York, NY 10016

ISBN 0-7818-0633-X

Printed in the United States of America.

CONTENTS

SI'IMEM VETCHI'IVO

Tua tuu hiapsimmake into tu'uwapo inime Yoem noki livrom ya'awak bwe'ituk wa Yoemra ketun waka vem nokta eiya into a sauwa inime wasuktiam weye'epo.

Si'ime wa yo'ora aet liohbwaniawa bwe'ituk vempo inim bwan bwiapo hiapsaka waka vem nokta a nookaka nah kuaktek. Vempo ket nah vuhtia ket wame ili uusim yeu kateme ket tuu hiapseka ameu Yoem nokpo nookak. Ume uusim véa ket waka Yoem nokta vem kovapo a namyak hunuen véa ian tahtia ket wa Yoem noki ketun inim anîapo ket ili nokwa. Wáate ket inim aane tua waka vem nokta a tuu eiya into ama vutti a nake, ka a ta'aruvaeka ea.

Hunuensan wame yo'ora into wame ehkuelampo tekipanoame nau eaka inime livrommet tekipanoak. Inime livrom si'imem vetchi'ivo.

Enchim tuu hiapsimmak into tu'uwapo inime livrom sauwane. Inia velekika enchim mampo taawak. Tua Lios em chiokoe u'uttesiavu, si'ime yeu tahtia.

PREFACE

The Yoeme language is an oral, largely unwritten tradition. The *Yoeme-English/English-Yoeme Standard Dictionary* contains over ten thousand words in both Yoeme and English. This bilingual dictionary is also of use to scholars, and is the first large dictionary of the language.

The 'Dictionary' is organized alphabetically from Yoeme to English, and English to Yoeme. A complete guide to Yoeme spelling and pronunciation is given. Directions for use (including abbreviations used) precede the Yoeme-English section.

The *Yoeme-English/English-Yoeme Standard Dictionary* can be used at all levels to teach Yoeme. It is a resource for students, teachers, parents, and others interested in this beautiful language. It will be especially useful in the years to come, as people gather, edit, and enjoy the literature from Yoeme culture.

It is hoped that this *Yoeme-English/English-Yoeme Standard Dictionary*, which is the first lengthy dictionary of a Cahitan language, will be the start of a dictionary tradition in this field. It is also hoped that it can be translated into Spanish for use in Mexico.

ACKNOWLEDGMENTS

This dictionary could not have been written alone. We thank all who have helped us. We give special thanks to the following people for their kind help and support:

Our Elders, for the knowledge and for welcoming us into their homes: Estefana Garcia, Maria Murrieta, Luis Ochoa, Maria Ochoa, Manuel Valencia, and Juanita Paula Valle;

Our Elders who have helped in the past: Anselma Tonopuame'a Anguis (deceased) and Rosario Bacaneri Castillo, Tomas Martinez (dec.), Francisca Martinez (dec.), Romana Sanchez (dec.), all of Marana; Ignacio Sombra, Antonia Flores, Vicente Molina, Teresa Baltazar, Vicente Baltazar, all of Potam; Alfonso Leyva Flores (dec.) of Las Guasimas; and Jose Maria Jaimez of Compuertam.

Our Yoeme Bilingual Teaching Assistants and Instructional Specialists for their help and encouragement in reviewing the manuscript: Jenny Cancio, Rosa Estrella, Sophia Morales (Johnson Elementary); Maria Cupis, Maria Palanes (Lawrence Elementary); Frances Delgado, Susana Garcia, Eulalia Valenzuela (Richey Elementary); Sam Castillo, Feliciana Martinez, Jenny Murrietta (Hohokam Middle School);

To Luis Valenzuela Sr., who began working in the 1940s on a Yoeme and English dictionary to preserve the Yoeme way of life.

To the Pascua Yaqui Tribe for their kind heart and strong support throughout this endeavor;

To the Bilingual Education and Hispanic Studies Department, Tucson Unified School District, for support during a very early phase of this work;

To the Arizona Humanities Council for financial help in the earliest stages of work on the dictionary;

To the published and unpublished works of Jean B. Johnson, Dr. Fernando Escalante, John Dedrick, Dr. Jacqueline Lindenfeld, Dr. Eloise Jelinek;

And last, but not least, to Dr. Larry Evers (Department of English, University of Arizona), the Bureau of Applied Research in Anthropology (University of Arizona), Alan Ferg (Archivist, Arizona State Museum), and Tumacacori National Historic Park.

F.S.M.
H.V.
D.L.S.

ACKNOWLEDGMENTS

HOW TO USE THIS DICTIONARY

Each main entry consists of four parts: the entry, an abbreviation for the part of speech, and a definition with any relevant grammatical or other information following in parentheses. Note that the definition may be expanded to include Spanish translations at a later date.

There are several conventions that must be noted.

1. Some nouns (mass nouns) may require the plural suffix -m; where possible, these are defined with the English plural suffix -s in parentheses (see ainam).

2. In Yaqui, as in English, there are words that sound alike, but mean different things (homonyms). These are listed separately and indicated by subscripts; see hoa₁ 'do, make' and hoa₂ 'put, place them'.

3. There are a number of pairs of homophones that are distinguished by stress. Such pairs are historical accidents, and are distinguished in written Yoeme by accent marks over the stress vowel; see véa 'then' and veá 'skin, hide'. There are only fourteen such pairs, and thus there is need to only write stress marks on these roots (and their derivatives), not on all the words in the language, for which stress is predictable.

4. Sometimes it is helpful to cross-reference one entry with another ("cf. ha'abwek" means to also consult the entry for ha'abwek). This is common where there are two stems for singular and plural (suppletive stems), and where there are synonyms or words closely related in meaning.

There are three kinds of information that are included after an entry in ( ).

1. The first kind of information includes variants and synonyms. For example, tatte 'choke on food' cross-references the dictionary user to hukte 'choke on liquids' and vice-versa.

2. The next information listed is about suppletive stems. This will include sg. for "requires singular subject" or pl. for "requires plural subject", or else sg. obj. for "requires singular object" or pl. obj. for "requires plural object". The entry for naa kaáte indicates that this verb requires a plural subject, and also tells the reader that the singular form is naa weye.

3. The third kind of information is grammatical. For nouns, this may include a locative form (loc.). For adjectives, this may

13

include the past tense form (pst.) and plural (pl.) if these forms are not predictable. For verbs, the forms listed are the past tense form (pst.) if irregular, the combining form (comb.; if this is the same as the entry, the virgule ~ is inserted as comb.), and the reduplicated form. For example, the entry muuke 'die' tells the user, after noting information about suppletive forms, that the past form is muukuk, the combining stem is muk-, and the reduplication is mumuke. For more on combining stems and reduplication, please refer to Appendix A ("Yoeme Alphabet and Spelling").

If there is more than one definition for an entry, the grammatical information is given after all the definitions have been listed. For example, nasonte 'harm, ruin, spoil' has a secondary definition 'break down (referring to machines)', and the grammatical information is listed after both senses.

ABBREVIATIONS

<	derives from
->	becomes
=	equals
aff.	affectionate
adj.	adjective
adv.	adverb
col.	collective
comb.	combining form
cf.	compare, see also
conj.	conjunction
derog.	derogative
d.o.	direct object
dv.	ditransitive verb
emph.	emphatic form
ex.	example
exp.	expression, phrase
fem.	female speaking
fig.	figurative
fut.	future
gen.	generic term
hab.	habitual
imp.	imperative
interj.	interjection
iv.	intransitive verb
lit.	literally
loc.	locative
masc.	male speaking
n.	noun
neg.	negative
num.	numeral
obj.	object(ive)
paus.	pausal form
pl.	plural
pl. obj.	plural object (used alone, this indicates that a plural object is required)
pn.	pronoun
poss.	possessive
postp.	postposition
pref.	prefix
pres.	present
pst.	past
ptc.	particle

rdp.	reduplication (means habitual, progressive, or distributive; "no rdp." means that a reduplicated form is not usual)
refl.	reflexive
resp.	in or as a response
s.	song language
ser.	sermon style
sg.	singular
Son.	Sonoran usage
sp.	species
Sp.	Spanish
subj.	subject(ive)
suf.	suffix
syn.	synonym
tv.	transitive verb
var.	variant(s)

YOEME-ENGLISH DICTIONARY

A

a *pn.* her, his, its; her, him, it (*cf.* apo'ik)
a"ache *rdp.* of ache, laugh
a"ansu *rdp.* of ansu, finish up
a"awa *rdp.* of a'awa, ask for
a'a'ate *rdp.* of a'ate, carry on head
a'aakta *rdp.* of aakta, put on head to carry
a'aetua *dv.* be cussing someone out
a'amu *rdp.* of amuse, go hunting
a'ana *tv.* dress (with a or au; ~-, *rdp.* a'aana)
a'aniame *n.* helper, assistant
      emo ~ *n.* colleague, ally
a'asoa *iv.* fertile, able to bear children
a'asoaatua *tv.* deliver a child
a'asoatuame *n.* midwife (with yee)
a'ate *tv.* carry on head (a'ati-, a'a'ate)
a'ava *adv.* it ... here (with verbs of transfer such as toha or bwise); ~ toha. Bring it here.
a'avo *adv.* there (over there); Yuke ~ weye. Rain is coming.
a'avo aneme *n.* visitor
a'avose *tv.* feed visitors (aavos-, aavose)
a'awa *tv.* ask for (a'aw-, a"awa)
a'awe- *comb.* of aawe, be able
a'awek *pst.* of aawe, be able
a'awia *iv.* get fat; Tahkaim yee ~. Tortillas are fattening.
a'ayu *iv.* 1. there is/there are 2. be in stock (*cf.* kakkaitu) (*pst.* ayukan, ayu-); Aman muunim ~k. There are beans there. Ime livrom mesapo ~. The book(s) is/are on the table.
a'e *interj.* ay, well (*fem.*; *masc.* abwe)
aa *adv.* can, be able (*ex.* aa tottotte, flexible, can be bent); Aapo chea a vichaka ka aa weyentia. When s/he saw it, s/he was unable to move. Ketun usitaka ne ~ vuivuiten. As a boy, I could run.
    ~ hinu *iv.* afford (*lit.* can buy)
    ~ tekipanoa *iv.* be industrious
aa'akte *rdp.* of aakte, put on head
aache *iv.* 1. laugh 2. grin, smile (a'at-, a"ache)
aakame *n.* rattlesnake; *cf.* awa'ala
aakame nakapit *n.* type of rattlesnake (*lit.* deaf rattlesnake)
aaki *n.* pitahaya, organpipe cactus (*Stenocereus thurberi*), the fruit of which is a favorite food
aakta *tv.* put on head to carry 2. gore (~-, a'aakta); Tooro ne ~k. The bull gored me.

aakte *iv.* put on one's head (aakti-, aa'akte)

aamak *pn.* with her/him/it (comitative); *cf.* -mak

aamu *tv.* hunt (~~, a'amu)

aane *iv.* do; be around, about (*pst.* aayuk/auka; an-/au-/ane-; a'ane);
       tiusi ~, embarrassing; *ex.* kaupo aukamta, that which is in the
       mountains. noki ama aune, there would be talk; Itom ansuko
       yuktaetek. After we finished, it started to rain. Haise ~? How are
       you doing? Wepul choki kalalipapati ~. One star is twinkling.
       Amak ume miisim into ume totoim si haiti ama a'ane.
       Sometimes the cats and the chickens mess around in there.
       Abwe heewi ne ket kia enchim suate vicha enchim ovisi aneo
       huni'i. I'm bothering you when you're very busy. Sinkuenta
       peesom hiva ama aayuk. There was fifty dollars left over.

aapa *n.* harp

aapaleo *n.* harpist

aapat *pn.* in front of her/him/it, ahead of her/him/it (with verbs of
       motion)

aapo *pn.* he, she, it

aapolai *adv.* by one's self

aasa *n.* lips; rim of a pot

aasos *n.* garlic

aasowaara *n.* nephew, niece

aavo rukte *iv.* approach, get close to

aawam *n.* horn, antler (*comb.* awa-); U masokova ~ kottek. The
       dearhead's antlers broke.

aawas *n.* obscuring one's view

aawas kopte *tv.* forget (*syn.* veaskopte, wahkopte)

aawe *iv.* be able, know how to do a physical thing (*var.* aa; *pst.* a'awek;
       a'awe- or aawe-); *cf.* ta'a, hu'unea; Aa kuvahe hoa. He knows
       how to make drums. Aa warim hoa. She knows how to make
       baskets. Aa karote weetua. S/he can drive a car. U lootor ka
       ama ~. The doctor is not competent (*syn.* ka tu'i).

aayuk *iv.* 1. did, was (*pst.* of aane) 2. be room (*ex.* kampo ~, there is
       room in the yard)

abwa'atu *adj.* edible

abwe *interj.* well (*masc.*, *var.* bwe; *syn.* huntunko; *fem.* a'e); A: Emesu
       haisa aane—kave ko'okoe? B: Abwe Diosta ela'apo ian lautipo
       kave ko'okoe. A: How are all of you (in the family) doing—is
       everyone well? B: Well, God be thanked, just now no one is sick.
       A: Haisa ka womtek? B: Abwe heewi, apo chea a vichaka ka aa
       weyentia. A: Wasn't s/he frightened? B: Why yes, s/he was unable
       to move when s/he saw it.
       ~ he *interj.* well, yes

achai *n.* father (*masc.*; *s.* achali)
       ~ O'ola, God (*syn.* Itom ~)
       ~ Taa'a, Father Sun (the Creator in myths; *cf.* Lios Achai Ola)

Achai, Itom *n.* God, Jesus, Our Father

achali *n.* father (*s.*; = achai)

achaiwai *n.* father (as family head)

achakaari *n.* crab

ache'a *n.* one who laughs a lot (*var.* ache'era)

ache'era *var.* of ache'a, one who laughs a lot

achi *pn.* at/on her, him, it

aduana *n.* customs (at border)

advervio *n.* adverb

ae$_1$ *pn.* of her/him/it (with ichakte, rohikte, tiiwe)
> ~ amapo *adv.* after, behind
> ~ chaka'aku *postp.* beside
> ~ nachi *postp.* by, near (*resp.*)

ae$_2$ *n.* mother (*var.* aye); Itom Ae, the Virgin Mary

aechi *postp.* on

aepat *postp.* in front of; U hamut aepat weye. The woman is ahead.

aet *postp.* on her, him, it; *cf.* iat; Aapo ~ hiohte. S/he is writing about him.
Aapo Kahe'emetat livrom yak. S/he wrote a book about Cajeme.
> ~ ea *iv.* depend on someone; Apo aet ea. S/he depends on
> her/him.
> ~ eetu *iv.* be dependable
> ~ eewachi *iv.* be dependable
> ~ cha'aku *interj.* behind
> ~ hohowame *n.* bathroom stool
> ~ nooka *iv.* criticize
> ~ venta *tv.* slander

aetana *postp.* from/alongside her, him, it

agila *n.* eagle

ahi'itu *adj.* potable, drinkable

aho *n.* amaranth (*syn.* wee'e)

ahta *conj.* until, up to a certain point (*var.* ahtake); Ahta ke aman yahak.
They finally got there.

Ahteeka *n.* 1. Mexicano, Aztec 2. the Matachin dance

ai$_1$ *postp.* with (by means of)

ai$_2$ *interj.* wow; A: Im sofaapo chuvala yeesa. B: Heewi, tua su tu'i. ~
tu'isi bwalko. A: Sit here on the sofa for awhile. B: Yes, it's truly
good. Wow, and so soft.

ainam *n.* flour

aetua *dv.* swear, curse

affiler *n.* safety pine

aiya *n.* guasima (*Guazuma ulmifolia*), a medium sized tree with edible
fruit, the wood being used for the tampaleo's drum and drum
making in general

aki taaka *n.* organpipe cactus or pitahaya fruit

akia *n.* ditch, trench

ako *n.* sister (older; *fem.*)

akwo *n.* saguaro skeleton, dry saguaro ribs

ala *conj., interj.* 1. *conj.* if 2. *interj.* well now 3. contrastive particle; ian ~,
right now; ~ a tekipanoatek tu'i'ean. If s/he could work, it would

be good. ~ ian itou yevihne u heeka. Well, the storm is heading our way. Aman sahak ~ a teune. If they go there, they will find it. Hunuen a sikak ~tu'i machi. If you cut your hair like that, it would be good. Hunuen aayuk ~ tu'i. It's good for you to do that. A: Waáte ka yee nake. B: Aapo ~ yee nake. A: S/he doesn't care about other people. B: But s/he does care about others.

ala maachi *iv.* keep it up (said to a Pascola dancer as an encouragement when he is dancing); ~, pahko'ola, tua e sumwachim wokek. Keep it up, Pascola, you really have frightening feet (are dancing up a storm).

ala'akun *interj.* so it is, keep it up, atta boy

ala'amai *n.* bullsnake

alasu *interj.* 1. how nice (*resp.*) 2. yes, you're right; A: Hose pahko'ola yi'ivae. B: ~. A: Joe wants to dance pascola. B: That's good. A: U hamut tuu hiapsek. B: ~. A: That lady is really good hearted. B: You're right.

alavalo *n.* dawn service

alavansam *n.* 1. hymn, chant 2. the tuning and music used from the beginning of a fiesta until midnight (see soonim); Bwe chupuk u ~teame u naatei, kanaria. The alabanzas finish that which was started, the canarios.

alavea *interj.* I see, really?, is that so?; A: Maala ko'okoe. B: ~. A: Mother is sick. B: Oh, I see.

Aleluya *n.* Easter Sunday

alevenak yaa *tv.* copy

alevena *interj.* the same (in reply); A: Hoseta vena? B: ~. A: Like Joe? B: Just so/just the same.

alfonram *n.* rug

alhevra *n.* algebra

alilite *iv.* be loose (*pst.* ~n; aliliti-; no *rdp.*); In tamim ~. My teeth are loose. U sapti ~. The wall is loose.

aliliti *adv.* loose (with aane); Kuta ~ aane. The post is loose. Tamim ~ aane. The teeth are loose.

alkohol *n.* alcohol

allea *adj.* happy, content; lively, exciting; *cf.* allete'ea; Aleskau saka'apo tu'isi ~ machi. It would be exciting to go to Alaska.

alle'eetua *tv.* console

alleaka *adv.* happily

alleaka aman yevihne *exp.* good-bye (*lit.* happily you will arrive)

alleaka yeu matchune *exp.* goodnight (*lit.* may you come out happily in the morning)

alle'ela *iv.* has gotten happy

allete'ea *iv.* become happy, content

alletua *iv.* amuse

yee ~wame *n.* amusement

allewame *n.* health, fitness, well being

20

almanaake *n.* calendar

almario *n.* cupboard (especially standing)

alpes *n.* flag-bearer

altaria *n.* altar

alva *n.* dawn

alvanyi *n.* mason

am *pn.* them (*var.* ame)

ama *adv. var.* of aman(i), there; Siari bwa'amta bwa'awapo ~ aune.
       Vegetables are the best food.
        ~ hiove *tv.* try on
        ~ vutti *adv.* a lot, desperately
        ~ vutti machi, *iv.* be harsh
        ~ vuttia *iv.* exaggerate, say too much
        ~ weye *iv.* belong there, go there, fit in

amae *adv.* over there (*cf.* aman(i), wannavo)
        ~ yehte *iv.* change one's mind (*pl.* ~ hoote)
        ~ yeehte *iv.* always change one's mind (*pl.* ~ hohote)

amak(o) *adv.* sometimes; ~ aapo aavo yepsa. Sometimes s/he comes over.
        ~ weama *iv.* date (as a couple)

aman(i) *adv.* there (near speaker; *var.* ama; *cf.* amae, um, hunam(a),
       wannavo); Vempo totomekapo ~ vempo chea hooka. They have a
       monetary advantage.
       aman vicha, *adv.* toward over there

amapo *postp.* behind (not moving), at/on there (with a noun in *obj.* case,
       or the following paradigm: ne, ee, ae, itom, enchim, vempo'im)

amau vicha *adv.* backwards; Empo amau vicha weyeteka, empo hani em
       mala kokoe tatapne tea. They say if you walk backwards (at
       night) you will make your mother sick.

amawa *adv.* it ... to the back (with verbs of transfer or
       placement; *pl.* ~m); ~m hoa, set them in the back

amawi *adv.* towards there, behind, in the back (*resp.*)

ame *pn.* of am, them

amea *pn.* of them (with ichakte, rohikte, tiiwe)

amemak *pn.* with them (comitative)

amene *adv.* (so) much; ia ~, this much; veeki ~, so much; wa ~, that much

amepat *pn.* in front of them, ahead of them (with verbs of motion)

amet *pn.* at/on them

ametana *pn.* from/alongside them

ameu *pn.* to/into/beside/from them; *cf.* -wi, -u

amma'ali *adv.* 1. properly 2. medium in color (*cf.* kutwo)
       ka ~ anwame *n.* sin
       ~ aane *iv.* do the right thing, behave properly
       ~ hia *iv.* say the right thing
       ~ nooka *iv.* talk properly
       ~ siki *adj.* pink
       ~ suka *adj.* tepid/lukewarm

amoe *n.*, *iv.* 1. *n.* cooked grains 2. *iv.* get thick, agglutinate, increase in size by swelling (~-, a'amoe)

amto *pn.* from them

amu *n.* grandchild (of daughter; *fem.*)

amu- *comb.* of amuse, go hunting

amureo *n.* hunter

amuse *iv.* go hunting (*sg.*; *pl.* amuvo; *pst.* amusuk, amu-, a'amu)

amusuk *pst.* of amuse, go hunting

ana *comb.* of a, object marker and ne, I; Ana hu'une'eiyak waka ama tekipanoamta. I found out who works there.

andarera *n.* walker (for elderly)

anheles *n.* angel

anhelito *n.* little angel

anhelwarda *n.* guardian angel

anhenhivle *n.* ginger

ánia *tv.* help, aid, assist (~-, a'ania); Dios ket apo enchi ~ne. God himself will help you. Dios em chania. God help you (traditional greeting; *sg.* addressee; *pl.* addressee: Dios em chaniavu; see hiokoe, keche, kette). Tu'i u ~. It's nice weather. Ka tu'i u ~. The weather is not nice.
au ~ *iv.* defend self; ka aa au ánia, defenseless; Apo au ániane. S/he will defend themself.

ániawame *n.* assistance

anía *n.* 1. world 2. weather (*s.* aniwa); ~ au yoa, earthquake; ~ vuite, earthquake; Bwe'tuk yoko ~ ka tu'ivae. Because tomorrow the weather will not be good. Yoko ~ tu'ine. Tomorrow the weather will be good. Tu'i u ~. It's nice outside. ~ haisa maachi? What's the weather like? ~ ka tu'ivae. The weather looks bad.

anilio *n.* ring (finger)

anima *n.* soul

animalim *n.* beast, animal (particularly domesticated)

Animam *n.* Book of Departed Souls

Animam Mikwa *n.* All Souls Day (*lit.* Giving to Departed Souls)

anisim *n.* anise

aniwa *n.* world (*s.*; = ánia); Empo sewa yo huya ~ (*s.*). You (are) an enchanted flower wilderness world.

anoki'ichi *n.* liar; U ili o'ou tu'isi ~. The little boy is such a liar.

anoki'ichia *n.* lie, falsehood
~ta nooka *tv.* lie, tell falsehood (may also be used with the verb teuwa); Aapo ~ta neu teuwak. S/he told me a lie.

ansu *iv.* have just finished (~-, a"ansu)
nok ~ *tv.* conclude, summarize (orally)
hiohtei ~ *tv.* conclude, summarize (in writing)

ansuwa *iv.* end, terminate, be finishing up

antas *n.* litter (for holy figure)

ante *interj.* let's (used only for going; *cf.* te); Ante puevlowi. Let's go to town. Ante vihtammewi. Let's go to the movies.

antema *interj.* okay, let's go (*resp.* to antevu)

antevu *interj.* let's go (to *sg.* or *pl.* addressee); *cf.* antema

antihom *n.* eyeglasses (*Son.*; *cf.* leentim)

antuari *n.* whore, prostitute, loose woman

anwa *iv.* be there, be around; Wa'emammeu ~. They hang out at
       Guaymas.

apa *n.* grandfather (maternal)

apat *postp.* ahead of her, him, it
       ~ kivake *iv.* cut (in line)

apela *pn.* one's self, herself, himself (*var.* apola)

apelai *n.* 1. alone, single (unmarried) 2. old bachelor, old maid

apohtolo *n.* apostle

Apo'i *n.* the Devil (*lit.* he himself; the Devil's real name is not used
       because its use might summon him; if one whistles at night, the
       Devil will answer and lure the person into the wilderness)

apo'ik *pn.* her, him, it (*cf.* a; apo'ik is used to code different subject in
       subordinate clauses, while a is used to code same subject); I u
       tesoro ~ teaka'u. This is the treasure which he found. Apo
       hu'unea haveeta a vichaka'apo. He$_1$ knows the one who saw
       him$_1$. Apo hu'unea haveeta a vichaka'apo. He$_1$ knows the one
       who saw him$_2$. ~ a maka. Give it to her/him.

apola *var.* of apela, one's self

arau *n.* plough

arko *n.* arch

armorio *n.* cupboard

arosim *n.* rice

arte *n.* art

artikulo *n.* article

asafaata *n.* baking pan

asaroonim *n.* hoe

asautu *adj.* good at following orders

ase'ebwa *n.* father-in-law

asei tuuna *n.* olive

aseite *n.* oil, olive oil

aseka *n.* mother-in-law

aso'ola *n.* baby, infant; chuu'u ~, puppy; miisi ~, kitten; kava'i ~, colt

asoa *n.,iv.* 1. *n.* child (of either sex; *fem.*; *cf.* uusi, maara) 2. *iv.* give birth
       (~-, a'asoa)

asoakari *n.* placenta, afterbirth

asoavae *iv.* be pregnant

asu *n.* grandmother (maternal)

asukatua *tv.* sweeten

Asum Kawi *n.* Grandmothers' Mountain

asuuka *n.* sugar

at *pn. var.* of aet, on her/him/it

ata *pn.* we ... her/him (< a + te)

atala *adv.* on one's back; be inside out, upside down, backwards atbwa *tv.* laugh at (~-, a'atbwa); ne ~, laugh at me

ateka *interj.* let me see

atleta *n.* athlete

ato *pn.* from her/him/it; *cf.* -to

atte'a *n.* clothing, belongings, supplies; U vuuru uka ~ta pupuate. The donkey is carrying supplies.

atte'ak *tv.* own, possess (*pst.* ~an, attea-); Aapo karita ~. S/he owns a house.

atte'akame *n.* owner

atte'ari *n.* owned item

　　　im tahti ~ *n.* the sacred Yoeme boundary (*syn.* lindero)

atu'ulitu *adj.* loveable, likeable

atwame *n.* smiles, laughter

au₁ *postp.* 1. toward, into her/him/it 2. beside, next to her/him/it 3. from her/him (with verbs of transaction such as 'buy'); *cf.* -wi, -u

au₂ *pn.* herself, himself, itself; Wa bweha'i kechia ~ bwikria. The gourd also sings for itself (everything has a language of its own). In acahi chea Yoronata ~ vitlatia. My father saw the Llorona.

　　~ án'a *iv.* defend self physically

　　~ bwasa *iv.* purify self by smudging

　　~ hamutle *iv.* think of one's self as a woman (*ex.* sissy, effeminate, male homosexual)

　　~ hela *adv.* close, near; U kava'i au hela weye. The horse is walking close to him.

　　~ hima'ala, *iv.* let one's self go, go to pot, decline

　　~ hiokoe *iv.* be greedy, selfish, egotistical

　　~ hitale *iv.* be conceited, think one's self important

　　~ i'a *adj.* unkind, discourteous, cruel, brutal; bully

　　~ ___-le *iv.* self identify as (*ex.* ~ hapatle, self identify as Apache; ~ yoile, self identify as Mexican)

　　~ me'a *iv.* commit suicide (always in *pst.* me'ak or *fut.* me'ane)

　　~ nenka *iv.* surrender

　　~ nokria *iv.* defend self verbally

　　~ o'oule *iv.* think of one's self as a man (*ex.* tomboy, lesbian)

　　~ oule *iv.* brave, tough, courageous

　　~ sua *iv.* be careful, conscientious

　　~ tu'ure *iv.* be conceited, vain

　　~ uttia *iv.* boast; Vahim huvek kialikun tu'isi au uttia.

au'ori *n.* devil's claw (*Proboscidea parviflora*)

auka *iv. pst.* of aayuk; Haisempo ~? What happened to you?

aula *iv.* be wrong, be troubling (with haisempo); Haisempaula? What's the matter with you?

aula'apo *n.* where it is wrong

　　ko'okosi a ~'apo *n.* wound

aulim *n.* clams

aulireo *n.* clam gatherer

aulivea *n.* clam shell

ausu'uli *adj.* pure

       empo kia ota ~ *exp.* you are nothing but skin and bones

avachek *iv.* have an older brother

avachi *n.* brother (older; *fem.*)

avae *iv.* set corn

avah nawa *n.* cottonwood root, used for carving masks

avai *n.* corn on the cob, elote, fresh corn ear

       ~ choonim *n.* cornsilk

       ~ nohim *n.* green corn tamales

       ~ sita *n.* young corn (just developing on stalk)

avaniiko *n.* fan

avas *n. comb.* of avaso, cottonwood

       ~ naawa *n.* cottonwood root

       ~ veá *n.* cottonwood bark

avaso *n.* 1. cottonwood (*Populus sp.*), planted for shade, the boughs being used in rituals and the logs for ramada beams (Pascola masks are made from cottonwood because they are light in weight)
       2. the town of Alamos, Sonora

Avaso Kawi *n.* Cottonwood Mountain, a place in Rio Yaqui; Avas Kaura *adv.* from Cottonwood Mountain

ave *adv.* almost, be about to (*cf.* vatte); ~ ne muuke. I almost died. Em papa ~ yepsa. Your father is about to come home.

aveena *n.* 1. oats 2. cereal

avesu *adv.* almost; U yuku ~ itou yepsa. The rain is almost getting to us.

avesula *adv.* almost; U yuku ~. The rain is here.

avetuko *adv.* almost time for, in a while, tonight; Pahko ~ naatene. The ceremony will start tonight.

avi'itom *n.* habit (clothing; *syn.* santo supem)

aviasi—n *n.* airport

avo *adv. var.* of a'avo, there; ~ hela rukte. Come closer.

avogáo *n.* lawyer

avrekookim *n.* apricot

Avril *n.* April

awa *comb.* of aawam, antlers/horns

awa'ala *n.* sidewinder rattlesnake

awahkopte *tv.* forget (*var.* aveaskopte); *cf.* ta'aru

awakame *n.* horned one

awi$_1$ *adj.* fat, obese, chubby, corpulent; *cf.* topa'a

awi$_2$ *postp.* to her, him, it

awia *iv.* get fat, obese (~-, a'awia); Luis che'wasu ~. Louis is getting fat.

awilovolai *n.* husky, plump

awiria *tv.* fatten (~-, a'awiria)

Awohto *n.* August (*var.* Awosto); ~ 27-po, on August 27

aya'awi *n.* a type of squash

ayam *n.* rattles (musical; used by the Deer dancer and by Corn Wine singers; the rattles of the of the Matachin dancers, which are called wahi)

ayaman(su) *adv.* over there (*s.* = hunaman)

ayatana *n.* left (turn in Matachin dancing)

aye *n.* mother (*var.* of ae)

B

baas *n.* bus (*comb.* bah-); *ex.* bahta vovicha, waiting for the bus

behtab *n.* bathtub

beis *n.* base (in baseball)

bendisiroa *tv.* bless (*ser.*; *syn.* teochia)

bendisiroawame *n.* blessing (*ser.*; *syn.* teochiawame)

bet *n.* baseball bat

biblioteeka *n.* library

bomba *n.* balloon

bombam *n.* bomb

bombeo *n.* fire engine

bombiroa *tv.* bomb

bou *adj.* big, vast, enormous (*obj.* bo'uk, *pl.* bweere; *cf.* bwe'u); u ~ kaaro, the big car; Ume yoemem ~ bwiapo ho'ak. Those people live on a large land (the Tohono Reservation is large). Vempo bo'uk bwiak. They have a vast land. Uka ne bo'uk waata. I want the big one.

brocha *n.* brush

BW

bwa'awame *n.* food (*var.* bwa'ame); U hamut bwa'amta nu'upak. The woman bought food. Um bwa'ampo ona ama ve'e. The food needs salt.

bwa'e *tv.* eat (*pst.* bwa'aka; bwa'a-, bwabwa'e); Hitasa empo bwa'aka, sikilik tenekmochik? What did you eat, red-mouthed tortoise (from a myth)? Ian ketwo ne nohim bwa'aka. I ate tamales this morning.

bwa'ame *n.* food (*var.* bwa'awame)

bwa'amtakomweamapo *n.* esophagus

bwa'ari *adj.* eaten

bwa'arom *n.* lamb's quarters, purslane (*Chenopodium sp.*), used as a green

bwaana *iv.* cry, weep (~-, bwabwana; *comb.* bwan)

bwaata *tv.* stir, mix together (*syn.* kuuta; ~-, bwabwaata)

bwahi wikosa *n.* breechclout strings

bwahilovon *n.* wild cat, bobcat

bwahim *n.* diaper, loin cloth, breechclout (originally the Yoeme men's garb, today this is used for infants as a diaper and consists of a rectangular cloth tucked into a string around the waist; the diaper is changed but the string remains)

bwahsuma *iv.* braid

bwahsuma'i *n.* braid
> chonim ~ *n.* braided hair

bwai wikosa *n.* cord, belt

bwai yecha *tv.* 1. undress 2. get into someone's pants (have sex with)

bwakala *adj.* straddling with one's legs

bwakta *tv.* take out of a container (~-, bwabwakta)

bwaktai *adj.* 1. taken out, extracted 2. holowed out

bwala *n.* sheep

bwala aso'ola *n.* lamb

bwalareo *n.* sheepherder

bwalkimula *iv.* weak

bwalko *adj.* soft, smooth; ~ le, consider to be soft

bwalkote *tv.* 1. soften, smooth 2. tan hide (~-, bwalbwalkote)

bwalwotta *tv.* make feel weak, make tremble

bwalwotte *iv.* feel weak

bwan *ptc.* indeed (focus particle); *ex.* Seewam tua ~ uhyoi. The flowers sure are pretty. ~ enchi nattemain. It was you that (s/he) was asking for. A: Tu'isi tata. B: Heewi bwan. A: It sure is hot. B: Yes indeed.

bwan *adv.* weeping; ~ bwia *n.* this vale of tears (*lit.* weeping earth); bwan bwiapo, in this vale of tears; wame inim bwan bwiapo na kuaktisukame, those who have trod this weeping earth

bwani *n.* crybaby

bwánia *iv.* make a vow, promise for someone else (~-, bwabwania)
> au ~ *n.* promise (on one's own part; *syn.* promeesa)

bwanía *n.* wax

bwániari *adj.* bestowed a name by vow

bwanwame *n.* crying

bwaravoa *n.* wool

bwasa *tv.* cook it, bake it (bwasa'a-, bwabwasa)

bwassa'aka *n.* bird of prey (unidentified *sp.*)

bwase *iv.* cooking (bwas-, bwabwase)

bwasi *adj.* cooked, ripe

bwasia *n.* 1. tail 2. end, tail end (of a line)

bwasubwila *n.* yerba del indio (plant *sp.* used for toothe-ache)

bwatana *iv.* burn food (bwantan-, no *rdp.*)

bwatania *tv.* burn (food; ~-, bwattania; *cf.* taya); Aapo bwa'amta ~. He is burning his food.

bwawi *adj.* sharp (knife, scissors, axe, stick)
> ~ yotohta *tv.* make dull

bwawiteri *adj.* sharpened

bwawia *n.* sharpened end

bwawis *n.* barn owl

bwawite *tv.* sharpen (~-, bwabwawite)

bwe *var.* of abwe, well (*masc.*; in contemporary AZ, both men and women use bwe or abwe; *cf.* a'e)

bwe'ituk *conj.* because; Apo hiva yu move'ek ~ apo lovola kovak. He always wears a hat because he's bald.

bwe'u *adj.* big, large; pregnant (*pl.* bweere; *cf.* bou); Ume livrom ka ~. The book is not big. Ume livrom ka bwe'ebwere. The books aren't big.

  ~ choki *n.* morning star

  ~ ho'ara *n.* town, city

  ~ Hu'upam *n.* Valencia Village (settlement near Valencia and present-day I-19)

  ~ mam pusiam *n.* thumb

  ~m hiapsek *iv.* be courageous, brave

bwe'uria *tv.* enlarge, make bigger (~-, bwebwe'uria)

bwe'usi *adj.* large

  ~ aayu, grow tall (animals; *cf.* yo'otu); *ex.* ~ pahko, a large ceremony

  ~ yoiyiwa, large dance

bwe'uteta *n.* boulder

bwebwere *adj.* huge; Apo si ~m nakak. He has huge ears.

bwebbweka *adj.* wide

bweeka *adj.* broad, wide

bweere *adj.* big, large (*pl.*; *sg.* bwe'u; *cf.* bou); Aman ~ hoosom kawimpo hoho'a. Large bears live in the mountains.

  ~ chokim *n.* planets

bweha('i) *n.* half gourd (for dipper or resonator); bweha'apo, on the half gourd

bweka pa'aria *n.* plaza, open area

bwekasia *adv.* wide(ly)

bwekate *tv.* widen (~-, bwebwekate)

bwelta *tv.* turn, go around (~-; bwebwelta); Aapo karita k. He went around in the car. Vikammeu yeu ~k. They went to Vicam and back.

  yeu ~ *iv.* make a round trip/stop by/ visit (*syn.* yeu noite)

Bwetaewaim *n.* Holy Week

bwia *n.* 1. earth, land, soil 2. area, region, country; Ini si'ime Hiak ~. This is all Yoeme land.

  ~ Bwalko *n.* Big Flats (site of first Easter ceremony in Tucson area; in vicinity of present-day Miracle Mile and I-10)

  ~ mu'u *n.* burrowing owl

  ~ Toli, the Earth Rat who first brought music to the people

bwiara *n.* country, territory; homeland

bwiata vétuku *n.* underground

bwibwise *tv.* touch

bwíchia *n.* worm

    ~ voalam *n.* caterpillar

bwichía *n.* smoke

    ~ta hoa *iv.* be smoking, make a lot of smoke

bwih- *comb.* of bwise, catch it

bwiha *tv.* massage, rub (~-, bwibwiha)

bwihri *adj.* captured

bwihtua *tv.* let touch

bwihwa 1. *n.* capture (act of capturing) 2. *tv.* be captured, arrested

bwiichi *iv.* smoky, filled with smoke

bwiika *iv.* be singing (~-, bwibwika)

bwiikam *var.* of bwikam, songs

bwiiki *n.* sung

bwiiwi *n.* caterpillar

bwika *n.* song

    ~ hiawa *n.* rhythm and melody of a song

    ~ noki *n.* lyrics, song text

bwikleo *n.* singer (*syn.* bwikreo)

bwikola *adv.* around (*syn.* chikola)

bwikreo *n.* singer (*syn.* bwikleo)

bwise *tv.* 1. catch it 2. pass, hand it to one 3. capture, seize, arrest (bwih-, bwibwise)

bwisi *tv.* hold, grasp it (bwih-, bwibwisi)

bwisiria *n.* handle, lever

bwisiwa *iv.* be in captivity

bwisiwame *n.* captive

bwita *n., iv.* 1. *n.* excrement 2. *iv.* defecate (~-, bwibwita)

    ~ maival *n.* dung beetle

    ~ pattila *adj.* constipated

bwitchovia *n.* soot

CH

cha'abwa *tv.* patch (~-, chacha'abwa)

cha'aka *iv.* 1. be hovering, hanging, leaning 2. be like minded 3. be important (*ex.* aman wéepo ~, it's important to go) 4. be next in sequence 3. be next in sequence or agenda, moving behind (with the following paradigm: net, et, at/aet, itot, emot, vempo'imet) (*pst.* ~n, cha'a-, chacha'a; *cf.* chaya)

    nat ~ weye, follow/come after; Ini konti aet ~ weye. The procession comes next. Nat ~ weye si'ime was alavansa. All of the albanzas follow each other.

    nau ~ *iv.* be allied to

cha'akame *n.* ally (with *postp.* itamak, with us)

    nau ~ *n.* alliance

    yoemra nau ~ *n.* committee, board

cha'aparia *n.* 1. comb (of a chicken) 2. eaves, overhang of roof

cha'asaka *iv. pl.* of cha'asime

cha'asime *iv.* 1. billow (clouds) 2. walk (rain) 3. be flying along 4. glide
(*pl.* cha'asaka)

cha'atu *iv.* get together, collect, assemble (clouds; *s.* chatu)
nau ~ *tv.* connect

cha'atula *iv.* be hanging, hovering (cha'atu-, chacha'atu)

cha'atuwame *n.* connection

chaapa *n.* clothes pin

chaatim *n.* shot, injection

chachaeri *n.* cry, shout

chachaese *iv.* go to call, summon (*pst.* ~k, *comb.* chachai-, *fut.* chaene;
au = *d.o.*); Au ne chachaivae. I'll go call her/him.

chae *tv.* call, howl, yell, scream, whoop, call loudly (~-/chai-, chatchae);
Aapo senukut ~n. S/he was calling someone.

chahe *tv.* scrape bark off a tree with axe or machete (*pst.* ~n, chahi-;
chachahe)

chahi- *comb.* of chahe, scrape

chai- *comb.* of chae, call/howl

chaka'aku *adv.* on the corner

chaka'aria *n.* corner

chakaka'ati *adv.* sideways
~ weye, walking sideways

chakala *adv.* on its side, leaning; *cf.* chakula

chakalai *adv.* sideways

chake'etim *n.* jacket

chaketonim *n.* coat

chakiram *n.* elaborate necklace of many strands woven into a pattern of
adjacent horizontal diamond shapes, made of beads; Ume
hamuchim ~ kokam pahkota vetchi'ivo hoa. The women are
making chakiram for the ceremony.

chakkai *adj.* leaning

chakkui *adj.* bent, twisted, crooked

chakte *iv.* be dripping, trickling (chakti-, chakchakte)

chaktia *n.* drop

chakukte *iv.* go sideways (chakukti-, chakuchakute)

chakula(i) *adj.* crooked, tilted sideways, not level, uneven champu *n.*
shampoo (a native shampoo was made from the buffalo gourd,
and another from bamboo root)

chamta *tv.* split cane (~-, chamchamta)

chamte *iv.* be splitting cane (chamti-, chamchamte)

chamti *adj.* broken (*pst.* ~atukan)

chana *n.* blackbird

Chanatu *n.* Becoming a Blackbird (dance song)

chango *n.* monkey

chansa *n.* chance

chao *n.* chin, snout
~ voam *n.* whiskers, beard

chapa'a *adj.* pitched (roof, paper folded over)

chapa kari *n.* lean-to (*lit.* pitched house)

chapala *adv.* pressing together (flat surfaces); ~ mamak, have one's hands pressed together

Chapayeka *n.* masked Fariseo member (*lit.* folded nose)
  ~ yotui *n.* old man chapayeka mask

chapta *tv.* cut it with scissors (~-, chapchapta)

chapte *iv.* be cutting with scissors (chapti-, chapchapte)

chaptiam *n.* scissors

chasime *iv.* be flying, fly along (*var.* cha'asime; *sg.*; *pl.* cha'asaka)

chasisime *iv.* 1. blowing in the breeze, floating in air 2. float (*pst.* ~n; chasisim-; no *rdp.*)

chatu *iv.* assemble (clouds), cloud over (*s.*; = cha'atu); Kalasoiti hikauwi ~ko (*s.*), when the clouds gather brilliantly overhead

chatchae *rdp.* of chae, call

chava'im *n.* calf (of leg)

chavulai *n.* ponytail

chaya *tv.* tether it, hang it (chayá'a-, chatcha; *cf.* cha'aka)
  aet a ~ *tv.* attack
  yoemta ~ *iv.* execute by hanging

che *pn.* you (used in polite requests; *pl.* chem); Ne ~ vaulina. Wash my face. Ne che vovicha. Wait for me. Ne chem ho'okoe. You forgive me. Ne chem miika. Give me some. Ne chem pomtittua. Give me a drink. Ne che yentaa. Give me a smoke.

che'e suckle (chi'i-, cheche'e)

che'ewa *conj.* moreover

che'ewale *iv.* think highly of (che'ewali-, cheche'ewale)

che'ewasu *adv.* more and more (*var.* cheche'ewasu); Luis ~ awia. Louis is getting fatter and fatter.

chea *adv.* emphatic particle (*s.* chewa)
  1. more; ~ kia, tastier; A: Haisa pa'asim huhusai? B: E'e, pa'asim ~ momorao. A: Are raisins brown? B: No, they're really purple. A: Haisa plantano siki? B: E'e, plantano ~ sawai. A: Are bananas red? B: No, they're more yellow. Kaita ~ bwe'u? Can't you find something bigger to wear (said in teasing)? Kaita ~ ili'ichi? Can't you find something smaller to wear (said in teasing)?
  2. really; In achai ~ , Yoronata au vitlatia. My father really did see the Llorona. In Tio Lukas ~ hittoareotukan. My uncle Lucas was a healer. Te che hi'ibwa. We are eating. In chi'ilita ho'apo ~ vemela ili aso'ola katek. There is a new baby at my aunt's house.
  3. favorite; Hita bwa'amta empo ~ kiale? What is your favorite food? Hita yeewamta empo ~ tu'ure? What's your favorite sport?
  ~ chukula *adv.* much later
  ~ san tu'i *adj.*, *adv.* best
  ~ san tu'i~ ea *iv.* be (more) enthusiastic
  ~ tu'i *adj.* better

~ vatnateka *adv.* at the very outset, start

~ vatnatekai *adv.* long ago, once upon a time

~ waitana *adv.* further on the other side

~ wam vicha *conj.* furthermore

~ wannavo *adv.* beyond

~ watiawame *n.* 1. person who is spoiled (*lit.* one who is loved more) 2. pet, favorite

ka ~ tu'i *adj.* worst

cheaneakai *interj.* wonder of wonders, well as I live and breathe, it's a miracle you're here (expresses surprise at one's arrival); ~ im weama, I'm surprised to see you here.

cheeki *n.* check (bank)

chelechele'eti *adv.* on tiptoe (with weama)

Chepa Mochi Kawi *n.* Josephine's Turtle Mountain (name of folksong and character of the song)

chepta *tv.* jump over (~-, chepchepta)

chepte *iv.* jump, take a step, hop (chepti-, chepchepte)

aet ~ *iv.* step on

chepti *n.* act of stepping

cheptiwame *n.* step (stairs)

aet ~ *n.* rung (ladder)

chewasu *adv.* more

chi'i- *comb.* of che'e, suckle

chi'ichivo *n.* estafiate, sage, ragweed (*Artemisia* and *Ambrosia spp.*)

chewa *adv.* more (*s.*; = chea); Ayaman ne seyewailo, naiyoli yo tuku aniwapo, ~ yolemem (*s.*). Over there, I, in the flowered, cherished night world, I am more human.

chi'ila *n.* aunt (mother's older sister); *cf.* haaka, mamai, tia

chi'imu *n.* sty (in eye)

chi'itua *tv.* nurse (infant, baby animal)

chiachiakte *rdp.* of chihakte, splash

chiche'a *n.* slobbering, drooling

chiche'era *n.* one who always slobbers a lot

chichek *iv.* be drooling (*pst.* ~an, chit-)

chichi *n.* saliva

chichiam *n. var.* of chichiham

chichiham *n.* mistletoe (*Phorodendron californicum; var.* chichiam)

chichikla *adj.* combed, groomed (*sg.* a ~, *pl.* ama ~)

chihakta *tv.* splash it (chihakti-, chihachihakta); vaa'am ~, splash water

chihakte *iv.* splash (chihakti-, chiachiakte)

chihakti *n.* splash

chihaktia *tv.* cause water to splash from impact

chihchihtame *n.* masher

chispa *n.* spark

chihta *tv.* mashing it (*pl. obj.*; ~-, chihchihta)

chihtahko *adj.* slippery, smooth

chihte *iv.* be mashing (chihti-, chihchihte)

chihti *adj.* smashed, squashed (*pst.* ~ritukan)

chihtim *n.* mashed

chiihu *n.* indigo

chiinim *n.* cotton

Chiino *n., adj.* Chinese

chiiva *n.* goat

chiivam *n.* crowbar

chiivu *adj.* bitter

chiiwe *tv.* shell corn (chiu-, chichiwe); *cf.* hichiwe

chiiwi *n.* turkey (*syn.* koovo'e)

chike *tv.* comb one's own hair (chik-, chitchike); In chi'ila *Kentucky Friedpo* kateka au chiken. My aunt was sitting at Kentucky Fried (Chicken) combing her hair (tongue twister).

chikipona *tv.* tickle one (*pst.* ~n, chikipon-, chikipop—na)

chikitam *n.* gum (chewing)

chiklem *n.* gum (chewing)

chikola *adv.* around (*syn.* bwikola)

chikti *pn. adv.* 1. *n.* all, each, every, everyone 2. *adv.* even 3. *conj.* even though; ~ si'ime wepuali venasia nau tekipanoane. All will work together as one. ~ ketwo ne kafeta hiva hehe'e. I always drink coffee in the morning. Si'ime piisam avo toha momoeram ~. Bring all the blankets even the old ones. Vempo si'imekut noitek *Old Tucson* ~. They went all over, even to Old Tucson. Apo kaita aman tohaka huni chikti haivu aman weama. Even though he didn't take anything over there, he is already there (at a party).

    ~ mechapo *adv.* monthly (*var.* ~ metpo)

    ~ semanapo *adv.* weekly

    ~ ta'apo *adv.* daily

    ~ tukapo *adv.* nightly

    ~ wasuktiapo *adv.* yearly

chiktim *pn.* each and every

chiktu *iv.* become disoriented

chiktuachi *n.* confusing, disorienting, or unfamiliar place (*var.* chittuachi); Um pueblopo tu'isi ~. In that town it is very confusing.

chiktula *iv.* be disoriented, be lost (*var.* chittula; if one gets lost and wanders off in the desert, a little group of Surem will come along and guide the lost one back to his home)

chikul *n.* mouse; Ume ~im váchiata bwabwa'e. Mice eat up seeds.

chikul hu'i *n.* pincushion cactus (*Mammillaria sp.*)

chilik *n.* a bird *sp.*

chilikoote *n.* coral tree (the root is used in carving pascola masks because of the light weight of the cork-like root)

chiminea *n.* fireplace, chimney

chimta *tv.* touch, grab; kiss (~-, chimchimta)

chimti *adj.* touched, grabbed

chin sooka *n.* yearly cotton

chinchim *n.* chiggers, bedbugs, scabies

chinchintia *n.* thunder (loud); Yukeu si ~n. It was really thundering.

chinota kovak hair (curly, wavy)

chiokoe *ptc.* in: Dios em ~ utte'esia. Thank you (*cf.* hiokoe; ~ is a contraction of enchim and ~).

chipta *tv.* sipping it (~-, chipchipta)

chirikote *n.* coral bean (*Erythrina flabelleformis*), a tree growing in Sonoran mountains, formerly used for masks

chirimia *n.* oboe

chit- *comb.* of chichek, drool

chita vétala *adj.* smooth; Apo uka veáta ~ ~ a tu'utek. He cleaned the skin smooth.

chitahko *adj.* smooth, slippery

chitochitohte *iv.* slipping

chitohte *iv.* slipping (chitohti-, chitochitohte)

chitonia *tv.* plaster it (~-, chittonia)

chitoniari *adj.* plastered

chitwatte *iv.* spitting (chitwatti-, chitwatwatte)

chiva kovam *n.* goat heads, bullheads (vine with sharp thorns; *Tribulus terrestris*; *syn.* toorom, wicha'apoi)

chiu- *comb.* of chiiwe, shell corn

chiva'atu *n.* billy goat

chivehta *tv.* spread (particulate matter; ~-, chivechivehta)

chivehte *iv.* spreading particulate matter (chivehti-, chivechivehte)

chivehti *adj.* spread

chivelai *adj.* scattered

chivu si'ika *n.* gall bladder

cho'i *n.* paloverde tree (*Cercidium*); *cf.* vaka'apo

cho'ila *tv.* lasso

cho'oko *adj.* 1. salty 2. sour
    ~ vaso *n.* salt grass

cho'okote *tv.* make salty

cho'ola(i) *adv.* too high (garment, building; with katek)

choa *n.* cholla cactus (*Opuntia sp.*)
    ~ hipo'im *n.* Holy Thursday drink made from cholla

choachoakte *iv.* be sticky, gooey

choali *n.* lamb's quarters (*syn.* kapa)

choam *n.* crown of head

choawe *n.* caracara (hawk *sp.*)

chochona *tv.* hit one (~-, no *rdp.*)

choi *n. var.* of cho'i

choiti *adv.* in a flash

chokaroa *tv.* crash

choki *n.* 1. star (can be a nickname for children so that envious spirits can't take the child's identity by learning the child's real name)
    2. badge

Choki Araum *n.* the Big Dipper

    ~ hiisa *n.* comet (it is believed that a comet is the sign of bad things such as war)

    ~ Lo'i *n.* Lame Star (a Matachin dance tune)

    ~ tachiria *n.* starlight

chokinai *adj.* wrinkled

    ~k puhvaka a vitchu *iv.* scowl, frown

chokinakta *tv.* crumble, smash (~-, chokinakinakta)

chokinakte *iv.* get wrinkled

Coho Lo'i *n.* a dance tune

chokolaate *n.* chocolate

cholapelai *adj.* flabby

cholloi *n.* woodpecker

chom watte *iv.* blow nose (chom watti-)

chomim *n.* anus

chon weche *iv.* get bald

chona *tv.* punch (*pst.* ~n, chon-, chochona)

chone'ela *adj.* having a full head of long hair

chonekame *n.* one who has a choni (hair fetish)

choni *n.* hair fetish

    ~ kottila *n.* split ends (hair; *syn.* sea choni)

chonim vutta *tv.* let down one's hair

chookinai *adj.* wrinkled

choomek *iv.* have mucus

choomim *n.* phlegm

choonek *iv.* have head hair

choomo *n.* headdress, helmet mask used by the Chapayekas of the Fariseo Society (traditionally white, with black and red designs)

choonim *n.* 1. head hair 2. scalp fetish

choora *adj.* tall, skinny

choori *adj.* wrinkled

choorim *n.* men's underwear

choowe *iv.* drying up, get skinny (old age); wither, wilt (plants) (chou-, chochowe)

choparao *n.* raccoon (in older times, there was a Raccoon dance, as well as Deer, Coyote, and Nahi Water Fly)

chopo'oria *adj.* hilly (*pst.* ~tukan)

chopoi *n.* hill

choppoi *adj.* rough, uneven (terrain, surface)

choriiso *n.* sausage

chotcho'okoe *iv.* get salty (~-; only *pst.* and *fut.* usual)

chou- *comb.* of choowe, dry up

chove *n.* 1. buttocks 2. rear end (of automobile)

    ~po elesikile *exp.* it is going to rain (*lit.* there is itching in the ass)

chovikukta *tv.* bend, twist, crush, smash

chowia *iv.* dried up, withered (~-, chochowia)

chu *n. comb.* of chuu'u, dog

    ~ chae *iv.* bark (*syn.* voe, haiti chae)

    ~ ete *n.* flea

    ~ hamut *n.* bitch

chu'á- *comb.* of chuu'a, get stuck

chu'akta *tv.* glue it, paste it (~-, chu'achu'akta)

    sisiwokta nau ~ *tv.* weld

chu'akte *iv.* glued, pasted, attached (chu'akti-, chu'achu'akte)

chu'aktila *adj.* glued together; nat ~, *iv.* be stuck together

chu'ala *adj.* stuck (in mud; *pst.* ~tukan)

chu'ukam *n.* gum (tree), resin, pitch

chuchupame in: yee ~, *n.* ambitious person

chuchupe in: yeu ~, *iv.* develope, manifest, grow out of

chukta *tv.* cut with knife or saw (~-, chukchukta); wakasta ~, carve meat

chukatam *n.* black sap that seeps from mesquite trees (good for harp
    strings)

chukte *iv.* cutting with a knife or saw (chukti-, chukchukte)

chukti *adj.* cut

chuktia *n.* cut

chukui *adj.* black (*aff.* chukuli, *var.* chukuri; *pl.* chuchukui)

    ~ hœvahe *n.* black widow (spider)

    ~ kuta *n.* overgrown shrub with reddish brown wood; wood used
        for raspers for Deer Dance

    ~ teta *n.* magnetic stone (magnetic rock with powers; may be
        given to a person to keep the recipient in control)

    ~ vachi *n.* black corn

chukula *adv.* later

    aet ~ *adv.* afterwards

chukuli *adj.* black (*aff., var.* chukui)

    ama vutti ~ *adj.* swarthy

    ~ Poutela *n.* Little Black Cowbird (Deer song)

chukuri *adj.* black (*var.* chukui)

chumim *n.* vagina

chumte *iv.* 1. stuff one's self 2. hog food, not share food

chumti(a) 1. *adj.* rapid, fast, quickly (*var.* chumchumti is more formal;
    applied to water and animates; *cf.* uttea) 2. *interj.* hurry up, let's
    go; Hose ~ nooka. John talks fast. U o'ou ~ weye. The man walks
    fast. A: Haiavu ~ te katvae. B: Tu'i ma. A: ~! A: We still want to
    go. B: Okay, that's good. A: Come on, let's go.

    ~ hiavihte *iv.* pant, breathe hard

    ~ hita hohowa'apo *n.* factory

chumumutea *adj.* nervous

chumuria *n.* notch of an arrow

chuna huya *n.* fig tree

chunahkam *n.* mesquite flower; U ~ si tu'i hittoa ume riptiam vetchi'ivo.

Mesquite flower is very medicinal for pinkeye.

chunula *adv.* kneeling, on one's knees (upright, with calves against buttocks; *cf.* tonom)

    ~ **katek** *iv.* be squatting

chupa *tv.* 1. finish, complete 2. fulfill a vow 3. get married 4. create (chupá'a-, chuchupa); *cf.* ansu, yak; Huchi echat in ou asoa chupvae. My son is getting married next month.

chupa'awame in: yee ~, *n.* ambition

chupawame *n.* completed

    nau ~ *n.* couple

chupe *iv.* 1. get completed, finished 2. get married 3. become ripe (*pst.* chupuk, chup-, chuchupe)

chupi'iseka *adv.* coming into completion (with weye, ansime); Ini veá haivu ~ weye/ansime. This skin is already coming to completion.

chupia *iv.*, *n.* 1. *iv.* be complete (~-, chuchupia) 2. *n.* completed thing; Empo ka ~wa? Haven't they married you off yet?

chupiari *n.* 1. creature, completed one 2. unnatural, monstrous animal or person 3. gigantic snake or other giant animal living in caves outside physical reality that eventually outgrows its cave and must go to the sea to live, of human or animal in origin, usually destructive or frightening; it is accompanied by strong winds when it travels (see Suawaka); Ume Surem vo'ota pattak u ~ta ka aman kivake vetchi'ivo. The Surem blocked the road so the serpent could not enter.

chupiarim *n.* couple (married, dating)

chupuiwaim *n.* little pains in joints

chupuk *pst.* of chupe, finished

chutiam *n.* wood chips

chuu'a *iv.* get stuck (chu'á-, chuchu'a)

chuu'u *n.* dog (*comb.* chu); ~ aso'ola *n.* puppy

chuuna *n.* cultivated fig (*Ficus carica*)

chuune *tv.* suck (chuun-, chuchune)

    luuseta ~, suck on candy

chuutiam *n.* wood chips, cloth scraps

chuuva *adv.* for a while

    ~ vovicha, wait for a while

chuuyu *iv.* bloated, fat (~-, chuchuyu); Apo unna hi'ibwasu ~k. He ate too much and has heartburn.

chuvahko *n.* hurricane, strong wind storm

chuvala *adv.* momentarily; ~ ne vovicha. Wait a minute for me.

    ~ vetchi'ivo poke te yumhoivae. Because we want to rest a while.

    ~ koche, nap/doze off

    ~ vetchi'ivo, for a while, for a moment; chuvahko *n.* strong wind (*syn.* bwe'u heeka)

chuvalatuko *adv.* in a while

chuvva *adv.* for a moment
      yuin ~ *adv.* in a little while longer
chuvvatuko *adv.* in a little while
chuyula *adj.* bloated (*pst.* ~tukan, *fut.* chuyune)

D

diamante *n.* diamond
dies sentavo *n.* dime
diesempo *adv.* ten o'clock (*syn.* wohmanimpo)
Dios *n.* God (*var.* Lios)
Disiémbre *n.* December
disipulo *n.* disciple
distriito *n.* district
domisilio *n.* address
dosempo *adv.* twelve o'clock
      ~ tuka'ariapo, midnight (*syn.* nasuk tuka'ariapo)

E

e *pn.* you (*sg.*; = empo; with postposition vetchi'ivo); Alamachi, pahko'ola,
      tua e sumwachim wokek. Keep it up, Pascola, you're dancing up
      a storm.
e"ea *iv. hab.* of ea, think
e"eeria *rdp.* of e'eria, put away
e"eusiwa'apo *n.* hideout, hiding place
e'e *interj.* no; A: Haisa yuke? B: ~, ka yuke. A: Is it raining? B: No, it's
      not. A: Haisa sapawetne? B: ~, ka sapawetne. A: Is it going to
      hail? B: No, it's not.
e'eria *tv.* put away for safe keeping, save up (~-, e"eeria); Tomita ~ne.
      (I) will save some money.
e'eriari *n.* reserve, savings, cache
e'etbwame *n.* thief
e'ete *iv.* belch, burp (e'eti-, ee'e'ete)
e'etehome *n.* 1. storyteller 2. speaker, orator
ea$_1$ *pn.* of you (*sg.*; with verbs chihakte, rohikte, tiiwe)
ea$_2$ *iv.* think, feel like (*pst.* ean, *fut.* eene, e-, *hab.* e"ea; *cf.* machia,
      pensaroa); esuk, had thought; hiokot ~, feel miserable; ka
      hunen ~, *iv.* change one's mind; Ka a ~po ama yeu siika. It
      didn't come out the way he wanted it to. Aman katvaen ta vesa
      ka hunen e"eak. (They) were thinking of going there, but they
      changed their minds. Vemposu aman kat'ean, ta ka hunen ~.
      They should go, but they won't. Aapo karota hinuvaeka ~n. S/he
      was thinking of buying a car. Aapo haisa tua eene? B: Heitu.
      A: What will s/he feel like/be thinking? B: I don't know.

a ~o hoa *iv.* be inconsiderate, do as one pleases

aet ~ *iv.* depend on (on = aet)

aman ~ *tv.* decide; aman wéevaeka ~, I decided to go

ka tu'isi ~ *iv.* worry, fret

nau ~ *iv.* agree (share views)

tevei ~k *iv.* that's the way s/he is; Tevei eak numukne. He's always drinking.

ean *pst.* of ea, think

echi *pn.* at/on you (*sg.*)

echimu *n.* seed (for planting)

echo *n.* cardon cactus (*Pachycereus pectenaboriginum*; has rounded spines all around, and used as a hair brush after the spine tips are burned off)

~ taakam, cardon fruits

ee *pn.* you (*sg.*; with the postpositions vichapo, amapo)

ee'e'ete *rdp.* of e'ete belch

eecha *tv.* plant (et-, e'echa); Meecha tapuniak etni. When the moon is full, we'll plant.

eechi *iv., n.* 1. *iv.* be planted 2. *n.* plant

eene *fut.* of ea, think

eepat *pn.* in front of, ahead of you (*sg.*; with verbs of motion)

eerim *n.* thoughts

eesukim *n.* sugar ants

eetana *pn.* from, alongside you (*sg.*)

eete *iv.* belch, burp (eeti-, ee'e'ete; *fut.* may be used as *rdp.*); Na'aso va'awa yee e'etitua. Orange juice makes people burp (*syn.* Na'aso va'awa sep yee eetituane).

eetua *tv.* make suffer, make think

eetuame *n.* stimulus

eewame *n.* thought, idea

nau ~ *n.* unity

eeye *n.* red ant

ehea *n.* ironwood (*Olneya tesota*)

ehkaleam *n.* ladder

ehkalonim *n.* steps (stairs)

ehkina *n.* corner

ehkuela *n.* school

~ siime, go to school; Severiapo apo ehkuekuela. In the winter s/he goes to school.

ehkusao *n.* toilet, bathroom

ehootem *n.* green beans

ehpam *n.* sword

ehpeeko *n.* mirror

Ehpirito Santo *n.* Holy Spirit

ehso *tv.* hide, conceal (~-, e'ehso); e'ehsonpo, where they used to hide

ehtaka *n.* stake

ehtapia *n.* stamp

ehtapiaroa *tv.* stamp
ehtasión *n.* station

>tren ~ *n.* train station
>~m *n.* the Stations of the Cross

ehtasionaroa *tv.* park (vehicle; *Son.*, *cf.* parkiaroa)
ehtudiaroa *tv.* study (in order to learn; *cf.* mammate)
ehtuufa *n.* stove
eiya *tv.* care for, love (~-, e'eiya); In maala/ae ne ~. I love my mother. In achai/hapchi ne ~. I love my father. Hunuen ne am ~n. I thought about them.

>ka yoem ~ machi *iv.* be untrustworthy, unreliable
>yoem ~ *tv.* trust people

ekala *adv.* sitting with one's legs open (*syn.* ekka)
ekka *adv.* sitting with one's legs open (*syn.* ekala)
ela'apo *adv., interj.* let (*cf.* ela'aposu)

>1. *adv.* let, permit; Itepo nau ea uusim vétana ~ vempo tekipanoane. We agree that the children may work. ~ eu omtine ta kat monte. Let him be mad at you, but don't say anything.
>2. *interj.* so, .../so what?; A: Empo ko'okoe wetne. B: ~. A: You'll get sick. B: So what?
>Diosta ~ *exp.* God willing

ela'aposu *adv.* let; ~ hibwane. Let it eat. ~ vat weene. Let him go first.
elefante *n.* elephant
elektrisita *n.* electricity (*syn.* tahi)
elesiiki *n.* something that itches (*rdp.* e'elesiikia)
elesiikile *iv.* itch (*pst.* ~n, elesiikili-); In mamam ~ kavaekakai ne am wo'oke. My hands itch so I must scratch them.
elevéitor *n.* elevator
elevena *adv.* like you
elevenasia *adv.* in your manner
em *pn.* you (*pl.*; *sg.* empo)
emak *pn.* with you (*sg.*; comitative)
emepola *pn.* yourselves, you yourselves (*var.* empopola)
emo *pn.* you (*pl. obj.*; with postposition vetchi'ivo); your (*pl.*); yourself (*pl.*); herself, himself, themselves

>~ tu'ule *iv.* be having sex (*cf.* haana)
>~ yeewawame *iv.* be fondling, carressing

emoa *pn.* of you (*pl.*; with verbs ichakte, rohikte, tiiwe)
emochi *pn.* at/on you (*pl.*)
emopat *pn.* in front of you (*pl.*; with verbs of motion)
emot *pn.* at/on you (*pl.*)
émotana *pn.* from, alongside you (*pl.*)
emou *pn.* toward you (*pl.*)
épale *interj.* stop it, cut it out (to children; , e'e bale, no little boy; now used with children of both sexes)

empo *pn.* you (*sg.*; *pl.* em, enchim; *syn.* che, e, sem)
empola *pn.* yourself, you yourself
empopola *var.* of emepola, you yourselves
emvuudo *n.* funnel
enchi *pn.* you (*sg. obj.*)
enchiladam *n.* enchilada
enchim *pn.* you (*pl.*; *sg.* empo; *syn.* chem, em, sem)
enchimmak *pn.* with you (*pl.*)
enchimmet *pn.* at/one you (*pl.*)
enchimto *pn.* from you (*pl.*)
enchito *pn.* from you (*sg.*)
Enero *n.* January
enkaahe *n.* lace
ensalada *n.* salad
envidiak *iv.* be envious of; U Maria tu'isi Susanatat ~. Mary is envious
    of Susan.
eoktiachisi *adv.* smell foul, offensive
    ~ huwa *iv.* stink
    ~ maachi *iv.* seem offensive
eo'otea *iv.* be nauseated (*pst.* ~n, eo'ote'e-, eo'ote"ea); eo'oteo, when
    nauseated
epasoote *n.* epazote (*Cheopodium ambrosioides*)
epat *postp.* in front of you
erawen *tv.* expect, predict (erawi-, no *rdp.*); Ka te enchi ~n. We weren't
    expecting you.
erensia *n.* heritage (often used in sermons to denote what the Yoemem
    have inherited culturally and should preserve as God-given);
    Emo waka yo'ora lutu'uriata, polove ~ta hakwosa iat tiempopo
    waata. You want the elders' truth, the poor inheritance from
    the past.
Eskatel *n.* Scottsdale
et *pn.* at/on you (*sg.*)
eta *tv.* close (etá'a-, e'eta)
eta'ana *tv.* lock up, jail
eta'i *adj.* 1. closed 2. imprisoned, in custody
etahte *tv.* crack (etahti-, e'etahte)
etahtia *adj.* cracked
etapo *tv.* open up (~-, ettapo)
etapoi *adj.* open
etbwa *tv.* 1. steal 2. kidnap (~-, e'etbwa)
    ~ vicha *tv.* spy on
    ~ vichame *n.* spy
    ~ vitchu *iv.* be peeking
etbwaim *n.* hostage, stolen item
etbwareo *n.* bandit, thief
etbwari *n.* stolen item

etbwaria *dv.* steal from
etbwawa *iv.* be stolen
ete *n.* louse
ete'a *n.* one who always has headlice
eteo- *comb.* of eteho, speak
eteoreo *n.* storyteller; U yoem yo'owe si tu'i ~. The elder man is a very good storyteller.
eteori *n.* narration, storytelling; Um Yoem ~po u Yuku Namuta huvek. In Yoeme storytelling, Rain has Cloud as a wife.
eteho *iv.* speak, talk (eteo-, e'eteho); Inime waka hua ániata vichau vicha. These (are the ones who) are bringing up the talk about the wilderness world. Vempo tekilta nau ~. They're talking about work. Yoem nokpo te etehoim eteone. We will tell Yoeme stories.
etehoi *n.* 1. story, myth, legend 2. speech
    kia ~ *n.* story, tale (for entertainment)
etehoreo *n.* storyteller
etehowa *n.* meeting
etehowame *n.* conversation
etem *n.* lice, fleas (on animals)
eteme *iv.* delouse (etem-, etteme)
etleo *n.* farmer
etta *n.* plantation (what is planted)
    ~ tavokta, gather in the harvest
etwa *n.* planting, planting time
etwame *n.* agriculture, horticulture
eu *pn,.* to/into/beside/from you (*sg.*)
    ~ hoa *iv.* do as one pleases; *cf.* -u, -wi
    ~ kechia *exp.* to you as well (*resp.*)
euse *iv.* hide one's self (eusi-, e'euse)
eusi *adv.* secretly
    ~ katek *iv.* hiding out in back (*pl.* eusi hooka)
eusila *adj.* hidden
eusise *iv.* go to hide (*pl.* eusivo)
eusu *postp.* with you, to you
evanheelio *n.* gospel
eye'ekoe *n.* millepede

F

Fariseo *n.* Fariseo (member)
Fariseom *n.* Fariseo (Society)
fayalia *n.* opening, clearing, open area (*s.*; = pa'aria); ayaman ne seyewailo ~ta naishukuni weyekai (*s.*), over there in the flowered opening as I went walking...
Fevreo *n.* February

Finika *n.* Phoenix
firma *n.* signature
firmaroa *tv.* sign (*syn.* a teawam hiohte, a teawam yecha)
fonoora *n.* phonograph
fooko *n.* 1. light bulb 2. flashlight (*syn.* vateria)
fundasión *n.* foundation

G

galoon *n.* gallon
gannao *n.* lock (*syn.* lakim)
garaachi *n.* garage (for car repair)
gayeetom *n.* cookies
gahto *n.* wasteful one, costly one
gahtaroa *tv., iv.* 1. *tv.* spend money 2. *iv.* wear out
govierno *n.* government
gramo *n.* gram
grasia *n.* grace
gravadoor *n.* recorder (tape, videotape)
gravaroa *tv.* record (tape, videotape)

H

hi~- *pref.* used to derive intransitive verbs from transitive verbs (< hita, something)
ha'abwai *n.* things stood up (*pl.*; *sg.* kecha'i)
ha'abwek *iv.* standing up (*pl.*; *sg.* weyek; *pst.* ~an; hap-, haha'abwe); *cf.* hapte
ha'achihte *iv.* sneeze (*rdp.* ha'achihchihte); Senu ~ka huni mukne. One can even die from sneezing.
ha'achihtia *n.* a flower supposed to cause sneezing
ha'amu *iv.* climb up (~-, hahha'amu)
ha'amuria *iv.* increase
ha'ani *adv.* maybe (*var.* hani); Avo si'ime ~. I wonder if s/he is coming over. Manwetau nattemai haisa uka vachita vansuk ~. Ask Manuel if he already irrigated the fields.
haaka *n.* grandmother (paternal), aunt (paternal)
   ~ watte *iv.* cough up phlegm
haakam *n.* mucus, phlegm
haal *n.* hall (passage)
haamola *adv.* in bits and pieces (with aayu)
háana *adv.* in some way, some way or other, improperly; Pisam vétuku ~ nau anne. They're going to do something under the blanket (i.e., have sex).

~ aane *iv.* 1. clown around, act odd 2. misbehave

~ hiuwa *tv.* insult, tease with bad intent (-, hihiuwa; *cf.* hunniawa)

~ maachi *iv.* stuck up, snobby

~ nooka *iv.* mumble (with anger)

háania *iv.* make no sense (háaniu-, háana hihia)

Haapat *adj.* Apache

haareki *adv.* 1. over and over 2. one on top of the other

haate *iv.* gamble, bet, wager (~-, haha'ate)

haavi *n.* uncle (mother's oldest brother)

haawa *n.* vapor, steam

hachihte *iv.* sneezing (hachihti-, hachihchihte); Ne havachitivae su ne vevak. As I was about to sneeze, someone hit me.

hachin *adv.* somehow, someway

~ aane *iv.* behave oddly

~ huni'i *adv.* somehow, any old way; whatever; Aapo hachin huni a ya'ane. S/he will do whatever it takes.

~ maachi *iv.* be someway, unusual

~ ian teak? What is her/his name?

hachini *adv.* how?

haha'abwa *tv.* stand them up (~-, no *rdp.*)

hahame *tv.* catch up (haham-, hahhame)

hahase *tv.* 1. chase, pursue 2. follow a road (~-, haha-, hahhase)

tu'i voo'ota ~ *exp.* follow the good road (lead a good life)

hahateme *n.* gambler

hahau *tv.* pick up with hand (*pl.* obj; *sg.* tovokta; ~-, hahhau)

haiki *adv.* how many

haikimsia *adv.* what time is it?

hain *adv.* even though

~ huni *conj.* even though; Aapo ~ ko'okoeka huni aman siika. Even though he was sick, he went anyway.

haisa 1. *conj.* question marker (may occur with the clitic =su) 2. *pn.* what (in subordinate clauses) 3. *adv.* how; ~m hoovae? What do you want with them? ~ ne hoovae? What did you want me for? Ne o'outa weiya ~ kaita tekil ae vetchi'ivo? I have a man here; do you have any work for him? ~ u yoeme hamutta vitchu? Is the man looking at the woman? ~ chuu'u voe? Is a dog barking? Emesu ~ aane—kave ko'okoe? Is everyone well at your house? Ne ka hu'unea ~ em hiapo. I don't know what you said. Empo hu'unea ~ em hiakapo? Do you know what you said? Luisa ~ au ine'a? How's Louise feeling? Manwetau nattemai ~ uka vachita vansuk ha'ani. Ask Manuel if he already irrigated the fields.

~ a machiaka'apo *n.* form, shape

~ machi tehwa *tv.* describe

haisaka(i) *adv.* why

44

haisamaisi *adv.* how well
haisaula *exp.* what's wrong?
haiseakai *exp.* what are you thinking?
haisempane *exp.* how are you?
haisempaula *exp.* what's wrong
haisempea *exp.* how are you feeling? (in terms of emotions; < haisa empo ea); *cf.* haisempo emo ine'a
haisempia *exp.* what did you say?
haisempo emo ine'a *exp.* how are you feeling? (health); *cf.* haisempea
haisem toko *exp.* so what (it's none of your business)
haisia'ani *adv.* why not?
haisintoko *exp.* so what? (it's none of your business)
haita *tv.* despise, be disgusted by
haitauhoa *tv.* make dirty
haitaula *iv.* be messy
haitauya'ala *iv.* dirty, soil self
haiti *adv.* undesirable, messy, dirty, annoying
  ~ aane *iv.* 1. be undesirable 2. mess around 3. fussy, pesty; Uma miisim into ume totoim si haiti ama a'ane. The cats and chickens sometimes mess around in there.
  ~ chae *iv.* bark (*syn.* chu chae, voe)
  ~ eetua *tv.* bother, annoy
  ~ maachi *iv.* be dirty, filthy, impure
haiti(m) *n.* mess; Ume into bwan hunulevevena ~ a'ane. They are like that, they make too much of a mess. Haitim hia! You guys are making too much noise!
haitia *n., iv.* 1. *n.* noise, racket (*syn.* haitiuwame) 2. *iv.* talking bad (haitiu-, haiti hihia)
haitiachi *adj.* bothersome, disgusting
haitiachisi maachi *iv.* bothersome, annoying
haitiu- *comb.* of haitia, talking bad
haitiuwame *n.* noise
haitivetchi *adj.* awfully big
haitowikti *adv.* snapping a bow (*s.*)
haituya'ala *iv.* be dirty, soil one's self; Ili uusi ~. The baby soiled itself.
haituwikti *adv.* snapping
haiva *n.* crab
haiveleki *adv.* same amount
haivetchi *adv.* how big?
haivinuri *adj.* bought (< haivu hinuri; *pst.* ~tukan); Ume na'asom ~tukan. The oranges were already bought.
haivu *adv.* already, still (*syn.* tevei); Apo ~ koche. She's already asleep. Uusim, ~ kokot oora. Children, it's time for bed.
  ~ humak *adv.* about, more or less; Haivu humak mamni meecha ama vivitwakai. It was seen about five months ago.

haiwa *tv.* look for, search (*var.* hariwa; hariu-, hahariwa); wooki ~,
  tv. track; Haisa a hita bwa'amta hariune? What kind of food are
  you looking for?
hak *adv.* somewhere (*resp.*)
  ~ huni *adv.* anywhere; Hakhuni yesa'e. Sit anywhere (*sg.*)
    Hakhuni hoye'em. Sit anywhere (*pl.*)
  ~ huni kikkivakenme *n.* busybody (someone who gets involved
    or interferes; *lit.* one who enters anywhere)
hakala *n.* grandchild (son's child; *fem.*)
hakia *n.* arroyo, wash
hakku'uvotana *adv.* from any which way
haksa *adv.* where
haksaweka(i) *adv.* eventually; ~ véa u voo'o im wam vo'otene. Eventually
  the road will be made through here.
haksiani *adv.* where now?
hakta *tv.* inhale (~-, hakhakta)
hakta'apo *adv.* days ago, for days; A: Maria su? B: Nu chea ~ muksuk.
  A: Where is Mary? B: She has been dead for days.
haku'u *pn.* where? (*resp.*); A: Tomi ama karipo ayuk. B: ~? A: The money's
  in the house. b: Where?
haku'uvo *adv.* from where
haku'uvotana *adv.* from which side
hakuni *adv.* where, anywhere (*cf.* hauvicha); A: Maala siika. B: ~?
  A: Tusonewi. : Mother went out. B: Where to? A: To Tucson.
hakunsa *adv.* where
hakunsempo siika *exp.* where are you going?
hakwa'am huni *adv.* wherever; Empo hakwa'am huni sahak.
hakweeka *adv.* at some time
hakwo *adv.* when, at one time; Tusonpo ~ muina katekan. In Tucson, at
  one time there was a mill.
  ~ huni'i *adv.* whenever; Vempo hakwo huni vem e"eak saka'ane.
    They can go whenever they want.
  ~ katriam *n.* people of the past
  ~ siikame *n.* what happened in the past
hakwosa *adv.* in times past (does not occur alone); ~ iat tiempo, in the
  past (*var.* ~ iat tiempopo)
halahte *iv.* gasp for air (halahti-, no *rdp.*)
hale'emu *adv.* at some point or other
haleki *pn.* few (*obj.* ~ka); Aapo ~k eu teuwane. He'll say a few things
  to you.
halekisia *adv.* little by little, gradually (*re:* event, not plan; *cf.* yaa); Ket ~ au
  hapsakane. We will proceed (with the event in progress) gradually.
haleppani *adv.* so long (a length); ~k empo waata? What length do
  you want?
haliwaka *iv.* look for tracks (*s.*; = hariwa)
halla'i *n.* friend; ~ bwise, make friends
hamhamti *adv.* falling and breaking

hamta *tv.* break (brittle things, but not wooden; ~-, hamhamta); *cf.* kotta

hamte *iv.* break (brittle things; hamti-, hamhamte)

hamti(a) *adj.* broken (*var.* hamtila)

hamtila *adj.* 1. broken (*var.* hamtia) 2. on one's own; Itom karita
  ventaanau ~. Our house's window is broken. Ventaanam ~.
  The windows are broken. Piiso ~. The floor is in disrepair.

hamuchia *adj.* female; bwala ~, female sheep

hamuli *n.* great grandfather

hamut *n.* woman

hamutreo *n.* womanizer

hamyo'ola *n.* old woman

hana *comb.* of haana, in some way/improperly; ~ ne vitchu. S/he's staring
  at me (oddly, for bad reasons).
    ~ aane *iv.* be goofing off
    ~ hiuwa *iv.* insult, slander (*d.o.* = au)

hana'aka *interj.* you bet; You bet, of course, sure; ~ ti hiaka a yopnak. He
  answered, "you bet!"

hani *var.* of ha'ani, maybe; U hamut ~ mulatea. They say the woman is
  sterile. A: Huana ~ ko'okoe tea. B: Ka tea; lutu'uriapo ko'okoe.
  A: They say that Jane may be sick. B: It's so; it truth, she is sick.

hania *iv.* make no sense, say improper things (< hana + hia; haniu-)

hantiachi *adj.* 1. dreadful 2. disrespectful 3. promiscuous (*cf.* hu'i)

Hapa'achi *n.* Apache

hapchi *n.* 1. father (*fem.*) 2. title of respect used by a woman to a man
  (his reply is maala)

hapsaka *iv.* 1. float 2. stand on something that is moving (*pl.*; *sg.* siksime)

hapte *iv.* stand up (*pl.*; *sg.* kikte; ~-, hahapte); *cf.* ha'abwek

harahte *iv.* crack (skin; harahti-)

harekisia *adv.* over and over again (*var.* hareki, harekisi)

hariu- *comb.* of haiwa and hariwa, look for

hariwa *tv.* look for (*var.* haiwa; hariu-, hahariwa)

haroroti(a) *adv.* making a dragging sound
    ~ weama *iv.* drag one's feet

hasohte *iv.* breathe hard (hasohti-, hahasohte)

hateka *interj.* let me see

hato'i *n.* bow guard

hatteiya *iv.* fearless
    ka yee ~ *tv.* be fearless
    kaveta ~ *tv.* fear no one

haula *n.* cage

hausa *adv.* which way; Huan ~ vicha siika? Which way did John go?

hauvicha *adv.* where to? (*cf.* hakuni); A: Maala siika. B: ~? A: Mother
  went out. B: To where?

hava *interj.* go ahead

have *pn.* who (*obj.* haveta, *poss.* haveeta; *cf.* havee, senu); ~ huni'i,
    pn. anyone, whoever; ~ aman weyek? Who was that walking over
    there? ~ sakvaita bwa'aka? Who ate the watermelon? Empo ~ta

vitchu? Who are you looking at? Aapo ~ta tomita miika? Who did s/he give the money to? ~ huni waka uhbwanta in mampo yechane. Anyone could put a sacred request in your hands. Ne hu'uneak ~sa ama tekipanoa. I found out who works there.

havee *interj.* who? (*resp.*)

haveeta *pn. poss.* of have, who; A: ~ kari? B: A kariwa. A: Whose house is this? B: Her/his house. A: ~ laapisim? B: In paapisim. A: Whose pencils are these? B: They're my pencils.

havele *iv.* be snobby (haveli-, no *rdp.*)

havesaka *adv.* about to, on the verge of

haveta *pn.* which one?

havetuk(o) *conj.,adv.* 1. *conj.* if 2. *adv.* almost time for

havohti *adv.* thudding (*var.* havohavoti)

hávoi *tv.* miss out on food (*pl. obj.*; ~-, no *rdp.*)

havói *n.* grandfather (paternal)

havoli *n.* grandchild (son's child; *var.* havori; *masc., aff.*)

havorai *n.* daughter-in-law

hawa'i *n.* co-in-law (persons who are both in-laws to the same family)

hawassate *iv.* steam

he'e *tv.* drink (*pst.* he'eka, hi'i-, hehe'e); Aapo hiva yu vino hehe'e. He's always drinking wine. Chikti ketwo ne kafeta hehe'e. I always drink coffee in the morning. Tuuka ne kafeeta ~ka. Last night I drank coffee.

he'okte *iv.* have the hiccups (*pst.* ~n, he'okti-, hehe'okte)

he'oktiam *n.* hiccups

hechihtia *tv.* scratch (*pst.* ~k, no other tenses usual)

heeka *n.* 1. air, wind 2. dawn wind (*s.*); *iv.* blow
    ~ lu'ute *iv.* suffocate

heeko *n.* desert broom (*Baccharis sarothroides*), a common desert shrub
    ~ nawia *n.* burro bush, a slender shrub with sticky resin in twigs (*Hymenocla monogyra*)

heela *adv.* 1. close, near 2. nearly
    au hela, close by/near her, him or it; U kava'i au hela weye. The horse is walking close to him. Neu hela rukte'e. Move closer to me.
    avo ~, not far away
    ~ ansime *iv.* approaching (with au)
    ~ ho'akame *n.* neighbor (*syn.* vesiino)
    ito ~ ansime, approaching us

heelai *adv.* slightly; awi ~, slightly fat; cho'oko ~, slightly salty; ochoko ~, slightly greasy; wakila ~, slightly skinny

heemam *n.* liver

heewi *interj.* yes

heewi'ibwan *interj.* why, yes indeed

heewima *interj.* yes, then

heitu *interj.* I don't know

heka'ula *adj.* have a nervous tick (*pst.* ~tukan, *fut.* heka'une) hekam *n.* canopy

hekka *n.* 1. shade 2. ramada (*syn.* rama) 3. shadow

heloko *adj.* gelatinous

hemaha'achim *n.* lungs

henom *n.* shoulder; ~mpa ne wante. My shoulder hurts. ~ mechi, on
the shoulder

heohomte *iv.* be dusk, twilight; ~o ki'muk uume uusim. The children
went in at dusk.

heohomteo *adv.* in the evening, at dusk

heohtek *iv.* have scar tissue, get a boil from a burn (*cf.* vooyo)

heoko kuta *n.* globe mallow (*Sphaeralcea sp.*; *syn.* ochoko kuta)

heoko vachi *n.* large-eared corn

heota *tv.* wipe self (~-, heoheota)

hepa *interj.* hey (attention getter)

hepela *adv.* side by side

hepelam(su) *adv.* in a row; Aapo ume voteam hepelam am ha'abwak. He
stood the bottles in a row.

hero'ochia *n.* phlegm

heseim *n.* brown tepary beans (see se'elaim)

Hesu Krihto *n.* Jesus Christ

hewi *ptc.* (forms tag question); Aapo Hiaki, ~? Sh/e is a Yaqui, isn't s/he?
Empo chuu'uta kopte, ~> You want the dog, don't you? Empo si
emo uttia, ~? You like yourself, don't you?

hewite *tv.* say yes, respond affirmatively (*pst.* ~k; no other tenses usual)

hewiteria *tv.* give permission, permit, let (~-, no *rdp.*); Ka am ~'e. Don't
give them permission.

hi- *pref.* used to derive intransitive verbs from transitive verbs (< hita,
something; many examples follow)

hi'i- *comb.* of he'e, drink

hi'ibwa *tv.* eating (*pl. obj.*; ~-, hihi'ibwa)

hi'ibwase *iv.* go to eat (*pl.* hibwavo)

hi'ibwatua *tv.* 1. spoonfeed, handfeed 2. graze cattle

hi'ibwehe *iv.* digging (hibwe-, hi'ibwehe)

hi'ibwatua *tv.* spoonfeed, handfeed

hi'ika *tv.* sew, mend (hi'ik-, hihi'ika); Aapo pantaloonim ~. She's sewing
the pants.

hi'ikia kova'ala *n.* pin (sewing)

hi'ikiam *n.* needle

hi'ikia kovalam *n.* sewing pins, straight pins

hi'ikri *adj.* sewn, stitched

hi'ito *n.* palojito, a tree (*Forchammenia watsoni*), the fruit of which are
baked overnight in an underground oven

hi'u *n.* greens (in general); ~ne. will gather wild greens

hi'use *iv.* go to gather greens (*pl.* hi'uvo)

hia *iv.* 1. be sounding, vocalizing 2. be named 3. sound a certain way
4. marker of indirect discourse (hiu-, hihia; the *pst.* te'eka and
comb. ti'i- are used if 'sound a certain way' is intended);

U maakina hachin ~. The machine sounds funny./The machine is making an odd noise. U maakina hachin hian. The machine was sounding funny. U maakina hachin hiune. The machine will sound funny. U maakina hachin te'eka. The machine made an odd noise. U maakina hachin ti'ine. The machine will make an odd noise. Ori nen ~? What's her/his name? Ume kampaanim ~. The bells are ringing. Vempo inen ~ ke in wawai hani kunavae tea. They say that my cousin is going to get married. Kiihcul aman ~. A cricket is chirping.

hiabwia *n.* pole for gathering saguaro

Hiak *n. comb.* of Hiaki, Yaqui
    ~ chana *n.* blackbird (large *sp.*)
    ~ pahko *n.* Yoeme religious ceremony
    ~ vivam *n.* Yoeme tobacco
    ~ Vatwe *n.* Yaqui River

Hiaki *n.* Yoeme

Hiakim *n.* Yoeme country; ~meu ne siime. I'm going to the Yaqui country.

hiapsa *iv.* be alive, survive (hiapsi-); Hohokam im ~n. The Hohokams lived here. Aapo im vinwa ~k. He lived here a long time.

hiapsek *iv.* concentrate, have one's heart in it; Eme aet ~. Your heart is really in it.

hiapsi *n., iv.* 1. heart, soul, spirit 2. *iv.* live; vinwa ~, live a long life; Aman weye in ~. There goes the love of my life.
    ~ kuakte *iv.* change (heart, mind)
    tu'i ~mak *adv.* with good heart (with faith, love and devotion)
    chikti ~mak *adv.* wholeheartedly
    ~ ka luluteme, *n.* life everlasting
    ka tu'i ~mak *adv.* with a bad heart

hiapsim *n.* hearts (in cards)

hiapsitua *tv.* 1. give life to 2. feed someone

hiapsiwame *n.* life

hiavihmumuke *iv.* gasp, be short of breathe, suffocate

hiavihte *iv.* breathe (*pst.* ~n, hiavihti-)

hiavihtei *n.* breath

hiavihtetua *tv.* revive, resuscitate

hiawai *n.* sound (*ex.* kusik hiawaik, have a loud sound)

hiawi *n.* sound, noise, voice

hibwane *exp.* have something to eat

hibwe- *comb.* of hi'ibwe, dig

hibwisia *n.* handle (on ceramics or cooking vessels; *syn.* nakam, ears)

hicha'abwa *iv.* patching (~~, hihitcha'abwa)

hichike *iv.* sweeping (hichik-, hitchike); pisopo ~, sweeping the floor

hichikia *n.* broom

hichikri *adj.* swept; Santo tevatpo ~. The main plaza is swept.

hichiwe *iv.* be shelling corn (hichiu-, hichichiwe)

hichikia *n.* broom
hichoila *tv.* lasso, rope (~-, hihichoila)
hichupa *iv.* completing, fulfilling (vow), harvesting (~-, hitchupa)
hichupak *n.* crops, harvest
hihha'aria *iv.* wave hand, fanning (~-, hihihha'aria)
hihikubwa *iv.* be pointing at (with hand)
hihima'awa'apo *n.* cemetery (*syn.* kampo santo, sementeri)
hihinkolame *n.* runner, racer
hihinume *n.* buyer
hihiohtame *n.* writer, author
hihipaksiawa'apo *n.* laundry (place)
hihittohame *n.* delivery person, trucker
hihiutua *tv.* sound, blow to make a sound
hihiwame *n.* beverage, drink
hiho'ori *adj.* woven
hihoa *tv.* weave, knit (~-, hihiho'a)
hihoaleo *n.* weaver
hihsoa *iv.* poke, prick (~-, hihihsoa; *var.* hissoa)
hihsova *n.* grill
hihsovai *n.* barbecued meat
hihyokame *n.* artist
hiikia *iv.* leak
hiisa *n., iv.* 1. *n.* topknot, headdress, helmet mask 2.. *iv.* sprouting,
        budding; Maso awam hisane. The deer's antlers will unfold (s.).
hiite *tv.* roll up
hiitewa *n.* talking, discussion, council
hiitewame *n.* council, conference
hiiwe *tv.* 1. check on, look in on 2. sample, taste 3. look out for
        (hiu-, hihhiwe)
hik *comb.* of hi'ika, sew
        ~ maakina *n.* sewing machine (*syn.* maakina)
hikachi *n.* top, apex
hikaiwame *n.* attention
hikama *iv.* be packing
hikat *adv.* on top, high
hikattana on/from the top
hikau *adv.* at/towards the top (*syn.* hiakwi; *s.* hikawa)
        ~ cha'atula *iv.* be footloose, carouse, carry on
        ~ vicha *adv.* 1. uphill 2. towards north
        ~ yehtela *adv.* ahead, advanced in position
        mekka ~ *adv.* way up
hikawa *adv.* at/towards the top (s.; = hikau)
hikawi at/towards the top (*syn.* hikau); Chukui Kawi ~ ha'amuk, climbed
        to the top of Black Mountain; tolo pakun ~ (s.), up to the blue
        light outside
hikima *tv.* put away clothes, pack (hikim-, hihikima)

51

hikka *tv.* hear, listen, understand (*var.* hikkaha; hikkai-, hihikkaha)

hikkaha *tv.* 1. *var.* of hikka, hear 2. obey (hikkai-, hihikkaha); A ~k. (S/he) heard it. Ka ~. Don't listen. Ne waka chuu'u voemta ~k. I heard the dog that is barking. Ne chuu'uta voemta ~k. I heard the dog barking. U ili o'ou a ~k. The little boy obeyed him.

hikkubwa *iv.* point at (at = -u; ~-, hihikkubwa); Aapo mapau iae ~k. S/he pointed at the map.

hiko'a *iv.* chewing (hiko'o-, hihiko'a)

hiline *iv.* be cautious, prudent (hilin-, hihiline)

hilinwachi *adj.* dangerous

hilukiam *n.* rasper (*aff.*; *var.* hirukiam)

hima *tv.* 1. leave (behind) 2. abandon, desert 3. divorce (himáa-, himma and hihima)

hima'a *iv.* bury (~-, hihima'a)

hima'ako *iv.* cut wood (~-, himma'ako)

hima'ari *n.* 1. neglected, abandoned (place, house, field, village) 2. separated person (marriage, couple)

hima'aripo *n.* grave site, grave

hima'awa *n.* burial, funeral

himo'ote *tv.* leave in another's care, leave behind intentionally; (~-, hihimo'ote); *cf.* kopta

himsim *n.* mustache

himucha *iv.* be bereaved; *cf.* muucha

himuchala *adj.* bereaved

hina *tv.* hoe, chop weeds (~-, hinna)

hina'atua *dv.* tell on someone, inform (~-, hihina'atoa)

hinaikia *tv.* count (~-, hihinaikia)

hinaikiari *n.* already counted

hinaikiawakame *n.* sum, total

hinanke *n.* meeting (of persons or objects)

hinavaka *iv.* preach (*syn.* hinavakawamta ya'a)

hinavakawame *n.* sermon

hine *tv.* use as a cover (hin-, hinne and hihine)

hinepo *tv.* uncover, unveil, take cover off of (~-, hinnepo); Aapo a ~k. S/he uncovered it.

hiniam *n.* shawl

hinilwachisi *adv.* dangerously; Apo ~ aane. S/he's living dangerously.

hinko'ola *tv.* race (~-, hihinko'ola)

hinne'u *tv.* save (~-, hihinne'u)

hinne'uri *adj.* rescued, safe, saved

hinneola *tv.* take over, take control

hinneuwa *iv.* be saved

hinte *iv.* be covered up (~-, hihinte)

hintoa *tv.* cover with (~-, hihintoa)

hinu *tv.* buy (~-, hihin); Chino tiendapo ~ri. It was bought at the Chinese store. Inepo paanim Mariatau woi peesopo ~k. I bought the bread from Mary for two dollars. Empo ka yoemta maakinata ~ne? Is it not that man's car that you are buying?

hinuri *adj.* sold

hiohte *tv.* write about (about = *d.o.*; ~-, hihiohte); Aapo aet ~k. S/he wrote about her/him.

    a teawam~, sign (signature; *syn.* firmaora, a teawam yecha)

hiohtei *n.* alphabet, written, writing

hiohteme *n.* writer; secretary, clerk

    hiokoe *tv.* forgive one, confess (~-, hihiokoe); Apo ameu au hi~. She's apologizing to them.

    au ~ *tv.* 1. apologize, ask for forgiveness 2. be stingy; Apo au au hiokoe. = 1. He's asking him for forgiveness. 2. He's being stingy to him.

    Dios enchi ~ utte'esia *exp.* Thank you (*sg.* addressee).

    Dios enchim ~ utte'esia *exp.* Thank you (*pl.* addressee; *var.* Dios em chiokoe utte'esia).

    ne ~ *exp.* please, excuse me

    ta chuvala ne ~. Pardon me/excuse me.

hiokoewame in: emo ~, *n.* apology

hiokole *tv., n.* 1. *tv.* pity (hiokoli-, hihhiokole) 2. *n.* compassion, sympathy; A: Tua ne lotte. B: Enchi ne ~. A: I'm really tired. B: I feel sorry for you.

    ian lautipo te enchi ~ *exp.* our deepest sympathy (addressed to someone in grief; *lit.* right now we pity you)

hiokoliwame *n.* act of compassion

hiokot *adv.* pitifully

    ~ a hiawak, put someone down/demean

    ~ aane *iv.* be suffering

    ~ ea *iv.* feel miserable, be needy

    ~ hiawa *tv.* disparage

    ~ hoa *tv.* punish one, mistreat one

    ~ maachi *iv.* pitiful, painful, pathetic

hiokotwachi *adj.* pitiful

hioptua *tv.* confuse, cause to make a mistake

    hioria *iv.* 1. fast ritually 2. take it easy, get well (~-, hihioria)

hiosia *n.* 1. paper 2. venereal disease

    ~ nooka, *iv.* read

    ~ ta'a, *iv.* be literate

    ~ tomi, *n.* paper money, bills

    ~ totohame, *n.* messenger, ambassador

hiove *tv.* try on; make a mistake (hiop-, hihiove)

    ama ~ *tv.* try on (*ex.* pantolonim ~, try on pants; vochampo ~, try on shoes; kamisolam ~, try on shirts)

    ama vutti ~ *iv.* blunder

hiovek *adj.* mistaken

hioveka *adv.* by mistake

hiovila *tv.* 1. try, attempt 2. try on clothing 3. try out (~-, hihiovila); Ana ~vae. I want to take it for a test drive.

hiovukun *adv.* maybe, might; ~ huni ka kotne. You might not sleep.

hiowa *n.* Holy Week restrictions

hiowame *n.* mourning, mourning restrictions

hiowane *n.* ritual fasting

hiowe *n.* chicura, canyon ragweed (*Ambrosia ambrosioides*)

hipaksia *iv.* be laundering (~-, hihipaksia)

hipetam *n.* bed

hipeteka *iv.* make out bed (hipetek-, hipeteteka)

hipette *iv.* make mats (~-, hihipette)

hipi'ike *iv.* wring, squeeze (hipi'ik-, hihipi'ike)

hipi'ikim *n.* milk (*syn.* leechim)

hipona *iv.* beat drum, play music in general (hipon-, hihipona)

hiponreo *n.* musician

hiponreom *n.* band (musical group)

hippue *tv.* own, possess, have; keep (hippœ'u-, hihippue); Ne ika laapista ~. I own this pencil.

> ama ~ *iv.* have writing; hiosia kaita ama ~n, the page was blank

hipu'uwa *iv.* be kept; Ume yaaven im ~. The keys are kept here.

hipuyesa'alim *n.* a salamander *sp.*

hiruke *tv.* play musical rasp (hiruk-, hihiruke)

hirukia aso'ola *n.* rasp (musical; small)

hirukiam *n.* rasp (musical)

hisika *iv.* cut hair (~-, hissika)

hisikareo *n.* barber

hissa *tv.* throw, broadcast, toss (particulate matter; ~-, hihissa)

hissoa *iv.* poke (~-, hihissoa; *var.* hihsoa)

hisuma *tv.* tie it up (~-, hissuma)

hisumai *adj., n.* 1. *adj.* bundled, wrapped 2. *n.* package

hisumia *n.* 1. bundle, package, burden 2. bandage

hisumiam *n.* pascola's strips of black cloth

hita *pn.* what, thing, something, which; ~ mesapo kattek. There is something on the table. Aman ne hita vichak. I see something. ~ mesapo katek? What's on the table? Empo ~ hinuk? What did you buy? Aapo ~ enchi makne? Will s/he give you anything? Yo—ko ~sa te hoone? Are we doing anything tomorrow? Empo ~ yeu a puane ti ea? Which do you think he will pick (*var.* ~ empo yeu a puane tia?) ~ kolor pinturata empo sauwavae em kari yoka vetchi'ivo? What color are you going to paint your house?

> ~ hoa *tv.* be doing something
>
> ~ huni'i, *pn.* anything, whatever
>
> ~ ta'ame *n.* expert
>
> ~ ta'awame, *n.* knowledge
>
> ~ tattaame, *n.* pyromaniac, firebug
>
> ~ tenku *iv.* imagine

~ tuttu'ule, *n.* curious, nosey

~ vetchi'ivo, *exp.* for what purpose?

~ wohowohoktame *n.* drill (tool)

~ yeu siika *exp.* something happened (emergency, crisis)

hitaa *interj.* what? (questioning expression)

hitasa *pn.* what is it?

hitasempo *exp.* what do you ___? (< hita + sa + empo); ~ bwa'avae? What do you want to eat?

hitasempoa *exp.* What are you doing?; A: ~? B: Ika ne hoa. A: What are you doing? B: I'm working on this. A: ~ tuuka yaak? B: Uka ne yaak. A: What did you do yesterday? B: I worked on that. A: ~ yo—ko ya'ane? B: Ika ne yo—ko ket ya'ane. A: What are you going to do tomorrow? B: Tomorrow I'm going to work on this.

hitasu *adv., interj.* as if, what if

hitatua *adv.* what could it be?

hitaven *pn.* something else

hitcha *tv.* hang out (clothes) (hitchá'a-, hihitcha)

hitcha'ala *iv.* hang out (laundry)

hitcha'ari *adj.* hung out

hite'i *n.* fishing net

hitevi *n., iv.* curer who uses spiritual healing as a primary therapy; *cf.* hittoareo

hitta *iv., n.* make, set fire (~~, hihitta)

hitta'areo *n.* one who clears a field by burning

hitto *tv.* cure, heal (~~, hihitto); yee aa ~, know how to cure; Maala aa ~. My mother can cure.

hittoa *n.* medicine; Wa ili ~ta vetchi'ivo te aman a makne. We will give him something for the small amount of medicine.

hittoareo *n.* herbalist, one who cures with herbs and medicinals; *cf.* hitevi)

hittoha *tv.* deliver, transport (~~, hihittoha)

hittohakame *n.* the one who has delivered

hittowa *iv.* become cured (*pst.* ~k, ~n; no other tenses usual); Huana ~k. Joan was cured. Aapo ~n. S/he was being cured.

hituni hoa *exp.* do as one pleases (< hita huni hoa)

hiusaka *iv.* be sounding (~~, hihiusaka)

hiu- *comb.* of hia, sound

hiutua *tv.* ring (doorbell, bell)

hiuwa *iv.* they are saying, it is being said that ...

hana ~ *iv.* insult, slander (*d.o.* = au); Aapo hana a hiuwak. S/he insulted/slandered her/him.

hiva₁ *interj.* here!; A: ~ peeso. B: Vusan tomi em nakulia. A: Here's a dollar. B: (And here's) seventy-five cents back.

hiva₂ *adv.* only, just; Ini hiva kaita intoko. This is all; there is nothing else (that's all there is). Aapo hiva aman si'ime. He's the only one going. Aapo ~ aman simne. He's the only one going over there.

Vai peesom ne ~ nesitaroa. I need at least three dollars.

~ ka *exp.* except; Si'ime aman saka ta Luis hiva ka aman siime. Everyone went except Louis.

~ naeni *adv.* exactly

~ veeki *adv.* same amount of

~ vena *adj.* same

~ venaku *adv.* in the same place

hiva₃ *adv.* always

~ vetchi'ivo *adv.* forever

~ vetchi'ivo hiapsiwame *n.* eternal life

~ yu *adv.* from then on, all the time, continually, constantly; Hiva yu namuke. S/he's always drunk. Aapo hiva yu hi'ibwa. S/he's always eating. Apo hiva yu huname supek. She always wears the same dress.

~ yu hoone *iv.* continue

hivatua *adv.* maybe so, could be, perhaps; A: Im kompai hani aavo weye tea. B: ~. A: They say my compadre is coming. B: Maybe that is so. Vempo ~ aman katne. They might go. Hunakiasachi ~ amemak siika. Apparently she went with them. ~ yo—ko yaine. Maybe he'll come tommorow.

hivep- *comb.* of hiveva, hit

hivatune *iv.* will be, will come about; Ini tekil ~. This work will come about.

hivavendaku *adv.* at the same place

hiveva *tv.* hit it, strike it (hivep-, hivveva)

hivevia *n.* 1. slash 2. club, stick (for shinny or golf)

hivoa *iv.* be cooking (hiv—o-, hivovoa); Hamutta ~u su yuktaitek. While the woman was cooking, it started to rain.

hivoleo *n.* cook

hivoo- *comb.* of hivoa, be cooking

hiwise *tv.* saw (hiwis-, hiiwise)

hiyoka *iv.* be painting (hiyok-, hiiyoka)

ho'ak *iv.* live, dwell, reside (*pst.* ~an, ho'a-, hohho'a and hoho'a)

ho'akame *n.* 1. household member 2. inhabitant

ka im ~ *n.* stranger, foreigner

ho'apo *adv.* at home; Chema ~ katek. Chema is at home.

ho'ara *n.* 1. household 2. village, pueblo 3. home village, home town 4. neighborhood; Eme ~po teopok? Do you have a church in the village? ~po ehkuelak into tiendak. There's a school and a store in the village.

bwe'u ~, town/city

ho'aram *n.* village

ho'arau wáate *iv.* be homesick

ho'opo *n.* a tree *sp.*

ho'opo *adv.* on the back (*cf.* hoo'o, back)

~vaari *n.* wetback (*syn.* mohao)

ho'otia *iv.* snore (ho'otiu-, hotitihia)

hoa₁ *tv.* 1. do, make 2. live, reside (*pst.* yaak, ya'a-, hohoa); Yo—ko hitasa te hoone? What are we doing tommorrow? Vaavu puatota ne yaak. I made a dish from clay.
  a eu ~ *tv.* do as one pleases; Uusi a eu ~. The boy does as he likes.
  a au ~ *iv.* take one's sweet time
  koko'osi a ~ *tv.* injure
  veuti ~ *tv.* waste; Vempo veuti am ~. They're wasting them/it.

hoa₂ *tv.* place them (*pl. obj.*; *sg. obj.* yecha; ~-, hohhoa)

hoa'ate *iv.* move (change residence); Tusoneu ne ~. I'm moving to Tucson.

hochi *adj.* 1. fine 2. finely ground; Haivu ~. It's already fine. Use'e si ~. This is very fine. Tu'isi ~ vachitamake paanim yaak. She made bread with fine corn flour.

hohhote *rdp.* of hoote, be sitting

hohohna *n.* acacia *sp.*

hohootua *dv.* make someone do something

hohoova *n.* jojoba (*Simmondsia chinensis*)

hohoria *dv.* make or do for; Maala hiva ne yu anis teeta ~ ne ko'okoeu. Mother always makes me anise tea when I am sick.

hohoroi *adj.* bumpy

hohowame *n.* usual, customary, ordinary

homotu *iv.* be a beggar (*pst.* ~k, ~n)

hoiwa *iv.* get used to (*d.o.* = au; ~-, hohoiwa); Apo ranchopo ~k. He got used to it at the ranch. U ili hamut au ~k. S/he got used to the little girl.

hoiwai *n.* companion

hoiwala *iv.* be used to; Im ne ~. I'm used to this place.

hokoptui *n.* widow, widower

hokte *iv.* wheezing (hokti-; no *rdp.*)

hoktia *n.* whooping cough

hoo ota *n.* backbone, main beam

hoo'o *n.* back (body part); *loc.* hoochi, on (the) back

hooka *iv.* sit down (*pl.*; *sg.* katek; *imp.* hooyo'em, *pst.* ~n, hoo-, hohoye); *cf.* hoote; Vahi muu'um huyapo ~. There are three owls in the tree. Vahi mansaanam mesat ~. There are three apples on the table. Saalapo siiyam ~. There are chairs in the living room.

hookame *pn.* those present, audience (*lit.* seated)

hoome *n.* 1. inhabitant 2. native 3. citizen

hoomo *n.* beggar

hoona *n.* oven

hoopea *iv.* be enthusiastic (with hita as *obj.*)

hoori *n.* place that has been sat in

hooria *dv.* do something for someone else

hooso *n.* 1. bear (animal) 2. a tree *sp.*

hoosom *n.* sickle

hoote *iv.* sitting (*pl.*; *sg.* yehte; ~-, hohhote); (*cf.* hooka)
  amae ~ *iv.* change one's mind (*pl.*)
  amae hohote *iv.* vacillate, change mind often (*pl.*)
hooti *adv.* snoring (with hia)
  ~ koche *iv.* be snoring
hootu *iv.* flexible (agreeable), amenable, cooperative
hoovo'e *n.* orange-red ants
hoowa *iv.* 1. be going on 2. to do to 3. be making; *cf.* hoa$_1$; kari ~, be
  making a house; hain huni ka howaka, even though nothing is
  done to them
hooye *iv.* sit down (*pl. imp.* hooyo'em); *cf.* hooka, yeesa
hope'era *n.* cheeks (one with big cheeks)
hopem *n.* cheeks
hopo *n.* a tree with large leaves
hopo'orosim *n.* necklace (of pascola or deer dancer; made of abalone
  shell)
horoi *adj.* uneven, bumpy (*pl.* hohoroi)
Hose *n.* Joseph
hota *tv.* soften (*cf.* bwalkote), grind finely (~-, hohota)
hoteka *iv.* sit down Sewau ~ te. We sit down to flowers (to the
  instruments used by deer singers).
hotekate *iv.* sit down to; Vesa te sewam ~. Let us sit down to the flower
  (deer singers' instruments).
hoteel *n.* hotel
hotolai *adj.* hollow (something hemispherical; *pl.* hohotolai)
hovei *n.* palm tree *sp.*
hovo hi'ibwa *iv.* eat one's fill
hovoa *iv.* get full, satiated (hovo'o-, hohovoa and hovvoa); Tua véa hovo
  hi'ibwa vaane. He wants to eat his fill.
hovoi *adj.* full
hoyo *n.* poison
  ~k, be poisoned; Hivatua ~k. Maybe it's poisoned.
hu *comb.* of hu'upa, mesquite
  ~ bwan'am *n.* mesquite gum
hu'i *n.* penis
  kuta ~, *iv.* be promiscuous (of a man; *cf.* hantiachi)
hu'u *pn.* that
hu'ubwa(su) *adv.* in a while
  ~ nanateme *n.* beginner
  ~ yo'otume *n.* young man
hu'ukte *iv.* be choking (hu'ukti-, huhu'ukte); *cf.* hukte
hu'uktia *tv.* choke (~-, huhu'uktia)
hu'unakiachi(sia) *adj.* 1. obvious 2. apparently not amiable; U
  hamut ~ machi aane. The woman doesn't appear to be amiable.
  ka ~ *adj.* confusing; *cf.* chiktuachi
hu'unakte *tv.* create (deliberately; hu'unakti-, no *rdp.*); Itom Achai O'ola
  itom im ~k. God made us here. ~ka hunuen aayuk. He did it on

purpose. Itom Ya'akame Achai O'ola inim bwan bwiapo itom ~kame. Our Old Father who made us on this weeping earth is our creator. Dios Surem ~k. God made the Surem.

hu'unaktei *n.* 1. creation, creature 2. planned thing

hu'unea *iv.* be knowledgeable (hu'une-); *cf.* aawe, ta'a; Aapo ka ~ hakun vicha aa wenelu. S/he doesn't know which way to go. Ne ka ~ haisa em hiapo. I don't know what you are saying. Ne ~k havesa ama tekipanoa. I found out who works there. Empo ~ haisa em hiakapo? Do you know what you said? Ne ~ hita in ya'anepo. I know what I will do. Ne ka ~ hita em teuwa'u. I don't know what you are saying. Apo ~ haveeta a vichaka'apo. He$_1$ knows who saw him$_1$. Apo ~ haveeta apo'ik vichaka'apo. He$_1$ knows the one who saw him$_2$.

hu'uneiya *tv.* 1. know 2. acknowledge 3. realize 4. find out (~-/hunei-, hune"eeiya); Apo lutu'uriata ~k. S/he realized the truth. Ta vesa ne kia lautipo avo huneivaeka weama. But I came quickly to find out. In a ~po vempo aman yahak. As far as I know, they arrived there.

hu'uneiya vaane *iv.* be nosey (with si'imek as *obj.*)

hu'uneiyawame *n.* 1. something known, fact, knowledge 2. consciousness

hu'uneiyawari *adj.* known

hu'unewame *n.* knowing

hu'upa *n.* mesquite (*Prosopis sp.*); ~naposa ket hittoa sauwa. Mesquite is used for medicinal purposes.

  ~ hamuchia, *n.* female mesquite

  ~ keka'a *n.* catclaw acacia (*Acacia greggii*)

  ~ o'owia *n.* male mesquite

  ~ taakam, *n.* mesquite bean pods (*syn.* pechita)

hu'uwasu *iv.* be freezing (~-, huhu'uwasu)

hua *comb.* of huya, wild

  ~ ko'oko'im *n.* chiltepin

  ~ koowi *n.* peccary, javelina

  ~ miisi *n.* wild cat

  ~ Yoeme *n.* O'odham, Pima, Papago

Huan *n.* John

hubwa *comb.* of hu'ubwa, young, early

  ~ heela *adv.* recently

  ~ hiva *adv.* just recently (*ex.* ~ hiva ansuk. It just finished.)

  ~ kupteo bwiikam *n.* early evening songs

  ~ yo'otu *n.* young man

hubweela *adv.* 1. recently 2. fresh (baked, cooked); ~ yuke. It rained recently. Huan aman ~ siika. John went there recently. Paanim ~ ya'awa. The bread is fresh.

hubwiva *adv.* just recently

hubwuni *adv.* always, constantly; ~ tomita reewe. He's always borrowing money.

huchahi *n.* a hawk *sp.* (*var.* hucha'i)

59

huchahko *n.* Brazil wood (*Haematxylon brasiletto*), a spiny shrub used for the notched raspers and rasping stick; Inian hia wa ~. The Brazil wood sounds like this.

huchi(a) *adv.* again, next; ~ avo weye. It's coming again.

    ~ **aane** *tv.* repeat (action)

    ~ **mechat** *adv.* next month

    ~ **senu** *adv.* again, one more time, another; Apo huchi senu karota hinuk. S/he bought another car.

    ~ **teuwa** *tv.* repeat (verbally)

    ~ **vicha** *adv.* back again

Hudio *n.* Jew (*var.* Hurio)

hue'ena *adj.* mean, cruel, bad tempered, evil

huevena *pn.* many, much (human; *syn.* vuu'u); ~ka im aane. There's a lot of people here. ~ka a vichak. Many people saw her/him. Inepo ~m vichak. I saw a lot of them. ~ hamuchim ka tekipanoa. There aren't many people working.

huevenasi *adv.* many times

Hueves *n.* Thursday

huha *iv., tv.* 1. *iv.* fart 2. *tv.* sting (~~, huhha and huuha); *cf.* huuha; Mumu ne ~k. The bee stung me.

huham *n.* fart

huhteme *n.* 1. whale 2. dolphin, porpoise

huhu'ubwa *tv.* smelling it, sniffing it (~~, huhhu'ubwa)

huhupwa *iv.* getting married (of a man); *cf.* kukunawa

huiwa₁ *tv.* sense (premonition, especially when an older child senses that another child is on the way and pouts; *pst.* ~n, ~~, huhhuiwa); Aapo a ~n. S/he sensed it before it happened. U ili usi waivaeka a ~. Because the child is going to have a sibling, s/he is huiwa.

huiwa₂ *n.* 1. arrow 2. ammunition

    ~ **to'oria** *n.* quiver

hukta *tv.* smell it (~~, hukhukta)

huktila *adj.* choked

hukte *iv.* choke on liquids (hukti-, hukhukte; *cf.* hu'ukte, tatte); chichiae ~, choke on one's own saliva

hulen *adv.* that's why

hulentuko *adv.* for that reason

hulensan *adv.* that's why

Hulio *n.* July

Hurio *n. var.* of Hudio, Jew

huma'aku *adv.* maybe, perhaps

humak *adv.* 1. it would be better if ... 2. maybe (*var.* ~u'u); haivu ~ *adv.* about, more or less; Haivu humak mamni meecha ama vivitwakai. It was seen about five months ago. Apo ~ aman aane. S/he might be there. Apo ~ yeu yeune. S/he may go out to play.

    ~ **huni'i** *adv.* maybe; ~ te lauti sahak tu'ine. It would be better if we left early.

humaksan *adv.* maybe so

humaku'u *adv.* maybe, perhaps, probably (*var.* humak)

huna *pn.* that; Apo hiva yu ~me supek. She always wears the same dress.

huna'a *pn.* that (*emph.*)

huna'aka *interj.* of course, indeed; A: Empo muunim waata? B: ~. A: You want some beans? B: Sure.

hunaen *adv.* like that

hunaet *adv.* on that

hunak(o) *adv.* then; In maala ~ ka ne yo'otuko chin puppuane. Back then when I was still a child my mother used to pick cotton. A: Mil novesiento sinkwentai siatepo chin puppuan? B: Heewi, ~. A: Did she pick cotton in 1957? B: Yes, then. ~ apo yepsak. Then s/he came. ~ véa apo yepsak. And *then* s/he came.

hunaksan *adv.* then, and then, from then on; ~ aapo hiva yu au susua. From then on, she took good care of herself.

hunaksu *adv.* 1. what if 2. and then what (in relating story or event); A: Yoeme kari veppa kom wechek. B: ~. A: That person fell from the roof. B: And then what happened?

hunakteka *adv.* deliberately, on purpose, intentionally; Apo ~ a too vuitek. He left him behind on purpose.

hunaktekame *n.* creator (with yee)

hunakvea *conj.* and then; A: ~ simne u maaso? Heewi, inime vahim chupuko. A: And then the deer will go out? B: Yes, when (we) finish these three (songs).

hunalensu *interj.*, *adv.* 1. *interj.* likewise (in reply) 2. *adv.* equally (*var.* hunanensu); Waka'a pueplo yo'oweta intok waka'a wiko'i ya'urata ket hunalensu si'imeta tu'urisuk. The governor and the war leaders all wanted him equally (Cajeme). A: Tua Dios em chiokoe utteasia. B: Heewi, empo ket ~. A: May God forgive you strongly. B: Yes, and you likewise.

hunalevena *iv.* alike

hunam(a) *adv.* over there (farther than aman or um); ~ kom wechek. It fell down over there.

hunama wo'i *n.* streaked coyote *sp.*

hunaman(i) *adv.* over there (*s.* ayamansu)

hunanakle *iv.* aim at (with aet)

hunanensu *adv. var.* of hunalensu, equally

hune'ela *adj.* empty (*pl.* hunne'ela)

huneewam *n.* knowledge, wisdom

hunen *adv.* thus; ~ hiuwa. That's what they say.

hunuensan *conj.* that is why; U yoeme si omte, ~ apo ka wotte. The man is very angry, so he is keeping silent.

hunensu *interj.* that's why

hunera *adj.* ugly, plain; Kaarom nau tahtekapo unna huneraikan. The auto accident was terrible.

61

huneram *n.* voices that speak from where a dead person slept or sat

hunerasi anwa *iv.* be wild (in behavior)

huni *adv.* so, thus

      ka ~ *adv.* never again

Hunio *n.* June

hunneiya *tv.* belittle; U hamut hiva yee ~. That woman is always belittling people.

hunniawa *tv.* 1. make fun of, tease 2. deride, malign (~-, huninniawa; *cf.* hana hiuwa); Aapo hiva yee ~ne. He is always putting people down.

hunta *n.* gathering, meeting, assembly

huntuk *conj.* for that reason

huntuko *interj.* well, ... (*syn.* abwe)

huntuksan *conj.* that is why

hunu *pn.* that (*obj.* uka, *pl.* ume; *var.* u, nu; *emph.* huni'i, hunu'u, *obj.* hunuka); Abwe heewi ne ket kia enchim suate vicha enchim ovisi aneo huni'i. Well, I'm bothering you while you are busy. A: Em maala ka im katek? B: ~, au ne chaivae. A: Is your mother home? B: Yes, I'll go call her. A: Katin Peo sehtul ama wam weeka a vichaktia. B: ~ ne ka a hu'uneiya. A: Once Peter saw it going around. B: Well, I didn't know that.

hunulevena *adv.* like that (*var.* nulevena, hunulevevena)

hunuen *adv.* thus

     ~ eiya *tv.* assume

     ~ maachi *iv.* that's the way it is

     ~ yee eiyame *n.* assumption

hunueni *adv.* really

hunuensan *adv.* that is why; Vocham kanna'ana, ~ u nana ka am waatan. The shoes are not alike; that's why the girl didn't want them.

hupa *n.* skunk; Hupa hu'upapo vétuku kateka huvam ~k. The skunk sitting underneath the mesquite farted stinkingly (traditional tongue twister).

hupsi *n.* guayparin, tree of life, holywood (*Guaicum sp.*), a heavy hardwood that will sink

hupti *adv.* fast, quickly, rapidly (human growth; with yo'otu)

hupvawame *n.* bride-to-be (*syn.* huvituvaeme)

Hurasim *n.* Chapayekas

Hurio *n., adj.* Jew(ish)

hurisiaal *n.* police officer (*Son.*; *cf.* polesia)

husai *adj.* brown; Paapam huhusai. Potatoes are brown.

husaite *tv.* brown

husali *adj.* brown (*aff.*)

husama *adj.* brownish; Ne hikat ~ waiwanola cha'aka (*s.*). I dangle brownish on the top.

husari *adj.* brown (derogatory)

hutta *tv.* give a rash (~-, huhutta); Pantaloonim a ~k. The pants are giving him a rash.

hutte *iv.* get a rash (hutti-, huhutte)

huttiam *n.* skin rash

hutu'uki *n.* a small shrub *sp.*

huu *pn.* that (near; *var.* u)

huuha *tv.* bite (insect), sting (~-, huhha); *cf.* huha

huuki *n.* pit house

Huuras *n.* Judas

huuri *n.* badger

huuva *iv.* smell, stink (*pst.* ~kan, ~-); opposite of winhuva; Im huhhvae. It stinks in here.

huuve *iv.* marry (of men), take a wife (hup-, huhuve)

huuvi *n.* wife (*masc.*; *cf.* huviawai)

huva'asam *n.* venereal disease

huvachinai *n.* stinkbug

huvae toosa *n.* spider web; U huvae tosa si tu'i hittoa chuktiam vetchi'ivo. Spider web is good for cuts.

húvahe *n.* spider (*gen.*)

huváhe *n.* bebelama, chaste tree (*Vitex mollis*), a tall tree with a thick trunk

huvakvena *n.* a medicinal plant (*Bursera laxiflora*)

huvaria *n.* lower back

~po ko'okoe *iv.* have hemorrhoids

huvekame *n.* married man

huviawai *n.* 1. wife (in general; *cf.* huuvi) 2. housewife

huvituvaeme *n.* bride-to-be (*syn.* hupvawame)

huweetem *n.* toy(s)

huya *n.* 1. plant, tree, bush 2. branch 3. wilderness (*comb.* hua; *obj.* huata; *syn.* pocho'oria)

~ Ania *n.* Wilderness World (natural world, wildwood; desert, brushland, and river areas outside the realm of town; physical manifestation of the yo an'a)

~ ko'oko'i *n.* chiltepin, wild chile (*Capsicum annuum*)

~ kuu'u *n.* agave

~ Nokame *n.* the Talking Tree (*syn.* Kuta Nokame)

~ ro'akteme *n.* tumbleweed (*syn.* mo'oko)

~ tatakame *n.* fruit tree

~ vakulia *n.* branch

~ wakia *n.* hay, straw

huyaute *iv.* go to the bathroom outside (huyauti-, huhuyaute)

huyu *pn.* that (farther away; *cf.* hu); ~ka neu toha. Bring me that one. ~ husai. That one is brown.

huyuka'a *interj.* that (*resp.*)

huyu'u *pn.* that one (*emph.*)

I

i *pn.* this (*var.* nii; *obj.* ika; *pl.* ime); A: Hita sempoa? B: Ika ne hoa.
   A: What are you doing? B: I'm doing/making this.
ia *pn.* this (inanimate); ~ veeki, this much
i'a *iv.* be cruel (with au); U ili o'ou au ~. The little boy is cruel. U o'ou si
   au ~. The man is a brute.
ia veppani *adv.* this size
ia vetchi'ivo *conj.* because of this
iae *adv.* with this
iamak *pn.* with this
ian *adv.* 1. now 2. today (*paus.* iani); ~ maasu eme'e a vicha in kari haiti
   machi. As you can see, my house is a mess.; Hitasempo bwa'aka
   iani? What did you just now eat? Apo ian a hinuk. S/he bought
   it today.
      ~ katriam *n.* contemporaries, people of today
      ~ lautipo *adv.* at this very instant, right now
      ~ maasu *adv.* as you can see
      ~ tukapo *adv.* tonight
      ~ tahti *adv.* up tom now (*syn.* ~ kamti used in Sonora)
      ~ weeme *iv.* be happening to
ianriapo *adv.* at this time
iat *adv.* on this; *cf.* aet
iatana *adv.* from/on this side
ichakte *iv.* get bored of (of = nea, ea, ae, etc.; ichakti-, i'ichakte)
ichaktiachi *adj.* boring
ii'i *pn.* this one (in response; *obj.* ika; *pl.* ime'e)
iiket *pn.* this one (*obj.* ikaket, *pl.* imeket); Hiakim nassuaka'u ~ kaivu
   ta'aapo a koptane. The Yaquis who fought on this occasion will
   never be able to forget it to this day. ~ tu'i. This one is good.
   Maria ikaket nu'uka. Mary took this one.
iivo *adv.* on this side, from this side
ilempo *adv.* in this way
ileni(a) *adv.* this way
ili *adj.* small, little, few
      ~ aache *iv.* snicker, giggle
      ~ chivu *n.* kid (goat)
      ~ chu'u *n.* puppy
      ~ hamut *n.* little girl
      ~ Hu'upam *n.* Little Mesquites (former Yaqui settlement in
         Marana area west of old Casagrande highway)
      ~ kava'i *n.* colt
      ~ kucha'ara *n.* teaspoon
      ~ mam pusiam *n.* little finger
      ~ misi *n.* kitten
      ~ o'ou *n.* little boy
      ~ omte *iv.* be grumpy

~ pato *n.* duckling
~ teta *n.* pebble
~ totoi *n.* chick
~ uusi *n.* child
~ voo'o *n.* path
iliikim *adv.* a little bit; Aapo ~ waata. S/he wants a little bit.
ilikkani *adj.* narrow, small (area)
ilippani *adj.* short
ilitchi *adj.* small, little (*pl.* illichi)
illichi *pl.* of ilitchi, small
illikim *adv.* in little bits, in small portions; ~ am miika, gives them little
     portions
im *adv.* here (*var.* nim)
im tahti atte'ari *n.* the sacred Yoeme boundary (*syn.* lindero)
im vicha *adv.* from over here
imcha *adv.* hereabouts
ime *pn.* these
imi'i *adv.* over here; *cf.* im, wakin
imin *adv.* over here
in *pn.* my
in yeu *adv.* from here
inaeko *adv.* about this time
inchektaroa *tv.* inject
indulhensia *n.* indulgence
ine'a *iv.* feel, sense (ine'e-, i'inea)
ine'e *comb.* of ine'a, feel
ine'etua *tv.* make someone feel
ineete *iv.* get well, convalesce (~-, i'ineete and inneete)
inen(i) *adv.* like this
inepat *pn.* in front of me (with verbs of motion)
inepo *pn.* I
inepola *pn.* myself
inia vetchi *adv.* this size
iniamak *adv.* in this way
inian *adv.* in this way (*syn.* iyilen)
iniavu *adv.* last year
ini'i *pn.* this one (*resp.*); A: Have yo'ok? B: ~. A: Who won? B: This one.
inikun *pn.* so this is the one; Ala ~ maiso yoleme, hunukun maiso
     yoleme, ~ tua maiso yoleme. So now this is the deer person,
     so he is the deer person, so he is the real deer person.
inilen *adv.* in this way
inim(i) *adv.* right here
iniminsu *adv.* over here (*s.* iyiminsu)
inivo *adv.* from this side (*cf.* wanna'avo)
iniwa *pn.* this is (the) ___; ~ itom lutu'uria. This is our truth. ~ woi vahi
     lutu'uria. This is the two-three truth (said at the end of a speech
     or oration).

inopat in front of me

insinio *n.* insignia

into *conj.* and, while; Senu huena, senu into tuu hiapsek. One is mean, while the other is good hearted (said of twins). Apo na'asom hinuka ~ plaatanom. He bought oranges and bananas.
> ka into *adv.* quit (for good); Apo ka ~ yenvae. S/he wants to stop smoking.

intok(o) *conj.* when

intuchia *adv.* again, once again

isla *n.* island

itepo *pn.* we; *cf.* te

itepola *pn.* ourselves

ito *pn.* us (with *postp.* vetchi'ivo)

itoa *pn.* of us (with verbs ichakte, rohikte, tiiwe)

itochi *pn.* at/on us

itom *pn.* us, our

Itom Achai *n.* the Lord's Prayer

Itom Ae *n.* the Virgin Mary

itomak *pn.* with us (comitative)

itomto *pn.* from us

itopat *pn.* in front of us

itot *pn.* on/at us

itotana *pn.* from, alongside us

itou *pn.* toward/into/beside/from us; *cf.* -wi, -u

itou aneme *n.* guest, visitor

iva'achaka *tv.* embrace, hug (ivacha'a-, ivachacha'e)

iva'anama *tv.* hold in arms, cradle, embrace while moving around (iva'anam-, iva'ananama); *cf.* puanam; ~ sisime, go along cradling in one's arms

ivakta *tv.* cuddle, hug, embrace (~-, i'ivakta)

ivakte *iv.* be bunching things in arms (said of another person; ivakti-, i'ivakte)

ivo(su) *adv.* on this side of

iyilen *adv.* in this way (*syn.* inian)

iyiminsu *adv.* over here (*s.*; = iniminsu)

K

ka *adv.* not; U yoeme ~ hamutta vitchu. It's not the woman that the man is looking at. U yoem hamutta ka vitchu. The man is not looking at the woman.
> ~ a'asoa *adj.* sterile (female)
> ~ aawe *iv.* unable, cannot
> ~ allea *iv.* be upset
> ~ alleaka taawak *iv.* be disappointed

~ amma'ali *adj.* improperly, badly
~ au hiokoe *iv.* generous
~ au sua *iv.* be careless
~ au vitchu *iv.* ignore (*d.o.* = au)
~ au yo'oritevo *tv.* solicit sex
~ bwasi *adj.* raw, uncooked, hungover
~ chan(san), not even (~ chansan ne sevek. I'm not even cold. I ~ a naken. S/he didn't ever care for her/him. Ka chan a miikak. S/he didn't even give her/him anything.)
~ chupia incomplete, unmarried
~ haiki *adv.* not many
~ haitimachi *iv.* be pure, clean
~ ho'akame *iv.* be homeless
~ ho'otu *iv.* misbehave, stubborn
~ ho'otu *iv.* be impossible
~ hu'unakiachi *iv.* unfamiliar, vague, confusing
~ hu'uneiyawame *n.* secret (unknown)
~ huni *adv.* never again
~ huuva *iv.* weak (odor)
~ huvek *iv.* unmarried (man)
~ kia *iv.* be bland, tasteless
~ kolorek *iv.* drab, colorless
~ kunak *iv.* unmarried (woman)
~ kusisi *adv.* secretly (without noise)/stealthfully
~ lulu'uteme *adj.* everlasting, eternal, enduring, lasting
~ maachi *adj.*, *n.* 1. *adj.* dark 2. *n.* Hell
~ Machikuni *n.* Hell (*lit.* no light; *cf.* Tahita Vetepo)
~ machikun *adv.* into darkness
~ machileu *adv.* in the dark
~ mamachi *iv.* be invisible, dark
~ mekka *iv.* near (with aane)
~ mekka ko'omi *adj.* shallow
~ nanancha *iv.* be different
~ nanau hita ta'a *iv.* know unequally
~ nanaumachi *iv.* be mixed
~ nanawichi *iv.* uneven
~ nappat *adv.* not as before
~ nareempani *adv.* uneven in length
~ nokame *n.* dumb person
~ nooka *iv.* mute
~ nu'utu *iv.* unobtainable
~ nuklak *iv.* eternal, unending, perpetual, lasting
~ oviachi *adj.* easy, simple
~ pappea *iv.* listless, lethargic
~ pasaroa machi *iv.* be unbearable, dreadful
~ suak *iv.* crazy, senile

~ ta'awak *iv.* unknown
~ tamek *iv.* toothless
~ tea *exp.* it's so, really
~ tekwak *iv.* have little meat
~ tekipanoa *iv.* be unemployed
~ tekwak *iv.* be skin and bones
~ tiiwe *iv.* bold, daring
~ tu'i *iv.* bad, harmful
~ tua suak *iv.* slow, stupid
~ tua yuma'i *iv.* deformed, mentally retarded
~ tu'ure *tv.* oppose, object
~ tu'uriwa *n.* opposition, objection
~ u'use *iv.* sterile (male)
~ utte'ak *iv.* weak
~ vaeka *exp.* need, require (*cf.* vaeka)
~ vaekai *adv.* must (*cf.* vaekai)
~ vamvamse *iv.* be unhurried
~ vehe'e *iv.* cheap
~ vehetuari *iv.* unpaid
~ viohko *adj.* dull (not sharp)
~ voochak *adj.* barefoot
~ vovicha *iv.* be impatient
~ wotte *iv.* quiet, taciturn, reserved (~ wotti-, ~ wotwotte)
~ yantiachi *iv.* naughty, misbehave
~ yantimaachi *iv.* unsteady
~ yee hatteiya *tv.* be fearless
~ yee nake *tv.* be uncaring
~ yee tu'ure *iv.* 1. not care for 2. be prejudiced
~ yee yo'ote *iv.* 1. come onto sexually (to unwilling person)
    2. rape, molest, violate; ka a yo'orivae, coming onto
    her/him
~ yeeka *iv.* weak, unable to move
~ yo'ori machi *iv.* be disreputable
~ yoem eiya *tv.* mistrust
~ yoem eiya machi *iv.* be fickle
~ yu'utu *iv.* be immovable,stubborn
~ yuma'i *iv.* be a freak, unnatural
ka'ayu'e *tv.* unable to unfasten or open 2. unable to convince or control
kaachin *pn.* nothing; Neemak ~ machi a takea. As far as I can tell, it's
    okey with him.
    ~ maachi *exp.* nothing (in response to greeting)
kaakaatia *iv.* caw
kaakuni *adv.* nowhere, anywhere
kaal *n.* lime
kaama *n.* bed
kaapa'i *n.* palate

kaapam *n.* cape, cloak

kaape *n.* coffee

kaaro *n.* automobile; ~ lauti weye. The car is going slowly.

Kaarom *n.* Big Dipper (Yoemes see the Dipper as a big four-wheeled cart with a long tongue; the stars represent the seven original Yaqui towns, and now the seven sacraments)

kaasoyoi *adj.* bright (*syn.* kalasolai)

kaata *n. obj.* of kari, house

káate *tv.* build (house, building)

kaáte *iv.* walk (*pl.*; kat-, kakate; *cf.* weye); Ite pueplo konila naa ~n itom wawaim vitvaekai. We walked around the village to see our relatives.

kaave *pn., adv.* 1. *pn.* no one (*var.* kave; *obj.* kaveta) 2. *adv.* absent; Em yoemiam kave ko'okoe? Is everyone well at your house? Emesu haisa aane—kave ko'okoe? Is everyone (in the family) well (more usual way of stating this)?

kaavetuk *iv.* disappear (of an individual or a group)

kaavo *n.* corporal

kaayam *n.* street; Huevena kaarim u kaayet ho'oka. There are a lot of cars on the street.

kaayo *n.* callus

kafe *n.* coffee (older *var.* kape)

kafeteera *n.* coffee pot, tea kettle

Kahe'eme *n.* 1. Jose Maria Leyva 2. Ciudad Obregon

kahho'ota *tv.* thaw (~-, kahhoota)

kahho'ote *iv.* melt (kahho'oti-, kahhoote)

kahón *n.* box

~ pattiria, lid (for box)

kahtiiwo *n.* penance, punishment

kahtiiyo *n.* castle

kahtikaroa *tv.* punish; Diosta itom aet ~kai huni wam hua ániapo, kaupo ket hooka wame santo iglesiam. Even if God doesn't punish us with it, there are still the holy churches over there in the wilderness world, in the mountains.

kaila *n.* light (pre-dawn)

kaita 1. *pn.* nothing 2. *num.* zero; Aapo ~po enchi ánia. S/he is not helping you in anything (not towing the line, freeloading).

~ chea bwe'u? Can't you find something bigger to wear (said in teasing)? ~ chea ili'ichi? Can't you find something smaller to wear (said in teasing)?

~ ea *tv.* have no compassion on

~ hoa *iv.* be idle, have time to, be free

~ hu'uneiya *iv.* innocent

~ nake *iv.* negligent

~ suale *iv.* heathen, unbeliever

~ vaesae *iv.* ungrateful

~ vetchi'ivo tu'i *iv.* useless, worthless, good for nothing (either
    from laziness or lack of knowledge)
~po taawak, be left with nothing (fame, charm)
~po taawala, be deluded (be a castle in the air)
~po tawane, won't amount to anything
~po tawavae, on the brink of
~po tawasuk, be a has been
kaitatu *iv.* disappear
kaitu'una *adv.* enormous amount; ~ au mikkak. He took too much food.
kaivala *interj.* it can't be (< kaivu + ala, if)
kaivu *adv.* never
kaka *adj., n.* sweet, candy
kakae *iv.* be sweet (~-, kakkae)
kakalo *iv.* be swinging; huyapo ~, swinging through the trees;
    kulumpiopo ~, swinging on a swing
kakava *iv.* lay eggs
kakava'ekame *n.* person(s) mounted on horseback
kakawa *n.* sweets (baked goods and/or fruit)
kakawaate *n.* peanut
kakkai *iv.* get sweet
kakkaitatu *iv.* never be in stock (*cf.* a'ayu)
kakkavetu *iv.* 1. not show up, not attend 2. vanish, disappear without
    trace; Ume wikichim ama ~k. The birds simply disappeared.
kalahko *adj.* clear (transparent)
kalahkoa *tv.* make clear
kalalai *adj.* weak
kalalipapati *adv.* twinkling (with aane); Wepul choki ~ aane. A star is
    twinkling.
kalasolai *adj., n.* 1. *adj.* bright, brilliant (*syn.* kaasoyoi) 2. *n.* Tucson
kalasoiti *adv.* brilliantly, brightly
kalavera *n.* skeleton (*syn.* ohta)
kama$_1$ *n.* squash
kama$_2$ *n.* caiman
kaamara *n.* camera
kamachiako *adv.* at night (*syn.* tuka'apo), during the night (*syn.*
    tuka'ariapo)
kameeyo *n.* camel
kaminaroa *iv., n.* 1. *iv.* go in procession (from church to ramada or back)
    2. *n.* such a procession; *cf.* hinanke
    ~ bwikam *n.* processional song
    ~ sonim *n.* processional tune
kaminaroawa *n.* a procession in progress
kamisetam *n.* undershirt
kamisoolam *n.* shirt
kamisoolamte *iv.* put on a shirt
kampaani *n.* bell

kampamento *n.* camping place

~ kus *n.* cross at camping place

kampani sewa *n.* bellflower

kampiuter *n.* computer

kampo *n.* camp

~ Dies *n.* Camp Ten (former Yaqui settlement in near Mesa, Arizona)

~ santo *n.* cemetery (*syn.* hihima'awa'apo; after a soul has become a star, it is free to roam all over the world, and that at where its body rests others can come to communicate with it and also find peace)

~ sewa *n.* wild flower (*gen.*)

~ Uno *n.* Camp One (former Yaqui settlement near Yoem Pueblo)

~ Vuuru *n.* Mule Camp (former Yaqui settlement Yoem Pueblo)

~ Wiilo *n.* Camp Skinny (former Yaqui settlement in the Marana area)

kamta *tv.* crush (~-, kamkamta)

kamti *adv.* in: ian kamti, up to now (*Son.*; *syn.* ian tahti)

kamukta *tv.* take drink, hold liquid in mouth

kamula *adv.* with pursed lips, holding liquid in mouth

kanal *n.* canal

kananam *n.* bandoleer, bullet belt

kanario *n.* canary

kanariom *n.* first tune played or danced

kanela *n.* cinnamon

kannao *n.* pomegranate

kanoa *n.* boat

kanoareo *n.* boatman

kanteela tachiria *n.* candle light

kanteelam *n.* candle; Tua te ~mak haiwakka huni'i. Truly we will be looking for them with candles (candles as a prayer).

kantileom *n.* candelabra

kantina *n.* bar, saloon, tavern

kantoora *n.* hymn singer (*syn.* koparia)

kanutio *n.* a plant *sp.* (*Ephedra sp.*)

kapa *n.* lamb's quarters (*syn.* choali)

kape *n.* coffee (*var.* kafe)

kapetai *n.* 1. captain 2. head of the Fariseos

kapinteo *n.* carpenter

kapirotaaram *n.* bread pudding

kapitulo *n.* chapter

kapo sewa *n.* waterlily

kaponte *tv.* castrate

kapontei *adj.* castrated

kapyeo *n.* cowboy

karakte *iv.* break a bone; wok ~k, broke a leg

kareeta *n.* car, cart
karenam *n.* chain
kari *n.* house, building (*obj.* kaata)
       techoa ~ *n.* jacal/wattle and daub house
       sankoa ~ *n.* brush house/wickiup
karipo waiwa *adv.* inside, indoors
karoote *n.* stick (weapon), club
karpa₁ *n.* tent
karpa₂ *n.* goldfish
karpeeta *n.* carpet (*syn.*hipetam); Wa ~ yo'oriwan. The carpet was
      respected.
karsel *n.* jail, prison
karsetiinim *n.* socks; ~po wokte, put on socks
karsetiinte *iv.* put on socks
karta *n.* letter
kartam *n.* mail
kartoon *n.* cardboard box
kartuunim *n.* cartoons
karuucha *n.* wheelbarrow
kat *conj.* don't (*cf.* -'e, -'em); ~ hunuen aane. Don't do/be like that.
      ~ televisionta vivitchu. Don't watch so much television.
      ~ sisime. Don't be going (there).
kataro *n.* cold (illness)
katchaka *iv.* be going (*pl.*; *sg.* weesime)
kate *interj.* won't
katek *iv.* be sitting, be situated (*sg.*; *pl.* yeesa; *pst.* ~an, yeh-, yeyesa);
      cf. yehte; Kosinapo meesa ~. There's a table in the kitchen.
      Saalapo soofa ~. The sofa is in the living room.
katem *pn.* don't (*lit.* not you); ~ a kopkopta. Don't forget this.
      ~ emo ko'okosoa. Don't hurt yourself.
katema *iv.* walk (*pl.*; *sg.* weyema; *syn.* weama)
katim *pn.* not them; ~ houvoa. They never get full.
      ~ hikkaha. They don't listen.
katin *interj.* remember...; ~ sauko seewam, naoto'oria into negrita tu'isi
      tu'i taiwechiata vetchi'ivo. Recall that elderberry, naoto'oria and
      negrita is really good for a fever.
kati'ikun *interj.* don't you remember?; Kooni, hitasa mahaika, saiyula
      vo'oki? ~ vaka hiuwata mahai (*s.*)? Crow, what are you afraid of,
      all huddled up? Don't you remember that reed arrow?
kati'inia *interj.* don't you remember?
katom *n.* ball of wood or bone used for shinny (taahivevia)
katriam *n.* people (with ian, hakwo)
katte *exp.* we don't; ~ kaáte., We don't walk.
kau *comb.* mountain
      ~ chani *n.* a curcubit *sp.* (*Ibervillea sonorae*)
      ~ chuuna *n.* wild fig (*Ficus sp.*)
      ~ kokovi'iku *n.* canyon

~ mochik *n.* mountain tortoise
~ sapo *n. var.* of sapo
~ siiva *n.* cliff, precipice
~ tavachin *n. var.* of tabwiko seewa
~ vattai *n.* dock (*Rumex hymenosepala*; the roots of which are
used for gum disease, as a mouthwash, and for fever)
kausi *conj.* even though; ~ au oileka huni aman siika. Even though he is
not brave, he still went. Empo ka yo ~ wolekame, hitasa haliwa?
You who do not have enchanted legs, what are you looking for?
kauwam *n.* mother's milk
kava'e refers to horseback (not used alone)
aa ~ *iv.* able to ride (horseback)
kava'i *n.* horse (*comb.* kavai)
kavaeka *adv.* must; ~ te pueplou noitine. We must go to town.
kavai *comb.* of kava'i, horse
~ aso'ola *n.* colt
~ hamuchia *n.* mare
~ siila *n.* saddle
~ sisi *n.* mushroom
kavai siisi *n.* mushroom
kavam *n.* 1. egg(s) 2. testicles
Kavansam *n.* a dance tune
kavavoa *n.* sheep pelt, wool, fiber
kavayeo *n.* cowboy (*var.* kapyeo is used by older people)
Kavayo *n.* Cavalry Society member
Kavayom *n.* Cavalry Society
kaveta *pn.* no one (*obj.*; *cf.* kaave); hatteiya, *iv.* be fearless; yo'ore,
iv. impolite, rude
kawi *n.* 1. mountain 2. as a modifier this may indicate a wild variety of a
plant; (*ex.* kawi bwa'arom, a large kind of purslane that grows in
the mountains)
~ vo'okame *n.* mountain range
kawis *n.* fox
kayayati *n.* background noise
kayehon *n.* alley
ke *conj.* before
ke'e *tv.* bite it (*pst.* ~ka, ki'i-, keke); Vaakot yee ~! The snake bites!
ke'esam(i) *n.* first; ke'esam konti, first procession; Ii'i ke'esami. This is
the first.
ke'ewe *iv.* get wood (~-, keke'ewe)
kecha *tv.* 1. erect 2. stop the flow of 3. turn off (machine); (*cf.* patte)
(kechá'a-, keecha); U tapon va'ata ~. The plug stopped the water.
kecha'i *adj.* erect(ed) (*sg.*; *pl.* ha'abwai)
keche *adv.* how; A: ~ allea? B: Ket tu'i. A: How are you doing? B: Just
fine. Dios em chania, ~ allea. Hello (traditional greeting; *pl.*
addressee, Dios em chaniavu, kettekevete allea; *cf.* hiokoe, kette).
kechia *adv.* also

73

kee *adv.* not yet; kee yepsak, hasn't gotten here yet; Vempo ~ yaka. They haven't arrived yet.

kee vach'a *adv.* not yet

keekam *n* sores, mange, skin disease

keekim *n.* cake (dessert)

keesum *n.* cheese

keka'a *adj.* mangy

kekeka *rdp.* of weyek, be standing (*sg.*)

kemkemti *adv.* noisily; ~ weye, going along noisily

kensur *n.* cancer

kepa cha'atu *iv.* come together and drizzle rain a long time (re: clouds; used only in *pst.*)

kepe *iv.* close eyes (kup-, kepikepikte)

kepta *tv.* put in mouth (~-, kepkepta)

kesiktila *adj.* scraped (skin)

ket *adv.* 1. also 2. self; Dios ~ apo enchi an'ane. God himself will help you.

kette *adv.* still; Dios em chiokoe, ketne allea. God keep you (traditional greeting; *pl.* addressee, Dios em chiokoe, ~ allea; *cf.* hiokoe, keche).

ketun(ia) *adv.* still, since; Aapo'ik ketun ama tekipanoao tu'iakan. As long as she was working there, it was good.

ketwo *adv., n.* morning; Ian ~ hitasempo bwa'aka> What did you have to eat this morning?

ketwosu *adj.* already to go in the morning

keve'ete *tv.* carry in mouth (keve'eti-, kekeve'ete); Chuu'u ili wiikitta ~. The dog has a little bird in its mouth.

kevenia *n.* castor bean (plant; *Ricinus communis*), used for treating fevers and headaches (leaves are soaked in water and mixed with lard and ashes and applied to large areas of body to be replaced as needed)

kevenia váchia *n.* castor bean (seed)

ki'i- *comb.* of ke'e, bite

kia₁ *adv.* only, just; Kia waka nokta enchim a mahtane, vichau vicha. Just this talk will teach you, in the future.
    ~ etehoi *n.* legend, myth
    ~ hiapsa, lead a boring existence, just existing (*cf.* tuu hiapsekame)
    ~ nooki *n.* rumor, scandal
    ~ su *adv.* just so
    ~ valichiapo *iv.* pretend
    ~ pueplom, *n.* people without official ceremonial duties
    ~ veha *adv.* just so
    ~ yoemem *n.* ritually poor people

kia₂ *adj.* delicious (*pl.* kikkia); Amak ka ~. Sometimes they're not delicious.

kia₃ *iv.* fit into (~-, kikkia); Ume na'asom kahapo ~. The oranges fit into the box. Ama ne kiapea o'oven ta ne unna awi. I would like to fit into it, but I am too fat.

kiakama *n.* squash (variety with a throat)

kiale$_1$ *tv.* like, prefer, relish (kiali-, kikkiale)

kiale$_2$ *exp.* you just; ~ ka hikkaha. You just don't listen.

kiali *adv.* even though; Aapo kiali yo'otakuni tekipanoa. Even though he is old, he is still working. ~ ne eu nookan. That's why I'm talking to you.

kiali'ikun *conj.* that is why

kialim *adv.* they just (< vempo + kia); Kialim ka monteka sahak. They just left without saying anything.

kiasi *adv.* deliciously; ~ weche, hit the spot (satisfy); ~ ne wechek. That really hit the spot.

kiavea *tv.* 1. practice it 2. pretend (~-); ~ hiapsa, have no imagination, be locked into the daily grind

kichichite *iv.* swarm, wriggle

kichichiti *adv.* swarming, wriggling; ~ aane, feel something crawling up pants or sleeve

kiichul *n.* cricket

kiima *tv.* 1. bring them 2. insert them (*pl. obj.*; *sg. obj.* kivacha; kimá'a-, kikkima); U li hamut kiosiam kechapo ~. the girl is inserting flowers erect.

kíimu$_1$ *tv.* attack one

kiímu$_2$ *iv.* enter (*pl.*; *sg.* kivake; kimœ-, kikkimu)

kiivi *n.* permanent smile (because of facial features)

kik- *comb.* of weyek, be standing (*sg.*)

kikkia *rdp.* of kia$_2$ and kia$_3$

kikichiite *iv.* swarm, wriggle; ~ aane, feel something crawling up pants or sleeve

kikkimuwa'apo *n.* entrance

kiksime *iv.* be standing on a moving object (*sg.*; *pl.* kiksaka)

kikte *iv.* 1. stand up 2. stop (machine) (*sg.*; *pl.* hapte; ~-, kiikte); *cf.* weyek

kiktekte *pl.* of weyekte, walk

kilogram *n.* kilogram

kilometer *n.* kilometer

kimuria *n.* entrance

kinakte *iv.* squint, grimace, make a face (*d.o.* = au; ~-, kinakinakte); Aapo ne ~k. S/he gave me a dirty look. U ili o'ou au ~k. The boy squinted at him.

kinder *n.* preschool, daycare, kindergarten

kisaroa *tv.* fry it

kisaroari *adj.* fried

kitara *n.* guitar (*var.* kita)

kitareo *n.* guitar player

kitokte *iv.* contract (body)

kitta *tv.* pinch (~-, kikitta)

kitte *iv.* kneading (kitti-, kikitte)

kittim *n.* dough

kivacha *tv.* bring (*sg.* obj; *pl. obj.* kiima; ~-, kikkivacha)

kivake *iv.* 1. enter, go in 2. soak in (*sg.*; *pl.* k'imu; kivak-, kikivake);
  Vaa'am bwiapo kom ~k. The water soaked into the ground.
  apat ~ *iv.* cut in line
Kiyohtei *n.* Altar Guild member
Kiyohtei Yo'owe *n.* Altar Guild head
Kiyohteim *n.* Altar Guild
klasse *n.* class; vat ~, first class; sewundo ~, second class
ko'a *tv.* chew it (ko'o-, koko'a)
ko'apa'im *n.* a plant used to treat snake bite,; infections, and sores
ko'arek *iv.* wear a skirt (*pst.* ~an, koko'arek)
ko'ari *adj.* chewed
ko'arim *n.* skirt, dress
ko'arite *iv.* put on a skirt
ko'ate *iv.* put on a skirt (~-, koko'ate)
ko'o- *comb.* of ko'a, chew
ko'obwabwa'i *n.* crane (bird)
ko'oko *adj.* 1. hot, spicy 2. painful
ko'oko'era *adj.* unhealthy
ko'oko'i *n.* chile, pepper
Ko'oko'im *n.* Cocorit
ko'oko'itu *iv.* become hot from chiles (~-)
ko'okoa *n.* illness, sickness, disease; plague, epidemic
ko'okoe *iv., n.* 1. *iv.* be sick (*pst.* ~n, ~; not other tenses usual) 2. *n.* pain;
  Aapo vinwa ~k. S/he was sick for a long time.
  ~ weche *iv.* get sick
ko'okoeme *n.* sick person, patient
ko'okole *iv.* be in pain (ko'okoli-, kokko'okole); Maria henompo ~. Mary
  hurts in the shoulder.
ko'okosa *adv.* injuringly
  ~ hoa *tv.* 1. injure 2. beat, hit, strike (*cf.* chona) 3. torture (*pst.* ~
  yak, *comb.* ~ yá'a-)
ko'okosi *adv.* painful
  ~ a aula'apo *n.* wound
  ~ aane *iv.* be in pain
  ~ aayu *iv.* injure one's self; Kuruestau ka hihikubwawa;
  bwe'itukmampusiam hunak ~ ya'ane. Don't point at
  the rainbow; otherwise, one gets sores on the fingers.
  Kaveta ~ yak? Did it injure anyone?
  ~ hoa *tv.* torture; Aapo chuu'uta ko'okosi hoa. S/he is hurting
  the dog.
ko'omamaya *tv.* knock down with rock (ko'omamaya'a-, ko'omamama)
ko'om(i) *adv.* down, below, under, downward (*var.* kom); hunum ko'omi,
  below there; mekka ko'omi, deep
ko'omisu *adv.* down here; Apo a'avo ~ a tohak. He brought it down here.
  Vaiwa sililiti ~ yuyumao (*s.*). Coolingly, drizzlingly, downward it
  reached.

ko'orai *n.* dandelion

koa *n.* corral (*var.* kora); ~u, to the corral

koakta *tv.* turn it (~-, koakoakta)

koakte *iv.* turn, change course, diverge (koakti-, koakoakte)

koapa'im *n.* yerba de la golondrina (*Euphorbia sp.*, including *E. polycarpa*), members of the spurge family closely related to the poinsettia growing at high altitudes; used medicinally

koate *iv.* build a fence

Koasepe *n.* Corasepe

koche *iv.* asleep, sleeping (*sg.*; *pl.* kokoche; *pst.* kochok, kot-, kokkoche)

koche'a *n.* sleepyhead (*var.* koche'ela, koche'era)

koche'ela *n.* sleepyhead

kochi'ise *iv.* bed down, go to bed (*sg.*; *pl.* kokotvo)

kochimai *n.* lobster

kocho'i *n.* breast, chest, bosom

kochok *pst.* of koche, be sleeping
 sutti ~ *iv.* be fatigued, bushed, zonked

kochokame *n.* sleeper; ~ ka hita nu'une. Whoever falls asleep won't get anything.

koelai *adj.* round, conical

kohakte *iv.* revolve (kohakti-, kohakohakte); Ta'ata im ~u ne siika. When the sun was blazing here, I went.

kohtumre *n.* society (religious)

Kohtumre Ya'ura *n.* Lenten Society

kok- *comb.* of kookak, wear a necklace

koko *iv.* dying (*pl.*; *sg.* muuke; koko-, kokko)
 ~ Ania *n.* world of the dead

kokoarim *n.* dead people

kokoche *iv.* sleeping (*pl.*; *sg.* koche; *pst.* kokochok, kokot-, kokkoche)

kokovi'iku *adv.* in the corner (inside; *cf.* kovi'iku); ~ chiktia, in every corner/in all the corners

kokkocheme *n.* sleeper

kokome *n.* dying ones

kokomola *adv.* all over; Ayamansu sewailo yo huya saniloa vevetana weyeka, sea ~ awakai, yo vaa'ampo komsu vuitekai (s). Over there, walking from the flowered wilderness grove, with flowers all over your antlers, you run down to the enchanted waters.

kokot oora *n.* bedtime

kokotvo *iv.* bed down, go to bed (*pl.*; *sg.* kochi'ise)

kokowa *iv.* dying (*sg.*; *cf.* mumuke; koko-)

kokowame *n.* death

kokte *tv.* put around neck, put on a necklace (~-, kokkote)

kola waari *n.* square basket with square top

kolaroa *tv.* filter, strain

kolaroari *adj.* strained, filtered

kolcham *n.* quilt

kolehio *n.* college

Kolonia Militar *n.* Colonia Militar

koloorim *n.* color

koloroosa *adj.* pink (*syn.* sikhewei)

Kolos *n.* Colos

koludo *n.* a large, curious looking animal like a kangaroo or
large rodent which appears to reprimand people who have
been remiss in their duties, or to remind them to go home
from a festivity

kom *adv. var.* of ko'omi, down(ward)

~ cha'atu *iv.* decrease, subside (pain; kom ~-)

~ chepte *iv.* get down, step down, dismount (*ex.* karivempa kom
chepte *iv.* get down off the roof)

~ po'okte *iv.* bend down, stoop

~ vicha *adv.* downward, to the south

~ watwatte *iv.* fall (*pl.*; *cf.* kom weche)

~ weche *iv.* go down in price

~ wechila *adj.* fallen down

~ weye *iv.* go down, descend

komae *n.* godmother, comadre (female ceremonial sponsor)

kombilaroa *tv.* invite (*syn.* nunu)

kome'a *n.* runt (*derog.*; *var.* of kome'ela)

kome'ela *n.* short person (*cf.* kome'a)

komersiál *n.* advertisement, commercial

komia *n.* arm (bench, chair)

komona *iv.* get wet (komon-, kommoma)

komonia *tv.* moisten (~-, kokkomonia)

komonla *adj.* wet

kompae *n.* godfather, compadre (male ceremonial sponsor)

kompania *n.* company, corporation

kompaniya *n.* the music and tuning used during the second part of a
ceremony (see soonim, partiyo, unna vahti)

kompanyaroa *tv.* accompany

Kompuertam *n.* Compuertas

konfimaroa *tv.* confirm

konfimaroawa *iv.* be confirmed

konfimaraowame *n.* confirmation

koni woki *n.* crow's foot (plant)

konila *adv., postp.* around (motion)

Konkista *n.* the bringing of Christianity

konkistaroa *tv.* conquer

konlotor *n.* conductor

konseho *n.* advice

konseharoa *tv.* advise

konta *tv.* surround (~-, konkonta)

konte *iv.* go around, surround (konti-, kokonte); Vempo bwe'u
pa'ariapo ~. They are making a large surrounding.

konti *n.* 1. surrounding (by Fariseos) 2. procession (circular; *cf.* kaminaroa)

~ Voo'o *n.* the Way of the Cross

kontiwa *n.* procession

kontiwame *n.* procession (ceremonial)

koochim in: vaa ~, shrimp

kookak *iv.* wear a necklace (kok-, kokoka)

kookam *n.* necklace

kooko *n.* coconut

kookta *tv.* pull apart, pry loose (~-, kookookta)

koola *n.* glue

koomim *n.* arm(s)

koomora *n.* chest of drawers, bureau

koona *n.* crown (object)

kooni *n.* crow (bird)

koopa *n.* cup

koopia *n.* copy, facsimile

koorte *n.* court (law)

koova *tv.* beat, win, defeat; gain it, earn it (ková'a-, kokova); yuin tomita koova); Haikik empo koovak? How much have you earned? Itom peloteam ume Marana peloteam ~k. Our baseball team beat Marana's.

koove *tv.* leave behind, forget (*syn.* kopta; *pst.* ~k, no other tenses usual)

koovo'e *n.* turkey (*syn.* chiiwi)

koowe *iv.* swinging, hovering (*pst.* ~k, no other tenses usual)

koowi *n.* pig, hog

~ veyootam *n.* black oak, Emory oak *(Quercus emoryi; cf.* kusim)

kooyo *n.* oyster

kopaalim *n.* incense

kopaaroa *tv.* charge, bill (~-)

kopalai *adj.* quiet, still, peaceful

kopan *adv.* resting, relaxing

kopana *iv.* picnic (kopan-, kokopana); Huyavetuk te kopanne. We will eat under the tree.

kopanpahko *n.* ceremony (daytime)

koparia *n.* female hymn singer (*syn.* kantoora)

~ Yo'owe *n.* head hymn singer

Kopariam *n.* Singer Society (of hymns)

kopela *adj.* sliced (*pl.* kokopela, sliced in pieces); Aapo kutata ~ chuktak. He chopped the log in two.

kopelachukta *tv.* cut into short pieces

kopta *tv.* forget, leave behind unintentionally (~-, kopkopta); *cf.* himo'ote; Ka ne a ~. I can't seem to forget it.

kopte *tv.* desire, attracted to (kopti-, kopkopte)

aet ~, long for, yearn, have an urge to; Ne aet kopte tu'isi ne a chochonpea. Right now, I just want to punch him.

koptiachi *iv.* be desirable, be unable to keep one's hands off (*pst.* ~tukan, *fut.* ~tune; *d.o.* = aet); Aapo aet ~. S/he couldn't keep her/his hands off. U ili uusi si aet ~. the little boy couldn't keep his hands off it. U meesa tu'isi aet ~. The table is so desirable. U veeme tu'isi aet ~. The girl is very desirable.

koptiwame *iv.* envious, jealous; aet ~, be jealous of her/him

kora *n.* fence, corral

korate *iv.* fence something (koati- or korati-)

koreo *n.* post office

koreom *n.* notice, notification

koriente *n.* current (water)

kortiinam *n.* curtain

korvata *n.* tie (clothing)

kosina *n.* kitchen; ~po ehtuufa katek. There's a stove in the kitchen.

kot- *comb.* of koche, be sleeping

kotkottia *tv.* make sound when laying an egg (chicken)

kotpea *iv.* be sleepy; *cf.* kotpet'ea

kotpet'ea *iv.* get sleepy

kotta *tv.* break it (~-, kotkotta)

kotte *iv.* break (solid materials, such as wood, bone or metal; kotti-, kotkotte); *cf.* hamte

kottia *adj. var.* of kottila, broken

kottila *adj.* 1. broken 2. bankrupt 3. spoiled (*var.* kottia); mam ~, broken or sprained hand/arm; Pueta ~. The door is broken (*syn.* pueta wechia).
 ~ choni *n.* wavy, curly hair

kouria *tv.* swing, shake, wave (~-, kokouria; *cf.* wiuta)
 bwasiata ~ *tv.* wag the tail

kouvate *iv.* wag head, move head side to side (often with kom;)

kova *n.* 1. head 2. roof (of car) 3. person in charge; In achaita tosa ~k. My father has gray hair.
 ~ wante *iv.* have a headache
 ~ suawak *iv.* be intelligent

kova'a(ra) *adj.* big-headed

kova'atua *dv.* make earn; Veinte peesom senu ta'apo ~wak. He was paid twenty dollars a day.

kovahamte *iv.* be deep in thought, concentrate (kovahamti-, kovahamhamte)

kovahamti *adv.* 1. breaking one's head 2. mind wreaking (difficult mental work); Huan ~ wechek. John fell and broke his head.

kovak *iv.* have a head

kovalam *in:* hi'ikia ~ *n.* sewing pins, straight pins

kovameheria *n.* forehead

kovanao₁ *n.* governor, leader of a religious society

kovanao₂ *n.* creosote (*Larrea divaricata*)

kovanao kuta *n.* staff (ceremonial)

kovat *adv.* on one's head

kovatarau *n.* matavenado (spider)

kovate *tv.* 1. sink in (memory) 2. move head from side to side 3. place on head 4. put on a garment above the wait (*cf.* wokte) (~-, kokovate)

kovavae *tv.* compete (with emo, each other)

kovawa *iv.* lose (game, war, competition) (~-; not used in future; *cf.* kova'ana, might lose)

kovea *n.* oyster shell

kovi *n.* corner

kovi'iku *n.* corner; *cf.* kokovi'iku

kovi'iria *n.* corner (of a room)

kovre *n.* copper

kowema *iv.* be hovering (*cf.* koowe; *s.* koyowe)

kowi waakas *n.* pork, ham

kowia *tv.* turn (crank, handle; ~-, kokowia)

kowikta *tv.* gather into skein (~-, kokowikta)

kowikte *tv.* bend (~-, kokowikte)

kowila *adv.* around (circumference)

kowilai *adj.* round

kowi tami *n.* a shrub *sp.* with large thorns

koyoolim *n.* 1. jingle bells 2. a belt of such bells (has seven bells representing each of the original Yoeme villages; worn by the Pascola dancer; the number also refers to the number of main stars in the Big Dipper, and the number of Christian sacraments); Ume ~ ume pahko'olata wikosam into ume wovusan ~ Yoem pueplom natoan. The *koyolim* is the Pascola's belt, and the seven bells represented the seven Yoeme towns.

koyoreo *n.* oyster gatherer

koyowe *iv.* be hovering (*s.*; = kowema)

kreema *n.* cream

Krihmem *n.* 1. Christmas holidays 2. Christmas presents

Krihto *n.* Christ

kuachi *adj.* squatting, spread out
Kau Kuachi *n.* Squatting Mountain (in a Deer song)

Ku Wiikit *n.* a multicolored, resplendent bird that is a mythological character; (one of the first creations, he was plain but is transformed into the most colorful bird (the parrot) with help from his feathered brothers)

kuakta *tv.* 1. turn 2. convert (~-, kuakuakta)

kuaktala *iv.* be turned around

kuakte *iv.* 1. turn around 2. move about (kuakti-, kuakuakte)

kuaktiteam *n.* earth rotation naming ritual for infants

kuarta *n.* 1. room 2. bedroom; ~po hipetam weyek, ket kamam vo'oka, ket ropeo katek. In the bedroom, there is a mat, a bed, and a closet.

kuartel *n.* barracks, fort

kucha'ara *n.* spoon

kucha'arata aman susuta *iv.* be a busy-body, have one's finger in everything (*lit.* have a spoon in everything)

kuchi suaripo *n.* knife wound

kuchi'im *n.* knife, dagger

kuchichi'itia *iv.* creaking, squeaking (kuchichi'iti-, no *rdp.*)

kuchu *n.* fish

kuchukuupe *n.* scale (fish)

kuchuleo *n.* fisherman (with net)

kuchusua *iv.* fish (with net; ~-)

kuchuwam *n.* pimples (facial)

kuenta *n.* story

kuera *n.* string (for musical instrument)

Kuera Moelam *n.* Old Strings (Pascola dance song; *syn.* Moela Wikiam)

kuetem *n.* rockets, fireworks (rockets and firecrackers are used at ceremonial occasions such as processions and baptisms to carry messages to Heaven)

kueyo *n.* collar

kuhte *iv.* cross self (~-, kuhkuhte)

kuhteerim *n.* anger (feeling)

kuhteiya *tv.* hate, dislike, detest (*d.o.* = au; ~-, kuhte"eiya; *cf.* kuhtea); Aapo au ~. S/he is angry with her/him. I o'ou ika yoemta ~. The man is angry with this person. Apo am ~. S/he hates them.

kuhtewame *n.* anger (act of being angry)

kuhti maachi *iv.* resent, hold a grudge

kuhtiachi *adj.* unsociable, contemptible; Hu yoeme tu'isi ~. That person is hateful.

kuka *n.* vinorama (tree)

kukaracha *n.* cockroach

kukunawa *iv.* getting married (of a woman); *cf.* huhupwa

Kukupa *n.* Cocopa

kukupapa *n.* echo; Ume uusim chaeme ~. The yelling children are making an echo.

kukupopoti *adv.* the sound made by quails; Hakun ~ hiusakai? Why do they go *kukupopoti*?

kukusa *n.* Sonoran bumblebee

kukusi(a) *adv.* noisily (*s.* kukusiata)

kukusiata *adv.* noisily (*s.*; = kukusia); hakun ~, hiokot sem hiyawa (*s.*), they go somewhere, loudly, sounding pitifully

kuliichi *n.* silverfish, flies

kulpa *n.* fault, blame

kulpak *iv.* be guilty

kulpakame *n.* guilty party

kulparoa *tv.* blame, accuse, criticize; Apo ne ~ ne tepuam kottak tia. He accused me of breaking the axe.

kultivaroa *tv.* cultivate

kulumpio *n.* swing (playground)

    ~po kakalo *iv.* be swinging

kulupti *adv.* occasionally

    ~ wéeme *adv.* once in a while

kumkumti *adv.* beating (heart), clacking, thudding, clip-clop (sound of horses' hooves on ground/pavement)

kumplimento *n.* fulfillment, completion

kumsakam *n.* eyebrow

kumti *adv.* boom, clank

kumui *n.* uncle (mother's older brother)

kumula *adv.* holding water in mouth

kun *adv.* maybe

kunakame *n.* married woman

kunavawame *n.* groom, husband-to-be (*syn.* kunawaituvaeme)

kunawai *n.* husband (in general; *cf.* kuuna)

kunawaituvaeme *n.* groom, husband-to-be (*syn.* kunawame)

kunwo *n.* desert hackberry (*Cettis pollida*)

kup- *comb.* of kepe, close one's eyes

kupahe *n.* a bird *sp.*

kupek *iv.* be shut (eyes)

kupikte *iv.* shut eyes

kupikupikte *iv.* blinking; *cf.* kepe

kupitomte *iv.* faint, blackout

kupte *iv.* be late, evening, get late; ke ~, before it gets late

kupteo *adv.* late afternoon, towards evening, getting late (day's end)

    ~ weye *iv.* fall (evening)

kurai *adj.* mixed (with nau)

kurues *n.* 1. rainbow 2. boa (snake); ~tau ka hihikubwawa; bwe'ituk mampusiam hunak ko'okosi ya'ane. Don't point at the rainbow; otherwise one will get sores on the fingers. Kat ~ta hikkubwa bwe'ituk em mam pusiam chuktana. Don't point at the rainbow or your finger will be cut off.

kurula *iv.* be tangled up (with nat)

kus *n.* cross (traditionally the Yoemem had a Sun symbol, similar to the Maltese cross)

    ~ mayor *n.* village cross (*syn.* kus yo'owe)

    ~ yo'owe *n.* village cross (*syn.* kus mayor)

kusaroa *n.* different tuning

kusaroapo *adv.* cruciform, cross-shaped

kusi$_1$ *adj.* loud

kusi$_2$ *comb.* of kusim, acorns

    ~ ouwo *n.* oak tree

kusia *n.* windpipe, larynx, flute

kusiareo *n.* flute player

kusim$_1$ *n.* acorn(s)

kusim₂ adv. loudly (with bwaana, bwiika, but not nooka); cf. kusisi
kusisi(a) adv. loudly, aloud (with bwiika, aache, nooka, hibwa, hipona);
     U maso bwikame si kusisisia hiruke. The Deer Singer rasps
     very loudly.
     ka kusisi, adv. secretly (without noise)/stealthfully
kut comb. dark
          ~ horoi adj. dark (interiors)
          ~ tenei adj. dark figure (not clearly distinguishable because
               of darkness)
kuta n. stick, pole
          ~ chuktireo n. woodcutter, logger
          ~ ete n. termite
          ~ hu'i adj. promiscuous male
          ~ huiwa n. wooden-shafted arrow (as opposed to cane-shafted)
          ~ kuta naaka n. tree mushroom (lit. wood ear)
          ~ naawa n. tree trunk, stump
          ~ Nokame n. the Talking Tree (syn. Huya Nokame)
          ~ wiko'i n. bow (weapon)
          ~ wikui n. iguana
          ~ wisa'e n. ladle;
kutana n. throat, neck (throat)
          ~ kutte iv. have a sore throat
kutapapache'a n. swallow (bird)
kutareo n. person who sells wood
kutko adj. dark (color); ~ siari, dark green
kutsa'ite iv. get to be dusk
kutsa'iteo, adv. at dusk; Haivu ~. It's already dusk. ~o te yahak. We
     arrived at dusk.
kutta tv. tighten it (~-, kutkutta)
kutte 1. iv. be tightening (kutti-) 2. n. tuning
kutti n. tightened
kuttia tight
kuttiria n. corset, girdle
kuttiwame n. tuning (musical)
kutvea adv. dark(ly), in silhouette (with weye); ~ veati kaáte ume
     naamum. The dark clouds are rolling in.
          ~ kaáte, be silhouetted
kutvene adj. dark (color)
kutwatwatte adv. in the dark
kutwo adv. dark part of a hollow area
kuu'u n. mezcal, agave, maguey (Agave spp.), the hearts of which
     were formerly roasted and used as a vegetable and for an
     alcoholic beverage
          ~ viino, n. agave wine
kuucho n. scar

kuuku *n.* white-winged dove
kuume *tv.* chew, gnaw
kuuna *n.* husband (woman speaking of her own)
kuunak *iv.* married
kuupis *n.* firefly
kuuria *tv.* 1. turn, wind 2. stir (not food) (~-, kukuria)
kuuru *iv.* be tangled (kurœ-, kukuru)
kuurum *n.* flea (sand)
kuuse *iv.* play the flute (*syn.* tiitua), blow (wind instrument), honk (car)
kuusi *n.* loud sound
kuusim *n.* rosary
　　　~ Taewaim *n.* Holy Cross Day
kuuta *tv.* stir, mix (*syn.* bwaata; ~-)
kuuti *adj.* mixed; Ume munim nau ~. The beans are mixed.
kuutia *iv.* buzz, roar (insects), hum (insects)
kuvaeleo *n.* drummer (fife-drum player)
kuvahe *n.* a small type of drum
kuvahileo *n.* drummer (*cf.* kuvaeleo)
kuvia 1. *tv.* turn, twist, screw (~-, kukuvia) 2. *adj.* twisted
kuviari *iv.* turned, screwed
kuvikuvi'itatame *n.* revolving thing
kuvvi'ita *tv.* twisting, screwing

L

La Vataya *n.* a dance tune
laakria *n.* brick (*var.* laakrio)
laakrio *n.* brick (*var.* laakria)
laapis *n.* pencil
laatiko *n.* 1. date (fruit) 2. date palm (*Phoenix dactylifero*)
laautia *adv.* slowly
laaven *n.* violin
laavos *n.* nail
laavohtua *tv.* nail
lairavistam *n.* binoculars
lakim *n.* lock (*syn.* gannao); Apo yaavem ~po suutak. S/he stuck the lock
　　　on the door.
lakron *n.* thief (*syn.* e'ebwame)
lampa(ra) *n.* lamp
lamina *n.* sheet (metal)
lansam *n.* spear
lapala *adv.* with limbs folded (with mamak, wokek)
laplapti *adv.* trotting, loping (with weye)

laureel *n.* oleander (*Nerum sp.*)

lauti *adv.* 1. immediately, early (with weye, yepsa) 2. as soon as
   with -kai); Aapo ~ weye, Mayo heelai. S/he came early, just
   like a Mayo. Apo ~ a yaak kartata nu'ukai. She did it as soon
   as she got the letter.

lautipo immediately, right away

lavatorio *n.* laboratory

laveleo *n.* violinist

lecheria *n.* dairy

lechuuwa *n.* lettuce

leechim *n.* milk (*syn.* hipiikim)

leepe *n.* orphan

lei *n.* law

lelo *n.* clock, watch

Lencho *n.* Lawrence

letania *n.* litany

leuleuti *adv.* cautiously (with weye)

levelai *n.* piece

libra *n.* pound (measure)

lihlihti *adv. var.* of lilihti

lihtaroa *tv.* prepare

lihto *adj.* ready

lihtonia *n.* ribbon

liima *n.* lime (fruit)

liimam *n.* file (tool)

liimon *n.* lemon

liipo *n.* depot

lilihti *adv.* sparsely (may refer to materials blown by the wind;
   var. lihlihti, rihrihti); Huya anwa sea lihlihti heka (*s.*). The
   wild world is blowing brush (flowers and leaves) around.

limohna *n., tv.* 1. *n.* ceremonial solicitation 2. *tv.* donate; Aapo
   enchimmeu ~vae tia. It looks like she wants to donate something
   to you.

limohnaim *n.* 1. song (devotional) 2. donated song (one played by
   amateurs after the morning service)

lindero *n.* the sacred Yoeme boundary (*syn.* im tahti atte'ari)

linia *n.* line, boundary; Hunak in apa ~ta pasaroaka apo a uhteawam
   nakuliak bwe'ituk apo ka ume Yoim Yukataneu yeu a toi'ean.
   When my grandfather came across the border he had to change
   his name to a Spanish one so the Mexicans wouldn't deport him
   to Yucatan.

linteena *n.* lantern

Liohta vaesaene *exp.* Thank goodness!

liobwánia *tv.* thank someone for something

liohbwana *n., iv.* 1. *n.* thanks (formal) 2. *iv.* give thanks (liohbwan-,
   liohbwabwana)

liokis *adj.* free (no cost)

lionoka *iv.* praying

lionokri *n.* prayer

Lios *n.* God (*var.* Dios)

Lios Achai O'ola *n.* God the Old Father (the Creator; in myths, the Creator is called Achai Taa'a, Father Sun; the Creator lives in heaven (the Sun), the center of our universe, and source of energy)

Lios emak weye *exp.* goodbye (*lit.* God go with you)

lipti *adj.* blind

lisensia *n.* license, permission (*syn.* heviteria)

lisensiaria *tv.* license, give permission

litro *n.* liter

livra *n.* pound (measure)

livrom *n.* book; Ume ~ bwe'u. The book is big. Ume ~ bwe'ebwere. The books are big.
~ nooka, *iv.* read

lo'alai *adj.* slender, thin (*ex.* stick)

lo'i *adj.* crippled, lame

lochi *n.* hump, hunchback

Lomiinko *n.* Sunday

lomti patti *adj.* covered (with tarp, blanket)

lonchi *n.* bag or box lunch

loonam *n.* canvas, tarp

loora *n.* glory, heaven, Holy Saturday

loote *n.* lot (land)

lootor *n.* doctor, physician (*var.* lotoor)

loovo *n.* wolf

lopola *n., adv., postp.* 1. *n.* side 2. *adv./postp.* side by side; ae ~ weye, walk next to her/him

lopte *iv.* cast a shadow (re. clouds; lopti-, loplopte)

loseena *n.* dozen

lotlotte *iv.* get tired; *cf.* lotte

lotoor *n.* doctor (*var.* lootor)

lotte *iv.* be tired (lotti-, lotlotte); Tua ne ~. I'm bushed/exhausted. Kuta chukteka in komimpo ne ~k. My arms are tired from cutting wood.

lottemcha *adv.* as if tired, look tired

lottia *tv., n.* 1. *tv.* tire (~-, lolottia) 2. *n.* weariness

lottiachi *adj.* tiresome, hard, difficult, fatiguing

lottila *adj.* tired; *cf.* yumia

lovolai *adj.* humped, rounded, spherical

lovola hoo'ok *iv.* be hunchbacked

lovola kovak *iv.* bald, round-headed

lovola mamak *iv.* 1. have one's hand in a fist 2. have deformed (curled) hands

lu'ula *adj.* 1. straight 2. noon (with certain verbs)
    im ~, *adv.* straight through here; Im ~ witti weene. Go straight
        through here.
    wam ~ *adv.* straight through there U teopo im ~ katek. The
        church is straight ahead.
    ~ katek *iv.* be noon; haivu ~ yehte, almost noon
lu'uta *tv.* 1. use up 2. finish, complete (~-, lulu'uta);
    Aapo tomita ~k. S/he used up the money.
lu'ute *iv.* 1. be completed, finished 2. pass away (die) 3. vanish, disappear
    (lu'ut-, lulu'ute); Hakun tiempopo ~k huname'e. In the past they
    disappeared.
lu'utia *tv.* finish up, consume (~-, lulu'utia)
lu'uturia *tv.* use up someone else's food or resources (~-, lu'ulu'utaria).
lutu'uriatia *iv.* assert
lula katek *adv.* noon, midday
lula yehteo *adv.* towards noon
lunar *n.* mole (on body)
Lunes *n.* Monday
lutu'uria *n.* truth (especially as evidenced by one's actions and by
    fulfilling commitments; *cf.* manda); In ~ta yi'ine. I will dance my
    truth (spoken by a Matachin dancer).
lutuchuktiwa *n.* removal of mourning
lutula *adv.* candidly, frankly, straightforwardly
lutupahko *n.* death anniversary
luusem *n.* candy, sweets
luusim *n.* tail lights (on car)
luutu *n.* mourning cloth (black)
    ~k, *iv.* be in mourning
luutum *n.* death anniversary (the black luutu yarn it cut by the meastro
    in the morning after the night's prayers; this is a pahko held a
    year after the wake); Ume ~ si yo'oriwa bwe'ituk ini véa uka
    hiowamta hichupane. Death anniversaries are very respected
    because they signify the end of mourning.

M

ma₁ *ptc.* 1. elicits support from listener 2. look at (points something out)
    (*var.* maa); Hi'ibwa ma. Let's eat. Aapo ma ian lautipo sootak.
    Look at him, he must have gotten pad today. Maa=su Huan
    yepsak? So why did John come?
    ~ hakwo *adv.* you see, a long time ago
    ~ ian *adv.* and now, told you so
ma₂ *n.* mom, ma
ma'a *tv.* bury (~-, mama'a)
ma'ari *adj.* buried, plastered; techoa ~, plastered with mud
maachante *n.* customer, client

maachea *conj.* so why

maachi *adj.*, *iv.* 1. *adj.* clear, lighted, focused 2. *iv.* seem, appear; be light, daylight (*fut.* mach'ne, *pl.* mamachi); Haisa ~ ume ili uusim. Little children are like that. Kaachim maachi. There's nothing wrong (conventional reply).

maachil *n.* scorpion

maaka *n.* hammock, crib

maakina *n.* 1. machine 2. car, automobile 3. sewing machine (*syn.* hik ~)

maala1 *n.* 1. mother 2. title of respect used by a man to a woman (*n.* reply to hapchi)

maala2 *n.* female child (*masc.*)

maala mecha muuke *iv.* be a lunar eclipse

maaso *n.* whitetail deer

maasu *adv.* how come; ~ sesehtul amemak eteho? How come he talks to them little by little?

Maates *n.* Tuesday

maatum *n.* charcoal

maavis *n.* lark

Maayo1 *n.* Mayo

Maayo2 *n.* May

Maayom *n.* the Mayo country

macham *n.* thigh

mache'etam *n.* machete

machi'iheka *n.* dawn wind

machi'ira *n.* sister-n-law

machi'itana *n.* dawn (*var.* machiatana; *s.* mayachiala)

machia *iv.* 1. appear 2. think to be the case that (~-, mamacha; *s.* machiwa; *cf.* ea, pensaroa); Aapo tomita ho'arapo au ~n. S/he thought that the money was at home. In chi'ila haivu mukiataka huni a hiapsiwa kosinapo yeu ma~. The ghost of my dead aunt appears by the kitchen.

machiak(o) *adv.* in broad daylight; Vempo machiak hita etbwak. Something was stolen in broad daylight.

machiauvicha *adv.* toward dawn

machiku *adv.* in the light; ka ~, in the dark; ~ weama, walking in the light

machillia *n.* east, dawn (*s.*; *syn.* machia)

machiria *n.* light, day

machiwa *iv.* appear (*s.*; = machia)

machu'unama *tv.* hold in hand, grasp (machu'unam-, machu'unanama)

machuktia *n.* handful

machusaka *iv.* make it through the night (with aet yeu); Nian eme a hu'uneyaka aet yeu ~. This you (must) know to make it through the night.

maehto *n.* maestro (lay priest), teacher

maehto yo'owe *n.* head maestro

maestra *n.* teacher

mahai *adj.* scared, afraid
mahaika *iv.* be afraid; Hiatasa ~? What are (you) afraid of?
mahatua *tv.* frighten
mahau *n.* freshwater turtle
mahe *iv.* be scared, avoid people (with yee; mah-, mammahe)
mahiwa *iv.* scared (of a group), panic
mahkara *n.* pascola mask
mahkoapa'i *n. Euphorba sp.*
mahkome'ela *n.* a deer *sp.*
mahmahtame *n.* teacher
mahta *tv.* teach (~-; mahmahta)
        Mahta Me'a *tv.* Killing the Deer ceremony
mahtawame *n.* student, apprentice
        yee ~ *n.* teaching
mahti *adj.* taught
mahveá *n.* deer skin
maiko bees' nest, wasps' nest
maikuchi *n.* rim (of drum)
maineo *n.* sailor
maisi *adv.* seemingly, appearing as if; vempo ko'oko ~ aane, as if they
        were in pain or doing something painful; Ko'oko ~ au hoa. It
        looks as if s/he is hurting themself.
maiso *n.* old deer (elder)
maisooka *n.* tarantula
maival *n.* mayate (green beetle *sp.*)
maka *dv.* give (with the understanding of eventual return; mak-, mamaka;
        cf. miika); maksukan, had already given t; Aapo ne tomita ~k.
        S/he gave me money. Aapo ne tomita ~k. S/he gave me some
        money (to be repaid).
mako'ochini *n.* guamuchil tree (*Pithecellobium dulce*) 2. tamarind
makri *n.* gift
maksaewa *iv.* supposed to give; Ika ne enchi ~. I am supposed to give this
        to you.
makucha *n.* native tobacco
Mala Meecha *n.* Mother Moon; Taa'a Mala Mechata me'ak. There was a
        lunar eclipse.
malehto *n.* lay priest
Malekos *n.* Mark
mali *n.* fawn (*s.* = malichi, malit)
malichi *n.* fawn (*s.* mali)
malinchi *n.* apprentice Matachin member
malit *n.* fawn (*s.* mali)
malokai *adv.* altogether
malon *n.* ground squirrel (*Sp. juancito*)
mam *n.* hand;
        ~ kalalai *n.* weakness in one's hands

~ kavam *n.* biceps
~ kitoktia *tv.* make a fist
~ ottam *n.* hand bones
~ pusia sutum *n.* fingernail
~ pusiam tottote'epo *n.* knuckle
~ tohte *iv.* clapping
~ veta'aku *adv.* in one's palm
~ vetaria *n.* palm (hand)
mamachi *iv.* be seen, appear (*fut.* ~tune)
mamachiku(n) *adv.* right out in the open; U maaso ~ hi'ibwan. The deer
  was eating right out in the open. U maaso ~ weama. The deer is
  walking right out in the open.
mamachisi(a) *adv.* (out) in the open; U maaso ~ weama. The deer is
  walking around in an open area. U maaso ~ hi'ibwan. The deer
  was eating in the open (visible, but perhaps not unprotected).
mamai *n.* aunt (father's younger sister), uncle (father's younger brother)
mamaiwachi *adj.* scary, frightening
mamak *iv.* have hands
mamaka *tv.* have one's hands on (*syn.* aet mamne)
mamam *n.* paw
  ~ tottotte'epo, *n.* wrist
  ~mea, *adv.* by hand
mamato *tv.* imitate, copy (~-, no *rdp.*)
mamma *iv.* touch, move hands; handle (*pst.* ~n, ~-, no *rdp.*); aet ~, put
  one's hand on; Ka aet ~ iniachi. Don't touch this. Ka kia huni
  have aet ~ne. Not just anyone can handle it.
mammahe *iv.* be easily frightened
mammatchu *rdp. rdp.* of matchu, become morning
mammatte *tv.* notice, observe; study (observe closely; *cf.* ehtudiaroa);
  know well
  aet ~ *tv.* instruct, give lessons to
  vat a ~ *tv.* think over, consider
mammattewame *n.* comprehension, understanding
mamne *tv.* have one's hands on (with aet; *syn.* mamaka)
mamni *num.* five
  ~ sentavo *n.* nickel (coin)
  ~ takam *num.* hundred
mamnimpo *adv.* (at) five o'clock
mamnisia *adv.* five times
mampusam *n.* finger(s)
mamte *tv.* touch it with hand (~-)
mamtepachi *adv.* while resting one's hand; Aapo weche aet ~. While
  resting his hands, he fell.
mamyam *n.* a plant used for greens, perhaps black nightshade (*Solanum
  nigrum*)
  ~ Siarim *n.* Green Spinach (Pascola dance tune)

mana *tv.* set, put on flat surface (maná'a-, mamana); Muunim ama ~ka.
    She put the beans in a pot to cook.
mana'aria *n.* mold (for shaping things)
manda *n.* vow
mandamento *n.* commandment
manek *iv.* be situated (massive object; *pst.* ~an, *fut.* mammanne, *rdp.*
    mamane)
manharoa *tv.* drive (vehicle)
maniheo *n.* driver (vehicle)
mansaana *n.* apple
mansaniya *n.* 1. chamomile 2. a tree *sp.*
manso *adj.* tame, gentle
manteeka *n.* lard
manteelim *n.* tablecloth
mantekia *n.* butter, margarine
mantekiatua *tv.* spread butter; Inepo paanim ~k. I buttered the bread.
manto *n.* cultivated morning glory (*Ipomoea carnosa*)
Mao *adj.* Mayo
        Mao noka *iv.* speak Mayo
        Mao noki *n.* the Mayo language
maohte *tv.* clear (land; maohti-, no *rdp.*)
maomeo *n.* acrobat (*var.* maromeo)
mapa *n.* map; Aapo ~u imak hikkubwak. S/he pointed at the map
    with this.
mapoa *n.* bracelet
mareha *n.* wave (water, air)
mariposa *n.* moth
markaroa *tv.* mark, tag
Markoopa *n.* Maricopa
marooma *iv.* do acrobatics (~~, mamarooma)
Marso *n.* March
martiom *n.* hammer
martiresi *n.* martyr
masa *n.* 1. wing 2. Matachin wand (*syn.* palma)
        ~ vaite *iv.* flapping its wings
masa'asai *n.* coral vine, queen's wreath (plant; *Antigonon leptopus*; *lit.*
    winged older brother)
masa'asali *n.* queen's wreath (*s.; syn.* masa'asai)
masatana *n.* turn right
masiwe *n.* centipede
maso *comb.* of maaso, deer
        ~ bwasia, *n.* deer tail
        ~ bwika yo'owe, *n.* head deer singer
        ~ bwikam, *n.* deer songs (the Deer songs ask and call the Deer
            from the East; the Deer dancer is our link to the perfect
            world of the Sea Ania)
        ~ bwikame, *n.* deer singer(s)

~ kova, *n.* deer head
~ kuta, *n.* Mormon tea, a herb (*Ephedra sp.*)
~ nehhawa bwikam, *n.* deer running song
~ pipi, *n.* a common vine found especially in mesquite trees
  (*Sarcostemma sp.*; *lit.* deer tit)
~ sutum, *n.* deer hoof
~ ye'eme, *n.* deer dancer
~ yeu weye, *n.* third song played or danced
Masokova *n.* Dear's Head (mountain in *Son.*)
masoleo *n.* deer hunter
mata *n.* metate, grinding stone
mata'e *n.* kit fox
Matachin *n.* 1. Matachin Society member 2. referring to this Society
~ kovanao *n.* head of the Matachin Society
~m *n.* Matachin Society
matchu *iv.* 1. become morning, break (day) 2. stay up all night, keep vigil
  (~-, mammatchu)
matchu vicha bwikam *n.* toward morning songs
matchuk(o) *adv.* 1. at daybreak 2. the day after tomorrow
mate *n.* cicada
matriis *n.* womb
maukaapo *adv.* before dawn
maukaroa *iv.* get up before dawn, get up early
maukaroapo *adv.* before dawn
mavem *n.* a plant *sp.*
maveta *tv.* accept, receive (mavet-, mavveta)
mavetla *adj.* accepted, received Havu a ~tukan. S/he's already been
  accepted. It's been received already.
mawokte *iv.* put on shoes and socks
maya *iv.* 1. toss at, hurl at (at = *d.o.* in Yoeme) 2. be struck by lightening
  (mayá'a-, mama or mamaya)
maya'i *n.* fire already built
mayachiala *n.* dawn (*s.*; = machi'itana)
mayoa *n.* edge
me'a *tv.* kill (*sg. obj.*; *pl. obj.* sua; me'e-, no *hab.* for *sg.* for which use
  yee sussua)
mechi *postp.* on
me'e- *comb.* of me'a, kill (*sg. obj.*)
me'gliya *n.* jeans, pants
meecha *n.* 1. moon 2. month; tasaria mechat, in the summer months;
  chikti mecham, every month; Meecha tapuniak etne. We'll plant
  when the moon is full. 3. wick (candle)
mecha *comb.* of meecha, moon
~ kari, *n.* halo around the moon
~ muuke *iv.* be a lunar eclipse (during a lunar eclipse, people
  make noise and shout to wake the Moon out of her sleep;
  pregnant women should not watch an eclipse or even go

outside or the Moon will eat the unborn child which will then be deformed)

mechawa *n.* facial discoloration, liver spots, pregnancy mask

meesa *n.* table

mehe'eria *n.* forehead (in: kova ~; kova mehe'eku, on the forehead)

Mehiko *n.* Mexico

meka'atana *adv.* from far away

mekhikachi *adv.* too high, out of reach

mekka *adv.* far; mekka ko'omi, deep, down deep; ~ kom wechek. He fell way down.
> ~ hela *adv.* a little too far
> ~ vicha *adv.* far away

mekka'e *interj.* back off, get away

mekkaikut *adv.* in a faraway place
> ~ weama *iv.* be abroad

memoria *n.* memory; tu'ik ~kame, one with a good memory

meram *n.* stockings

merkao *n.* market; ~po, at the market

metela *iv.* have legs crossed

metro *n.* meter

mielim *n.* honey (*syn.* mumu ~)

mihmo *adv.* by one's self; Apo ~ au koko'osi yak. He himself injured himself.

miika 1. *dv.* give (for keeps, without expectation of eventual return); mik-, mimika; *cf.* maka; Aapo ne tomita ~k. S/he gave me some money. Tua wa maso bwikreo yo'owe ka amau vicha viva mimika. The head deer singer does not give cigarettes to those behind him. Dios taewaim ne ~. God gives me the days. Aapo ne tomita kiikak. S/he gave me the money (as a gift).
> animam ~ *dv.* give food to the departed 2. *tv.* serve (food beverage)

miiki *n.* gift

miil *num.* thousand

miina *n.* mine (ore, minerals)

miisa *n.* mass (ceremony; *comb.* misa)

miisam *n.* host (in communion)
> ~ bwa'e *tv.* take Holy communion
> ~ teuwa *tv.* say mass (*syn.* misate, misa hoa)

miisi *n.* cat

miiya *n.* mile

mik- *comb.* of miika, give

mikkoi *adj.* left-handed

mikko'otana *adv.* on the left

mikwame *n.* gift, item given (with yee); Ika yee makwamta, enchi ne makvae. This gift I want to present to you.

mil *num.* thousand (*comb.* of miil)

milagroso *n.* miracle
mimika *n.* giver, donor
    au ~ *tv.* assure
mina *n.* mine (mineral)
minai *n.* melon, cantaloupe
mineo *n.* miner; I ~ta karitukan. This was a miner's shack.
Miokoles *n.* Wednesday
misa *comb.* of miisa, mass
    ~ hoa *tv.* say mass
    ~ vicha *tv.* hear mass
misate *iv.* say mass (*syn.* imsa hoa)
    ~wa *iv.* mass is being said
misterio *n.* mystery
mo'a *n.* tassel (corn), head (grass, grain), tuft
mo'el *n.* sparrow, wren
mo'oko *n.* tumbleweed
mo'ola *n.* pile, heap
mo'one(wai) *n.* son-in-law
mocha'ala *adv.* in clusters, in a group, in a pile
mochakte *iv.* assemble, gather as a group (mochakt-, mochamochakte)
mochila *n.* bag, knapsack
mochik *n.* tortoise
Mochika Kawi *n.* Turtle Mountain (in a song)
mochomo *n.* driver, leaf-cutter ants
moe'esom *n.* tonsils
moela *adj. var.* of moera, old (inanimates)
moera *n.* 1. old (inanimates), worn out, tattered (*s.* molewa) 2. used
    terms (n *pl.*); Hunu o'outa maakina tu'isi ~. That man's vehicle is
    really run-down.
mohakta *tv.* take apart (~-, mohamohakta)
mohakte *tv.* crumble, tear apart; look over, look through (mohakti-,
    mohamohakte)
mohta *tv.* grind finely to a powder, pulverize (finer than tuuse; ~-,
    mohmohta)
mohtasa *n.* 1. mustard 2. a wild plant, possibly tansy
mohte *iv.* disintegrating, rotting, crumbling (mohti-, mohmohte)
mohti *adj.* powdered, pulverized
mohtiari *n.* powder
mohtia *tv.* cause to disintegrate
moi- *comb.* of mooye, wear out
moina *tv.* shoot (~-, moimoina)
moita *tv.* plow (~-, momota); Tua tu'i ~k. He really plowed up a storm.
moite *iv.* be plowing (mohti-, momote)
molestaroa *tv.* bother, molest (*syn.* suate vicha)
molewa *n.* old, tattered (*pl.* ~im; *s.*; = moela)
momo'oti *iv.* mumble (for discretion; with nooka)

momochala *adv.* in groups

momoi *adj.* ripe, mature; *cf.* bwase, momok

momoik *adj.* ripening

momoti *adv.* murmuring (with hia, nooka)

momotia *iv.* be murmuring (momotiu-; < momoti + hia)

Monaha *n.* Matachin leaders

monte *iv.* speak, comment (only in negative); ka au ~k, didn't speak to
him; Kat ~k. Don't say anything.

monti *adv.* in heaps, piles

monto *tv.* pile (~-, momonto); Ama a ~. Pile it there.

moo *comb.* of moro, moor

moono *n.* 1. monkey (*Son.*; *cf.* chango) 2. doll

moochi *n.* a plant *sp.*

mooroma *n.* foreman

moosen *n.* sea turtle

mooye *iv.* wearing out, getting old, rotting (mo-, momoye)

morao *adj.* purple

mordida *n.* bribe

morea *n.* witchcraft

moreak *iv.* 1. have wisdom 2. have psychic abilities

moreakame *n.* intelligent person, one have ability; ~ ka ko'oko'ita
bwabwa'e. Smart/psychic people can't eat chile (folk belief).

Moro *n.* 1. the manager of the pascolas 2. manager (*gen.*)

    ~ kuta *n.* the pascolas' manager's stick

    ~ Ya'ut *n.* head of the Moor Society

Morom *n.* Moor Society

Moroya'uchim *n.* Moor society

mortifikaroa *tv.* mortify

moso'okia *n.* ring (for carrying pots)

motcha *n.* heaps, piles

    ~ kaáte *iv.* walking, clustering

motchala *adv.* in a group, in a pile

motcho'okoli *n.* horned toad

motoor *n.* motor, engine

move'i *n.* hat

    ~te, put on a hat

movekta *tv.* turn upside down, overturn (~-, movemovekta)

movekti *adj.* turned upside down

movektia *n.* crown, apex, top

movektiam *n.* 1. cloth wimple for covering head of deer dancer 2. head
covering for women and men carrying the holy images; itom Ae
movektiam, embroidered headcloth

movela *adv.* upside down

moyok *adj.* rusted, rotting, dilapidated

muevlem *n.* furniture

muhe *tv.* shoot (*pst.* muhuk, mui-, mumuhe; *cf.* muuripo)

muhiri *adj.* shot
muhsu *adv.* with one's head down
muhte *iv.* 1. genuflect, venerate, worship 2. confirm (muhti-, muhmuhte)
muhti *n.* 1. devotion, worship 2. confirmation
muhtila *adj.* confirmed
mui- *comb.* of muhe, shoot
muhuk *pst.* of muhe, shoot
muina *n.* mill
muk- *comb.* of muuke, die (*sg.*)
mukila *n.* recently deceased
   ~ velaroawa *n.* wake (ceremony)
mule'etam *n.* crutches; ~mea weama, walk on crutches
muliliti *adv.* bop up and down (with kaate)
mumuhe *tv.* be shooting (mumui-)
mumui- *comb.* of mumuhe, be shooting
mumu *n. comb.* of muumu, bee
   ~ kari *n.* bee hive (*cf.* mako)
   ~ va'awa. *n.* honey
mumum *n.* honey
mun *comb.* of muun, bean
   ~ chihtim *n.* mashed beans
   ~ nohim *n.* bean tamales
   ~ ro'ovoim *n.* cooked beans
   ~ va'awa *n.* bean broth, bean soup
   ~ vakim *n.* cooked beans
   tosai ~im *n.* lima beans
mundo *n.* world (*ser.*; *syn.* ánia)
munyeeka *n.* doll
mureo *n.* ocotillo (*Fouqueria splendens*)
musa'ala *adj.* funny, amusing; ~ maachi, be funny
musa'aule *tv.* consider funny (musa'auli-, mumusa'aule)
museo$_1$ *n.* senita (*Lophocereus schotti*), a small cactus similar to
   organpipe
museo$_2$ *n.* museum
musiko *n.* musician
musukte *iv.* bow one's head (musukti-, musumusukte)
musula *adv.* sitting with head down
muteka *n.* pillow
muu'u *n.* owl
muucha *tv.* lose someone through death, be bereaved; *cf.* himucha
muuke *iv.* die (*sg.*; *pl.* koko; *pst.* muukuk, muk-, mumuke)
muukia *n.* ghost, apparition
muula *n.* 1. mule 2. sterile; U hamut han mula tea. They say the woman
   is sterile.
muukuk *pst.* of muuke, die (*sg.*)
muumu *n.* bee; *cf.* mumuli

muun *n.* bean
muura *n.* mule
muuripo *n.* wound (from a shot)

N

na *pn.* I (*ex.*: Tua na tu'ure ka taawak. I really stayed happy with it/really
    enjoyed it.)
na'aka *interj.* yes, okay, of course
na'aso *n.* orange; ~ va'awa, orange juice
na'ateo *iv.* tattle, accuse, gossip about (~-, nana'ateo)
na'atua *tv.* inform, tell on (~-, nana'atua)
na'ikiari *adj.* counted
na'ipisim *n.* cards (playing)
    ~ yeewa *tv.* play cards
na'ivuke *iv.* be jealous (*pst.* ~n, *fut.* na'ivukne, other tenses not usual)
na'ivuki *adj.* jealous
na'ove *iv.* be hoarse, have laryngitis (na'op-, nana'ove)
na'ulai *adj.* narrow (passage)
naa *adv.* about, around; Um itot cha'aka ~ katne. They will be hot on
    our heels.
    ~ kaáte *iv.* walking around (*pl.* ~ rehte)
    ~ kouvate *iv.* move head
    ~ mamma *iv.* gesture, gesticulate
    ~ siime *iv.* travel about (*sg.*; *pl.* ~ saka)
    ~ toha *dv.* distribute (natoi-, naatotoha)
    ~ weye *iv.* walking around (*sg.*; *pl.* ~ kaáte, ~ rehte)
    ~ yeecha *iv.* move head from side to side
    ~ yehte *iv.* move around; U miisi ~ vuite. The cat is running
        around.
naachepte *iv.* jumping
naachi *postp.* beside, next to
naahi *n.* sweat bee
naaka *n.* lady (in address), daughter, young woman
naakoa *tv.* be drunk, dizzy (*pl.*; *sg.* naamuke; ~-, nanaakoa)
naakoriam *n.* drunks
naama *tv.* herd them
naamu *n.* 1. cloud 2. Cloud, the wife of the Rain (Yuku; when they fight,
    he yells at her producing thunder and glares at her making light-
    ening and she cries producing rain)
naamukuk *pst.* of naamuka, get drunk
naamucha *tv.* make dizzy or drunk (naamuchá'a-, naamumucha)
naamuk *adj.* cloudy
naamuke *iv.* get drunk, dizzy (*sg.* ; *pl.* naakoa; *pst.* naamukuk, naamuk-,
    namumuke)

naamukia *n.* 1. drunk 2. rabid
  chuu'u ~, a rabid dog
naamumuke *iv.* dizzy
naamutu *iv.* get cloudy (~-); *cf.* nanamutu; namutakai ne (*s.*), I, being
  a cloud,...
naapo *adv.* 1. nearby 2. next to; Huan ne ~ katek. John is sitting next to
  me. Huan tua ne ~ yehte. John is really trying to sit next to me.
naarechi *adj.* same size
naate *tv.* begin, start (~-, nanate); Huanita haisa ehkwela ~suk. Jane has
  started school already.
  ~ bwikam *n.* beginning songs
naatetua *tv.* make begin, turn on (machine)
naateéka *adv.* in the beginning, since the beginning; U karo ~ tu'isi hiva
  weama. A car runs really well in the beginning.
naatei *n.* something in progress; ~ haivu weye. The event is already
  in progress.
naateka *adv.* since starting, since the beginning; Ketwo ~ tekipanoa. He's
  been working since the start. Unampo ~ tekipanoa. S/he'e been
  working since one o'clock.
navetana *adv.* from that side
naavo *n.* prickly pear cactus (Opuntia spp.; every living thing has a spirit,
  so when gathering cactus fruit one may jump at and yell at the
  plant to scare away the spirit)
naavuhtia 1. *adv.* straight through, beyond 2. *conj.* furthermore
naawa *n.* root
naawe *iv.* chasing, pursuing (<naa + weye); U hamut wait ~. The woman
  is chasing from the other side.
naaya *tv.* light, build a fire (nayá'a-, nanna); *cf.* naiya, naya'i
nahi *var.* of nahi, sweat bee
  ~ Bwikam *n.* Sweat Bee song
nahiveva *iv.* move or swing from side to side (nahivep-, nahivveva)
nahkuakte *iv.* pace, turn about
nahsa'akaria *n.* branch; ~po, on the branch
nahsuareo *n.* fighter, warrior
nahsuawa *n.* battle, war
naiki *num.* four; Aapo ~m waata. S/he wants four.
naiki tomi *n.* fifty cents
naikia *tv.* count (~-, nanaikia)
naikim *adv.* apart
  ~ wiike *tv.* pull apart, analyze
  ~ wikwame *n.* analysis
naikimpo *adv.* (at) four o'clock
naikiawa *iv.* be counted
naikimte *tv.* 1. separate, divide (*pl. obj.*) 2. unravel (*pl. obj.*) 3. distribute
  (*pl. obj.*) 4. *iv.* scatter, spread out (~-, nanaikimte)
naikimtei *adj.* divided, separated

99

naikisia *adv.* four times

> naikiwe *adv.* in four ways

nainasukuni *adv.* in the middle (*s.*; = nasuku, nasukuni); huya ~ (*s.*), in the middle of the wilderness

naiya *iv.* add wood to fire (~-, nanaiya); *cf.* naaya, naya'i

naiyoli *n.* cherished

naiyote *tv.* 1. tempt 2. corrupt, lead astray (naiyot-, nanaiyote)

naiyotela *adj.* corrupt

naka woho'oria *n.* ear hole

naka'ara *n.* 1. one with large ears 2. Chapayeka mask with pointed ears

nakam *n.* ear(s)

nakapit *n.* deaf

nakate *tv.* pay attention to, listen to (~-, nakkate)

nakkaim *n.* Santa Cruz prickly pear cactus (has purple pads; Opuntia violacea)

nake *tv.* care about, want, love (nak-, nannake)

nakouvate *iv.* move head from side to side (*var.* nakovakovate in deer songs)

nakulia *n.*, *tv.* 1. *n.* change (money) 2. *tv.* exchange, trade (~-, nanakulia); A: Hiva peeso. B: Vusan tomi em ~. A: Here's a dollar. B; (Here's) seventy-five cents back (as change).

nakwa *iv.*, *n.* 1. *iv.* be cared for 2. *n.* loved one, someone who is cared for

nakwame *n.* act of caring for (with yee)

nam *pn.* I-them; Yoko ~ vitne. I will see them tomorrow.

nakatavaku *adv.* in the area behind one's ears

nama *var.* of namaka, hard

namaka *adj.* hard (physical property), stiff, tough (*var.* nama)

namakasia *adv.* strong (mentally, physically)

namamachi *adj.* transparent, clear

namu vakot *n.* marine tornado, waterspout

namuli *n.* great grandmother

namulia *iv.* cloud over (*s.* = nanamutu)

namulopte *iv.* begin to cloud over, be overcast (namulopti-)

namuriute *iv.* be a cloudburst

Namu Riutine *n.* Clouds Will Break (Pascola dance song)

namurokoa *n.* algae

namuwam *n.* cataracts

namya *tv.* 1. absorb mentally, digest 2. integrate (~-, nanamya); Inepo a bwisek into in kovapo ~k. I caught it (an idea) and absorbed it.

nana *n.* little girl

nana'ana *pn.* same, uniform; ~ te. We are the same.

nana'anate *tv.* make the same

nanahria *tv.* dodge, avoid (~-, no *rdp.*)

nanahsuame *n.* fighter

nanale *tv.* avoid, miss, avoid meeting (nanali-, no *rdp.*) voota ~ *tv.* miss the road

naname *iv.* be staggering (~-, no *rdp.*); ~ka weye, be staggering like
    a drunk
nanamutu *iv.* get cloudy (*pst.* ~n; *s.* namulia); *cf.* naamutu
nanancha *pn.* same, equal, both; ~ ka totomek. Neither of them
    has money.
    ~ tutu'i *adj.* average, of usual quality
    ~ wasukate *iv.* be the same age
    ~ veeki *iv.* same amount
    ~ vehe'e *iv.* same cost;
nanancha wasukte *iv.* be the same age
nanau *adv.* like, similar
    ka ~ machi aane *iv.* be various, be a variety
    ~ hia *iv.* have a consensus
    ~ machi *iv.* be similar, alike
nanawichi *adv.* equally
    ka ~ *adv.* uneven
nanke *tv.* meet (nanki-, nannanke)
nanna *rdp.* of naaya, light it
nao *n.* cob, corncob
    ~ Ania *n.* Corncob World
naolai *adj.* narrow (re: passageway, hall)
naoto'oria *n.* a medicinal plant *sp.*
naowo *n.* a plant *sp.*
naposa *n.* ashes
napo *comb.* of naposa, ashes
    ~ Sauwa *n.* Ash Wednesday (*lit.* use ashes)
    ~ vaki *n.* nixtamal, hominy (*lit.* boiled ashes)
    ~ Wisa'im *n.* the Milky Way
nappat *adv.* no longer, not as before (ka ~; nappat does not occur by itself)
naranhao *adj.* orange (color)
nareechi *adj.* same size, length, area (*pl.* nanareechi)
nareempani *adv.* same length
nareki *adj.* same (amount or volume; *pl.* nanareki); Ume soto'im ~. The
    pots (hold) the same amount.
nasa *adv.* here and there
nasion *n.* nation, country
nasonte *tv.* 1. harm one, ruin, spoil 2. break down (machine)
    (~-, nanasonte); Yee nanasonteme amak ousei si a'ane. The ones
    who harm people sometimes change into mountain lions.
nasontela *adj.* disarrayed, messed up, damaged
nasonti *iv.* ruined, blotched (~-)
nasontu *iv.* wear down, break down (~-, nanasontu)
nassakariam *n.* branch (tree)
nassua *tv., n.* 1. *tv.* fight, battle (~-, nanassua) 2. *n.* war, battle (real or
    ritual); Vempo tomita nau ~. They are fighting over money.
nassuawa *n.* warfare

nassuawame *n.* fighting, strife; ~ tu'isi ka tu'i kia kaita tu'uwata hiva itou nunnu'upa. Fighting is no good; it never brings anything good to us.

nasukria *n.* center, middle; Im ~ u wikia. This is the center of the string.

nasuktukaria bwikam *n.* midnight songs

nasuk(u) *adv.* in the middle, among (*var.* nasukuni; *s.* nainasukuni)
>~ amani *adv.* in half
>~ mam pusiam *n.* middle finger
>~ tuka'apo *adv.* at midnight
>nau nasuk *adv.* in between

nasukuni *adv. var.* of nasuku, in the middle

nat *postp.* on each other
>~ monti *iv.* be stacked
>~ cha'aka *iv.* be glued together
>~ chu'aktila *adj.* stuck together
>~ hooka *iv.* be on top of each other
>~ tente *iv.* be kissing (nat tenti-, nat tetente)
>~ to'oka *iv.* be in layers, be layered

natcha'abwai *tv.* patch together

natcha'aka *adv.* 1. one after another 2. stuck together; ~ kaáte, walking one after another (a Matachin dance formation)

natchi'ika *n.* nit

natesuwak *iv.* has already started (used only in *pst.*)

natoa *tv.* represent, symbolize

natoi- *comb.* of naa toha, distribute (*cf.* naa)

natpat *adv.* not anymore, (in: ka ~; natpat does not occur by itself)

nattemai *tv.* ask about, ask for (~~); Aet pappeaka nian ket eme a ~ne. Vigorously, like this, you will also question it. Manwetau ~ haisa uka vachita vansuk ha'ani. Ask Manuel if he already irrigated the fields.

nattemaiwame *n.* the act of asking, question

nattepola *adv.* in bunches

nau *adv. var.* of nawi, together; ~ chopola hooka. They sit next to each other (houses). ~ em nemo toha ian lautipo, vario karim vetchi'ivo (poster slogan). Get together now for barrio housing. Senu totoi into woi ili totoim ~ vahi. One hen and two chicks make three altogether. Ume o'owim tekilta ~ eteho. Those men are talking together about the work.
>~ cha'atu *tv.* unite
>~ chaya *tv.* fasten, join
>~ chupwame *n.* couple (man and woman)
>~ eewame *n.* unity
>~ nasuk *adv.* in between; u trake woi pueplom ~ nasuk vo'okame, the railroad between two towns
>~ tahte *iv.* collide, clash
>~ toha *tv.* gather, collect, assemble

~ vicha *adv.* face to face
~ yaha *iv.* collect, assemble as a group
naup- *comb.* of nauve, be hoarse
nausu *adv.* together
nauto'oria *n.* herb *sp.*
nauve *iv.* be hoarse, have laryngitis (naup-, nanauve)
nava'asom *n.* pocket knife
Navilan *n.* Christmas
navo sitoi'm *n.* prick pear jelly
navo taaka *n.* tuna (prickly pear fruit)
Navahoa *n.* Navojoa (*lit.* prickly pear town)
navuhti(a) *adj.* transparent (with maachi or mamachi); ~ vicha, further-more; Navuhti vicha ket te enchimmeu nattemaivae.
Furthermore, we want to ask you something.
~ vicha *iv.* clairvoyant
~ yee vicha *tv.* read someone's mind
navuhtia *adv., conj.* 1. *adv.* straight, beyond, head-on, directly 2. *conj.* fur-thermore; Ian véa ~ hita weye? What happens next? U em uusi chea ~ mahtana. Your child will be taught better.
ama ~ *adv.* in addition to
nawa *exp.* combination of nau (together) and a (it/her/him); Vempo nawa toha. They are gathering it together.
nawa kookta *iv.* uproot (*syn.* nawapona)
nawa'achaya *tv.* put together, assemble (~-, nawa'achatcha)
nawa'acha'abwa *tv.* patch, mend (~-, nawa'achacha'abwa)
nawapona *tv.* uproot (*syn.* nawa kookte)
nawi *adv.* together
nawi wo chume'a *n.* coward (*lit.* scared asshole)
nawi'o *n.* white paloverde (*Acacia willardiana*)
nawia *n.* weakling, coward, scaredy-cat
nawit *pn.* both; ~ mamni wasuktiapo aayuk. Both took five years.
nawite *tv.* weaken someone (~-, nanawite)
nawitu *iv.* be weak, faint
naya'i *n.* fire (already built)
nayeehte *iv.* move in place, fidget, rock back and forth; Tren ~sime. The train is rocking back and forth.
ne *pn.* me, I (*emph.* nee; *s.* ni); A: Hitasempo yo—ko ya'ane?
B: Wako'ita ne ya'ane. A: What are you doing tommorrow?
B: I'm making a griddle.
nea *pn.* of me (with verbs ichakte, rohikte, tiiwe)
neche *pn.* you/me (*sg.*; *pl.* ~m; used in giving commands); ~ vicha. Look at me. ~m hiokoe. Have pity on me.
nechi *pn.* at/on me
ne'e *iv.* be flying (*pst.* ~ka, ni'i-, nenne'e)
ne'esa *n.* mother's older sister
ne'otula *iv.* stutter (*pst.* ne'otukan, *fut.* ne'otune)

nee *pn.* emphatic form of ne, me; Uka chuu'uta ~ voemta hikkahak. I heard the dog that was barking at me.

nee hiokoe *exp.* please, pardon me

nee'o *n.* stutterer

neeka *tv.* miss (target or opportunity; nek-, *rdp.* is neneeka)

negrita *n.* an herb *sp.*

nehpo *pn.* I, me (*emph.*; var,. nepo, nee)

nehunwa *tv.* invite formally (~-, nenehunwa); *cf.* nunu; Itom ~. S/he invited us.

nemak *pn.* with me (comitative)

nen *adv.* ; Ori ~ hia. What's her/his name?

nenenkame *n.* seller, merchant (with hita)

nenenmkiwa *iv.* be for sale

nenka *tv.* sell (nenki-, nennenka)
    au ~ *iv.* surrender

neo'okai *n.* mockingbird

nepo *var.* of nehpo; ~ ala ta'a, I know it; ~ la taya, I know it (*s.*)

nersi *n.* nurse

nesau *n.* command, order

nesauri *n.* law, order, commandment; Diosta ~, God's laws

nesawe *tv.* command, order (nesau-, nessawe)
    si ~'a *iv.* be bossy

nesaweme *n.* commander, director, supervisor, government

nesawi *n.* rule, commandment; Wowmamni Nesawim, the Ten Commandments

nesitaroa *tv.* need (*syn.* waata); Inepo tomita ~, Mariata in ae vehe'etuane'u. I needed money, so Mary lent me some.

net *pn.* at/on me

netana *pn.* from, alongside me

neto *pn.* from me

netane *tv.* ask for, beg for; mooching (netan-, nettane)

netanria *dv.* ask for (~-, nettanria)

neu *pn.* to/into/beside/from me; *cf.* -u, -wi

newosio *n.* 1. business 2. affair, matter, concern
    nepo kaita ama ~k *exp.* it's none of my business

ni *pn.* I, me (*s.*; = ne)

nian *adv.* like this; ~ hia, sound like this; ~ au hahase was bwiika. The songs follow each other like this.

nii *pn.* this (*obj.* ~ka; *cf.* i)

nim *adv.* here (*cf.* im)

nini *n.* tongue

ninnituame *n.* flyer, pilot

no'asi *adj.* half full; noasnakuku, in two; A: Kafeta waata? B: No'asik. A: Want some coffee? B: Just half (a cup).

no'ocha *iv.* want to be babied, be a wimp (with au)

no'ochia *iv.* act childishly (with au; ~-, nono'ochia); Lupe au ~. Lupe is acting/talking childishly. U ili hamut au ~. The little girl is acting childishly.

no'ochiamsa *adv.* childishly; au ~ nooka, talking childishly

Noche Weena *n.* Christmas

noha *iv.* make tamales (nohi-, nonoha)

nohim *n.* tamales

noinoiteme *n.* regular visitor

noita *tv.* take someone over (~-, noinoita)

noite *iv.* visit (*d.o.* = eu; noiti-, noinoite; near *syn.* pasiyaroa, which is a less formal or necessary visit); Maria avo ~k. Hita haiwan? Kia avo pasiyaloan. Mary came over. What was she looking for? Only visiting. Chea ne lautia avo emou ~k tu'i'ean. I want to come see you all soon.

noitekame *n.* visitor

noitine *iv.* go visit

nok *comb.* of nooka, talk
   ~ bwikam *n.* poem
   ~ bwibwikame *n.* poet
   ~ hiawai *n.* voice
   ~ hikkaila *tv.* take, heed (advice)
   ~ nassua *tv.* quarrel; Vempo nau emo nok nassuan. They were quarreling.
   ~ omte *iv.* complain

nokapo amani *adv.* according to

noki hoowame *n.* grammar

noki weye *iv.* be a scandal

nokita kuaktala *n.* pun

nokiu vicha yecha *iv.* translate

noklutu'uri *n.* scripture

nokria *dv.* 1. speak on someone else's behalf 2. defend someone 3. recommend, endorse; Wame a ~, waka hua ániapo, waka sea yolemta ~ ala. They speak for the wilderness world, the deer.

noktehwa *n.* advice, counsel

noktohame *n.* messenger

noktotohame *n.* messenger, ambassador

nokvehe'e *tv.* contradict (~-, nokvevehe'e)

nokwa *iv.* be gossiping about (*d.o.* = -tat); U Mariatat ~. They're gossiping about Mary.

nokwa'apo *adv.* in one's own language; Aapo a ~ nooka. S/he's speaking in her/his own language.

nokwame *n.* act of talking
   yet ~ *n.* gossip

nonnoka *tv.* gossip about (with yet)

nonnokame *n.* talker, gossiper

noono *n.* night-blooming cereus (*Peniocereus greggi*)

nooka *iv.* talk (nok-, nonoka; *s.* noyoka)

aet nooka *iv.* be gossiping about; Vempo aet ~. They're gossiping about it.

livrom ~ *iv.* readnooki *n.* word, language

noolia *interj.* hurry up!

notta *dv.* 1. return a favor 2. pay back 3. take revenge (~-, notnotta; i.o. = aet); aet a ~, return a favor/pay back; Aapo aet a ~k. S/he paid him back (aet = her/him)/S/he got revenge (aet = on her/him). Aapo u hamuttat a ~k. She took revenge on the woman.

notte *iv.* be returning (notti-, notnotte)

novena *n.* novena

novia *n.* girlfriend

novio *n.* boyfriend

noyoka *iv.* talk (*s.*; = nooka); Ala senu kuta kun ~i (*s.*). One stick might be talking, talking.

Noviemre *n.* November

nuasi *adv.* half, half way; kafeta ~ k ne mika, give me half a cup of coffee

nu'e *tv.* 1. get, acquire 2. photograph (*pst.* nu'uka, nu'u-, nunu'e); Aapo paanim Mariatau nu'uka. S/he bought the bread from Mary. In achai mumu mielim nu'uvae um mumu hoarapo. My father is going to gather honey from the bee hive.

nu'uka *pst.* of nu'e, get

nu'upa *tv.* bring, deliver, receive (~-, nunnu'upa); ~suwak, already brought; Nassuawame tu'isi ka tu'i kia kaita tu'uwata hiva itou nunnu'upa. Fighting is no good; it never brings anything good to us.

nu'uria *dv.* fetch, get for someone; Na'asom a ~ne. Get him some oranges.

nu'ute *tv.* save, set aside food (~-, nunu'ute); *cf.* yeu'ave'a

nu'uteria *dv.* save food for someone

nuevempo *adv.* (at) nine o'clock (*syn.* watanimpo)

nuhmeela *n.* youth, young man

nuki *adv.* so long, so much; Vaa'am ~akan. The water was up to here.

nukisi(a) *adv.* so much, so high, to a great or certain extent; Tu'isi ne enchi aet vaesae Diostau nukisia. I'm really grateful to you for this all the way up to God. Tu'isi ne enchi aet vaesae Diostau ~. I'm really grateful all the way up to God.

nuksaka *tv.* take away (*pl. obj.*; *sg.* nuksime; *pst.* nuksahak, nuksaká'a-, nuksasaka)

nuksiime *tv.* take away (*sg. obj.*; *pl. obj.* nuksaka; *pst.* nuksiika, nuksim-, nuksisime)

nulevena *adv.* like that (*var.* hunulevena)

numero *n.* number

nunu *tv.* invite (informally; ~-, nunnu); *cf.* nehunwa

nunu'e *tv.* grab, seize (nunu'u-, nunnu'e)

nunu'eme *n.* buyer, procurer

nunu'ubwa *tv.* have on one's person, have in one's possession (~-, nunnu'ubwa)

106

nunuwa *iv.* be invited
nuu'u *n.* sack lunch
nuudo *n.* knot

O

o₁ *interj.* oh, yes; Kat uka mun soto'ita kom tave o empo huynak
     a hamtane. Don't drop that bean pot or you will break it.
     A: Vempo uka em ili ou asoa *ringboi*'i'a. Nu su véa ama weyetea.
     B: O heewi. Kaachin maachi hunu'u. A: They want your little
     son to be a ringboy. B: Oh yes, there's nothing wrong with that.
     A: Havesa u sea hamut? B: Abwe in koomai Martinata ili hamut
     asoa, Anhelita. A: O. A: Who is going to be the flower girl?
     B: Well, my comadre Martina's little girl, Angela. A: Oh.
o₂ *conj.* or; Empo ian haivu simvae ~ chukula? Do you want to go now
     or later?
o"omte *rdp.* of omte, get angry
o"ove *rdp.* of oove, be lazy
o"ouva *rdp.* of ouva, be difficult to do
o'a *n. var.* of o'ola, old man
o'ola *n.* old (person, animal), old man (*var.* o'a, oora)
O'ola Hahawa *n.* pursuit of the Old Man
o'omtak *pst.* of omta, dislike
o'omtila *adj.* angry
o'omtitua *tv.* make angry; Maria kaita vetchi'ivo au ~. Mary is making
     herself angry for no reason at all.
o'ora *n. var.* of o'ola, old man
o'oream *n.* brains
o'ou *n.* man, male (*pl.* o'owim)
     ~ au ouleme *n.* macho, virile, masculine
o'ouwia *n.* male; bwala ~, male sheep
o"ouva *iv.* get tired of; *cf.* ouva
o'ovek *interj.* yes, that is so; A: Empo tekipanoa? B: ~. A: Are you
     working? B: Yes, that is so.
o'oven *adv.* nonetheless; Aman te saka ~. We are going nonetheless.
     Apo yee mahtavao ~. She wants to be a teacher. Tomita vempo
     eriavae ~. Tomita vempo eriavae ~. They try to save money to
     no avail.
o'owia *n.* masculinity
ochoko *adj.* greasy
ochoko kuta *n. var.* of heoko kuta, globe mallow
ohelaata *n.* tin can, can (food)
ochompo *adv.* (at) eight o'clock (*syn.* wohnaikimpo)
ofesiina *n.* office
ohelata *n.* tin can, canned goods
ohvo *n.* blood

~ wikia *n.* vein

~ wo'ote *iv.* bleed

~ yehtela *n.* bruise

ohvora *iv.* be in heat, have one's period (*pst.* ~tuka'a, *fut.* ~tune)

Oktuvre *n.* October

omme *n., interj.* 1. *n.* friend (male to male) 2. *interj.* hey, man (*masc.*)

ommo'okoli *n.* Inca dove

omo'ocho *n.* turtle *sp.*

omochi *adv.* at the wrong side

omola *tv., n.* 1. *tv.* shift piles 2. *n.* something put or pushed aside

omola *adv.* outside, to the side

omot *adv.* somewhere else; Aapo ~ siika. S/he went somewhere else.

omot rukte *iv.* move (residence)

omta *tv.* dislike, hate, detest (with/at = eu; *pst.* o'omtak, ~-, o"omta); Aapo
    enchi ~. S/he dislikes you.

    yee ~ *tv.* despise, hate

omte *iv.* 1. get angry 2. growl (*d.o.* = au; omti-, o'omte and o"omte); ke a
    o'omteo, before s/he gets mad; neu ~, angry with me; Aapo eu ~.
    S/he is mad at you.

    nok ~ *iv.* complain

    tu'isi ~ *iv.* be furious

omteka a vitchu *tv.* glare at (*d.o.* = "at")

Omteme Kawi *n.* Angry Mountain, the sight of the Talking Tree that pre-
    dicted the coming of the Europeans as well as telling the future
    of the Yoeme people; it vibrated like an earthquake to attract
    attention to what it was trying to say

omtemta puhvak *iv.* be scowling

omtemtavena *iv.* look as if angry

omtiteam *n.* nickname; Fredi ~. He's nicknamed Freddy.

omtiteatua *tv.* nickname

omtiteatuari *adj.* nicknamed

omtiwame *n., iv.* 1. *n.* anger 2. *iv.* get angry

onawatte *iv.* mine salt

onchempo *adv.* (at) eleven o'clock

ono'e *n.* barrel cactus (*Ferocacus spp.*)

onsa *n.* ounce

ontua *tv.* salt (~-, o'ontua)

oobwa *iv.* choke on (obwá-; choke on anything but liquid; *cf.* hukte)

oona *n.* salt

oora *n.* hour

ooro *n.* gold

oove *iv.* be lazy (-st. ~n, ~-, o"ove)

oove wechia *iv.* laziness

oove weeche *iv.* get lazy

Opata *n.* Opata

oppoa *iv.* weep (~-, o'oppoa)

oppoam *n.* tears

oraario *n.* schedule

orarioroa *tv.* schedule

oraroa *tv.* pray (*syn.* lionoka)

orasion *n.* prayer (*syn.* lionokri)

ore *tv., iv., n.* 1. *tv./iv.* uh (used when searching for a verb; ori-) 2. *n.* what's it, what's her/his name; oritukan Porfiirio Diastukan, it was in the days of Diaz

oregano *n.* oregano

orekan *iv.* do such and so (used when searching for a word)

ori *n.* ah, uh, umm (used when trying to think of a word); ~ im ~ maala weama enchim teovachiavae tia. Uh, this lady, uh, looks like she is going to bless you. A testamento tian, porke ini ~ u vatnataka u yo'ora... tekipanoasuk. They call it a testament because, uh, in the beginning the elders worked on it. ~ nen hia? What's her/his name?

oripo *adv.* uh, umm (used when trying to think of an adverb); ~ yukuk. It rained somewhere.

orno *n.* oven

ospitaal *n.* hospital

ota *n.* 1. bone 2. skeleton (*syn.* kalavera) 3. chaff (from thrashing; *syn.* sankoa) 4. trunk or stem (tree, plant)
kia ~ ausu'uli *iv.* be just skin and bones
~ ausu'uli *adj.* bony

ou apelai *n.* single man

ou asoa *n.* son (female's male offspring)

oule *iv.* be brave, courageous (with au; *pst.* ~n, ouli-, o'oule)

ousei *n.* 1. mountain lion (*s.* ouseli) 2. lion; Yee nanasonteme amak ~ si a'ane. The ones that harm people sometimes change into mountain lions.

ouseli *n.* mountain lion (*s.* ; = ousei)

ousi(a) *adj., adv.* 1. *adj.* hard (physical property), sturdy, strong 2. *adv.* much (with much energy); *syn.* unna, yuin; ~ bwana, cry a lot; ~ maachi, looks sturdy; ~ tekipanoa, work hard; ~ yukuk, rained really hard; Tuka kupteo tu'isi ~ yukuk. Yesterday afternoon it rained really hard.

ouva *iv.* 1. be difficult to do 2. be lazy, not feel like doing (*pst.* ~n, ~-, o"ouva; o'ouva, get tired of); au ~, neglect one's self; Tekilta ne ~. I don't feel like working.

ouvam *n.* coals, embers

ouvatu *iv.* get to be hot (coals)

ouwo *n.* tree, bush; na'aso ~, orange tree; piocha ~, chinaberry tree

ove'a *n.* lazy bones, one who is habitually lazy (*var.* ove'era; *pl.* o'ove'am); U yoeme tu'isi ~. That man is lazy. U yoeme tu'isi ~tukan. The man was lazy.

ove'era *n. var.* of ove'a, lazy person

ove'eso *n.* 1. ram (sheep) 2. mountain sheep

ovetave in: yee ~, make one lazy

ovewechila *adj.* having become lazy

ovi eiya *iv.* think something is hard to do

oviachi *adj.* 1. difficult, hard 2. complex, complicated

ovisaane *iv.* be busy

ovisi *adj.* busy

      ~ aane, be busy; ~ te aane. We're busy.

owilai *adj.* curved, circular

oyoven *adv.* even though (*s.*; = o'oven); Kia ne huyapo ka yeu
      machiata, vuite ~. I am running, although I am unseen in
      the wilderness (*s.*).

P

pa'akta *tv.* lift with a lever (~-, papa'akta)

pa'akun(i) *adv.* outside (*var.* paku); Pa'akuni! Get out! (*pl.*) addressee, ~
      em katvo, go outside (*pl.*); Tutulik e kare into paku ket ume
      seewam tu'isi uhyoi. You have a beautiful house and outside the
      flowers are very pretty.

pa'aria *n.* yard, plaza, clearing, open area (*s.* fayalia)

pa'asi *n.* raisin

paakam *n.* hay

paalam *n.* shovel

paanim *n.* bread

      ~ pa'asek *n.* raisin bread

paapa *n.* potato (originally thought to be poisonous)

paare *n.* priest

paaros *n.* jackrabbit

passo *n.* step (*ser.*; *syn.* woki)

paavo *n.* peacock

paato *n.* duck (*syn.* vetayeka)

paayum *n.* necktie, neckerchief, handkerchief

      ~ kooka *iv.* wear a necktie

pahko *n.* 1. ceremony (religious celebration; this may be a town
      ceremony, or a household ceremony in which a delegation
      from the church of maestro, cantoras, and Matachin dancers
      are hosted by the pahkome and the pahko'olam) 2. gathering
      (social event)

      ~ suma'i, *n.* person obligated to give a ceremony (*syn.* pahko
         sumawakame)

      ~ vanteam *n.* flag (ceremonial)

      ~ vichame *n.* spectators (at a ceremony)

      ~ yo'owe *n.* sponsor of a ceremony

      ~ ya'ut *n.* the person in charge of a ceremony

pahko'ola *n.* pascola, who entertains at pahko ceremonies and interacts in ritual drama with the Deer dancer; the pascola is supposed to be the historian who passes on oral tradition, and is the auxiliary host (see pahkome) to the church delegation during a household pahko

pahko'ola atte'a *n.* pascola paraphernalia

pahkome *n.* 1. fiestero, ceremonial sponsors (of the Blue and Red societies that present the Moors vs. the Christians on the town's feast day) 2. household pahko sponsors (a man and a woman, usually husband and wife) who are assisted by the pascolas (pahko'ola)

pahkowame *n.* act or event of doing a ceremony

Pahkua *n.* Old Pascua, Pascua

Pahsiko *n.* Frank

pahteelim *n.* pie, pastry

Pasihka *n.* Frances

pahmo *n.* muscle spasm

pahti *n.* poison

pahtiam *n.* aspirin

pahtitua *tv.* poison

　au ~ *tv.* over medicate

　kuchum ~ *tv.* poison fish

pake *conj.* because, so that

pala *adj.* entire, whole (archaic)

　~ an'a *n.* universe (*lit.* endless world)

　~ vato'i *n.* Christianity, Christendonm

　~ vato'ora *n.* Christianity, Christendom

palma *n.* Matachin wand (*syn.* masa)

paloma *n.* 1. moth 2. pigeon

pamiita *n.* a small bush, the seeds of which are used for cleaning the digestive system

pan hoa *iv.* make bread

panaleo *n.* baker (*var.* panreo)

panreo *n.* baker (*var.* panaleo)

pa *n.* son; Pa vina weye. Son, come over here.

papa *n.* father, dad; Vanseka lauti au chaine bwe'ituk em ~ have yepsa. Hurry and call her quickly because your father is about to come home.

papachihtim *n.* mashed potatoes

papalote *n.* 1. kite 2. windmill

pappea *iv.* energetic, enthusiastic, have energy for (pappé'e-, no *rdp.*); Kaveta au ~. No one has the energy for it.

　ka ~ vo'oka *iv.* lying listlessly

pappewame *n.* the quality of being energetic; U ~ tua tu'i. To have energy is really good.

paraliista *iv.* be paralyzed

parke *n.* park

parkiaroa *tv.* park (vehicle, AZ.; *cf.* ehtasionaroa)

parkiaroawa'apo *adv.* in (the, a) parking lot

paro hoo'o *n.* person who can easily make up (*lit.* jackrabbit back)

parteera *n.* midwife; (*syn.* hamut an'a aso'amta, woman who helps in birthing)

partiyo *n.* the music and tuning that is used in a ceremony from dawn until the end of the fiesta (see soonim, unna vahti, komapniya)

pasaheo *n.* passenger

pasaroa *tv., iv.* 1. *tv.* pass (*syn.* aet wam siime) 2. *iv.* happen 3. *iv.* experience hardship; 4. *tv.* pass a test; Haivu te a ~k. This has already happened to us. Iniavu te ka tu'isi a ~k. Last year we had a hard time.

    tu'isi ~ *iv.* have a good time

pasaroa machi *iv.* be bearable

paseo *n.* mangrove

pasia *tv.* ride (vehicle); kavaipo ~, ride on horseback; karota ~, ride in the car

Pasihka *n.* Frances

Pasihko *n.* Francis

Pasioneom *n.* all the persons of a village engaged in the Easter ceremonies

pastelim *n.* pie

pasiyaloa *iv.* visit, tour, make the rounds (with au; ~-, pasiyayaloa); Vempo eu ~. They are visiting you.

patala *adv.* to the brim (with tapuni)

patalai *adj.* flattened, crumpled, formless

pato pusim *n.* a red flowering vine of Sonora (*lit.* duck eyes)

patpattame *n.* lid, cover

patta *tv.* cover, barricade (~-, patpatta)

patte *iv.* 1. be constipated 2. be stopped up, be closed firmly (*pst.* ~k, *fut.* pattine); U pueta ~k. The door slammed shut (by itself).

patti(la) *adj.* closed, covered

pattiria *n.* top, lid, stopper

    kahoon ~ *n.* lid (for box)

pawis *n.* wild parsley

payaaso *n.* clown

pe'ela *adv.* bent (re: any bipedal); ~ cha'aka, stand bent/stooped over; ~ chovek, with butt sticking out

peche'eku *adv.* in the/a crack; ~ a haiwa, look for it in the crack

peche'eria *n.* crack; chove ~, crack in the buttocks

pechita *n.* mesquite bean pod (*syn.* hu'upa taakam)

peena *n.* pain, suffering (*ser.*; *syn.* wantia, ko'okoe)

peeni *n.* penny

peenta *tv.* pawn it (~-, peepenta)

peenti *n.* pawned item

peera *n.* pear

Peesio *n.* Hermosillo

peeso$_1$ *n.* prisoner

peeso$_2$ *n.* dollar, peso

peesote *tv.* capture, jail, take prisoner (peesoti-, pepeesote)

peesotu *iv.* be imprisoned (~-)

pehta *tv.* explode, blow up (~-, pehpehta)

pehte *iv.* exploding, bursting (pehti-, pehpehte); U tanki ~k. The tank exploded.

pehtivuite *tv.* squash, run over; Karo chuu'utat pehtivuitek. The car ran over the dog and smashed it.

peina *n.* comb

    ete ~ *n.* comb for hair lice made from the burr of echo cactus

pekador *n.* sinner

peloteam *n.* baseball team

peloota *iv.* play ball (~-, pepeloota and peloota)

pelootam *n.* ball (sports); *cf.* voola

pempe'im *n.* heel

penaroa *n.* penance

pensaroa *tv.* think (analyze, intend to do; *cf.* ea, machia); Aapo ~n. S/he was thinking about it. Aapo karota hinuvaeka ~n. S/he was thinking about buying a car.

    kia ~ *iv.* wonder

Peo *n.* Peter

peonasim *n.* peas

pepeesote *rdp.* of peesote, capture

pepiino *n.* cucumber

periko *n.* parrot (*syn.* tavelo)

perioriko *n.* newspaper

pesaroa *tv.* weigh

pesekte *iv.* confess (pesekti-, pepesekte); Aapo paratau ~k. S/he confessed to the priest.

pesektiwame *n.* confession

Pessio *n.* Hemrosillo

petakia *n.* chest, trunk

petala *adv.* prone, on one's stomach

petta *tv.* cut (anything; ~-, pepetta)

peuta *tv.* butcher (peuti-, peupeuta)

peute *tv.* be butchering (peuti-, peupeute)

piano *n.* piano

pichel *n.* pitcher

piesapo *adv.* continuously, over and over, repetitiously (like a broken record; *var.* piesa)

pihkan *n.* fiscal

pihtoola *n.* pistol

piichel *n.* pitcher

piike *tv.* wring (pipiik-, pipiike)

piiki *iv.* dive (piki-, pipike); vaapo kom ~, dive into the water

piiko *n.* bill, beak

piikom *n.* pick (tool); Aapo palam into pikom sauwa. He uses a shovel and pick.

Piima *n.* Pima

piine *tv.* suck out (pin-, pipine)

piino *n.* tamarisk, salt cedar (*Tamarix aphylla*)

piinsam *n.* tweezers

piipa *n.* pipe; In ~ ne ta'aruk. I lost my pipe.

piisa *iv.* be sensitive (with tam, tooth/teeth); *cf.* pipisa tam ~k *iv.* have sensitive teeth

piisam *n.* blanket; Vempo Tusoneu vemela ~ hinuk. They bought a new blanket in Tucson.

piisi *n.* a erect shrub *sp.* with thorn used for Christmas trees

piiso *n.* floor

piitau yoa *iv.* shiver (< piiti au yoa)

piiye *n.* foot (measure)

pikacho *n.* mountain peak

pikokame *n.* cone (shape)

Pilaato *n.* Pontius Pilate

pino moraom sesewame *n.* shrub tamarisk (*Tamarix ramosissima*)

pintura *n.* paint

piocha *n.* chinaberry tree (*Melia azedrach*), used as a medicine

piopiokti *adv.* chirping (with hia); *cf.* piupiuti

pip aso'ola *n.* nipples

pip kuttiria *n.* brassiere

pipi'ike *tv.* wring, squeeze (pipi'ik-; no *rdp.*)

pipim *n.* breasts

pipisa *iv.* be sensitive (with tam, tooth/teeth); *cf.* piisa tam ~ *iv.* have sensitive teeth (enamel worn off)

pisaroon *n.* blackboard

pitta *tv.* press, (a surface; *cf.* yotta), crush, smash (~-, pitpitta)

piupiuti *adv.* chirping (with hia); *cf.* piopiokti

plaano *n.* model, plan, design

plancham *n.* iron (for clothes)

plancharoa *tv.* iron clothes

plantano *n.* banana, plantain

po'okte *iv.* bend, stoop, double over (po'okti-, popo'okte)

po'ola *adv.* stooped over

    ~ cha'aka *adj.* stooping

    ~ cha'atu *iv.* duck (head)

pochilai *adj.* short (string, rope)

pocho'oku *n.* wilderness

    ~ kowi *n.* peccary, javelina

pocho'oria *n.* desert, wilderness, the bush (*syn.* huya)

podoroso *n.* powerful (*syn.* utteak)

pohporo *n.* match
pohta *tv.* boil (~-, pohpohta)
pohte *iv.* boiling (pohti-, pohpohte)
pohtia *tv.* boil for someone (~-)
pohtisom *n.* false teeth
poke *conj.* because; Chuvala vetchi'ivo ~ te yumhoivae. Because we want to rest for a while.
pokti *adv.* plop, plunk
polesia *n.* police officer (**AZ**; *cf.* hurisiaal)
polesiam *n.* the police (collectively)
polia *n.* termite
polopolohti *adv.* in a dripping manner
poloove *adj.* poor
polovesi(a) *adv.* poorly, humbly
pomahe *n.* a tree *sp.*
pompa *n.* pump
pomparoa *tv.* pump
pompomti(a) *adv.* in a thudding manner (re: water drum)
pomta *tv.* take a drink (~-, pompomta)
pomte *iv.* gulp, swig, take a drink (pomti-, pompomte)
pomtitua *tv.* give someone a drink (but not of water; *cf.* vahi'itua)
pon- *comb.* of poona, beat
pona *tv., iv.* 1. *tv.* pull out, pluck (*pl. obj.*; pop—na) 2. *iv.* fall out
  chon ~ *iv.* pick cotton
  voa ~ *iv.* fall out (hair)
  voam ~ *iv.* pluck down feathers
poochi *adj.* short
poona *tv.* 1. bang, beat, knock, pound 2. mash, shred 3. play (instrument, radio, phonograph) (pon-, pópona; *cf.* hiponna); Yo—ko empo puetata ponne. Tommorrow you will be knocking at the door.
pooso *n.* well (water)
poota *tv.* push aside (with yeu; ~-, popota); yeu a ~k, pushed it aside
poote *n.* loose dirt
poove *adj.* poor, destitute
poowim *n.* newt, salamander
pópona *tv.* be beating, knocking (*rdp.* of poona)
popóna *tv.* pull up, uproot (popon-, poppona)
poponna *rdp.* of poona, beat
poposiula *adj.* rusty
poposiwe *iv.* rusting (poposiu-, poposisiwe)
porke *conj.* because
porowi *n.* salamander (*var.* poowi)
portinera *n.* purse
posoim *n.* posole, hominy stew
  tiiko ~ *n.* wheat stew
  mun ~ *n.* hominy and bean stew

pota *tv.* throw up dirt tailings by digging (~- or potán-, popota)
Potam *n.* Potam
potán- *comb.* of pota, throw up dirt
potta *tv.* stuff one (with food), overfeed (~-; *rdp.* not usual)
potte *iv.* have indigestion (potti-, popotte)
pottila *n.* indigestion
poute'ela *n.* cowbird (brown)
presensia *n.* presence (*ser.*)
prinsipal *n.* main, primary, principal
profeta *n.* prophet; Inim yeu yumak ~m. Here the prophets arrived.
promeesa *n.* promise (*syn.* au bwánia)
proyekto *n.* project
pu'akta *tv.* lift, pick up (~, pu'apu'akta)
pu'akte *tv.* load (pu'akti-, pupu'akte)
pu'akti *n.* 1. load 2. pack
pu'ate *tv.* carry, transport, take along (pu'ati-, pupu'ate); *cf.* weiya
pu'ilai *n.* 1. peak, pinnacle 2. cowlick 3. unique, in a class of it's own
    4. by her/his/it's self; Wa kawi apela ~ weyek. The mountain is
    standing by itself.
pua *tv.* 1. pick (crops) 2. choose, select, appoint (with yeu) (~-, puppua);
    Aapo chin puppuan? Did s/he used to pick cotton? U hamut
    taho'ota yeu ~. The woman picked out the cloth. Vempo
    kovanaom yeu ~wak. They appointed a governor.
puanam *adv.* with something upright in one's arms
    ~ sisime *iv.* go along holding something erect in one's arms
puanama *tv.* carry a person (puanam-, puananama)
puato *n.* plate, dish
publikaroa *tv.* make known, publish
puchi yena *iv.* be puffing a cigarette
puentes *n.* bridge
pueplo *n.* village, town (opposite milieu of the yo an'a; in the town there
    is order and the supernatural is represented by statues and
    images in the church)
puerto *n.* port, harbor
pues *interj.* well
pueta *n.* door, car door
    ~ bwisiria *n.* door knob/door handle
puh *comb.* of puusi, eye
    ~ aso'ola *n.* pupil (of eye)
    ~ chaka'ariam *n.* a look out of the corner of one's eye
    ~ chaka'ariam véa a vitchu, looking at her/him out of the corner
    of one's eye
    ~ mayoa *n.* eye socket
    ~ se'eve'im *n.* eyelashes
puhta *tv.* blow away, spray (~-, puhpuhta)
puhte *iv.* open one's eyes (puhti-; the tense forms of remte are often used)

puhtia *adj.* bloated, obese, overweight; Manteka, tahkaim bwa'eka kia ~m vena. Eating butter and tortillas makes them fat.

puhtua *dv.* give someone the evil eye; Aapo a ~k. S/he gave her/him the evil eye.

puhtuari *n.* given the evil eye

puhva *n.* face

puhvaka *adv.* facing; ~ weye, stand facing a certain direction; Apo wam vicha ~ weyek. S/he is standing facing away.

puhveá *n.* eyelid

pulgada *n.* inch

puppua *rdp.* of pua, pick

puntam *n.* points (engine)

pusiyesa'ala *n.* salamander

putte *iv.* shoot bow or a gun (putti-, putputte); putekame, one who shoots; putputeme, one who shoots well

puul *n.* pool, billiards

puusim *n.* 1. eye 2. hole (in flute) 3. headlights (of car) (*comb.* puh-, *obj.* puhta)

~ tutucha *iv.* wink; O'ou hamuttau ~ tutuchan. The man winked at the woman.

R

ra'ati *adv.* sound of something brittle clanging

raadio *n.* radio

Raahum *n.* Rahum (comes from rahukte, become hard from evaporation)

raaya *n.* groove; Veáta tu'uteteko se'eta ka sauwane bwe'ituk ~m hunk ya'ane. In cleaning the skin, you can't use sand because you will make grooves (in the skin).

rahukte *iv.* become hard from evaporation (with nama)

rama *n.* ramada (*syn.* heka)

Ramos *n.* Palm Sunday

rancheo *n.* rancher

rancho *n.* ranch

rahukte *iv.* cake, dry out (food; rahukti-)

rauta *tv.* rinse (~-, raurauta)

ravikte *iv.* twist ankle (ravikti-, no *rdp.*)

reata *n.* lariat

reemam *n.* oar, paddle

reepam *n.* earring

regaalo *n.* gift, present

rehte *iv.* walking (*pl.*; *sg.* weama; rehti-, rerehte); Itepo tasariapo huyapo rerehte. In the summer we go hiking.

rei *n.* king

reina *n.* queen

relikia *n.* relic
rema wiike *tv.* row (boat)
remoa *tv.* alternate (~-, reremoa)
remta *tv.* look at, watch (~-, remremta)
remte *iv.* open one's eyes (remti-, remremte)
rentaroa *tv.* rent
repikte *iv.* blink eyes (repikti-, repirepikte)
repooyo *n.* cabbage
restaurante *n.* restaurant
retraato *n.* photograph
retratoroa *tv.* photograph (*syn.* nu'e)
reuwa *tv.* loan, borrow (reuw-, rereuwa); Tu'isi ne em siya reuwne. Let
        me borrow your chair. Empo em siya nee reuwak. You loaned
        me your chair. Mesata chuvala nee reuwa. Let me borrow the
        table for a while. Inepo tomita Hoseta reuwak. I loaned money
        to Joe.
revarua *n.* yeast
revei *n.* piece
revekta *tv.* crumble (*ex.*: bread, clods, adobes, old bricks; ~-, reverevekta)
revekte *iv.* be crumbling, cracking (revekti-, reverevekte)
revektia *adj.* crumbled
reverevekti *adv.* piece by piece, piecemeal
        ~ weche *iv.* fall apart/fall to pieces
rewi'ise *iv.* go to borrow (*sg.*; *pl.* rewi'ivo)
rihhu'utiam *n.* deer hoof belt
rihrihti *adv. var.* of lilihti, sparsely
rii'itia *iv.* jingling
Riingo *n.* Anglo
rikora *n.* rich
Ringo *comb.* of Riingo, Anglo
        ~ Bwia *n.* the United States of America
        ~ noka *iv.* speak English
        ~ noki *n.* the English language
ripte *iv.* pinkeye, have eye infection (ripti-, ripripte)
ripti *n.* blind person
riptiam *n.* pinkeye
riuma *n.* rheumatism
riuta *tv.* fracture (~-, riuriuta); Apo wok otata ~k. S/he fractured her/his
        leg bone.
riute *iv.* fracture (in process of fracturing; riuti-, riuriute); Ota ~k. The
        bone was fractured.
riutia *adj.* fractured
ro'iro'ikti *adv.* limping
ro'akta *tv.* roll up (~-, ro'aro'akta)
ro'akte *iv.* be rolling, tumbling (ro'akti-, ro'aro'akte)
ro'aro'akteme *n.* acrobat (*syn.* maromeo)

rohikte *iv.* 1. be sad, lonely, bored (of = nea, ea, ae, etc.) 2. miss a person or place (rohikti-, rohirohikte)

rohiktiachi *adj.* 1. boring 2. sad

roira a desert shrub with small orange berries (*Lycium andersoni*; *var.* roiya)

roiya *n. var.* of roira

roosa *n.* rose

roovo *n.* wolf

ropeo *n.* closet

roppo'otiam *n.* maypole or maypole dance

ropropte *iv.* be sinkable, submergible

ropte *iv.* sink, submerge, drown (ropti-, ropropte); roptivae, one the verge of drowning/sinking

roptihinek *adj.* covered (with cloth)

roptila *adj.* sunk (in water; *cf.* tuttila)

rovoi *adj.* rounded

rovou hoo'ok *adj.* hunchbacked (*syn.* lochi)

ru'uru'uti *adv.* thunderingly

ru'uru'utia *iv.* be thundering (ru'uru'utiu-, ru'uru'uti hihia)

ruenasim *n.* peach (*syn.* rurahno)

ruera *n.* 1. wheel 2. steering wheel

rukta *tv.* move (~-, rukrukta); Puatota ne ~k. I moved the door.

ruktatu *iv.* movable (not used alone)
    aa ~ *iv.* be movable
    ka ~ *iv.* be immovable

rukte *iv.* move, stir (rukti-, rukrukte); Ime ne ~k. I moved over here.
    aavo ~ *iv.* approach, get close

rukti *adj.* moved (closer); U mesa avo heela ~. The table was moved closer (to use).

ruktiwame *n.* act of moving closer

rumui *n.* uneven

rupakte *iv.* blazing (rupakti-, ruparupakte)

rupaktiam *n.* flames

rurahno *n.* peach (*syn.* ruenasim)
    ~ ouwo *n.* peach tree
    ~ váchia *n.* peach pit

rurumui *n.* rough ground

rutukte *iv.* straighten out (rutukti-, ruturutukte); Wokim ne ~vae. I'm straightening out my legs.

ruura *n.* rue (leaves are warmed in a small amount of olive oil, and the solution is applied to ear for infection)

ruuse *tv.* 1. rub 2. scrub (rurus-, ruruse); mamam ~, rub one's hands together; Inepo in ili asoa rurussek. I rubbed down my little boy.

ruutia *iv.* 1. bang, explode, growl (stomach) 2. roar (train, rain, thunder, sea) (*pst.* ruutihiak, ruutihiu-, rurutia)

S

=sa *ptc.* interrogative particle; I hitasa? What is this? Haiki kuchumsa? How many fish are there?

=san *ptc.* however; Ne kaita yuumak in chu'usan hi'ibwak. I got nothing, but my dog did eat.

sa'abwaniak *pst.* of sabwa'ania, re-injure someone else

sa'awa *n.* sore

sa'ina *tv.* sift (~-, sasa'ina)

saake *tv.* toast grain (sak-, sasake)

saaki *adj.* toasted

saakim *n.* popcorn, parched corn

saala *n.* living room, parlor; ~po soofa into siiyam hooka. There is a sofa and chairs in the living room.

saalochi *n.* a plant *sp.*

saami *n.* adobe brick

saanto *n.* saint

saarten *n.* frying pan

saasaati noka *iv.* whisper

saavum *n.* soap

saawa₁ *n.* saiya, a plant *sp.* (*Amorexia palmatifida*)

saawa₂ *tv.* share; nau a ~, share it

saaweam *n.* pants, trousers; ~po wokte, put on pants

saawi *n.* cane (*Amoreuxia palmatifida*)

sabwa'ana *iv.* hit a sore spot, re-injure self (with au)

sabwa'ania *tv.* re-injure someone else (*pst.* sa'abwaniak, ~-, sasa'abwania)

sahti *adv.* sound of particulate matter impacting (grain, sand)

sai *n.* older brother (*masc.*)

saila *n.* younger brother (*masc.*)

saila maaso *n.* 1. the deer (in the deer dance) 2. deer dancer

saiyula *adv.* huddled

sak- *comb.* of saake, roast grain

    saka *iv.* go (*pl.*; *imp.* ~vo'em, *pst.* sahak, saká'a-, sasaka); this verb may be suffixed with the *comb.* of another verb to mean "____ while moving"); *cf.* siika)

    yeu ~ *iv.* go out, exit, leave; ke a ~o, before they go out

saka'atua *tv.* make leave, dismiss (*pl. obj.*)

saka'avo'em *interj.* go away! (*pl.*; *sg.* simise'e)

sakkau *n.* Gila monster

sakovai *n.* watermelon (*var.* sakvai)

saktuse *iv.* be grinding (saktuh-, saktutuse)

saktusi *n.* pinole, meal (flour)

salvaroa *tv.* save (*syn.* hinne'u)

sama'i *n.* uncle (father's older brother)

Samawaka Kawi *n.* a sacred mountain near Totoitakese'epo

sami hoa *iv.* make adobe; vaavoe sami hoa, make clay into adobe
bricks; Wempo vaavuta sami hoa. They are making the clay
into adobes.

samta *tv.* split cane (~-, samsamta)

samte *iv.* be splitting (can; samti-, samsamte)

san *ptc., adv.* however, only; Ne kaita yuumak in chu'u ~ hi'ibwak. Aapo
san ke tu'uli tomek. He, however, still has some money. Neu
kaita yuumak in chuu'u ~ hi'ibwak. There was no food for me;
only for my dog. Ne kaita yuumak in chu'usan hi'ibwak. I got
nothing, but my dog did eat.

San Huan *n.* St. John
San Huan Taewai *n.* St. John's Day, the beginning of summer;
San Huan Taewaipo u yoeme uva. One bathes on St. John's Day.

San Paasiko *n.* St. Francis

sana *n.* sugarcane

sana'im *n.* rib

sánake *iv.* really care for her/him; Hose ~. Joseph really cares (for John).

sanava *n.* corn husk

sanchina *adv.* unkempt (with kovak); ~ kovak, have messy hair

sanchivei *adj.* messy

sania *n.* grove

saniloa *n.* grove, woods

sankakam *n.* brown sugar

sankira *adv.* bristling, bushy (*syn.* sanvera); ~ kovak, be unkempt; ~ bwasiak,
have a bushy tail

sankoa *n.* 1. trash 2. chaff (in thrashing grain; *syn.* ota)
~ kari *n.* hut
~ monti *n.* trash heap, trash pile
~ wo'oti *n.* trash scattered or strewn about, litter

sankora *n.* 1. trashy person 2. drunk (person) 3. a particular pascola tune

sanku'ukuchi *n.* raven

sanooria *n.* carrot

Santa Kuusim *n.* May 3, the end of Lent; on this day, the ritual control of
the Fariseo Society ends until the following Ash Wednesday;
people make crosses of willow branches to put on house walls;
the old crosses are burned along with weeds and trash

santa puusim wiroa *n.* a plant *sp.*

santene *adv.* upright (with katek, weyek)

santo *n.* 1. saint 2. statue of a saint; Uka ~ta movela yechak apo hani
enchi ániane tea. If you put the saint upside down they say he
will help you.
~ hoa *tv.* consecrate (*syn.* santole)
~ Livrom *n.* Bible
~ supem *n.* habit (*syn.* avi'itom)
~ tevat *n.* ceremonial patio; Ume ~m altariapo hooka. The saints
are on the altar.

santole *tv.* consecrate (*syn.* santo hoa)

santora *n.* the complement of saints on an altar, the saints (*col.*)

sanvara *adv.* frightfully, horribly
~ bwana *iv.* have an awful cry

sanvera *adv.* bristling, bushy (*syn.* sankira)

sanveta kovak *iv.* have unkempt hair

sapa weche *iv.* snow

sapa wechia *adj.* 1. fallen (snow, ice) 2. frozen

sapak *adj.* icey

sapala *adv.* intersecting, crisscrossing; ~ teéka, lay it across; Vempo
kustata ~ teéka.

sapam *n.* 1. ice, snow; icile 2. ice-cream

sapo *n.* limberbush (*Jatropha cardiophylla*; *syn.* kau sapo)

sapti *n.* wall

sarhento *n.* sergeant

sarampionim *n.* measles

sarteen *n.* frying pan

sasavua *iv.* lather, get sudsy

sasavutua *tv.* soap, apply soap

sata *n.* red dirt (for property slip)
~ Kawi *n.* island in San Carlos Bay

satema *n.* buzzard (*gen.*; *cf.* wiiru, tekoe)

satemali *n.* mountain lizard (a lizard *sp.*)

sauko *n.* elderberry (*Sambucus sp.*)

sauwa *tv.* use, make use of (~-, sasauwa)

sauwari *adj.* usual
ka ~ *adj.* unusual

sauwawame *n.* use, adaptation

sauwo *n.* saguaro cactus (*Carnegiea gigantea*)

sauwo taaka *n.* saguaro fruit

sava *tv.* covet (especially food; ~-, sasava)

Savala *n.* Saturday

Savala Looria *n.* Gloria, Holy Saturday

savanam *n.* sheet (bed)

savatua *tv.* covet (especially food)

sawa *n.* 1. leaf 2. page

sawai *adj.* yellow; Kesum ~; kama ket ~. The cheese is yellow; the squash
is also yellow. Sanoorim naranhao into sasawai. Carrots and
orange and yellow.

sawaik kovak *iv.* be blond

sawali *adj.* yellow (*s.*)
~ wiikit *n.* Yellow Bird (a pascola and Deer dance song)

sawan *n.* arch (*syn.* arko)

sawaria *n.* jaundice

sawe *tv.* order, command, boss (saw-, sasawe)

saweam *n.* 1. trousers 2. underwear

saweate *iv.* put on pants

se *pn.* you (*sg.*; *pl.* sem; *syn.* che, e, empo; < haisempo); Sewa nat se weche vétuku (*s.*). You, under where the flower falls. Yoko vampo se heka (*s.*). In the spotted water, you drank. Ne se muteka teki (*s.*). I, you laid as a pillow. Se ka hikkaha. You don't listen. Se hiokot maachi. You look pitiful. Empo tiendau siime? Are you going to the store?

Se Chopoi *n.* High Town (Yaqui community near Chandler)

se'elaim *n.* white tepary beans (*cf.* heseim)

se'eparia *n.* sand dune, sandy area

sea *n. var.* of seewa, flower

Sea An'a *n.* the Flower World (supernatural world in the East, where all living spirits reside including those of animals, a utopia free from illness and care where our ancestors return after death; the Deer in the Deer dance is the link to this perfect world; *cf.* maso bwikam); I ili malit sea ániapo ho'ak. The little fawn lives in the Flower World.

sea choni *n.* split end (hair; *syn.* choni kottila)

Sea Hamut *n.* the Flower Woman (the interpreter of the Talking Tree; also called Yo Mumuli; some versions of the myth have both Sea Hamut and Yo Mumuli as twin sisters who do the interpretation)

sea hi'ika *iv.* embroider (*lit.* sew flowers); Apo aa sea hi'ika. She can embroider.

sea hikwame *n.* embroidery

sea taka *n.* spiritual body (*lit.* flower body), person with a sixth sense with intuitive knowledge of the future and therefore protected to some degree, has an aura-like force field around their body; persons with this have extra-sensory perception, self-awareness, keen judgment, assuring memory, and intelligence against evil powers

sea vachi *n.* variegated, multicolored corn

sea yoleme *n.* the Flower Person (the Deer in the Deer dance)

seariak *v.* overwhelm, overpower in thought or feeling; Ne a ~. I overwhelmed him.

seatakakame *n.* one who has seataka

seate *iv.* make artificial flowers

see pa'aria *n.* sand dune, dune

see'e *n.* sand

seechuktia *adv.* all of the sudden; Aapo ~ kokoe weche. S/he fell sick all of the sudden.

seekam *n.* armpit

seeka voam *n.* underarm hair

seekia *n.* ditch

seenu *num., pn.* 1. *num.* one 2. *pn.* someone 3. *pn.* other (*var.* senu; *obj.* senuku); ~ we'epo, on the other hand; Senu aavo weye. Someone is coming. Senuk ne vicha. I see one/someone. Senu hamutta hivane. Senu o'ou aman ho'ak. A certain man lives there. Ave kia, senu enchim kuta wisa'ei maya. Okay for now, someone may hit you with a wooden serving spoon (typical remark to a pascola). Senu hamutta hiva ne vicha. I see only one woman. Senukut kom wetne. That might fall on someone. ~ chake'etam ne vittua. Please show me another jacket.

Seeri *n.* Seri

seevo *n.* fat, tallow

seewa *n., iv.* 1. *n.* flower (flowers represent good, and help people fight against evil; flowers are symbolized by confetti, paper flowers, the Deer dancer's regalia, and other ritual items; when Christ died on the cross, his drop of blood that fell to the ground were transformed into flowers) 2. *n.* ceremonial work or labor 3. *n.* the love of one's life (*masc.*) 4. *iv.* blossom, flower; Aman weye in sewa. There goes the love of my life.

sehchuktia *adv.* suddenly, by surprise

sehtul(ia) *adv.* once

sekala *adj.* parallel

sekawam *n.* ribbon (of Matachin crown)

sekka'atana *adv.* on one side

sekola *adv.* with open arms (with cha'aka)

selwalka *n.* a type of squash

sem *pn.* you (*pl.*; *sg.* se; *syn.* enchim); Hiokot sem hiyawa (*s.*). They go sounding pitifully. Tu'i ~ ho'ak. You people live well (have a nice home).

semalulukut *n.* 1. hummingbird 2. lively person, live wire

semaana *n.* week

   ~po taewaim *n.* days of the week

sementeeria *n.* cemetery

semento *n.* cement, concrete

semta *tv.* stretch (~-, semsemta)

semte *iv.* stretch (semti-, semsemte)

sena'asom *n.* sistrum, disk rattle used by pascolas (*syn.* sonasom)

sene'eka *n.* spring (water)

sentavo *n.* cent

   dies ~ *n.* ten cents, dime

   mamni ~ *n.* five cents, a nickel

senteiya *n.* thunderbolt

sentiirom *n.* senses (of perception); mamni ~, the five senses

sentro *n.* downtown, civic center

senu *num., pn.* 1. *num. var.* of seenu, one 2. *pn.* someone 3. a, an (*obj.* ~k); ka ~k vena, not like each other/not like any other; ~ we'epo, at once (in a single instant); ~ wéeme, in other words/in another vein; ~ aman weye. Someone is walking over there. ~ minaita bwa'aka. Someone ate the cantaloupe. Empo ~k vithcuk. You were looking at someone. Aapo ~k tomita mikne. S/he will money to someone. ~ we'epo a yak. S/he did it at once. ~ wéeme ama aayuk. There's another point/facet to that.

senu taka *num.* twenty
senu we'epo *adv.* in a way, under one condition only
senu wechiapo *adv.* all at once, in no time at all
senyor *n.* 1. lord 2. God
Senyorta Hiavihteim *n.* God's Breathing (the first Pascola tune played
    after the opening of a pahko)
Senyorta pahko *n.* a pahko held by a family during Lent, involving
    feeding many of the villagers, including the ceremonial people
    (*syn.* Waehma pahko)
sep(ia) *adv.* right away (*var.* sep, sepsu); Au chachaewak ~ yepsak. When
    they called him, he came right away. Aapo ~ o'omtek. Right
    away he got angry. Si ka aman wéevaetek sep nokne. If you don't
    want to go, speak right up.
sepio *n.* toothbrush
sepsu *adv. var.* of sep(ia), right away
Septiemre *n.* September
serafin *n.* seraphim (*var.* serafinesi)
sermonia *n.* sermon
seruuchom *n.* saw (tool)
servisio *n.* service, assistance
sesevea *rdp.* of sevea, get cold
seva *n.* barley
seve *adj., iv.* 1. *adj.* cold 2. *iv.* be cold 3. homosexual (male or female);
    ke ~o, before it gets cold
seve meecham *n.* winter, winter months
seve'e choa *n.* jumping cholla (*Opuntia fulgida*)
seve'i *n.* eaves, overhang
seve'im *n.* fringe
sevea *iv.* get cold (sevé-, sessevea); Vaa'am ~k. The water got cold. Enerot
    hani sevevae tea. They say it will be cold in January. *Flagstaff*
    po tu'isi sessevea. It gets cold in Flagstaff.
sevele *iv.* feel cold (*pst.* ~n, *fut.* seveline; for other tenses, forms of
    chuvakte are used)
severia *n.* 1. winter 2. cold (sickness; *syn.* kataro); ~po, in the winter; ~po
    tu'isi seve. It gets very cold in winter.
sevi *n.* jumping cholla
sevis maso *n.* mule deer
sevo'i *n.* fly (insect; *s.* sevoli)
sevoli *n.* fly (insect; *s.*; = sevo'i)
sevora *n.* onion
sewa *n. var.* of seewa, flower (often used as a nickname for children
    because envious spirits could take a child's identity by finding
    out their real name)
    ~ Hamut *n.* the Flower Woman
    ~ tomte *iv.* blossom
    ~ yoleme *n.* flower person
sewailo *adj. var.* of seyewailo, flowered (*s.*)

sewalka *n.* a type of squash

sewaivampo *n.* flower water (the water of the water drum used during a Deer dance which is sacred during the ceremony; the Deer comes to the water to drink and play, and the water may be thrown at spectators after the Deer dance is over)

sewatua *tv.* decorate with flowers

sewatuari *adj.* decorated with flowers, bedecked; U kus yo'owe ~. The village cross is decorated with flowers.

sewundo *n.* second (in position or turn)

sewuraroa *tv.* secure, make secure

seye *n. var.* of seewa, flower

seyewailo *adj.* flower-covered, flowered (*s.* sewailo; ~ is often used in song language as well)

si$_1$ *adv.* very; U kuvaleo si a hipona. He's a good drummer.

si$_2$ *conj.* if, whether; Apo aman wee'ean ~ tomeko. He would go there if he had money. Ne ka hu'uneiya ~ apo aman weene. I don't know whether he'll go.

~ kaa *conj.* unless, if; Si kaa ama wevaetek sep nokne. If you don't want to go, speak up.

si'ibwia *adj.* numb

si'ika *n.* bladder

si'ime *pn.* all, everyone, entire (*obj.* ~k)

si'ime wa'a *pn.* all of it, all of them; Si'ime wa'a yoemta allea. All of humanity is happy.

si'imek *adv.* completely, wholly, entirely

si'imekut *adv.* all over

si'imekunvicha *adv.* in all directions

si'imekuttana *adv.* from all directions

si'imem *pn.* all of it/them, everybody, everything; ~ nu'e. Get all of it.

si'imenawi *adv.* altogether

si'ite *iv.* in: vaa ~, be sprinkling

si'ita *tv.* in: vaa ~, sprinkle it

si'iya *n.* chamomile

sia bwakta *tv.* disembowel

siakikichiite *iv.* get green, bud out

sialapti *iv.* verdant, covered with green

siali *adj.* 1. green 2. pale 3. inexperienced (*var.* siari)

siali muunim *n.* green beans

siam *n.* intestines

siari adj 1. green 2. raw, crude; Ehootem lechuwa into sisiari. The string beans and lettuce are green. ~ si ayuk. It (vegatation) got very green.

~ bwa'ame *n.* vegetable

~ maival *n.* mayate, a green Mexican beetle

siari tomi *n.* paper money, dollar bills

siasaalai *adj.* greenish

sihho'ote *iv.* drizzle (rain; *syn.* sio yuke; sihho'oti-)
sihoniam *n.* rash
sihpattila *iv.* have urinary problems (*pst.* ~tukan; only the *pres.* and *pst.* are usual)
siika *iv.* 1. *pst.* of siime, go (*sg.*) 2. shrank; Vai wasuktiam ~k vempo karota hinuvaen. After three years passed they were wanting to buy a car. In pantolonim nau ~. My pants shrank.
siiku *n.* navel, umbilical cord
siila *n.* saddle (in: kavai ~, saddle)
siime *iv.* go (*sg.*; *pl.* saka; *imp.* simise'e, *pst.* siika, sim-, *hab.* sisime; may be suffixed to the *comb.* of another verb to mean "____ while moving"; *cf.* -sisime); Apo woi veemelam mapoasimvae um pahkowi. She has two new bracelets to wear to the ceremony.
aet ~, *iv.* pass (*syn.* pasároa; aet = *d.o.*); Aet ne wam siika. I passed her/him/it.
wam ~ *iv.* cross, traverse
yeu ~ *iv.* come out
siirisiiriti *adv.* buzzing, rattling (rattles); Yoyo a'akame sevipo vo'oka, ~ hia (s). Enchanted snake lying in the cholla, going zzzz.
siise *iv.* urinate (sis- or sih-, sisse)
au ~ *tv.* relieve one's self
siisi *n.* urine
siiva₁ *tv.* carve (wood); pare, peel (sivá-, sisiva); *cf.* vesuma, vekta
siiva₂ *n.* cliff, precipice
siiva wiikit *n.* cliff bird (*s.*)
siivo *tv.* 1. harm, damage 2. curse, hex (siv—, sisivo)
siiya₁ *n.* 1. chair 2. car seat (in Arizona; used in the *pl.*; *cf.* vanko)
~ rueratame *n.* wheelchair
siiya₂ *n.* hose
sika *tv.* cut (hair; siká'a-, sisika); Itom achai Luista ~k. Our father cut Louis' hair.
sikamtachi *adv.* in the past; U wasuktia ~ tu'isi ko'okoewak. In the past year there was much sickness.
sikharai *adj.* red-faced
sikhewei *adj.* pink (*syn.* koloroosa)
siki *adj.* red; Kannao ~; wichalakas ket ~. The pomegranites is red; so it the cardinal. Tomaatem si~. Tomatoes are red.
Sikil Kawi *n.* Red Mountain, an enchanted mountain near Guaymas
sikili *adj. var.* of siki, red
sikisa hoa *tv.* redden
sikisi *iv.* become red (*pl.* si~)
sikite *tv.* redden
sikkucha'a *n.* coral snake
sikropo'i *n.* a plant *sp.*
siksiktia *iv.* shuffle

siktavut *n.* red racer (snake)
sikupuriam *n.* kidneys
silate *tv.* saddle
silikte *iv.* sprain (ankle)
silili'iti *adv.* trickling (sound)
silolote *iv.* be drizzling (siloloti-)
silosiloti *adv.* drizzle (*s.* = sio)
silweela *n.* prune
simise'e *interj.* go away (*sg.*; *pl.* saka'avo'em)
simla *adj.* 1. happened, past 2. gone; Hunain yeu ~. It came to pass.
simtua *tv.* make leave
sina *n.* a cactus *sp.*, crawling in habit *(Stenocereus alamosanus)*
sink *n.* sink
sio yuke *iv.* drizzle (*syn.* sihho'ote; *s.* = silosiloti)
siok yoene *exp.* cheer up, keep your chin up (said to a person who is sad
      or in mourning)
sioka *iv.* be lonely, sad (siok-, sisioka)
sioktua *tv.* hurt, make sad
siosioti *adv.* rusting sound (with hia)
siotia *iv.* hiss
sipa *tv.* cool it down (sipá'a-, sisipa)
sipe *iv.* get cool (sip-, sisipe)
siper *n.* zipper
sirko *n.* circus
sipepe'eti *adv.* the sound of big raindrops impacting; ~ yuku, be raining
      loudly
siririti *adv.* sound of sand or grains shifting or pouring; (*syn.* sisiti; used
      with hia)
sisioka *iv.* get lonely, sad; *cf.* sioka
sisi'ibwa *iv.* be chapped (~-, no *rdp.*)
sisi'ibawala *adj.* chapped
sisia *adv.* smelling like the sea or ocean (with huva)
sisime *iv. hab.* of siime; kia ~, wander off, have mental problems
sisivome, yee *n.* witch
sisiwooki *n.* iron, metal
sisteema *n.* system
sita$_1$ *n.* young, developing corn ear
sita$_2$ *tv.* sprinkle (with vaa, water)
sita'avau *n.* huevito *(Vallesia glabra)*, an evergreen shrub used for
      drumsticks and for eyedrops
sitepo(lo) *n.* a plant *sp.*
sito'im *n.* jelly, gell
siuta *tv.* tear (~-, siusiuta)
siute *iv.* be torn (siuti-, siusiute)
siuti *adj.* torn apart
siutila *adj.* torn (*var.* siutia)

Siva Kovi *n.* Cliff Corner (Yaqui community near Yuma)

siviviti *adv.* whistling (any whistling sound; with hia)

sivo'oli *n.* tadpole

sivori *adj.* bewitched (therefore sick or listless)

siwe *iv.* grow (plants), sprout (siu-, sisiwe); aa ~ capable of growing; Im minaim aa siwe. Melons can grow here.

soa *tv.* poke, prick, puncture (~-, sossoa); *cf.* hihsoa

soari *adj.* pricked

sochik *n.* bat (animal); bats are common in Yoeme myths and stories; in the story of how Voovok (Toad) brought the rain back from Yuku (Rain) by borrowing Bat's wings

soita *tv.* lift (~-, soisoita)

sokiktu *iv.* become hoarse

sokiktula *iv.* be hoarse temporarily (*pst.* sokituk, ~-, sosokiktu)

sola *adj.* transparent, glistening (*s.*; = soolai); vaiwa ~ voyoka (*s.*), lying fresh with dew

solaar *n.* property, land; Hunaman in hoara ~po. Over there (is) my home.

soliaroa *iv.* get sunstroke, heatstroke

sololoi *adj.* plastic; Puato ~to ya'ari. The dish is made of plastic.

solti *adv.* stealthily, sneaking, skulking

~ weye *iv.* sneak, skulk

sombriya *n.* umbrella

somo'ochia *n.* foam, suds, lather

sonasom *n.* disk rattle (an older usage; *syn.* sena'asom)

sontao *n.* soldier

sontaom *n.* army

sooda *n.* carbonated beverage, pop

soofa *n.* couch (sofaapo, on the couch)

sooka *adj.* in: chin ~, perennial cotton

sookte *iv.* come loose, fall apart (sookti-, soosookte)

soolai *adj.* sheer, see-through, transparent (*s.* sola)

alambre ~ *n.* wire mesh

taho'ori ~ *n.* sheer cloth

kari ~ *n.* transparent house

soonim *n.* dance tune (Pascola, Matachin, etc.), the unwritten music associated with the Deer, Pascola, and Matachin dances (the alavansam is used from the beginning of the fiesta until midnight, when the worlds turns; the kompania is used from then until dawn; and the partiyo is used from dawn until the end of the ceremony)

Sooria *n.* Enchanted Mountain, southern boundary of the Yaqui lands

soosa *n.* plants of the nightshade family (Solanum *sp.*)

sooso *iv.*, *n.* 1. *iv.* get stickers (sos—, sosso) 2. *n.* thorn, sticker 3. *n.* bullheads, goat heads (plant)

soota *iv.* be paid (~-, sosota)

soovre *n.* envelope

soparoa *n.* enough, sufficient quantity; Inepo ~ta he'eka. I had enough to drink. A: Empo watek waata? B: ~. A: Do you want some more? B: No. That's enough.

sopi'ichim *n.* overripe fruit

sopo'ochi *n.* fallen saguaro fruit

soso'oki *adj.* pocked

sosoko *adj.* rough (surface), scaly (skin); ~k veákan, had rough skin

sosso *rdp.* of sooso, get stickers

sossoa *rdp.* of soa, poke

soto'i *n.* olla, pot, kettle (*obj.* soto'ota, *comb.* soto'o-)

soto'ote *iv.* make pottery

soute *iv.* go down (re: swelling; souti-, sousoute)

soute'ela *n.* magical deer

sova *tv.* roast (~-, sosova); *cf.* hisova

sovaroa *tv.* rub, massage (for health)

=su *ptc.* attached to any part of speech (*cf.* su, -suk)
1. as (attached to verbs); Aapo hi'ibwakasu tattek. As s/he was eating, s/he choked.
2. do, did (emphasis; attached to adverbs, pronouns, and nouns, especially in song language); may have a sense of obligation; Vemposu aman katne, ta ka hunen ea. They should go there, but they won't. Itom to'osiika, isu yoyo an'a (*s.*). It left us, this enchanted world. Sewailo malichi su siika. The flowered fawn did go. San Huan San Pasihkota wiko'ita su kottak. St. John did break St. Francis' bow. Vempo su? And them (what about them)?
3. where; Davidsu? Where is Dave?
4. it is because; Aaposu ka hikkahaka woho'oriapo kom wechek. It is because s/he did not listen that they fell into the hole. Aapo su lottila. Because s/he is tired (*resp.*). Aapo su siika. Because s/he went (*resp.*).
5. question marker (may be used with the question marker haisa); Em maala su hoa'po katek? Is your mother at home? Emesu haisa aane—kave ko'okoe? Is everyone well at your house?
6. what if; Huan Lupeta vichak su? What if John did see Lucy?
7. focus marker on adverbs (especially adverbs of location); *ex.*: che'ewasu, more and more; nausu, really together; komsu, downward; Empo amansu wee'ean. You should go there. Notteka toloko bwiapo komsu siika (*s.*). Returning, you did go down in the light blue earth.

sua₁ *tv.* 1. kill 2. fish with a net (*pl. obj.*; *sg. obj.* me'a; ~-, sussua)

sua₂ *tv.* take care of, guard, watch over, protect (~-, susua); em ~. Take care (*sg.* addressee); ~'em. Take care (*pl.* addressee); Hunaksan aapo hiva yu au susua. After that, s/he always took care of themself. Emo e ~ne waka ka em ta'amta eu nokao. You be careful when a stranger talks to you.

suak *adj.* clever, smart, shrewd
suale *tv.* believe (sual-, susuale)
sualsi *adv.* believable
    ~ **maachi** *iv.* honest
sualwachi *adj.* trustful
sualwame *n.* belief
suame *n.* agent
suan- *comb.* of suawa, be watched
suatam vicha *tv.* butt in, interrupt
suate vicha *tv.* bother, disturb;
suatea *iv.* be uncomfortable, worried, concerned, anxious
suati *adv.* irritating
    ~ **aane** *iv.* be misbehaving
    ~ **eetua** *tv.* irritate one
suatia *tv.* bother, disturb; Ka te a ~. Don't bother us.
suatiachi *adj.* irritating
suatiachisi maachi *iv.* be irritating
suavusa *iv., tv.* 1. *iv.* wake up 2. *tv.* awaken (~-, suavuvusa; *var.* vusa); Ian ketwo ne ~k. This morning I woke up. Ian ketwo ne in saela ~k. This morning I woke up my younger brother.
suawa *iv.* 1. be watched 2. be on probation (suan-, susuawa)
suawak *iv.* have common sense
suawak in: kova ~, be intelligent
suawaka *n.* 1. meteorite 2. Meteorite, a supernatural being that descends as a meteorite to earth to protect people from chupiarim (he is a short, fat dwarf and the son-in-law of Yuku, Rain; he carries a rainbow in his hand and strike the chupiarim from above, usually striking mountains in which they dwell)
suawame₁ *n.* slaughter, killing
suawame₂ *n.* protection
sueram *n.* sweater
suerom *n.* IV (intravenous food and/or medication)
suerte *n.* luck
suertek *iv.* be lucky
suka *adj.* warm
suka yoene *exp.* warm yourself, come in and warm yourself
sukaria *tv.* warm (~-, sukkaria)
sukawa *n.* warmth
sukawe *iv.* warm one's self (sukau-, *rdp.* susukawe, sukkawe)
suke *tv.* scratch (*pst.* susukuk, susuk-, sussuke)
sukkai *adj.* warm
suluú- *comb.* of suulu, slip

sulumai *n.* a marine bird *sp.* that slides into the water

sulwachi *adj. var.* of sunwachi, horrible; ~ si aane. He's acting
dangerously, foolishly.

sum- *comb.* of suume, sink

suma *tv.* tie (sumá'a-, susuma)

suma'i *adj.* tied; pahko ~, one obligated to give a ceremony (*syn.* pahko
sumawakame)

sumawakame *n.* one who is tied
pahko ~, one obligated to give a ceremony (*syn.* pahko suma'i)

suma'ariam *n.* bandage

sumeiya *tv.* be afraid or suspicious of (of = *d.o.*); Apo enchi ~. S/he is suspicious of you.

sumia *iv.* be flat (tire; *pst.* sumuk, went flat)

sumuk *pst.* of sumia, go flat (tire)

sunsunte *iv.* crawl (re: caterpillar, inchworm), be stretchable; *cf.* vo'osime,
waka'anama, waka'ate

sunsunti *adv.* swiftly (with weye)

sunwachi *iv.* horrible, fierce, frightening

supem *n.* shirt, blouse

supete *iv.* put on shirt or dress (~-; *cf.* wokte); vepa ~, put on a shirt of blouse

supetua *tv.* dress one

supe yecha *iv.* undress (*pl.* supem watta)

Surem *n.* 1. the ancestors of the Yoeme (at the time of the Talking Tree,
many people stayed, but those who did not wish to be baptized
and remain in a world that would change greatly left into the
hills, caves, and ocean, becoming insects, animals; those who left
became immortal, while those who stayed to be baptized became
mortal; a dance of farewell was held by the ones who left) 2. the
susuakame (*fig.*)

suru bwikam *n.* messenger songs

sussuale *iv.* believe in certain things (with hita)

susuakame *n.* intelligentsia, intellectuals; *cf.* surem

susuame *n.* caretaker, care provider
chivam ~ *n.* goat-herd
bwalam ~ *n.* sheepherder

susukipo *n.* wound (from scratching, mauling)

susukuk *pst.* of suke, scratch

susuluwa'apo in: kom ~ *n.* slide (playground)

susuta *tv.* dip

sutala *adv.* with legs extended

sutoha *tv.* 1. leave, abandon 2. release

sutsutti *adv.* chugging (with weye)

sutta *adv.* with legs extended straight out (with wokek)

sutta'a *adv.* forcefully
~ chochona *tv.* hit someone with one's fist; *cf.* sutti
~ veévak *tv.* really hit her/him/it hard

sutte *tv.* stretch (legs, arms)

   vata ~ *iv.* have a rash in one's crotch

sutti *adv.* with maximum impact; *cf.* sutta'a

   ~ kochok *iv.* be bushed, zonked, fatigued

sutum *n.* nail (body part), hoof, claw; maso ~, deer hooves; misi ~, cat claws

sutu'ura *n.* a shrub *sp.*

suulu *iv.* slide, slip (suluú-, susulu; *ex.*: va'apo ~, slide into the water)

suume *iv.* sink (of water, tide, reservoirs; *pst.* suumuk, sum-, susume); *cf.* ropte, wo'okte

suumeiya *tv.* frightened of; Aapo taewalita ~. S/he is afraid of the day.

suumuk *pst.* of suume, sink

suut *n.* suit (clothing)

suuta *tv.* penetrate, insert into, shove in (~-, suusuta); Yaavem puetapo ~. The key is stuck in the door. Apo yaavem lakimpo ~k. S/he stuck the key in the lock.

suva'i *n.* quail (*var.* suva'u, *s.* suwali)

suva'u *n.* quail (*var.* suva'i)

suwali *n.* quail (*s.*; = suva'i, suva'u)

suvina *tv.* end, finish up, terminate (suvin-, suvvina)

T

ta *conj.* but, however; ~ inepo haivu kotpea. But I'm already sleepy. Haivu te katean ~ hu ketun lotte. We should leave, but s/he's still tired.

ta vesa *conj.* but, however, but now (*var.* ta véa); Matachinim yi'ivaen, ta vesa ayam kottek. Ta véa nee yoemnoka. But at least I speak Yoeme. Tua ka tu'iakan ta vesa ian ili tu'isi weyemta vena. It wasn't going too well, but now it's a little better.

ta'á- *comb.* of ta'ewa, be popular

ta'a *tv.* 1. know, know how 2. recognize, discern 3. know a person, have someone's number, read someone like a book (~-, tatta'a; *s.* tata'a); *cf.* aawe, hu'unea; au hiosia ~, know how to write; waka hamutta ~, know that woman (acquainted); Yoem nokta ~, speak Yoeme; Havetuni ~. S/he recognizes anybody. Ne ka enchi ~n. I didn't recognize you. Aapo ~ta ~k. S/he learned the truth.

ta'abwi *pn., adj.* 1. *pn.* other, another 2. *adj.* different 3. *adj.* wrong choice of two alternatives (*pl.* tatta'abwi, *obj.* ~k, *pl. obj.* tatta'abwik); ~ ánia, another world; Au nokwau tattabwisusu hia. He started saying other things. ~k hinuk. S/he bought another. Ne ~ tekilta enchim makne. I'll give you another job. Uka senu chake'etam ne vittua. Please show me the other jacket. ~ hamut haani yevihne tea. Another woman is supposed to show up. Unume chake'etam ta'abwi. That's the wrong jacket. U hamut Huantamak

133

tekipapanoa ta apo ian ~ tekilta teak. That woman used to work with John, but now she found a different job.

ta'abwisi *adj.* different, strange, odd (with maachi)

ta'abwikut *adv.* 1. pre-occupied 2. have mind elsewhere, have mind on something or someone else 3. on someone or something else (re: blame); Aapo ~su a kuparoa. S/he blamed it on someone else.

ta'ale *iv.* consider to be knowledgeable; hita au ~, know a subject in depth

ta'ame in: hita ~, *n.* expert, authority

ta'apea *iv.* be curious

ta'apo *adv.* in the way (you) know it, in your own words; Em a ~ amani a teuwan. Say it in your own words.

ta'aru *tv., iv.* 1. *tv.* lose 2. *iv.* get lost 3. *iv.* lose one's mind (~-, tatta'aru); A ~tu. It gets lost easy. Hoseta te ~k. We've lost Joe. Hose tomita ~k. Joe lost the money. In yaavem ne ~k. I lost my keys.

ta'arula *adj.* lost (with au); Apo au ~mta hariwa. He is looking for the lost one.

ta'arutua *dv.* confuse, disorient

ta'awame *n.* known

ta'ewa *iv.* popular, famous (*pst.* ~n, ta'á-)

ta'ewachi *adj.* recognizable

ta'ewak *adj.* noted, famous

ta'ewame *n.* 1. known, famous 2. knowledge, fact

taa *n. comb.* of taa'a, sun

~ bwasi *adj.* sunburnt

~ himsim *n.* ray, sunlight

~ machiria *n.* sunlight

~ mukia *adj.* sunstroke

~ tachiria *n.* sunlight

~ yeu katek *iv.* clear (of weather)

taa'a *n.* sun; ~po, in the sun; Ika yo ~ta yo vali huakte, waim ake yewilu siika sewailo malichi (s). When the enchanted sun turns (the east) cool, with that the flowered fawn went out. Hakunsa weye wa taewai? Waka taewaita, waka machiriate weiyamta, waka achai o'olata ito vepa katekamta, inian a teuwa waka ~ta. Where is the day going? The day, the one that carries the light, the old father sitting above us, in this way the sun is called.

~ muuke *iv.* be a solar eclipse

~ta kom weche vetana *adv.* west

~ta vitchu *n.* 1. sunflower 2. a plant like sunflower, non-seasonal and common in disturbed areas (*Verbesina encelioides*)

~ta yeu weye vetana *n.* east

taabwiko *n.* bird of paradise plant

taahivevia *n.* hockey, shinny

taaka *n.* fruit, nut

hu'upa ~ *n.* mesquite bean

taakam *n.* pustules (*lit.* bodies)

taakialia *conj.* even so

taamu *iv.* faint, pass out, be knocked out (tamœ-)

taasa *n.* cup

taata *n.* uncle (mother's younger brother)

taavu *n.* rabbit (cottontail), cottontail

taawa *iv.*, *tv.* 1. *iv.* stay, remain 2. *tv.* leave behind unintentionally (tawáa-, tatawa); Dios aapo enchim ~. God be with you. Dios apo enchimmak ~. My God stay with you. Inen enchim mampo taawane, wa lutu'uria. It is in your hands that this truth will stay. Aapo ho'arapo a ~k. S/he had him stay home.
aman ~ *tv.* flunk, fail a test; *cf.* pasaroa
ka tu'isi ~ *iv.* come to a bad end
kaitapo ~k *iv.* was left nothing (fame, charm)
kaitapo ~la *iv.* be nothing (be a castle in the air)
kaitapo tawane *iv.* will get burned out (wont' amount to a hill of beans)
kaitapo tawavae *iv.* be on the brink of disaster
kaitapo tawasuk *iv.* be a has-been
aman tawala *iv.* stayed behind

taawe *n.* hawk (*gen.*)

tabwiko seewa *n.* 1. a plant *sp.* related to poinciana and Mexican bird-of-paradise (*Caesalpinia gillesei*; *syn.* kau tavachin) 2. *var.* of tavachin

tachiria *n.* 1. light (of fire) 2. halo (of saint or holy figure) 3. grace (*syn.* grasia); U Senyoa itom ya'uchiwa Dios ~ta Hiakimeu kom vittua. The Lord, our leader, sends down his grace to the Yaquis.

tachuela *n.* tack (metal)

taewai *n.* day, date (*s.* taewali); semanapo ~m, days of the week

taewali *n.* day (*s.*; = taewai)

tah- *comb.* of tase, cough

taha *iv.* get burned (tai-, tataha/tattaha)

tahek *iv.* 1. shine 2. be on (of lights or electricity) (*pst.* ~an)

tahi *n.* 1. fire, flame 2. electricity
~ kawi *n.* volcano
~ wiko'i *n.* gun

tahita tutuchame *n.* fireman

Tahita Vetepo *n.* Heaven (*lit.* where the fire is burning; after death, the soul becomes a star, first traveling to Heaven, the Sun, taking three days; those without a good heart eventually also reach the Sun and become stars after returning to Earth to atone for their wrongs)

tahkae *iv.* make tortillas (~-, tatahkae)

tahkai kuchu *n.* flounder (*lit.* tortilla fish)

tahkaim *n.* tortilla

tahkali *n.* cedar

taho haiti machi *n.* laundry, dirty clothes

taho'o(ri) *n.* clothes, clothing; taho'opo, on the clothing; ~tat yukuk. It rained on the clothes.

tahta *tv.* 1. touch 2. bump into, hit with an impact (~-, tahtahta); Karo a ~k. The car hit him. Maria a mam ~k. Mary touched her/him on the hands.

tahte *iv.* bump into (tahti-, tahtahte); Aapo hiva mesau tahtahte. S/he's always bumping into the table.

tahti(a) *conj.* until, till, up to; ian ~, up till now (*syn. Son.* ian kamti); im tahti, up to here; yeu tahti, throughout; Luneseu ~ ima ne. I'll be here until Monday. Maranau ~ ne wokim siika. I walked till I got to Marana.

tahtiavu *adv.* throughout

taiweche *iv.* have a fever (taiwet-, taiweeche)

taiwechia *n.* fever; ~ta vetchi'ivo totoi kavata kokoemta vepa am ruruhne. For fever, a hen's egg must be rubbed over the sick person's body.

taiwet- *comb.* of taiweche, have a fever

taiwo *adv.* 1. east 2. upriver 3. the upriver area (villages of Ko'oko'im, Vahkom, Torim, Vikam)

taka *n.* body, carcass

taka huni *adv.* also, even though; Aa semalulukut taka huni toloko huapo sika (*s.*). The hummingbird also went into the light blue wilderness world.

takalai *adj.* Y-shaped, forked

Takalaim *n.* enchanted mountain northwest of Guaymas (*lit.* forked)

take *tv.* dust, shake out (*pst.* ~n, tak-, tataki)

takea *tv.* hire

takease *tv.* ask a favor or for a job

tako *n.* a native palm *sp.* (*Sabal uresana*)

tako voo'o *n.* palm road

tako waari *n.* palm basket

Tako'ouvaawa *iv.* be time for Palm Sunday

Tako'ouvaawausu *adv.* just before giving out the palms on Palm Sunday; ~ sahak, just before they gave out the palms, they (had to) leave

Tako'ouwa *n.* Palm Sunday

takochae *n.* a bird *sp.*

taksi *n.* taxi

taksim *n.* tax; ~ vehe'etuaneekai, must pay taxes

tam *comb.* of tami, tooth
  ~ lotoor *n.* dentist
  ~ moera *n.* cavity (tooth)
  ~ wante *iv.* have a toothache

tamachia *tv.* measure; survey, lay out a building (~- tammachia)

tamachiko *n.* a children's game

tamahte *iv.* be bucking (tamahti-, tatamahte); U kava'i ~. The horse is bucking.

tamahtitua *tv.* make buck

tamahtivaawa *iv.* ride a bucking horse

tamahtiwa *n.* rodeo

tamekame *n.* shark

tami *n.* tooth; Tamim ta'aruka tenkuka'u tu'isi vinwa hiapsine tea. They say that if you dream of losing a tooth that you'll live a long life.

tamek, have teeth

tamim *n.* teeth; teeth of a musical rasp

tamko'okochi *n.* devil's claw

tampa'im *n.* molars

tampa *n.* drum (as opposed to the water drum)

tampaleo *n.* drummer

tanki *n.* tank

tanna *adv.* saggingly

~ ho'ok *iv.* have a sway back

tannai *adj.* sagging

tante *iv.* warp (tanti-, tantante)

taparea *n.* lid

taparia *n.* mouthpiece of a flute

tapehtim *n.* cane platform used as bed, table or shelf (especially for table on All Souls' Day and as bier for a deceased person)

tapekonariina *iv.* shield eyes with hand (from bright light or sun)

tapicha *iv.* fan fire

tapoon *n.* stopper, plug; dam

tapsiolai *adj.* thin (*pl.* tapsisiolai)

tapuna *iv.* get full (of liquid or particulate matter; tapun-, tappuna)

tapuni *adj.* full

tapunia *tv.* fill (~-, tappunia); Meecha ~k etne. When the moon is full, we'll plant.

hiosiam ~ *tv.* fill out (paper, form)

taravia *n.* spindle

Tarumaara *n.* Tarahumara

tare'eka *n.* bag, sack

tarima *n.* cot

taruk *n.* roadrunner

tasaria *n.* summer (*var.* tataria); ~po, in the summer; ~po tu'isi tata. It is very hot in the summer.

tase *iv.* cough (*pst.* ~n, tah-, tatase)

tasia *n.* coughing, cough

tata *adj.* hot (*pl.* tattae); ke ~o, before it gets hot

tata'a *tv.* 1. recognize 2. know (*s.*; = ta'a); Apo hamutta ~k. He recognized the woman. Sewa yoemta ka ~ (*s.*)? Don't you know that person?

tatai *iv.* 1. get hot, overheat 2. be in heat (~-, tattai)

~ mukuk *iv.* have heatstroke

tataka *n.* a fruit-bearing tree

tatakalim *n.* any forked object; Elapo yeu wene, vai ~ awakame (*s.*). Let him go out, the one with three-pointed antlers.

tataki *adj.* dusted

tatale *iv.* feel hot

tatap- *rdp.* of tatave, knock down

tataria *n.* 1. heat 2. *var.* of tasaria, summer

tatave *tv.* knock down, drop (tatap-, no *rdp.*; *var.* tave)

tatavuhte *iv.* sweating (tatavuhti-, no *rdp.*)

tatavuhtia *n.* sweat, perspiration

tatawiilo *iv.* turn around (~-, tatawiwilo)

tatchi'ina *n.* primrose

tate *n.* sinew, tendon

tatta'a *tv. rdp.* of ta'a, know: 1. learn 2. recognize 3. tavachi notice (~-, no
    rdp.); ian ala ana ~k, now I recognize her/him

tatta'awa *n.* recognition

tatte *iv.* choke on food (tatti-, tatatte); *cf.* hukte

tauhia *iv.* say to (tauhiu-, tauhihia); "Heewi," ~k. "Yes," s/he said.

tauna *n.* coffin, tomb

tavachin *n.* dwarf poinciana (*Caesalpinia pulcherrima*; *syn.* tabwiko seewa)

tava'i *n.* grass *sp.* used for thatch

tavawasa'i *n.* jaw

tave *tv.* knock down (*pst.* tatavek, tatap-, tatave)

tavelo *n.* parrot

tavilai *adj.* leaning

tavla *n.* board (wood)

tawaa- *comb.* of taawa, stay

tawi *n.* chest (body part)

taya *tv.* 1. burn, ignite, set fire to 2. turn on (electricity, lights) (tayá'a-,
    tatta); ~'avawa, it's going to be burned

taya'i *n.* burned thing

te *pn.* 1. we (*subj.* clitic) 2. let's (may lengthen preceding vowel);
    Periokikota te hinune. Let's buy a newspaper. Hita te bwa'ean.
    Let's get something to eat. Atneete. Let's laugh. Bwikneete.
    Let's sing.

te'ebwa *tv.* lick (~-, tete'ebwa)

te'ehma *n.* a tree *sp.*

te'eka *iv. pst.* of hia, sound

te'ine *iv.* moan (*pst.* ~n; *pres.* and *pst.* are the only tenses usual)

te'ite *iv.* trip, stumble (te'iti-, tete'ite)

te'ochia *tv., n.* 1. *tv.* bless one (~-, tete'ochia)

te'ochiawame *n.* blessing, benediction

=tea$_1$ *ptc.* quotative particle
    1. used in direct and indirect quotes; Vempo ha'ani a'avo katetea.
       They say that they are coming.
    2. used in giving names; Aapo Maria=ti teak. Her name is Mary.
    3. used with words that describe sounds (*var.* =tia, ti); Kumti
       wechek. It fell down with a thump.
    4. supposed to (*var.* ti); Ta'abwi hamut haano yevihne ~. Another
       woman is supposed to show up.

5. in truth (with negative); A: Huana hani ko'okoe tea. B: Ka tea; lutu'uriapo ko'okoe. A: They say that Jane is sick. B: It's so; in truth, she really is sick.

tea₂ *tv.* find (after having lost; teu-, tettea); tekilta ~, find work

teak *iv.* be named, be called (*pst.* ~an, tee-); Haisempo ~? What's your name? Ne Mariata ti ~. I am called Mary. Ne Mariata ti teepea. I liked to be called Mary. A: Aapo haisa ~? B: Aapo Hose-ti ~. A: What is his name? B: His name is Joe.

teaka *iv.* they say (*s.* telika); Aapo aa hita hoa ~i, takeawak. Because he knows how to get things done, they hired him.

teakame *n.* 1. name 2. title

team *n.* name (*var.* teawam)

teatua *tv.* name

teawam *n.* name (*var.* team)

tebwi *n.* datura, jimson weed (*Datura discolor*)

techi'ite *iv.* be scratching

techo *n.* ceiling

techoa *n.* mud; ~ kari, wattle-and-daub house; ~ ma'ari, plastered with mud

techoe *n.* bad sign, bad omen; Chukui vaesevo'i ~. A black butterfly is a bad omen (folk belief).

techom *n.* elbow

techuniak grubby

techuniam *n.* grime, filth

tee *n.* tea

teeham *n.* 1. hail 2. a game played with rocks 3. curved roofing tiles

téeka *n.* sky, heaven (*var.* teweka; the Yoeme concept of Heaven is that Heaven is the Sun, which is where our Creator lives in the center of our universe; when a person dies, they journey to the Sun in three days; on the third day, the soul bursts out of the Sun as a star; even evil people become stars, but must first return to earth to atone for any evil deeds)
  ~ sevo'i *n.* horse fly

teéka *tv.* lay it across (tek- and tek'-, teteka)

teéki *n.* laid

teeko *n.* boss, supervisor, director, manager

teekuku *n.* dust devil, whirlwind; U tekuku tevesi siika. The dust devil went a long way.

teeni *n.* mouth

teeso *n.* cave, den, lair; tehpo, in the cave

teevo *n.* an edible wild green

teevat *n.* patio, yard

teeve *adj.* tall, long (*pl.* tetteve; *cf.* tevesi); U tren si ~. The train is long.

teewa *tv.* find (teu-); Haksa chea inepo waka yo'ora lutu'uriata chea tu'ik inepo teune? Where am I going to find the best of the elders' truth?

tehale *tv.* 1. use up, finish off 2. destroy (*pl. obj.*; tehal-, tetehale) tehkiak *iv.* hold a job

tehwa *tv.* 1. inform, show, tell 2. explain 3. notify (~-, tetehwa); Inika
si'imeta ka ~suk. They never told me all these things.

tehwak in: a ~, *n.* warning

tehwawame in: yee ~, *n.* announcement

tekama *tv.* be laying it (*cf.* teéka)

tekia *n.* talent, job, intended purpose

tekil *n.* work, job, task, duty; Hita ~ta empo hoa? What job are you
doing? Vempo ~ta nau eteho. They are talking about work.
~ hiosia *n.* job application

tekipanoa *iv., tv.* work (~-, tekipapanoa; this may especially refer to
planned activity for a specific purpose, especially the fulfillment
of a ritual vow; one's task in this sacred context is called sewa,
flower, instead of tekil, task/job); Severiapo te tekipapanoa. It the
winter, we usually work. U hamut Huantamak tekipapanoa ta
apo ian ta'abwi tekilta teak. That woman used to work with
John, but now she has another job.
aa ~ *iv.* be industrious

tekipanoapea *iv.* be enthusiastic, want to do

tekipanoareo *n.* worker

tekipanoawame *n.* work (act of working)

tekoe *n.* white-headed vulture

tekolai *adj.* round

tekowai *n.* master (of an animal or servant)

tekri *adj.* laid down

teku *n.* squirrel

tekuriam *n.* knob (on antler)

tekwa *n.* flesh, muscle, meat

tekwak *iv.* 1. be corpulent 2. be strong in taste or flavor (with yuin)
ka ~ *iv.* be skinny, meatless
yuin ~ *iv.* 1. be meaty, beefy (animals) 2. be muscle-bound
(people) 3. be strong in taste or flavor

telefon *n.* telephone

televisión *n.* television

telika *iv.* they say (*s.*; = teaka); Vanseka, yo ~ (*s.*). Go ahead, they say,
with enchantment.

tema'i *n.* tick (insect)

temahti *n.* sacristan

temai *tv.* ask (~-, tetemai); *cf.* nattemai; Aet emo ~ne, achaim. You will
question yourselves, fathers.

temasti *n.* sacristan

temu *tv.* kick (~-, tetemu)

temula *adj.* rolled up (in a ball)

tena'asam *n.* pliers

tenanchim *n.* female litter bearers

tenela(i) *adv.* erect, upright

teneror *n.* fork

tenevoim *n.* rattles (cocoon)

tenhaawa *iv.* breathe visibly (in cold; ~-, tenhahaawa)

teniente *n.* lieutenant

tenku *iv.* dream (~-, tettenku); ~po a vichak Itom Achai. S/he saw our father in a dream.

tenku an'a *n.* Dream World (the reality or medium in which the yo an'a is accessible to humans)

tenkuim *n.* dreams

      ka tu'i ~ *n.* bad dreams, nightmare

tenne *iv.* run (*pl.*; *sg.* vuite; tenni-, tettene)

tennei *n.* free-standing

tenveria *n.* lip

tenwe *n.* pelican

teochia *tv.* bless (~-, teteochia; *syn.* bendisiroa)

teokita *n.* silver

teopo *n.* church

      ~ kovanao *n.* head sacristan

      ~ santora *n.* the complement of saints of the church altar

tepa(n) *adv.* I think, I thought that ... (marks one's own opinion; often with su); ~ ne enchi a wetean. I thought you knew that. ~ ne am tutu'itean. I thought they were very good. ~ ne am atu'i hiapsektean. I thought they were good-hearted.

tepohti *n.* brand, branding iron

tepohtia *tv.* brand

tepua *n.* spur (of chickens)

tepuam *n.* axe

teput *n.* flea

tero'okim *n.* ankles

teru'usia *n.* wart

tesa *n.* a small tree *sp.* like acacia

tesia *n.* bundle or load of reeds (carried on back)

tesooro *n.* treasure

testamento *n.* statement

testiaroa *tv.* test

tesua *n.* clod, lump of dirt or clay

teta *n.* rock, stone

teta'ahao *n.* coyote gourd

tetam *n.* gravel

tetata yeu wike *tv.* mine (ore, minerals)

tetehwame in: yee ~, *n.* 1. warning 2. announcement

tettea *rdp.* of tea$_2$, find

tettene *rdp.* of tenne, run (*pl.*)

tettenku *rdp.* of tenku, dream

tetamatum *n.* coal
tetevaure *iv.* get hungry
tettenkume *n.* dreamer
teu- *comb.* of tea$_2$, find and teewa, find
teula *adj.* found
teuwa *tv.* affirm, acknowledge (teuwáa-, teteuwa)
     hita ~ *tv.* say something
teuwawa *n.* what is being said
teuwawame *n.* knowledge
     ka ~ *n.* secret
tevachia *n.* patio (*syn.* tevat)
tevai *iv.* starving
     ~ muuke *iv.* be starving (*pl.* ~ koko; *cf.* tevaure)
     ~ mukiari *n.* greedy person, glutton, hog (one who takes things
          so others can't have them; *pl.* tevai kokoarim)
tevat *n.* patio (*syn.* tevachia)
     ~ kus *n.* patio cross
     ~ te'ochia *n.* bless (ceremonial area)
tevatpo kus *n.* patio cross
tevaure *iv.* be hungry (tevauri-, tettevauri, tevvaure); (*cf.* tetevaure,
     tevai-)
tevauri *adj.* hungry
tevei *adv.* already (*syn.* haivu); ~ Tusaneu saka. They're already going to
     Tucson. Huan ~ aavo weye. John is already coming here.
     Apo ~ koche. S/he's already asleep.
     ~ eak *iv.* that's the way s/he is; Tevei eak namukne. He's always
          drinking.
tevesi *adj., adv.* 1. *adj.* tall (*cf.* teeve) 2. *adv.* a long way; ~ yo'otuk. It grew
     tall. U huya ~ weyek. The tree is tall. Ume huyam tettevesi
     ha'abwek. The trees are tall. Tekuku ~ siika. The dust devil went
     a long way.
tevoli *n.* clover (good for heart and blood diseases)
tevos *n.* gopher
tevote *tv.* greet (~-, tetevote); Heewi, aman ne ~ em yevisnewi. I send my
     greetings to where you will arrive.
tevotewa *n.* handshaking
tevotua *iv.* be greeting
tevuhlia *n.* rainy season, monsoons (*s.* tevulia); ~po, *adv.* during the rainy
     season
tevuhpo *adv.* during the rainy season
     tevuhlia *n.* rainy season (*s.*; = tevuhlia); ~po tu'isi yuyuke. During
          the monsoons, it usually rains a lot.
     ~ yuku *n.* monsoon
tewei *adj.* dark blue (*s.* teweli)
teweka *n. var.* of téeka, sky
teweli *adj.* dark blue (*s.*; tewei); Ayaman ne seyewailo ~ kauta heheka

vetukun koyowe (*s.*). Over there, under the shade of the dark blue, flowered mountain, I hover.

ti'i- *comb.* of te'eka, sounded

=ti(a)₁ *ptc. var.* of =tea; In achai chea Yoronata au vitlaitia. My father saw the Llorona.

tia *n.* aunt (either paternal or maternal); *cf.* chi'ila, haaka, mamai

tio *n.* uncle; *cf.* haavi, kumui, mamai, sama'i, taata

tiempo *n.* time

tienda *n.* store, shop

tigre *n.* tiger

tiikom *n.* wheat

tiiko posoim *n.* wheat stew

tiina *n.* tub

tiisa *n.* chalk

tiitua *tv.* make a sound; kusiata ~, play the flute (*syn.* kuuse)

tiiwe *iv.* be shy, bashful, ashamed (of = nea, ea, ae, etc.; *pst.* ~n, tiw-, tittiwe)

tiket *n.* ticket (*syn.* voleeto)

tinaaha *n.* jar

tinaaroa *tv., iv.* 1. *tv.* guess (infer) 2. *iv.* be lucky 3. *iv.* do by chance (~~); Aapo premiota ~k. He won the prize. Aapo numeerom ~k. S/he guessed the numbers.; Aapo loteria numeerom ~k. S/he won the lottery.

Tiniepla *n.* Tenebrae

Tinira *n.* Trinity (*var.* Trinira)

tinti *adv.* banging, clanging

tio *n.* uncle (maternal or paternal); *cf.* haavi, kumui, mamai, sama'i, taata

tiri'isia *n.* habit (gestural)

tiri'isiak *iv.* have a nervous habit

tittiwe *iv.* be easily embarrassed

tiukove *iv., n.* be in agony, be on one's deathbed (tiukop-, tiukokove)

tiura *n.* embarrassment, shyness, bashfulness

tiurame *n.* disgrace; tiurampo taawa, be in disgrace

tiusi *adj.* embarrassing (often with aane, maachi)

~ aayuk *iv.* was embarrassing; Ne tua tiusi aayuk. I was really embarrassed.

tiw- *comb.* of tiiwe, be shy

tiwe'e(ra) *adj.* shy

=to *ptc.* and so (points out an exception; from into, and); Enchimto ka ha'avosek? And they didn't pay you? Itomto ka vehe'etuak. And us he didn't pay.

to'a *tv.* pour, lay down (*pl. obj.*; to'o-, toto'a); kafeta yeu ~, pour coffee

to'e *iv.* be lying down (*pl. subj.*; *sg.* vo'ote; toto-, toto'e)

to'o- *comb.* of to'a, pour

to'ochia *n.* dust

to'ochiok *iv.* be dusty

to'ochorai *adj.* sheer, transparent (through thin cloth)

to'oka *iv.* be lying down (*pl.*; *sg.* vo'oka; *pst.* ~n, to'o-, toto'e; *s.* toyoka); *cf.* to'ote

to'ona *n.* guts, stomach lining

to'osaka *tv.* 1. leave off 2. lay while moving

to'osiime *tv.* 1. leave off, take along (*sg. obj.*) 2. to miss (*ex.*: Baas ne to'osiika. I missed the bus)

to'ote *iv.* lie down (*pl.*; *sg.* vo'ote; ~-, *rdp.* toto'e); *cf.* to'oka

tochopola *adj.* in white; ka ~ cha'ane, will not hang in white (will lie outside the Christian sphere)

toeyam *n.* towel

toha *tv.* take it, carry it (*sg. obj.*; pl *obj.* weiya; toi-, totoha)

　　nau toha *iv.* get together, come together on (with reflexive); Nau em emo toha ian lautipo, vario karim vetchi'ivo (poster slogan). Get together now for barrio housing.

tohakte *iv.* bounce (tohakti-)

tohakteme *n.* bouncing song (one with special rhythm that is difficult for the deer dancer)

tohsaalai *adj.* whitish

tohta *tv.* make fade (~-, tohtohta)

tohtaria *dv.* make fade (something of someone else's; *rdp.* tohtohtaria); Huana ne pantalonim ~k. Jane faded my pants. Pantalonim ne ~k. My pants faded on me.

tohtaroa *tv.* toast, parch (food)

tohte *iv.* fade (tohti-, tohtohte)

toiri *adj.* brought

toiwa *iv.* be taken, be carried (~-, totoiwa)

　　yeu ~ *iv.* be on trial

tokta *adv.* a lot, with force (with veéva, chochona); Aapo tikta vehetoak. He really paid him a lot. ~ chochonak. He really punched him hard.

tokti *adv.* too much

toktokta *adv.* smacking; Aapo ~ veévak. S/he really smacked it.

tolo *adj.* light blue (*s.*; toloko)

toloachi *n.* jimson

tolochivela *iv.* be scattered (dust)

toloko *adj.* light blue, grayish (*var.*, tooro, toroko; *s.* tolo; the blue in the Yoeme flag represents the open sky under which we all live together with no boundaries); Téeka ~; vaa'am ket ~. The sky is light blue; so is the water.

toroko huya *n.* a bush *sp.*

toma *n.* stomach (*loc.* tompo, in the stomach)

　　tompo wante *iv.* have a stomach ache

toma'arisi *n.* tomatillo (*Physalis sp.*)

tomaate *n.* tomato

tomahektek *iv.* have a miscarriage

tomi *n.* 1. money, cash 2. twelve and a half cents, two bits

　　woi ~ *n.* twenty-five cents

naiki ~ *n.* fifty cents

vusan ~ *n.* seventy-five cents

~ yo'o *iv.* earn money

tomi nakuliam *n.* change (money)

tomin *n.* coin

tomta *tv.* 1. tan (hide) 2. disentangle (hair) 3. make hair "alive" by combing it (~-, tomtomta); chonim ne ~, I make my hair alive by coming it

tomte *iv.* be budding, blossoming; have smallpox (tomti-, tomtomte)

tomti kateme *n.* future generations

tomtiam *n.* smallpox

tomtomtia *adv.* popping (sound), thumping

tonalai *adj.* warped

tonna *adv.* curved, arching, bent, twisted (with hoa, yak)

tonnai *adj.* warped

tonom *n.* knee

tonommea weyek *iv.* kneel

tonua *n.* joint, segment; second part of a song

toochivei *adj.* dusty

tooro *n.* bull

toorom *n.* puncture vine, bull's head, goat's head (*Tribalus terrestris; var.* chiva kovam, wicha'apo)

toorovoi *adj.* dusty

toosa *n.* nest

toosam *n.* baby blanket

topa'a *adj.* pot-bellied

topakta *tv.* wedge, lift with wedge (~-, toptopakta)

topechei *adj.* naked, nude

topol *n.* a small cat *sp.* (wild)

tori *n.* rat

Torim *n.* Torim (*lit.* rats)

tornio *n.* bolt

toro kapontei *n.* steer

toroko *adj. var.* of toloko, light blue

toroko huya *n.* a light blue plant *sp.* (probably *Kraneria grayi*)

toronha *n.* grapefruit

toroote *n.* a plant *sp.*

tosa'a kovak *iv.* have gray hair

tosa'a saweam *n.* underwear

tosai *adj.* white (*cf.* tossalai)

~ navo *n.* Indian fig (type of prickly pear)

~ kuchu *n.* fish *sp.* (*Sp.* corvina)

~sa yoka *tv.* whitewash

tosaite *tv.* whiten, whitewash (~-, totosaite)

tosali *adj.* white

tosisitia *adv.* crackling (sound)

tossalai *adj.* pure white

145

totenne *tv.* run away from

totenniwame *n.* the act of running away

totoi *n.* chicken

> ~ hamuchia *n.* hen
> ~ hisa *n.* comb (chicken)
> ~ kari *n.* chicken house
> ~ kava *n.* egg
> ~ o'owia *n.* rooster
> ~ woki *n.* a plant *sp.* used for greens

Totoitakuse'epo *n.* a sacred mountain, the highest peak in the Yaqui country, near Vacam (*lit.* where the rooster crows)

totta *tv.* fold (~-, tottatta)

totte *iv.* be curving, winding, folded (totti-, tottotte)

tottila *adj.* folded

tottotte *iv.* be flexible (*syn.* aa tottatu)

tovei *n.* a palm-like tree found in the mountains of Sonora

tovo'ote *tv.* carry with hands (*pst.* ~, tovo'oti-, totovo'ote)

tovokta *tv., n.* 1. pick up with hand 2. take over (*sg. obj.*; *pl. obj.* hahau; ~-, totovokta; *s.* tovokita) 2. *n.* harvest

tovoktia *tv.* pick up (*s.*; = tovokta)

tovuivuite *tv.* 1. avoid meeting or dealing with someone 2. run away from (*sg.*; with yee or *pl. obj.*; *pl.* totettene); Hunu yoeme yee tovuivuik. That man avoided everyone. U yoeme hiva ne ~. The man always avoids me. Apo ka a vitvaeka a ~. She doesn't want to see him so she avoids (him). U misi chu'uta ~. The is running away from the dog.

toyoka *iv.* be lying down (*pl.*; *sg.* toyoka; *s.*; = to'oka)

trampa *n.* hobo, tramp

trahte *n.* paraphernalia (ceremonial), gear, equipment

trake *n.* track, rail

traktor *n.* tractor

trank *n.* trunk (automobile)

tren *n.* train

> ~ traakem *n.* railroad
> ~ta weweamtuame *n.* engineer

triikim *n.* firecrackers (during processions, at certain times in ceremonies, people set off rockets and firecrackers to carry the message to Heaven and the people above)

Trinira *n.* Trinity

trivu *n.* tribe

trompeta *n.* trumpet

trono *n.* throne

trooke *n.* truck

troopa *n.* troop

tu'i *adj.* good, clear (understandable), correct (*pl.* tutu'i); U lotoor ka ~. The doctor is not competent (*cf.* aawe).

> tua ~, perfect; Hu kafe tua ~. The coffee is perfect.

~ hiapsek *adj.* kind, good-hearted (*var.* tu hiapsek)

~ machi *iv.* 1. be certain, known 2. be potentially good

~ Tukaria *n.* Christmas Eve

tu'i'ean *iv.* be useful; ~ kaaroko, a car is useful; ~ tomeko, it is useful to have money

tu'iria *iv.* get well, better (tu'i-)

tu'isi *adv.* 1. well 2. a lot, very, too much; U koreo ilitchi; u ehkuela ~ bwe'u. The post office is small; the school is very large. U parke ~ vasok. The park has a lot of grass. U usi ~ au sua. The child is cautious.

    ka ~ taawa *iv.* come to a bad end

    ka ~ a vicha *iv.* experience hardship (*syn.* ka ~ pasároa)

    ~ a vicha *iv.* have a good time

    ~ ... -ne *exp.* may; Apo tu'isi kampo yeune. S/he may play in the yard.

    ~ yeyewe *iv.* play fair

tu'isia *iv.* say good things

tu'ule *tv. var.* of tu'ure, like; sewata ~ka (*s.*), loving the flower; Ikasu yo taa'ata vali kuaktemta ~ka, saniloapo welama (s). Loving the coolness of the enchanted sun's turning, (I am) walking about in the grove. Aapo hekata ~. S/he enjoys the wind. U koowi techoata ~. The pig likes the mud. Aapo ume siki supem ~. The red dress appealed to her.

tu'ulemcha *adv.* as if liking or enjoying

tu'ulisi *adj. var.* of tutu'uli, beautiful

tu'uliwame *n.* the quality of being affectionate

tu'ure *tv.* adore; appreciate; like, prefer (*pst.* ~n, tu'uri-, tutu'ure; *s.* tuyule); Tu'isi au ~, kia kavetau nonoka. He likes himself so much that he doesn't speak to anyone.

    au ~ *iv.* be conceited

    ka ~ *tv.* object, oppose

    chea ~ *tv.* prefer

tu'uriwa *iv., n.* 1. *iv.* be cherished 2. *n.* treasure

    ka ~ *n.* objection, opposition

tu'ute *tv.* fix, repair, mend, clean up (~-, tutu'ute); Ventaanata ne ~ne. I'm going to fix the window.

tu'utei *adj.* fixed, repaired, cleaned

tu'uti *n.* repaired, cleaned

tu'uwa *n.* goodness; ~po, in goodness; ~t weyepo, sacred circumstances; Maria ~ta nooka. Mary is talking goodness (giving accurate, purposeful advice of religious intent). ~ta weyepo, ka huenasia hiuwa. Where there is goodness, no bad words are said. Nassuawame tu'isi ka tu'i, kia kaita ~ta itou nunnu'upa. Fighting is not good; it brings nothing good to us.

tua *adv., n.* 1. *adv.* truly, certainly, really 2. *n.* fact; A: ~ ne lotte. B: Enchi ne hiokole. A: I'm exhausted. B: I feel sorry for you.

~ Hiaki *n.* full-blooded Yaqui

~ maaso *n.* Coues whitetail deer

~ tu'i *adj.* perfect

~ vat Hiakim *n.* the first real Yoemes

tuaka in: wok ~, *n.* pine cone

tuata *n.* truth and goodness (< tu'uwata); ~ nooka, speak truth and goodness

tuata venasia *adv.* as if (as if it were a fact)

tucha'aria *tv.* erase, wipe out, blot out (~-)

tuchuk wiro *n.* toro prieto, a tree *sp.*

tuerka *n.* nut (with bolt)

tuivit *n.* killdeer (bird)

tuka an'a *n.* night world (*s.* tuka aniwa, a Deer song about evening on the earth and the way night comes)

tuka'apo *adv.* at night (*syn.* kamachiako); ~ ka amae rehtiwa. One should not walk backwards at night (especially westward; folk belief; thought to cause one's mother's death). ~ ka hitchiwa. No sweeping at night (folk belief; thought to cause bad luck). nasuk ~ *adv.* at midnight

tuka'ariapo *adv.* at night, during the night (*syn.* kamachiako); nasuk ~, at midnight

tuka'u *ptc.* deceased

tukaria *n.* night (tuka'apo, at night); Tukariau yu maka, haivu ko'okoe. By nightfall, s/he was already sick.

tukariau *adv.* by nightfall

tunikam *n.* ceremonial robe

turui *adj.* thick

turuik kovak *adj.* hard-headed

Tuson *n.* Tucson

tutta *tv.* 1. insert 2. go out for everything, be enthusiastic about anything (~-, tuttutta)

tuttala *adj.* inserted

tutte *iv.* sink into ground (liquid; tutti-, tututte)

tuttila *adj.* sunk, settled into ground; *cf.* roptila

tuttu'iria *iv.* improve

tuttuti *adv.* precisely, exactly; ~ Yoem noka, speak Yoeme fluently; ~ a ta'a, know it thoroughly

tuttutta *n.* nosey person (in: hahuni au ~); *cf.* tutta

tuttu'ule *tv.* like

tutu'uli *adj.* handsome, beautiful, pretty (re: animates) *cf.* uhyoi (*var.* tutu'ulisi)

tutucha *iv.* close one's eyes, blink; *cf.* paata, eta; pusim ~, winking one's eyes

tutuha *n.* mano (for grinding stone; *syn.* tuusa)

tutukam *n.* scree, gravel eroding from hillside or rock

tutukaviako *adv.* last night
tutusi *adj.* ground
tuu *adv.* well
~ hiapsek *adj.* kind, amiable
~ hiapsekame *n.* person with a good heart looking for spiritual
    empowerment)
tuucha *tv.* 1. extinguish (fire, light), turn off electricity 2. erase 3. turn off
    (electricity, lights) (tuchá'a-, tutucha); Kat am ~. Don't erase it.
tuuka *adv.* yesterday
tuuka ketwo *adv.* yesterday morning
tuuke *iv.*, *tv.* 1. *iv.* go out (fire, light) 2. *tv.* turning off (*pst.* tuukuk, tuk-,
    tutuke)
tuulisi *adv.* beautifully, enjoyably; Apo ~ hichike. She is sweeping
    beautifully.
tuusa *n.* mano (*syn.* tutuha)
tuuse *tv.* grind (coarser than mohta; tus- or tuh-, tutuse)
tuusi *adj.*, *n.* 1. *adj.* ground (*pl.* tutusi) 2. *n.* meal, flour
tuuva *n.* 1. tube 2. pipe (plumbing)
tuvukta *tv.* jump
tuvukte *iv.* leap, jump down (tuvukti-, tuvutuvukte)
tuwa'apo nooka *tv.* praise
tuwa'apo nokwame *n.* praise
tuyule *tv.* love (*s.*; tu'ure)

U

u *pn.* that (close; *var.* huu, hunu; *obj.* uka, *pl.* ume); Empo uka yoemta
    maakina hinune? Are you going to buy that man's car? Itepo ka
    u uusita chuu'u vitchuk. It was not the child's dog that we were
    looking at.
u"a *rdp.* of u'a, take away
u"ura *rdp.* of uura, take away
u'a *tv.* take away (u'áa-, u"a); *cf.* uura
u'ari *adj.* taken away; Vempo bwiata ~. The land had been taken away
    from them.
u'u *pn.* that (close; *emph.*)
u'ura *tv.* be taking away
u'use *iv.* be fertile, able to have children (man)
u'ute *iv.* strong (re: animals, humans; no tenses other than present usual);
    cf. utte'ak
uhbwana *tv.* make a ceremonial request (uhbwan-, uhbwabwana)
uhbwani *n.* ceremonial request
uhteak *iv.* be surnamed

uhteam *n.* last name, surname

uhu'u *tv.* take care of, raise children (~-, no *rdp.*); Aapo ili usita ~. She is
    raising a family.

uhu'ume *n.* care (re: children, elderly)

uhu'ureo *n.* babysitter

uhu'uwame *n.* taking care of children

uhyoi *iv.* 1. be beautiful 2. interesting (inanimates; *var.* uhyooli; *s.* usyoli);
    U teopo tu'isi ~. the church is beautiful.

uhyoisi(a) *adv.* beautifully (*s.* usyolisi); U altaria ~ seewak. The altar is
    beautifully decorated with flowers.

uhyooli *var.* of uhyoi, beautiful

uka *pn. obj.* of u, that (*paus.* uka'a)

ukkule *tv.* desire (re: especially food; ukkul-, no *rdp.*; *cf.* veutia); Haivu ka
    a ~. He has no desire for it.

ultimo *n.* last one
    chea ~ *n.* the very last one

um *adv.* there (close, but farther away than aman(i); *var.* yum); *cf.*
    hunam(a)

ume *pn.* those (close; *paus.* ume'e)

umu'u *adv.* there (close; *emph.*)

una vahti *n.* tuning used at midnight

unen *adv.* thus

Ungara *n.* Gypsy

universita *n.* university

unna *adv.* a lot, too much (excessive mount; *cf.* ousi, yuin); ~ yukuk. It
    rained a lot. Aapo ~ itom tekpanatua. He's making us work too
    much.
    ~ bwe'u *adj.* huge, gigantic
    ~ hi'ibwak *iv.* overate (*syn.* ama vuhti hi'ibwak)
    ~ kokoe *iv.* be an emergency (health)
    ~ va'ak *iv.* be watery, thin
    ~ vahti *n.* first harp and violin tuning used during a pahko
        (*cf.* kompaniya, partiyo)

unompo *adv.* (at) one o'clock

uppa *tv.* lift a baby

uppala *interj.* oof, upsy-daisy (in lifting a baby)

urnia *n.* bier

usi mukila pahko *n.* child's funeral

usi yeu yoemtu *n.* childbirth

usira *n.* children (as a group)

usiteeve *n.* child (tall)

usituwame *n.* childhood

usyol(i) *adj.* beautiful (*s.*; = uhyoi); yo huya aniwapo ~ machi hekamak
    (*s.*), in the enchanted wilderness world, beautiful in the dawn
    wind

usyolisi *adv.* beautifully (*s.* ; = ~ vaiwa sola voyoka) (*s.*), beautifully you lie laden with dew

ute *adv.* fast

utte'a *n.* strength

    sa ~ *exp.* why is it necessary, is it absolutely necessary; Sa utte'a enchi aman wéenepo?" Why is necessary for you to go there?

    ~ weye *iv.* speed

uttea'awa *n.* power, strength; peloteo ~, the ball player's strength; motor ~, the motor's strength

utte'ak *iv.* be strong (re: inanimates; *pst.* ~an, ~-, u'utte'a); *cf.* u'ute

utte'am *n.* cramp

utte'apo *adv.* by force (*ex.*: ~a nunu'e, take by force)

utte'esea *tv.* esteem, like someone very much (~-)

utte'esia *adv.* strongly; Dios enchi hiokoe ~. Thank you (*sg.* addressee). Dios enchim hiokoe ~. Thank you (*pl.* addressee).

utte'ewa *iv.* have strength, be strong (re: animates); (*cf.* utte'ak, u'ute)

utte(a) *adv.* 1. fast rapidly (used with inanimates; *cf.* chumtia) 2. strongly; U kaaro utte weye. The car is going fast.

uttia *tv.* 1. be proud of 2. to become one, look good on one (~-, u'uttia); Aapo ehkuelapo ~. S/he looks good in school. Ume supem hamuttat ~. The dress looks good on the woman. A ne ~n. I was proud of her/him. ~ si aane. S/he's doing something that people will be proud of. Hose au ~ tekipanoakai. Joe is proud of himself because he is working. Vahim huvek kialikun tu'isi au ~. He has three wives and is proud of himself.

uttiawame *n.* pride

uttisi(a) *adv.* extremely; Juan ~ tekipanoa. John is really quite a worker.

uuli *n.* rubber

uura *dv.* take away from someone (u'á-, u"ura; *cf.* u'a); Aapo livrom a ~k. S/he took the book(s) away from her/him.

uuse *tv.* father a child (uusi-, u'use)

uusi *n.* child, son (male speaking)

uusi hamut *n.* preteen girl

uusi yo'owe *n.* child (older)

uusira *n.* children, youth, young people

uuva *n.* grape

uva *iv.* wash one's self, bathe (uvá'a-, u'uva; *s.* yuva)

uva wiroa *n.* grapevine

uva'ala *iv.* bathed

uvva *tv.* bathe, wash someone (~-, u'uvva); kovata ~, wash someone's hair

V

va'achia *n.* olla (clay pot for water)

va'achise *iv.* go to get water (*sg.*; *pl.* vatvo; both used only in *pst.*)

va'ak *iv.* have water (river, container)

   ka ~ *iv.* be empty (have not water)

va'akam *n.* nut grass (*Cyperus sp.*), used as medicine

va'apo cha'asime *iv.* be bobbing (in water; *pl.* to'osaka)

va'apo weye *iv.* sail, go by boat

va'ari *adj.* moist, wet, damp, humid

va'ata *iv.* get water (vat-, vava'ata)

Va'atakomsika'apo *n.* place in the Rio Yaqui (*lit.* water went down)

va'awa *n.* 1. juice, broth 2. soup, stew 3. liquid excretion, pus

va'ayole *iv.* quench thirst (*var.* vaayole; va'ayoli-, va'ayoyole)

vaa *comb.* of vaa'am, water

   ~ chomek *iv.* have a runny nose

   ~ haitimachi *n.* dirty water

   ~ he'e *iv.* drink water

   ~ húvahe *n.* 1. octopus 2. water spider

   ~ koochim *n.* shrimp

   ~ kuvahe *n.* water drum

   ~ loovo *n.* sea lion

   ~ nuu'u *n.* thermos, water bottle, canteen, water gourd

   ~ puusim *n.* spring (water)

   ~ si'ita *tv.* sprinkle (vaa si'ita-, vaa sisi'ita)

   ~ si'ite *iv.* sprinkle (vaa si'iti-, vaa si'isi'ite)

   ~ vetuku *adv.* underwater

   ~ weye *iv.* flow

   ~ yepsak *iv.* be flooded

   ~ yoama *n.* amphibians and other aquatic animals (but not fish)

   ~ yoene *exp.* come get a drink of water

vaa'am *n.* 1. water 2. broth, liquid (vaau, to the water); vampo, in the water

vaachai *n.* jar (archaic word)

vaaho'oti *adv.* blaring, noisy (with hia; *syn.* ~ aache); Musikom ~ hipona. The music is blaring.

vaahta *tv.* loosen, take down (~-, vaavahta)

vaahtawa *n.* loosening, untying

vaaka *n.* cane, reeds (*Arundo donax*, giant reed; *Phragmites oustralis*, reed), used for many purposes (matting, basketry, arches, arrows, musical instruments)

vaaka huiwa *n.* cane arrow

vaake *tv.* boil food (vak-, vavake)

vaaki *adj.* boiled

vaakot *n.* snake; ~ tekukupo weama. Where a whirlwind stops, you'll find a snake (folk belief).

vaakot hiawai *n.* snake sound

vaala *n.* bullet

vaalai *adj.* loose (joint, hinges)

vaali *adj., n.* 1. *adj.* fresh, cool 2. *n.* freshness, coolness (*syn.* vai)

vaamse *adv.* in a hurry

vaanam *adv.* 1. downriver 2. the downriver area (the villages of Potam, Rahum, Wivisim, Veenem) 3. west (*cf.* taa'at)

vaane *tv.* irrigate, water (van-, vavane)

vaapo hiapsame *n.* aquatic biomass

vaario *n.* barrio, quarter, ward, suburb

vaasevo'i *n.* butterfly

vaaso *n.* glass (drinking)

vaasu *tv.* soak (vasœ-, vavaasu)

vaata *n.* crotch, groin (*loc.* vatapo)

vaata yehtepo *n.* march, bog, swamp (*lit.* where water collects)

vaataponame *n.* water-drum player

Vaatosaimpo *n.* place in Sonora (*lit.* place of the gulls)

vaatu *iv.* dash out (~-, vavatu)

vaavu *n.* clay

vaawe *n.* sea, ocean

vaawe *iv.* leak (vaw-, vavawe; re: roof); Kari ~. The roof is leaking.

vaaye *n.* valley

vacha'e *n.* kangaroo rat

vachi *n.* corn (seed, kernels)

    ~ vino *n.* corn wine

    ~ vino bwikam *n.* corn wine songs

vachi waasa *n.* corn field

váchia *n.* 1. seed 2. pit, stone (fruit)

vachía *adv., interj.* 1. *adv.* first (in position), turn (taking a ~) 2. *interj.* go ahead (*interj.*); Aapo ~. Let he/him go first. A: Empo ~. B: Chiokoe uttesia. Thank you.

vacho'oko *n.* salt water, saline solution

vachomo *n.* seep willow (*Baccharis salicifolia*)

vachu *interj.* hold it, one moment please

vae *adv.* by means of water

    ~ muuke *iv.* be thirsty (*pl.* ~ koko)

    ~ mukne *iv.* get thirsty (*pl.* ~ kokone)

    ~ weche *iv.* be foggy

    ~ wetvae *iv.* get foggy

vaekai in: ka vaeka, *exp.* need, allow for, require, must; Ka vaeka senu oorata emo makneekai trenta bwihvaeteko. You want to give yourself an hour if you're planning to catch the train. Ka vaekai empo a vehe'etuakai. You must pay for it. Empo ka vaekai aman noitenekai. You should go pay them a visit.

vaekio *n.* a plant *sp.* (*Sesbania exaltata*)

vaesevoli *n.* butterfly (*s.*; = vaisevo'i)

vaewa *n.* fog, mist (*s.*; = vahewa)

153

vaewaakas *n.* cactus wren

vaeweche *n.* dew, fog

vah- *comb.* of vaso, grass

vaha *iv.* swell (vai- or vahi-, vavaha; vahakan is used as the perfect instead of vasisuk)

vahewa *n.* mist, fog (*s.* vaewa)

vahewehcia *adj.* dew-laden

vahi *num.* three (*s.* vai)

Vahi Mariam *n.* the Three Marias

vahi'itua *tv.* give someone a drink of water

vahia *n.* bay (water)

vahima *iv.* wash hands (vahim-, vavahima)

vahimpo *adv.* (at) three o'clock

vahisia *adv.* thrice, three times

vahiwe *adv.* in three ways

vahiya *iv., n.* 1. *iv.* be swollen (*pst.* ~k) 2. *n.* swelling (*var.* vaiya); Aapo tu'isi wok ~. Her/his foot is swelling up. U ~ ka kom siika. The swelling went down. U ~ soutek. The swelling went down.

vahkom *n.* 1. lake, pond 2. Bacum

vahooti *adv.* loudly, boisterously

vahotiuwa *n.* loud background noise

Vahtekoim *n.* the Pleiades

vahu'uki *n.* boiled food taken out of pot

vahu'uri(a) *n., iv.* 1. *n.* hay, pasturage 2. *iv.* cut hay

vahu'urina *iv.* wash one's face (*s.* vaulina)

vahu'use *iv.* go for hay (*sg.*; *pl.* vahu'uvo)

vahume *iv.* swim (*pst.* ~n, vahum-, vavahume)

vahwiolai *adj.* plants (metaphoric for people)

vai$_1$ *num.* three (*s.*; = vahi)

vai$_2$ *comb.* of vaa'am, water

      ~ koko, *iv.* thirsty (*pl.*)

      ~ muuke, *iv.* thirsty (*sg.*)

vai-$_3$ *comb.* of vaha, swell

vai *adj.* fresh, cool (*syn.* vaali)

vai heeka *n.* cool breeze

vaikumareewi *n.* dragonfly

vaile *n.* dance (social event)

vaisae *iv.* be grateful (~~, vaisasae); Yoeme tua enchi ~. The man is really grateful to you. Apo a ~. S/he is thankful to her/him.

vaisaewame *n.* gratitude, thankfulness

vaisevo'i *n.* butterfly (*s.* vaesevoli); U chukui ~ techoe. The black butterfly is a bad omen.

vaita'a *tv.* misinform, deceive, fool (vaita'á-, vaitata'a)

vaita'awame *n.* fooling

vaite *tv.* flap, flutter (with masa as *obj.*; vaiti-, vaivaite)

vaitia *iv.* joking, teasing; ume usim nau ~. The children are teasing each other.

vaitiuwa *iv.* be chatting, joking (pastime)
vaitiuwame *n.* joke
vaivakuria *n.* small branch (tree)
vaiweche *n.* fog, mist
vaiya *n.* swelling
vak- *comb.* of vaake, boil food
vaka *comb.* of vaaka, cane
  ~ nawa *n.* reed root (used for shampoo)
  ~ Tetteve *n.* Bacatete Mountains (Yaqui stronghold)
vaka'apo *n.* Mexican paloverde (*Parkinsonia aculeata*; *cf.* cho'i)
vakalaume *n.* a bamboo *sp.*
vakasi—n *n.* vacation
vakau *n.* golden bamboo
vake'o *n.* cowboy
vakeeta *n.* leather
vakoe *n.* a plant *sp.* used for greens
vakoni *n.* a species of duck
vakot hiawai *n.* harp and violin tuning used for weddings
vakot muteka *n.* a plant *sp.*
vakot nini *n.* a plant *sp.*
vaksia *tv.* wash (not clothes, hands; ~-, vavaksia); *cf.* hipaksia; Aapo
  aso'ola toosam ~ne. She will wash the baby's blanket.
vakulia *n.* new shoot (plants), twig
vakuuna *n.* vaccine
valansa *n.* scales (for weighing)
vali yoe *exp.* come cool off
valepo *n.* desire, will
vali yoene *exp.* come and cool off
valiria *tv.* cool
valiaroa accepted according to rule or convention, count (in sports)
valichiapo *adv.* pretending; for the sake of argument (with kia); Kia ~ te
  tomita yewane. Let's play with the money just for pretend. Ka
  nau omte vetchi'ivo kia ~ hosom itom bwiapo nu'upavawatea.
  Not to get angry, but for the sake of argument, suppose that
  there were bears in our country.
valiliti *adv.* coolingly, refreshingly (*s.*; valisi); sia ~ yo hekame (*s.*), the one
  who is blowing enchanted green coolingly
valisi *adv.* coolingly, refreshingly (*s.* valiliti); ~ yuke, raining refreshingly
valle *n.* pail, bucket
valumai *tv.* wash (*s.*); kia ne seata ~ (*s.*), I am just washed by the flower
vamihtua *tv.* hurry; Itom maala Mariata ~. That woman is hurrying Mary.
vamse *iv.* be in a hurry (vamsi-, vamvamse); Aapo su ~ move'iwa
  to'ossika. Being in a hurry, he left his hat behind. Vempo si ka
  vamvamse. They don't hurry up.
vamsea *adv.* go ahead, you might as well; ~ weye, go ahead and go
vamseka *interj.* Nolia ~ emo a'ana. Hurry up and go ahead.
vamsi *adv.* in a hurry; Aapo hiva yeu ~ne. He is always in a hurry.

van- *comb.* of vaane, irrigate

vandeha *n.* pan

vanko *n.* 1. bench 2. car seat (in Sonora; used in the *pl.*; *cf.* siiya)

vannai *n.* pudding

vanreo *n.* irrigator (person)

vansea *adv., interj.* 1. *adv.* might as well 2. *interj.* go ahead; ~ weye.
Go ahead.

vanseka *interj.* 1. hurry 2. go ahead

vanteam *n.* flag; Ume Yoem ~ naiki chokim hippue; ume tevei, tosai,
into siki. The Yoeme flag has four stars; it is dark blue, white
and red.

vanteereo *n.* flag bearer (*syn.* alpes)

vanyo *n.* shower (for bathing)

variil *n.* barrel

varko *n.* ship

varnis *n.* varnish

varnistua *tv.* varnish

varvula *n.* valve

vasea *n.* dregs (of drink)

vaseka *n.* 1. flotsam, debris washed ashore 2. a plant *sp.*

vasevo'i *n.* a fly *sp.* (*lit.* water-fly; *s.* vaesevoli)

vasiwe *iv.* sprout (vasiw-, vavasiwe)

vasiula *n.* 1. shoot, sprout 2. descendent

vaso *n.* grass (*comb.* vah-; including *Bouteloua barbata* and other species)

Vaso Huuras *n.* Straw Judas burned during Easter ceremonies

vaso moela *n.* brush, dried area

vasou *adj.* to the grass

    ~ wattila *iv.* be free to do as one likes

    ~ wetla *iv.* while the cat's away, the mice will play

vasua *iv.* be cleansed by soaking or rain (*var.* vasula; ~-, vavasua)

vat- *comb.* of va'ata, get water

vat *adv.* first, foremost

    ~ tuuka *adv.* day before yesterday

    ~ wéeme *n.* basic, fundamental thing

vata *n.* crotch (*loc.* vata'apo)

vatan *adv.* at/to the right; ~ vétana, from the right; ~ vétana mampo
taawak, stayed right in the hands of; Se–or itom achai
Diosta ~ vétana mampo taawak. It (the truth) stayed in God's
right hand.

vatat *n.* small green frog *sp.* with long legs

vatatana *adv.* to the right

vatea *n.* mixing bowl

vateria *n.* 1. battery 2. flashlight

vatnaataka(i) *adv.* in the beginning, long ago (in mythic times) (*var.*
vatnaateka; this is used in narratives, sermons, and other formal
genres; *syn.* vinwatuko which is used in conversation); si
vatnaaaateka, very long ago; ~ aavo yaahisukame haivu kokosuk.

The one who came in the beginning haved already passed away.
chea ~ *adv.* at the very beginning, at the outset
vato'i *n.* baptized person, Christian; ka ~, 1. mean person 2. pagan
vato'o *adv.* in baptism
    ~ achai *n.* godfather (*masc.*)
    ~ ae *n.* godmother (*masc., fem.*)
    ~ asoa *n.* godchild (either sex; *fem.*)
    ~ hapchi *n.* godfather (*fem.*)
    ~ hiosia *n.* baptismal certificate
    ~ maara *n.* goddaughter (*masc.*)
    ~ teak *n.* first name, Christian name
    ~ uusi *n.* godson (*masc.*)
    ~ yo'owam *n.* godparents
vatosai *n.* seagull
vatowawame *n.* baptism
vatta *tv.* soak
vatte *adv.* almost (*cf.* ave); ~ne muukek. I almost died. ~ karita wechek. It
    (a tree) almost fell on the house.
vatvo *iv.* go to get water (*pl.*; *sg.* va'achise)
vatwe *n.* river
vaulina *iv.* wash one's own face (*s.*; vahu'urina)
vauwo *n.* pochote, ceiba tree (*Ceiba acuminata*)
vava'atoa , *tv.* 1. pour liquid on 2. butter someone up, flatter (~-, no *rdp.*)
vavaasu *rdp.* of vaasu, soak
vava'atua *iv.* throw water
vavasua *tv.* pre-soak laundry (*pst.* ~n, ~-; no *rdp.*); Ime saavom hunaka ~.
    The laundry is pre-soaking (in) the soap.
vavatria *tv.* haul water for someone
vavepiinim *n.* hair pin, bobby pin
vavi cho'ola *n.* lark
vavis *n.* a plant *sp.*, perhaps wild parsley (*Sp.* yerba manso)
vaw- *comb.* of vaawe, leak
vawa in: ka [noun] ~, be canceled, called off (*ex.* ka pahko vawa, be no
    ceremony)
vawe mayoa *n.* shore, coast, beach
ve'a *tv.* save, reserve (vi'i-, veve'a)
ve'e *iv.* be lacking, left over (*pst.* ~ka, vi'i-, veve'e); Maria im ~ka. Mary is
    absent. Ama ~. It is still lacking. Tomi Mariatau ~. Mary has no
    money. Um bwa'ampo ona ama ~. The food needs salt.
ve'ekame *n.* remainder, extra; Vempo waka bwa'am yeu ve'ekamta
    mikwak. They were given the extra food.
ve'ekik *adv.* so much
ve'emu *adv.* a certain distance or length; wai ~, as far as over there;
    wai ~ ha'amuk, climbed so far; kaita va vemu weamakasu (*s.*),
    walked so far away from
ve'okte *iv.* stick out tongue, be lightening (ve'okti-, ve'ove'okte)
ve'oktia *n.* lightening

ve'ove'okte *iv.* be lightening, stormy

véa *adv.* does, will, then (*ptc.* gives emphasis; it is placed after the clause
  constituent that is emphasized; used in song language and
  spoken Yoeme); Ian ~ yo ániapo bwiika. Now it is singing in
  the enchanted world. Nu su ~ ama weyetea. That's what goes
  in it (content of song, talk, ritual, or other event). Nasuk
  tukapo ~ sewa heeka ama weye. In the middle of the night,
  the Flower Wind goes there (*s.*) Sewa huli ~ ama weye. The
  Flower Badger *does* go there (*s.*) Hunak ~ aapo yepsak. And
  then s/he arrived. Aapo ~ bwikne. He will sing.

veá *n.* skin, shell, bark, rind; nasoveá, orange rind
  ~ huya *n.* a plant *sp.*
  ~ pua *tv.* take rind off squash
  ~ yecha *tv.* skin

veák vena *n.* a plant *sp.*

veakta *tv.* unroll, stretch out

veakte *iv.* be unrolling (veakti-, veaveakte)

veakti *iv.* turned over

veas(i) *postp.* behind, beside; on the other side

veaskopte *tv.* forget (*var.* wahkopte; veaskopti-, veaskopkopte; *ex.*: am veas
  ne koptek, I forgot them)

veasu *conj.* since; ~ empo ka a sualekai, ka into te enchi mahtavae. Since
  you don't believe, we're not going to teach you anymore. Vat em
  kaáte ~ eme ka itom vovitvae. Go ahead of us since you don't
  want to wait for us.

vechehta *tv.* roll up pants or sleeves (~-, vevechehta)

veeki *adv.* so much; ia ~, this much; wa ~, that much; Ia ~ka ama aayuk.
  There is this much there.

veeko *n.* abalone, abalone shell, mother-of-pearl

veelam *n.* sails

veelom *n.* veil

veeme *n.* girl, young woman

Veenem *n.* Belem

veerok *n.* disease (lip)

veete *iv.* 1. be burning 2. glow (veeti-, veveete)

veetia *iv.* be burned

véeva *tv.* chase, kick out (vep-, vevva)

veéva *tv.* hit, strike

veewa *n.* nonsense, gibberish

veewatia *adv.* 1. nonsense 2. brag, boast; complain, whine (said of
  a drunk or whining child) (with the verb hia: veewatiu-,
  veewatia hihia)

veha *adv., interj.* 1. *adv.* already, maybe (*var.* vesa) 2. *interj.* ready?;
  Apo ~ yo—ko humak yevihne. Maybe he will come tomorrow
  morning.

vehako *adv.* a while ago

vehe'e *tv.*, *iv.* 1. *tv.* betray, deceive 2. cost (so much) 3. *iv.* be expensive, costly, valuable (~-, vevehe'e); A: Paanim kafeta into hinuvae. B: Woi peesom vehe'e. A: (I) want to buy bread and coffee. B: That will be two dollars; Inime livrom tu'isi ~. These books are very valuable.

    au ~ *iv.* be one's own worst enemy; Huan aposu au vehe'e. John is his own worst enemy.

    yee ~me *n.* traitor

vehe'ebwan *iv.* be too expensive

vehe'eri *postp.*, *n.* 1. *postp.* against 2. *n.* enemy

vehe'eria *iv.*, *n.* 1. *iv.* cost, be worth 2. *n.* cost

vehe'etua *tv.* pay, repay; kaita am ~k, paid them nothing

vehe'etuari *adj.* paid

vehe'ewa *n.* price, cost, expense

veho'orim *n.* cachora (lizard *sp.*)

vehu'uku *n.* nook, cranny, crevice

vekta *tv.* shave, plane, scrape (~-, vekvekta)

vekte *iv.* be scraping (vekti-, vekvekte)

vekti *adj.* shaved, scraped

velaaroa *iv.* vigil, stay up

vele'ekatana *adv.* from side to side, from place to place

veleki *adj.* this much (*obj.* ~ka)

veletchi *adj.* size; Waka see'eta ~k huni te hakam vitne. We will see them (the truths of the past) the size of a grain of sand.

veliis *n.* suitcase

vélohko *adj.* bright, shining

vemela *adj.* new, innovative (*pl.* veemela; *cf.* wéemta); U hamutta kari ~. The woman's house is new. Aapo ~ maakinata hippue. S/he has a new car. Ume livrom ~. The book is new. Ume livrom veemela. The books are new. Vempo Tusoneu ~ piisam hinuk. They bought a new blanket in Tucson. Aapo ~ maakinata hinune. S/he's going to buy a new car.

Vemela Pahkua *n.* New Pascua

Vemela Wasuktia *n.* New Year

Vemela Vasuktiawi, Alleaka Te Au Yumak *exp.* Happy New Year

vemelasi *adj.* new (to position or situation); ~ au kikte, be new in a position

vemelate *tv.* renew, renovate (~-, vemmelate)

vemmucha *tv.* spank, whip (*syn.* vepsu; vemmuchá'a-, vemmumucha)

vempo *pn.* they

vempo'im *pn.* them; ~ mechi *pn.* at/on them

vempo'immet *pn.* at/on them

vempola *pn.* themselves

vemu *adv. var.* of ve'emu, a certain distance

vena *postp.* as, like; *cf.* venasi(a);, vévena; Aapo vepsuwamta ~. He looks like he's been beaten up.

venak(o) *adv.* same, like this; Ia ~ ne waata. I want something in this size.

venasi(a) *postp.* as, like; *cf.* vena; Aapo tomekamta venasia nau weye. S/he goes around as if they were rich.

> tuata ~ *adv.* as if; Huan tuata ~ hiune. John always has the best intentions.

vennikut *adv.* in a given direction, in far or unheard of places; hakun ~, in far away places; Hakun ~ te yeu noitek. Some where in far away places we visited. Apo hakun ~ a hahase. S/he chased her/him to the back of beyond/to unheard of places.

venta *tv.* 1. smear, spread 2. anoint (~-, venventa)

ventaana *n.* 1. window 2. windshield (on car); ~m tutu'uteme, *n.* windshield wipers

venveno'ote *iv.* flying in circles (venveno'oti-)

veohko *adj.* bright, shining

vepa *postp., n.* 1. *postp.* on top of, more than 2. *n.* roof; Karipo ~ kom chepte'e. Get down off the roof. I kama chea tu'i kia wai kamata ~. This squash is sweeter than that squash.

vepa supem *n.* blouse

vepasu *postp.* above, overhead

veppani *adj.* certain size

vepsu *tv.* spank, whip (*syn.* vemmucha; ~-, vevepsu)

vera'a voocham *n.* sandals

verai *adj.* flat (re: small items)

verduura *n.* vegetable

vesa₁ *interj.* okay for now

vesa₂ *adv. var.* of vesa, already

veseo *n.* calf (animal)

vesiino *n.* neighbor (*syn.* heela ho'akame)

vesiito *tv.* kiss (*syn.* nat tetente; ~-, vevesiito)

vesuma *tv.* skin, peel with axe or knife (~-, vevesuma; *ex.* bark); *cf.* vekta, siiva; na'asota ~, peel an orange

vetala(i) *adj.* flat, even, smooth (*var.* veta'i, in: wok veta'i, sole of foot)

vétana *postp.* 1. from 2. between (*cf.* nau nasuk); o'ou into ili o'outa ~, between the man and the boy; Itepo nau ea uusim ~ ela'apo vempo tekipanoane. We agree that the children can work. U hua misi kawim ~ kom yepsa. The bobcat comes down from the mountains (at night). Ume yoemem vatatana ~ kaáte. The men are coming from the right.

vetayeka *n.* duck (*syn.* paato)

vetchi *adj.* same size (*pl.* vettechi); ia ~, this size; Itom kari ia ~. Our house is this size.

vetchi'ivo *postp.* for
> 1. for the benefit of, for
> 2. for the purpose of, in order to (with a noun in *obj.* case, the combining form of a verb, or with the following paradigm: ne, e, a/ae, ito, emo, vempo'im); U ili usita hariune, me'e ~. He

is looking for the Child, in order to kill Him (nativity story).
U pahkota ~ ito nau tu'ute. We're getting ready for the
ceremony. Ume hamuchim revarua paanim hoa veloriota ~.
The women are making yeast bread for the wake.

3. be good for (remedy), intended for; hik ~, be intended for
sewing; Inime váchiam et ~. This is seed for planting. Katin
sauko seewam, naoto'oria into negrita tu'isi tu'i taiwechiata ~.
Recall that elderberry, naoto'oria and negrita is really good for
a fever.

chuvala ~, *adv.* for a little while

vetcho'oria *n.* crust

vetelai *adj.* flat

vette *adj.* heavy

yee ~ tave *iv.* will pull one down (health, emotion)

vettea *n.* weight

vétuku *postp.*, *n.* 1. *postp.* under 2. *n.* base, bottom; humaku ~, under
the ground

vétukuni *postp.* beneath

veuti *interj.* what a shame, what a waste; ~ munim woovo'ota. What a
shame they threw away the beans.

~ am hoa *tv.* waste; Vempo bwa'amta veuti hoa. They're wasting
food.

~ maachi *iv.* be desirable; Hamut ~ maachi. The woman is
desirable.

veutia *tv.* desire (re: anything, including food; *pst.* ~n, ~-; *cf.* ukkule);
Aapo ama vutti a ~. S/he desires it desperately.

kaita ~ *iv.* be wasteful

veutiachi *adj.* desirable

veutiachisi *adv.* desirably (often with maachi)

vevehe'eri *n.* 1. enemy 2. the Devil

vevepa *postp.* on top of; Kawim ~ rehte. (They) are walking on top of the
mountain. yo aniwata ~ (*s.*), on top of the enchanted world

vewichi *postp.* along side of, next to (*resp.*)

vewit *postp.* next to, at the same level

~ weye *exp.* be same age as; Ne vewit weye. S/he is the same age
as me.

vi'am *n.* nape (of neck)

vi'ita *tv.* twist, wind around, coil (~-, vivi'ita)

vi'ite *iv.* 1. be twisting 2. be on the verge of a bowel movement (vi'iti-,
vivi'ite)

vi'iti *adj.* twisted

vi'itia *iv.* be twisted, tangled

viakta *tv.* roll something up (~-, viaviakta)

viakte *iv.* roll over (viakti-, viaviakte); kom ~, roll downhill

vaa'a ~ *iv.* flood; Uka vaa'ata ~k ite hamuta te hinne'uk. When
the big flood came we rescued that woman.

viakti *n.* rolled over

viaktisime *iv.* be rolling

vicha₁ *postp.* toward

~u, in the future; Ta ~u ket Dios aapo enchim a mikne. In the
future, God himself will give it to you.

wam ~ *adv.* beyond; karipo wam ~, beyond the house

vicha₂ *tv., iv.* 1. *tv.* see; oversee, direct, manage 2. *iv.* look at (vit-,
viivicha, vivit-); In achai chea Yoronata au vichaktia. My father
saw the Llorona. Haivu numak mamni meecha ama vivitwakai.
It was seen about five months ago.

misa ~ *tv.* hear mass

yee ~ *tv.* read someone's mind (*lit.* see straight through people;
cf. ta'a)

vichapo *postp.* in front of (not moving; with a noun in *obj.* case, or with
the following paradigm: ne, ee, ae, itom, enchim, vempo'im)

vichame *n.* 1. spectator 2. overseer, superintendent, director

vichau *postp., adv.* towards; ~ itom to'osiika yoyo ániwa (s), towards
(where the sun sets) the enchanted world left us

vichau vicha *adv.* in the future; Vempo vichau vicha tekipanoa. They
work to the future.

vichau vicha weye *iv.* go forward, proceed

vichi'ise *iv.* go to see (*sg.*; *pl.* vitvo)

videotepim *n.* videotape

Vienes *n.* Friday

vihpa *n.* vespers

vihta *tv.* wrap (~-, vihvihta)

vihtam *n.* the movies, film

vihte *iv.* be wrapping (vihti-, vihvihte)

vihtei *adj.* wrapped

viicha *n.* wasp

viichi *adj.* bald; Luis kova ~. Louis is bald.

viika *iv.* 1. rot, spoil, decay 2. be infected (viká-, vivika)

~ huva *iv.* stink, smell bad

viino *n.* wine

viiva *n.* 1. tobacco 2. cigarette (cigarettes may be used to cure, or for
harming another person; a cigarette may be used to scout ahead
of a party)

vika *n.* arrowhead

vikala *adj.* spoiled, rotten, putrid

Vikam *n.* Vicam

viko *n.* bumblebee

víkue *iv.* whistle (*syn.* viute; vikœi-, no *rdp.*)

vina *adv.* toward over there, toward over here

~ weye. Come over here.

vina'avo *adv.* from over here, from this side (*cf.* vina)

vinakre *n.* vinegar

vinwa *adv.* long ago, for a long time; Haivu ~ yuke. It's been raining for a
long time.

vinwatu *iv.* be ancient
vinwatuk *adv.* delayed, too long
vinwatuko *adv.* a long time ago (in conversation; *syn.* vatnaateka is used
      in stories and sermons); si viiiiinwatuko, very, very long ago
viohko *n.* shiny object
viohkosi *adv.* sparkling (with aane)
violaroa *tv.* rape
visa'e *n.* gourd
visachia *n.* vomit
visata *iv.* vomit (visat-, vissata)
visikleeta *n.* bicycle
vit- *comb.* of vicha, to see
vit ta'a *tv.* recognize, know by sight
vitchime *n.* on-looker, someone making the rounds (visiting)
vitchu *tv.* 1. look at 2. observe (*pst.* ~-n, ~-, vivitchu); Hamut karim ~.
      The woman is looking at the houses.
      chokinaik puhvaka a ~ *iv.* scowl, frown
vitchume *n.* onlooker, bystander
vitchuwame *n.* observation
vittua₁ *dv.* show; Livrom ne ~. Show me the books. Peuta ne karita ~k.
      Peter showed me the house.
vittua₂ *tv.* send, dispatch
vitvo *iv.* go to see (*pl.*; *sg.* vichi'ise)
vitwame *n.* view
viute *iv.* whistle (*syn.* v'kue; viuti-, viuviute)
vivino(li) *n.* a plant *sp.*, bushy and sweet smelling
vivinwatu *iv.* take too long (~-)
vivinwatume *n.* someone who takes too long
viyateera *n.* wallet
vo'a *tv.* fish with line; *cf.* kuchusua
vo'areo *n.* fisherman, angler (with line; *cf.* kuchureo)
vo'arim *n.* fishing hook
vo'o hoa *tv.* 1. walk 2. travel, take a trip 3. be occupied with 4. lead
      one's life
vo'o hoame *n.* traveler
vo'oka *iv.* be lying down (*sg.*; *pl.* to'oka; *pst.* ~n, vo'o-,; *s.* voyoka);
      cf. vo'ote
vo'ose *iv.* go to lie down (*sg.*; *pl.* to'otek)
vo'osime *iv.* float 2. lie on a moving object 3. slither (*sg.*; *pl.* to'osaka;
      pst. ~n, vo'osim-, no *rdp.*); *cf.* sunsunte, waka'anama, waka'ate
vo'ote *iv.* lie down (*sg.*; *pl.* to'ote; ~-, vovo'e); *cf.* vo'oka; vo'ote'epo, where
      was laid
vo'otek in: *iv.* aet ~, be convicted (*lit.* lay it on her/him)
voa *n.* 1. fur, down, hair (not head hair) 2. feather (*gen.*)
      ~ rovoi *adj.* hairy, furry, fuzzy
      ~ weche *iv.* lose (fur, hair), molt
voak *n.* mold

voam *n.* fuzz, fur, down, body hair

voara *n.* 1. hairy 2. wooly caterpillars

voatu *iv.* grow hair, get moldy

vochata *iv.* put on shoes, tires

voe *iv.* 1. bark (*syn.* chu chae, haiti chae) 2. argue (with emo) (voi-, vovoe; *ex.*: am ~ne, get 'em; emo voi, *n.* exchange of [angry] words); Chu chukuli bwan ne voyeme. Yes, indeed, the black dog is barking at me (tongue twister). U chuu'um vovoe. The dogs usually bark.

voes *n.* ox

vohokta *tv.* bore, drill a hole

vohte *iv.* 1. be draining, emptying 2. have diarrhea (vohti-)

vohtek *iv.* be spilled, upset (re: contained item(s); with yeu)

vohtila *adj.* open at one end (bag)

vohtiwame *n.* one having diarrhea

voleeto *n.* ticket

volsa *n.* pocket

voo'o *n.* road, path (*loc.* voot); Wa yoawa tua inivo yeu siika, a sewa voota ye siika (s). The animal (deer) went out, went out on its deer road. Vaakot voot vo'oka. There's a snake lying on the road.
~ tottepo *adv.* at the/a bend in the road
~ta hahase, follow the road
tu'i ~ta weiya, follow the good road (lead a good life)
~ta tehwa, point out the way

voo hóowame *n.* journey, trip

voo toha *tv.* accompany someone a short distance

voocham *n.* 1. shoes 2. tires, wheels (of car); ~po wokte, put on shoes

vooda *n.* wedding

voohoria *iv.*, *n.* *iv.* 1. *iv.* lead a good life 2. *n.* event 3. *n.* life

voohtia *n.* diarrhea

voola *n.* 1. ball of string or yarn (*cf.* pelootam) 2. crowd, throng
~ yehtela *iv.* become tangled into a ball/have muscles knotted up

voolo *n.* gathering (social), baptism party

voonia *n.* cane, walking stick

voopo *iv.*, *n.* 1. *iv.* blister 2. *n.* blister, boil

voosa *n.* sack

voot *adv.* on the road (*loc.* of voo'o, road)

voote *n.* can, canned goods

voovok *n.* Colorado River toad; Vovok sikim lihtomaka kontituan. One processes with a toad tied with a red ribbon (folk belief).

vooyo *iv.* get a blister from abrasion (voyo-); *cf.* heohtek

vosime *iv.* *var.* of vo'osime, crawl

votea *n.* bottle

votiika *n.* drugstore, pharmacy

votoon *n.* 1. button 2. doorknob 3. handle (doors, furniture) 4. bulb (plant)

vovicha *tv.* wait for, await; be patient; Ume kopariam uka maehtota yevih
~. The cantoras are waiting for the lay priest to arrive. Apo si ~.
S/he is patient.

voyoka *iv.* lie down (*sg.*; *pl.* toyoka; *s.*; = vo'oka/to'oka)

voyola *iv.* blister (voyó-, vovoyo)

vu'u *pn.* many (nonhuman; *pl.* vu'um); *cf.* huevena; ~ kavam, many eggs;
Aapo ~m nautohak. He gathered many.

vu'uchi *n.* wattles (chicken, turkey)

vu'uria *iv.* to multiply; Vempo emo ~. They are multiplying.

vuam *n.* white cloth for deer dancer's deer head

vuhti *adv.* in: ama ~ hi'ibwak, overate (*syn.* unna hi'ibwak)

vuite *iv.* run (*sg.*; *pl.* tenne; vuiti-, vuivuite)

vuitilame *n.* fugitive

vuitiria *dv.* run for someone else

vuivuite *iv.* jog

vuivuiteme *n.* jogger

vuke *tv.* own, raise (animals)

vukek *iv.* have livestock

vuki *n.* pet, slave

vukiwame *n.* animal husbandry

vuru sisi *n.* a fungus (*Podaxis sp.*; *lit.* burro piss)

vusa *iv., tv.* awaken, wake up (vusá'a-, vuvusa; *syn.* suavusa, which is
more formal in diction)

vusa'ala *adj.* awake; Hose haivu ~. Joe is still awake.

vusan tomi *n.* seventy-five cents

vusani *num.* six

vusanimpo *adv.* (at) six o'clock

vusanisia *adv.* six times

vutta *tv.* untie, loosen , release grip (~-, vutvutta)

vutte *iv.* become untied, loose (vutti-, vutvutte)

vutti 1. *adj.* untied (*var.* vuttila) 2. *n.* harsh person 3. awesome,
wondrous, incredible
ama ~ *adv.* desperately; Aapo ama ~ a veutia. S/he desires it
desperately.

vuttia see ama

vuu'u *adj.* many (re: nonhuman); *cf.* huevena

vuuru *n.* ass, burro. donkey

W

wa'a *pn.* that

Wa'emam *n.* Guaymas

wa'akta *tv.* step over

wa'akte *iv.* open mouth (wa'akti-, wawa'akte); *cf.* waawakte

wa'am(i) *adv.* there (*var.* wam)

wa'itopit *n.* salamander, gecko

wa'ivil *n.* small turtle *sp.*

waacha *tv.* dry (wachá'a-, wawacha)

waakas *n.* 1. cow 2. meat, beef

waake *iv.* dry out, dry up (wak-, wawake)

waaket *pn.* that one (*obj.* wakaket, *pl.* wameket); ~ tu'i. That one is good. Huan wakaket nu'uka. John took that one. Aapo wameket bwa'aka. S/he ate those ones.

waante *iv.* run (*sg.*; *syn.* vuite; *pl.* tenne; ~-); tompo ~, have a stomach ache; Ne kovo ~. My head aches. Ne mam ~. My hand(s) hurt. Hamut kovo ~. The woman has a headache.

waari *n.* basket

waaria *n.* barracks, police station

waasa *n.* field

Waasimam *n.* Las Guasimas

waata *tv.* want, desire (~-, wawwa'ata)
    kaveta ~ *tv.* ignore/snub/dislike (*syn.* ka yee waata)

wáate *iv.* think of, remember (*d.o.* = au; waati-, wawáate); Au ne waawatek. I remembered it. Au ne wawatek. I was thinking about it. Huan a malawau ~. John is remembering his daughter.

waáte *pn.* others, some (people); ~ avo kaáte. Others are coming. Inepo ~m vicha. I see the others. ~ wanna'avo kaáte. Some people are coming from that other side.

waátem *pn.* more; Ne ketun ~. I want more.

wáateme *n.* one who remembers; a hitau ~, one with a good memory

waatia *tv.* want (~-, wawwatiawa)

waatiawa *n.*, *iv.* 1. *n.* desire, want 2. *iv.* be wanted

waatimachi *iv.* able to remember; Ke ne au ~. I can't seem to remember it. Ka ne enchi au waaticmahia. I thought you would never remember it.

waatiwame *n.* memory (with au)

waawa *tv.* roast in coals (wawá-)

waawakte *iv.* be yawning

wacha'a- *comb.* of waacha, dry

wacha'i *n.* dried

Waehma *n.* Lent

Waehma Mecham *n.* the Lenten season

Waehma pahko *n.* a household ceremony sponsored by a family during Lent to fill a vow, involving feeding many of the villagers and ceremonial people (*syn.* Senyorta pahko)

waevas *n.* a bird *sp.*

wah *comb.* waasa, field
        ~ hi'u *n.* spinach
        ~ kuu'u *n.* cultivated agave
        ~ wechia *n.* abandoned fields

wahi *n.* Matachin rattle

wahiwa *adv. var.* of waiwa, inside
wahreo *n.* field hand, agricultural worker
wahu supem *n.* underwear
wahuwa *postp. var.* of waiwa, inside of
wai$_1$ *n.* younger sister or brother *(fem.)*
wai$_2$ *pn.* that
~ ve'emu *n.* that long, that far (from one point to another)
~ veppani *adj.* that size
waichi *adv., interj.* 1. *adv.* (towards) around there 2. *interj.* go over there!
(said to divert a whirlwind or dust devil, while crossing one's
index finger and thumb, waving hand back and forth)
waihuiwa *n.* condition where a child senses another child in the womb of
mother and cries *(Sp.* chipili)
waik *num.* pair (with emo)
emo ~ *exp.* they're a pair
waim *comb.* step- (with kin terms)
~ achai *n.* stepfather
~ ae *n.* stepmother
~ maala *n.* stepmother
~ maara *n.* stepdaughter
~ uusi *n.* stepson
waimak *pn.* with that
wain(a) *adv.* 1. over there, from over there 2. from/on that side *(var.*
wainavo; *s.;* = wanna'avo); Inim ~ emou kom yaaha. They come
over here to you. Sea mochala awa ~ se vuite *(s.).* With a cluster
of flowers on your antler, you come running from that side.
wainavo *adv. var.* of waina (sense 2)
wait out there; *cf.* waitana; ~ naa weye, walking around out there
waitana *n.* (from/along the) other side *(var.* wait)
~ Tuson *n.* 39th Street Barrio (Tucson)
waivas *n.* guayabon (a plant *sp.*)
waiwa *postp.* inside of *(var.* wahiwa, wahumwa); karipo ~, inside the
house; Haisa u kannao siki ~? Is the pomegranate red inside?
~ supem *n.* underwear
waiwanola *adv.* dangling (with cha'aka)
waka *pn.* that *(obj.* of wa'a; *emph.* waka'a); A: ~ neu toha. B: Hita?
A: Waka'a. A: Bring me that one. B: Which? A: That one.
waka *comb.* of waakas, cow
~ chuktireo *n.* butcher
~ veá *n.* cowhide; Waka veáta vekta, chomota yavaekai. The
cowhide is being scraped to make a mask.
waka'anama *iv.* crawl (intentionally; waka'anam-, waka'ananama);
cf. sunsunte, vo'osime, waka'ate
waka'ate *iv.* crawl (because of inability to walk; *cf.* waka'anama;
waka'ati-, wawaka'ate)
wakahipi'ikim *n.* cow's milk

wakapoponi *n.* shredded meat, carne seca

wakas chuktireo *n.* butcher (*syn.* peotireo)

wakasek *iv.* have cattle

wakasim *n.* cattle

wakavaki *n.* meat and vegetable stew

wakawacha'i *n.* jerky

waki bwia *n.* arid lands

wakia *adj.* dry (*pst.* ~kan, wak-, wawakia)

wakila *adj.* 1. skinny, lean, weak, withered, frail 2. Father Time (Death
    personified as a skeleton) (*var.* wakira)

wakiltu *iv.* get skinny (~-)

wakin in: im wakin, over here; Aapo im ~ yeu yepsak. He came over here.

wako'i *n.* grill, comal

Waluupe *n.* Guadalupe (*var.* Waruupe)

wam *adv. var.* of wa'am(i), there

    ~ vicha *adv.* towards over there, beyond; karipo ~ vicha, toward
      or beyond the house

    -wame *suf.* thing(s)/one(s) being verbed (*ex.*: nu'uwame, things
      being procured; etbwawame, stolen thing or things);
      cf. -kame, -me

wamcha *adv.* there about

wamsu *adv.* over there

wana *adv.* from the side there; A: Larry ~ weye. Larry is coming.
    B: Hauvotana? From what direction?
    A: Wana'a. From that side.

wana'a *adv.* there (*emph.*)

wanna'avo *adv.* on/from the other side, on/from that side (*s.* waina;
    cf. amae, aman(i), inivo); Kawim ~ hoak. He lives on the other
    side of the mountain.

wanna'avotana *adv.* far side

wannavo *adv. var.* of wanna'avo

wantem *n.* gloves

wantaroa *iv.* suffer from (from = *d.o.*); Tatariata te ~. We are suffering
    from the heat.

wante *iv.* ache, hurt (body part; wanti-, wanwante); Ne kutana ~. I have a
    sore throat.

wantia *n.* sickness, pain

wanwoochim *n.* burlap

Wapa'im *n.* a mountain near Vikam

Warahio *n.* Guarajio Indians

wasu'uwila *n.* plant *sp.* (cure for pottila)

wasukte *iv.* become a year

wasuktia *n.* year

    ~ sikamtachi *adv.* during the past year

    ~ yuma *iv.* be the anniversary

wasuwasukteka *adv.* for years; Vempo hani ~ hiapsine tea. They say that they will live for years.

wata *n.* willow (especially *Salix gooddingi*, which is cultivated around houses for shade)

wata'akuli *n.* a lizard *sp.*

watakte *iv.* prepare for a trip (with yeu)

watanimpo *adv.* (at) nine o'clock (*syn.* nuevempo)

watiawame *n.* one who is loved

watta *tv.* 1. take off (clothes) 2. throw (with -po; ~-, watwatta) yeu ~ *tv.* throw out

watte *iv.* 1. fall down (with kom; *pl. subj.*; *sg.* weche) 2. return (*pl. subj.*; *sg.* wechise; watti-, watwatte); Teetam kom watwatte. (Look out for) falling rocks.
  heeka ~ *iv.* expel phlegm
  kawimmeu ~ *iv.* return to the mountains

wawá- *comb.* of waawa, roast in coals

wawaate *rdp.* of wáate, think of

wattila *adj.* fallen down
  vasou ~, *iv.* be free to do as one pleases (when the cat's away, the mice will play; *lit.* fallen to the grass)

wawai *n.* cousin

wawaim *n.* kin; si'ime ~, all of one's kin

wawaira *n.* cousins, clan, extended family

wawairi cousins

wawatitua *tv.* remind

wawwa'ata *rdp.* of waata, want

we'epo *exp.* in: senu ~, at once (in a single instant)

we'epul(ai) *num.* one, just one (*var.* wepul); *cf.* seenu, senu; Wepul chiva au ta'aruk. One goat got lost. Huan wepul ayam hamtak. John broke one rattle. Aapo wepul tahkaim kom tatavek. She dropped one tortilla. Chikti si'ime wepulai venasia nau tekipanoa. All will work together as one (bill board slogan).

weama *iv.* walk (*sg.*; *pl.* rehte, naa kaáte; weam-, wee-, weweama; *var.* weyema, *s.* welama); Sewa huya yeu ne weevalika... yeu ne sika (*s.*). As I walk along in the flowered wilderness..., I go out. Aapo huya hikut ~. S/he's in the top of the tree. Kari hikut ~. S/he's on top of the house. U mochik lauti weweama. The turtle goes along slowly. Tasairapo te huyapo weweama. In the summer we usually go on hikes. Hakunsa weama? Where is s/he?
  kia ~ *iv.* stroll, take a walk

weamtua *tv.* drive (vehicle), make walk (child); aa karota ~, be able to drive a car

weche 1. *iv.* fall down 2. *tv.* fall on (on = *d.o.*) (*sg.*; *cf.* wechi'ise; *pl.* watte; *pst.* wetchuk, wet-, weweche); Ne hiva yu weweche. I'm always

169

falling down. Vatte karit wechek. It almost fell on the house.

kiasi eu ~ *iv.* hit the spot (satisfy)

ko'okoe ~ *iv.* take sick/get sick

mampo ~ *iv.* be in the control of; U o'ou vem mampo wechek.
The man is in their control.

tu'isi eu weche *iv.* 1. respond to medication 2. come to
understand, acquire a taste for; Tu'isi neu wechek. I
responded to the medication/ I acquired a taste for it.

vaa'am kom ~ *n.* waterfall;

wechia *n., iv.* 1. *n.* fallen 2. *iv.* be fallen down (other tenses like weche;
syn. kottia); Heka ~. The ramada is fallen down. Sapti ~.
The wall has fallen down. Teecho ~. The roof has caved in (*syn.*
Vepa ~).

senu ~po, all at once; Huan senu ~po na'asom bwa'asuk. John
ate the orange all at once.

wechi'ise *iv.* be in the process of falling down, fall down (with kom;
sg. subj.; used only for present tense; *cf.* weche; *pl. subj.* watte)
2. return (*sg.*; *pl.* watte); huyau ~, return to the wilds; Huyau ~ka
siika wa maaso, ka into nottivaeka véa siika. The deer went to
enter the wilderness, never to return.

wechila *adj.* fallen

kom ~ *adj.* fallen down

wee₁- *comb.* of weye, go/walk

wee₂ *comb.* of wee'e, amaranth

~ vannaim *n.* amaranth pudding

wee'e *n.* amaranth, pigweed (especially *Amaranth palmeri*)

wéemta *iv.* be new (recent; ~-); *cf.* vemela

wéeme *exp.* in: senu ~, in other words/in another vein

wéeneme *n.* current affairs (in: ian ~, what is going on now)

weero *n.* light in complextion

weesime *iv.* be going (*sg.*; *pl.* katchaka)

wéetua *tv.* drive, steer (vehicle), back up (vehicle); aa karota ~, be able to
drive a car

weiya *tv.* 1. take, carry 2. act, carry out 3. conduct, guide, lead 4. take
through a procedure (*pl. obj.*; *cf.* toha; ~-, weweiya)
ka tu'i vo'ota ~ *iv.* be on the wrong track
tu'i voo'ota ~ *iv.* be following the good road (lead a good life)

weiyawa *iv., n.* 1. *iv.* be carried out 2. *n.* way something is carried
out, style u masobwikame ~, the way of carrying out deer
singing

welema *iv.* go, walk (*s.* = weama)

welisia *adv.* in: nat ~, ala in all (in making a conclusion)

wepe'im *n.* hips

wepu'ulai *pn.* one, only, single (*var.* wepul); *syn.* senu is used in counting;
~ venasi nau tekipanoa, working together as one; ~k ne maka.
Give me just one. Wepul taa'ata ya'ane. Draw one sun.

wepul *n. var.* of we'epul(ai), one; ~ hiosiata ne maka. Give me a flower. ~ choki kalalipapati aane. One star is twinkling.

wepulsi *adv.* once (one repetition)

wepultakana *adv.* on one side

weri *iv.* be related to; nemak ~, related to me

wetchime *iv.* stumble

wetchuk *iv. pst.* of weche, fall

wet- *comb.* of weche, fall (*sg.*)

wetepo'i *n.* gnat

weweamtuame *n.* driver (vehicle; *syn.* maniheo)

weweri *n.* relatives, kin; Vempo nau ~. They're all related.

weye *iv.* go, walk (*sg.*; *var.* wee; *pl.* kaáte; *pst.* ~n, wée-, weweye); U hamut vat wee. The lady is going first. Aet chukula maaso kechia yeu weevae. Later the deer wants to go out (after the first song). Heewi, pues ne weevae. Well, I guess I'll be going. Nu su véa ama weye=tea. That's what goes in it (ritual, prayer, song, etc.). Katin Peo sehtul ama wam weeka a vichaktia. They say that Peter saw it once going around. Heewi pues ne weevae. Well, I'll be going running along (on leave taking).

    ama ~ *iv.* belong, fit in, go in a certain place; Hunu etehoi ama weye. That story fits in there.

    karopo ~ *iv.* go by car

    trenpo ~ *iv.* go by train

    utte'a ~ *iv.* speed

    va'apo ~ *iv.* go by boat

    wikitpo ~ *iv.* fly, go by airplane

weyek *iv.* standing (*sg.*; *pl.* ha'abwek; *pst.* ~an); *cf.* kikte

weyekte *iv.* walk, takes steps (*pl.* kiktekte)

weyema *iv. var.* of weama, walk

weyeme *n.* custom, tradition; culture (anthropological sense)

wi'ika *n.* digging stick

wi'ira *adv.* drooping, sagging

    ~ cha'aka *iv.* be drooping

wi'ita *tv.* spin (thread)

wi'ite *iv.* make thread, be spinning

wi'okta *tv.* 1. unroll 2. take apart(~-, wiwi'okta); *cf.* veakta

wicha *n.* chips, splinters, kindling, thorn

wicha'apoi *n.* bullheads, goat heads (*Tribulus terrestris*; *syn.* chiva kovam, toorom)

wicha'arakim *n.* slingshot

wichakame *n.* 1. thistle 2. porcupine

wichalakas *n.* 1. cardinal (bird) 2. a Pascola song/dance played during kompaniya

wichik *n.* elf owl

wicho'e *n.* a plant *sp.*

wihhu'ute *iv.* carry on arm or back (wihhu'uti-, wiwihhu'ute) wihhu'utiria *n.* yoke

wihta *tv.* 1. sprinkle (re; particulate matter) 2. spin a firedrill to make fire (~-, wiwihta)

wihte *iv.* sprinkle (re: particulate matter; wihti-, wiwihte)

wii'i *n.* thread

wiike *tv.* 1. pull, stretch 2. draw, attract a crowd 3. ring church bell (wiik-, no *rdp.*); *cf.* wike, wikema; Vailam yee nau ~. A dance draws people.; Si senuk mukuk u kampaani wiikwa. If someone dies, the church bell is rung.
    yeu ~ *tv.* take it out/extricate

wiikit *n.* bird (*gen.*)

wiikwa *iv.* be rung (bell)

wiilo *n.* skinny person

wiiru *n.* turkey vulture

wiivis *n.* a bird *sp.*

Wikapa'am *n.* the Maypole Dance

wike *tv.* 1. take it out, extract (with yeu) 2. rub down (wik-, wiike); *cf.* wiike; Maala nee mam ~k. My mother rubbed my arm down.

wikema *iv.* be pulling; wiikema, keep on pulling

wikia *n.* string, rope, cord

wikiria *dv.* owe; a ~ tawa, remain in debt; Aapo nee mamni peesom ~. S/he owes me five dollars. Inepo tomita a ~n. I owed her/him some money.

wikiriame *n.* debtor

wikiriawame *n.* 1. debt 2. state of being in debt

wikit bwikam *n.* bird songs

wikit woki *n.* an edible wild green (*lit.* bird tracks)

wiko'i *n.* bow (weapon; *s.* wikoli)

Wiko'i Ya'ut *n.* Coyote Society

wikoli *n.* bow (*s.*; = wiko'i)

wikosa *n.* belt, waist

wikosam *n.* breechclout strings

wiksime *tv.* drag (~-, wiwiksime); Hamut kutata ~. The woman is dragging the stick.

wikui *n.* cachora (lizard *sp.*)

wilohko *adj.* delicate, thin, weak (people, animals); *cf.* vahviolai

winhuva *adj.* sweet smelling; Sewam ~. The flowers smell good.

winhuvasi(a) *adv.* sweetly; Ume kanteelam ~ veete. The candles are burning sweetly (giving off a pleasant odor).

wiroa *n.* vine (*gen.*)

wiroavakot *n.* vine snake

wisa'e *n.* large wooden cooking spoon

witalai *adj.* narrow (thin strip)

wite'eria *tv.* trap by netting (~-)

wite'i *n.* net, snare

witosa *n.* spider web, cobweb

witta *tv.* make a straight line (~-, wiwitta); U yoem yop'owe kutae ~k. The old man made a straight line with a stick.

witte *iv.* draw lines, write, make symbols (witti-, wiwitte)

witti *adv., adj.* 1. *adv.* straight, straight ahead 2. *adj.* correct(ed); Im luula ~ weene. Go straight through here. I voo'o ~ vo'oka. The road leads straight there. U hiosia ~. There's a lot of corrections on the paper.

witti nooka *iv.* talk straight

wituam *n.* charred bones

wi'ukta *tv.* swallow (~-, wiwi'ukta)

wi'ukte *iv.* swallow (wi'ukti-, wiwi'ukte)

wíuta *tv.* wave (~-, w'uwiuta)

wiúta *tv.* 1. tear down, demolish 2. spend (~-, wiwiœta); tomita ~, spend money; karita ~, tear a house down

Wivisim *n.* Huirivis

wo'i *n.* coyote; Woi ~ wo'olim wokim wo'oke. Two coyote twins scratching their legs (tongue twister).

    ~ bwikam *n.* Coyote songs

    ~ chomo *n.* Coyote dancer headgear (*syn.* ~ hiisa)

    ~ minai *n.* a plant *sp.* (*lit.* coyote melon)

    ~ sonim *n.* Coyote songs for pursuing the Deer

    ~ Yi'iwame *n.* Coyote dance (a Yoeme military society in which men are pledged as young boys to defend the Yoeme nation and initiated with a tobacco smoking ritual)

wo'oke *tv.* scratch (wok-, wowo'oke)

wo'okte *iv.* sink (in dirt, sand, or mud; wo'okti-; *cf.* ropte)

wo'olim *n.* twins (affectionate)

wo'orim *n.* twins; Senu huena, senu into tuu hiapsek. One is mean, while the other is good hearted (said of twins).

wo'ota *tv., iv.* 1. throw out 2. *iv.* spill out; separate (couple) (wo'oti-, woowo'ota); Aapo vaa'am yeu ~. She threw out the water. Váchiam yeu ~k. S/he accidentally threw out the seeds. Maria into Hose emo ~k. Mary and Joe got divorced. Emo ~k. The two of them separated.

wo'ote *iv.* 1. be spilled, strewn 2. be left by one's spouse (wo'oti-, woowo'ote)

wo'oti *adj.* spilled, strewn

wohana *tv.* dodge, try to get away from (wohan-, wohanna)

wohanria *tv.* avoid, dodge (~-)

wohmamni *num.* ten

    ~ ama mamni *num.* fifteen

    ~ ama naiki *num.* fourteen

    ~ ama senu *num.* eleven

~ ama vahi *num.* thirteen
~ ama vatani *num.* nineteen
~ ama vusani *num.* sixteen
~ ama wohnaiki *num.* eighteen
~ ama woi *num.* twelve
~ ama wovusani *num.* seventeen
~ taka *num.* two hundred
~ mpo *adv.* (at) ten o'clock (*syn.* diesempo)
~ sia *adv.* ten times

wohnaiki *num.* eight
~mpo *adv.* (at) eight o'clock (*syn.* ochompo)
~sia *adv.* eight times

wohokta *tv.* punch, drill hole (~-, wohowohokta)
wohokte *iv.* get a hole (wohokti-, wohowohokte)
wohoktila *adj.* pierced, punctured
woi *num.* two
~ tomi *n.* quarter (coin)
woi vahi *adj.* several (*obj.* woika vahika); Waka woika vahika lutu'uriata
ket inen kechia, eme a waata. It is these several truths you want.
Imin te yeu te hoteka, woika vahika sea hipetampo yeu te hoteka
(*s.*). Over here we sit out, several on the flower mat, sitting out.
woikatana *adv.* on both sides
woimpo *adv.* (at) two o'clock
woisia *adv.* twice, two times
woita *tv.* untie (~-, woiwoita)
woiwe *adv.* in two parts; ~ ama aayuk. There's two aspects to this.
wok *comb.* of wokim, feet/legs
~ chava'i, *n.* calf (leg)
~ hiapsi, *n.* sole
~ himari, *n.* a game like soccer
~ himawame, *n.* a game like soccer
~ koreo *n.* relay runner, messenger
~ kuria, *iv.* 1. tangle one's feet 2. trip over one's own feet
~ move'i, *n.* top of foot
~ ota, *n.* leg/foot bones
~ pusiam, *n.* toe
~ sutum, *n.* toenail
~ tate, *n.* tendon, nerves (of leg or foot)
~ techuniam, *n.* grime (foot)
~ tomam, *n.* calf muscles
~ tuaka *n.* pine cone
~ Vake'o, *n.* Walking Cowboy
~ veta'i, *n.* instep, sole (*loc.* wok veta'aku)
~ voo'o, *n.* trail, foot path, path
wokek *iv.* have legs, feet
wokim *n.* feet, legs (*s.* wole)

wokita hoa *tv.* take a step (slightly archaic in usage)

wokkoi *n.* mourning dove

wokkoi aaki *n.* a cactus *sp.*

wokla *n.* footprint, track; *cf.* chepti

wokleo *n.* infantry soldier, trooper

woko *n.* pine (tree; Pinus spp.)
  ~ taaka *n.* pine cone

wokovavase'ela *n.* swallow (bird)

wokte₁ *tv.* track (wokti-, wokwokte); ouseita ~, track a mountain lion

wokte₂ *iv.* put on pants (~, wookte); karsetiinim ~, put on socks; Aapo aana ~k. S/he dressed her/himself.

wokti *n.* step

woktesime *iv.* tread

woktua *tv.* dress someone

wokwante *iv.* pain (foot, leg)

wole *n.* legs (*s.*; = wokim); ~kame, one having legs

womta *tv.* scare, frighten, startle, astonish (~-, womwomta)

womte *iv.* be frightened, astonished (womti-, womwomte)

womtia *n.* sickness (from fright)

womtila *adj.* frightened

womtiwame *n.* surprise, astonishment, wonder

woo'o *n.* mosquito

woo'ochi *n.* grasshopper

wooho'oria *n.* hole

wooki *n.* foot, hoof, paw
  ~ haiwa, *tv.* track; Aman em a wooki haiwa. You are tracking it.

wookte *rdp.* of wokte₂, put on pants

woora *n.* cap

woosa *adv.* twice

wootovoli *s. var.* of wotovo

wotovo *n.* a shrub with white flowers (*Cardia parvifolia*; *s.* wootovoli)

wotte *iv.* in: ka ~, be reserved, taciturn (stem does not occur alone; wooti-, wotwotte)

wovusani *num.* seven

wovusanimpo *adv.* (at) seven o'clock

wovusanisia *adv.* seven times

Y

ya'a- *comb.* of hoa, do/make

ya'ane *n.* 1. shape, form 2. foundation

ya'ari *adj.* made; hunen ~, it has been made like that

ya'aria *dv.* make; Inepo karita a ~k. This house was made a long time ago.

ya'atek *iv.* quit (momentarily); Apo hiohte ~. He quit writing (for now).

ya'avae *tv.* try, attempt

ya'awak *adj.* made; I kari winvwatuk ~. This house was made a long time ago.

ya'e'etia *iv.* yelp (ya'e'eti-)

ya'uchim *n.* big beads in rosary

ya'uchiwa *n.* 1. leadership 2. God, Jesus

ya'ura *n.* 1. authority, leadership, reign 2. religious society 3. power, right 4. council

ya'uram *n.* government

ya'ut *n.* chief, leader

yaa *tv.* 1. do, make 2. proceed, go ahead according to plan 3. found, establish (ya'a-); *cf.* aayu, haleksia, yaate; A te a ya'ane. We'll go ahead (as planned). Vem nasionta ~k. They founded a nation. ili ___ta ~, shorten; Te ili orita te ya'ane. We'll shorten it.

yaaha *rdp.* of yaha, arrive (*pl.*)

yaak *pst.* of hoa, do/make

yaakame *n.* producer, maker, manufacturer

yaate *iv.* finish up, stop (activity) (yaati-, yaayate)

yaati *adj.* complete, end

yaatitua *tv.* stop

yaatituari *adj.* stopped, ceased, lapsed

yaave *n.* faucet; ~ chakte. The faucet is leaking.

yaavem *n.* key

yaayate *rdp.* of· yaate, finish

yaha *iv.* arrive (*pl.*; *sg.* yepsa; yai-, yaaha); yaahisukame, the ones that used to come; ~'em. Come in (polite invitation). Alleaka ~'em. Come in happiness.

yahame *n.* arriving persons

yai- *comb.* of yaha, arrive (*pl.*)

yaiwa'apo, nau *n.* conference

yamyamti *adv.* loudly (with nooka)

yantam *n.* tire (vehicle)

yantela *adj.* carefree, not worried, not concerned, confident (*var.* yante'ela; *cf.* suatea)

yantelwame *n.* peace, being calm and relaxed
    ~ yaa *tv.* make peace

yanti *adj.* quiet, peaceful

yanti maachi *iv.* peaceful, calm, quiet, still, well-behaved

yantia *iv.* behave

yantiachi *adj.* well behaved

yantitua *tv.* pacify, soothe; Apo ili usita ~. She is making the child quiet.

yaplo *n.* devil

Yasikue *n.* an enchanted mountain by Guasimas

yatitua *tv.* make stop; Apo a asoawa bwan ~. She is making her baby stop crying.

yatta *tv.* sip (*syn.* chipta; ~-, yatyatta)

yavarai *n.* flounder (fish)

yavemmea etapo *tv.* unlock

yayatitua *tv.* try to get one to stop crying

ye'e *iv.* dance (*pst.* ~ka, yi'i-, yeye'e); Have Maso yi'ivae ian tukapo? Who is going to dance the Deer tonight?

ye'eka *n.* one who danced

yea *adv. var.* of yea'a, out

yea'a *adv.* out, outwards (*var.* yea)

yeabwise *tv.* snitch, inform on (yeabwih-, yeabwibwise)

yeatoha *tv.* take outside (*sg. obj.; pl. obj.* yewamtoha; yeatoi-, yeatotoha); Inepo sankoata ~k. I took out the trash.

yecha *tv.* 1. put, set, place it 2. take off (clothing) 3. awaken, get someone up (*sg. obj.; pl.* hoa₂; yechá'a-, yeecha); Vempo tu'isi au a ~k am ánia"i'akai. They appealed to him to help them. Vempo haivu nau a yecha'alatukan vem hoarata naatevaekai. They have already made the arrangements to establish a village.

    au a ~ *dv.* make an earnest request

    teawam ~ *tv.* sign (signature; *syn.* firmaroa)

    nokiu vicha ~, *tv.* interpret, translate

yecha'ala *n.* plan, design

yecha'ari *adj.* set, appointed (date)

    ~ taewai *n.* date, appointment

yee *pn.* people in general (used only as an *obj.*)

    ~ a'asoatuame, *n.* midwife

    ~ a'awiria *iv.* fattening

    ~ hihittome *n.* doctor (*syn.* lootor)

    ~ eteoria *tv.* talk relate news

    ~ hihikkaituanme *n.* hearing aid

    ~ Hunaktekame *n.* Creator

    ~ kekeme *n.* biting animal or insect

    ~ mahte *dv.* teach

    ~ mahmahtame *n.* teacher

    ~ mikwame *n.* gift

    ~ nakwame *n.* caring, loving compassionate person

    ~ nanasonteme *n.* sorcerer, witch

    ~ omta *tv.* hate, despise

    ~ ovetave *tv.* make a person lazy; Apo ne ovetavek. He made me lazy.

    ~ sisivome *n.* sorcerer

    ~ sivowame *n.* curse, hex

    ~ sussuame *n.* killer, murderer

    ~ vaitatta'ame *n.* dishonest person

    ~ vaitatta'a *iv.* be a trickster, deceiver

    ~ vemmumucha *n.* whipper

    ~ vicha *tv.* read someone's mind

    ~ yo'ore *iv.* be respectful, considerate, polite

    ~ yo'oriwa, *n.* respect (the act of respecting)

    ~ yo'oriwame *n.* respect

yeecha *rdp.* of yecha, put

yeeka *iv.* 1. capable, able 2. dominate, govern (~-, no *rdp.*); ka mamam ~ *iv.* be paralyzed in the arms

yeepsa *rdp.* of yepsa, arrive (*sg.*)

yeesa iv sit down (*sg.*; used in *imp.* only); *cf.* yehte

yeete *iv.* doze off, fall asleep (~-, yeeyete)

yeetem *n.* drowsiness, sleepiness; ~ ne womtavae. I'm warding off sleepiness.

yeewa *tv.* 1. play with 2. caress, fondle (yewá-, yeyewa)

yeewari *adj.* has been played with

yeewe *iv.* play (yew-, yeyewe)

yeewi *adv.* towards outside (*var.* yeu); *cf.* yewim, pa'akuni

yehte *iv.* 1. sit down, settle down 2. land (ship, airplane) (*sg. subj.*; *imp.* yeesa'e, ~-, *rdp.* yehyehte, prob. yeehte; *pl.* hoote); *cf.* yeesa amae ~ *iv.* change one's mind

yehtetua *tv.* seat

yeka *n.* 1. nose 2. hood (of car)
   ~ pohna *n.* bloody nose
   ~ woho'oriam *n.* nostrils

yeka'ara *n.* big-nosed

yeleo *n.* refrigerator

yena *tv.* smoke (yen-, yeyena)

yepsa *iv.* arrive (*sg.*; *pl.* yaha; yevis- or yevih-, yeepsa); Yuku ~k. The rain came.

yepsame *n.* arriving person

yervawena *n.* mint (plant)

yet *adv.* 1. about, here and there 2. about other people; ~ nonoka. (S/he) talks about other people.
   ~ nokwame *n.* gossip
   ~ nooka *iv.* gossip

yeu *adv.* 1. out (*s.* yewi, yeulu, yewilu, yewulu) 2. outwards, towards outside (*var.* yeewi); ~ im kaáte, walking out; ~ im saka, (they) left
   ~ bwikam *n.* play songs
   ~ chuchupe *iv.* develop, manifest
   ~ hiiwe *iv.* peek out
   ~ kakatwa'apo *n.* exit (passage)
   ~ machia *iv.* appear (vision), come out (something new)
   ~ poota *tv.* push aside; yeu a pootak, pushed it aside
   ~ pua *tv.* appoint
   ~ sasakawa'apo *n.* branch off, exit (freeway)
   ~ siime *iv.* happen, occur, transpire
   ~ sikame *n.* event
   ~ tahtia *adv.* throughout
   ~ toha *tv.* deport (*sg. obj.*; *pl.* yeu weiya)
   ~ ve'e *tv.* exceed, surpass

~ vuite *iv.* escape (*pl.* ~ tenne)
~ watta *tv.* throw out
~ we *iv.* be coming up (sun, moon)
~ wo'ota, *tv.* throw away, throw out
~ wike *tv.* extract, withdraw, pull it out; Vempo orota
      kawimpo ~ wike. They extract gold out of the mountains.
~ wokte *iv.* take off (garments below waist)
~ yoemtu *iv.* be born
~ yoemtukapo *n.* birthplace
yeu'ave'a *tv.* save, reserve (yeu'avi'i-, yeu'aveve'a)
yeu'aveve'a *tv.* leave out, exclude
yeuleo *n.* player (game, sports)
yeulu *adv.* out (*s.*; = yeu)
yeusu *adv.* (*s.* yeulu)
yeuwame *n.* 1. game, sport 2. drama, skit
yevicha *iv.* have a particular attitude (with haana or tu'isi)
yevih- *comb.* of yepsa, arrive (*sg.*)
yevis- *comb.* of yepsa, arrive (*sg.*)
yevuku *n.* forager, hermit, hunter (forager)
Yevuku Yoeme *n.* Forager
yew- *comb.* of yeewe, play
yewá- *comb.* of yeewa, play with
yewa'ave'ene *tv.* leave out (for convenience)
yewamtoha *tv.* take out (*pl. obj.*; *sg.* yeatoha)
yeweli *adv. var.* of yewi
yewi(lu) *adv.* out (*s.*; = yeu)
yewulu *adv.* out (*s.*; = yeu); Aa sewailo malichi ~ siika (*s.*). The
      beflowered fawn went out.
yeye'eme *n.* dancer
yeyename *n.* smoker
yi'i- *comb.* of ye'e, dance
yi'ireo *n.* dancer
yi'iriawa *iv.* dance for someone
yi'itevo *iv.* sponsor a dance; Vempo yoko ~ne. They're sponsoring a
      dance tomorrow.
yi'itua *tv.* make someone dance
yi'iwa *n.* dance (event)
yi'iwame *n.* dance (act of dancing)
yo *adj.* enchanted (*s.* yosi)
    ~'ota hamne *iv.* will arrive in the presence of God
    ~ An'a *n.* Enchanted World (the supernatural world, the essence
      of the huya an'a or its spiritual dimension which gives
      humans, including the pahko'ola and Deer dancer, powers
      and ability to do perform the rituals connected with the Yo
      An'a; said to be reached in several days time or through a
      special caves or springs; *cf.* Sea An'a)

~ chiva'ato *n.* enchanted goat

~ hiapsiwame, *n.* eternal life

~ ho'ara *n.* enchanted home

~ Mumuli *n.* Enchanted Bee (*syn.* Sea Hamut; some versions of the myth have both ~ Mumuli and Sea Hamut as twin sisters who interpret for the Talking Tree)

~ Vaa'am *n.* Enchanted Water

~ vakau *n.* a bamboo *sp.* (perhaps *Chuskea* or *Arandinaria*)

~ ya'awa *iv.* become a leader

~ yi'iwak *n.* dance of enchantment

~ Yi'iwaka'apo, *n.* place where they had a dance of enchantment before the arrival of the Spanish which is barren, not even having weeds; the ones who rejected baptism went underground to form their own existence as Surem

~ ya'awak, *adj.* being completed (made into an elder by marrying one off)

~ yoleme *n.* enchanted person

yo'o *tv.* win (yo'—-, yoyo'o)

yo'okame *n.* victor, winner, champion

yoko muu'u *n.* spotted owl

yo'oliwa *iv.* be respected (*s.*; *cf.* yo'oriwa)

yo'ora *n.* elders, ancestors (*syn.* yo'owam)

yo'ore *tv.* respect, venerate (yo'ori-, yoyo'ore)

yo'ori *adv.* respectable (with maisi; *var.* yoriwa)

yo'oria *tv.* win for

yo'oriwa *iv.* be respected, sacred (*syn.* yo'oliwa); Wa karpeta ~. The carpet (the deer singers sit on) is respected.

taewai ~ *n.* birthday

yo'oriwame *n.* 1. respected person 2. respect

yo'oritevo *tv.* make self respectable (~-, no. *rdp.*)

yo'otu *iv., adj.* mature, grow old or tall (~-, yoyo'otu ~ yo'oyo'otu); hapti ~, grow tall (persons); tevesi ~, grow tall (plants); ke a ~o..., before it gets old (while still young)

yo'otui *n.* old person, elder (affectionate *var.* yo'otuli; *pl.* yoyo'otuim)

Yo'otui Hahawa *n.* Maundy Thursday (*lit.* running of the honored Old Man)

yo'oturia *iv.* raise (child); *tv.* grow (in skills or maturity; used with reflexive); Vempo emo ~. They are making themselves grow.

yo'owam *n.* elders (collectively), ancestors; *var.* yo'ora

yo'owe *n.* elder

yo'owe kus *n.* village cross

yoa *tv., iv.* 1. *tv.* shake, rock (cradle, hammock) 2. *iv.* tremble (*pst.* ~n, yoo-, yoyoa)

au ~ *iv.* shiver

yoawa *n.* animal (*gen.*); wild animals

~ lotoor *n.* veterinarian
~ noki *n.* language of the animals
~ta hippuwa'apo *n.* zoo
yoem *n. comb.* of yoeme, person/Yoeme (Yaqui)
    ~ chupia *n.* condemned person
    ~ noka *iv.* speak Yoeme
    ~ noki *n.* the Yoeme language
    ~ nokpo *adv.* in the Yoeme language
    ~ Pueplo *n.* Yoem Pueblo (at Marana)
yoeme *n.* person, human (*s.* yoleme; *comb.* yoem)
yoemia *n.* 1. family 2. the Yoemes (collectively) (*var.* yoemria)
yoemiak *iv.* have a child or children
yoemiarim *n.* children
yoemiawam *n.* offspring (children)
yoemra *n.* humanity
yoemria *var.* of yoemia, family
yoemte *iv.* make into a person (~-)
yoemtu *iv.* 1. be born 2. become an adult (~-)
yoemtukapo *n.* birthplace, (hometown in: a yeu ~)
Yoemtuwame *n.* being a person, Yoeme
yoene *iv.* (used in certain fixed invitations)
    siok ~ *exp.* cheer up, keep your chin up (even though you're sad
        or in mourning)
    suka ~ *exp.* warm yourself, come and sit by the fire
    vaa ~ *exp.* have a drink of water
    vali ~ *exp.* come cool off
yoeria *n.* insect, bug (*gen.*)
Yoeta *n.* sound of the spirit of the wilderness(or the spirit itself which
    roams the wilds whistling), sometimes thought of as a cowboy
yoh- *comb.* of yosia, warm up
yohte *iv.* 1. fall, drop (rain, precipitation, particles) 2. shed (fur) (yohti-,
    yohyohte)
Yoi *n.* Mexican
    ~ muunim *n.* black-eyed peas
    ~ noki *n.* Spanish (language)
    ~ sana *n.* sugarcane (*Saccharum officinarum*)
    ~ yi'iwa *n.* European dance
yoka *tv.* paint, mark, color (yoká'a-), (yoyoka)
yokak *adj.* colored
yoka'i *n.* picture, painting, mark
yoki *iv.* be stained (yok-)
yoko *n. comb.* of yo—ko, tommorrow
    ~ ketwo *adv.* tomorrow morning (*syn.* yokosu)
    ~ matchuko *adv.* day after tomorrow , tomorrow morning
yokok *adj.* stained

yokoriapo *adv.* the next day

yokosu *adv.* tomorrow morning (*syn.* yoko ketwo)

yokta *tv.* stain (~-, yoyokta)

yokte *iv.* stain (yokti-, yoyokte)

yokti *adj.* stained

yoleme *n.* person (in song language)

yoliwa *n.* sacred, respected

yoo- *comb.* of yoa, shake

yoo *adj.* old (animates)

    ~ chapayeka *n.* head Chapayeka

    ~ chupa *iv.* live to a ripe old age

    ~ hamut *n.* 1. older woman 2. woman in charge of a society

    ~ maehto *tn.* head maestro

    ~ monaha *n.* head Matachin dancer

    ~ pahko'ola *n.* head pascola

    ~ woo'ochi *n.* large grasshopper *sp.*

    ~ yuuma *tv.* overpower, conquer

yóoko *adj., n.* spotted, jaguar

    ~ muunim, *n.* pinto beans

yoóko *adv.* tomorrow

    ~ kupteo *adv.* tomorrow evening

yóokote *iv.* make multicolored

yoopi'opi'okte *iv.* go up and down

Yoroona *n.* the Llorona (folkloric figure); In achai chea Yoronta au vitlatia. My father saw the Llorona.

yoore *iv.* heal (any part of body; yoré'e-, yoyore)

yoosi *adv.* just because; Empo ~ta tekipanoa. Just because you're working...

yooyopna *rdp.* of yopna, answer

yoré'e- *comb.* of yoore, heal

yopna *tv.* answer, reply (~-, yooyopna); Iniamak emo nok ~, wa tampaleo into wa aapaleo. The fife-drum player and harpist answer each other in this way.

yopnawame *n.* reply, answer

Yori *n.* 1. Mexican (*var.* Yoi) 2. humanoid Chapayeka mask

yosi *adj.* 1. hot, heated 2. esteemed, venerable 3. enchanted (*s.*; = yo); *cf.* yossia; Ala aman tewekapo tua ~ maachi (*s.*). Well, there in heaven it truly appears enchanted.

    ~ eiya *tv.* adore, love, cherish

    ~ hia *iv.* say good things about

yosia *tv.* warm up (yoh-, yossia)

yossia *iv.* get hot, heat up readily (~-)

yotohta *iv.* become dull (used only with bwawi, sharp)

yotohti *adv.* with a thud or clank

yotta *tv.* depress, press a single spot (~-, yotyotta)

yotti *adj.* pressed (*ex.*: button); Haivu ~tukan. It was already pressed.

yotui kova *n.* a cactus *sp.*

yotuli *n.* old person

Yoyo Kawi *n.* Enchanted Mountain

yoyo'ora *n.* elders (collectively), ancestors

yoyo'otuk *adj.* big, old (*pl.*; *cf.* yo'otu)

yoyo'otukan *iv.* old-timer, long term resident

yoyo'owam *n.* ancestors

yoyoma *adj.* enchanting (*s.*)

yu *interj.* hey, look, behold (*var.* yuu at the beginning of an utterance);
    Vicha, yu! Hey, look~ Yuu, sochik! Look, a bat!

yu'a *tv.* push (yu'u-, yuyu'a)

yu'e *tv.* 1. able to open, unfasten, undo 2. able to convince; control, domi-
    nate, boss around (yu'i-, yuyu'e); Vempo ka am ~. They can't
    control them.

yu'u- *comb.* of yuume, get tired

yu'uni *adv., n.* 1. *adv.* much 2. *n.* plenty, abundance; *cf.* yuin(i)

yu'uria *tv.* push

yuin(i) *adv.*, 1. *adv.* a lot, much (amounts; *cf.* ousi, unna); ~ chuvva, in a
    little while longer
    ~ ea *iv.* feel better
    ~ tekwak *iv.* 1. be pleasingly plump, stocky (people) 2. be meaty
        (animals) 3. have a strong flavor

yuke *iv.* rain (*pst.* yukuk, yuk-, yuyuke)

yuku *n.* 1. rain (yuke'epo, in the rain) 2. paloverde beetle
    ~ bwikam *n.* rain song
    ~ chaktia *n.* raindrop
    ~ heka *n.* thunderstorm, storm
    ~ hima'i *n.* lightening strike, bolt of lightening
    ~ himak *iv.* be a lightening strike
    ~ Naamu, *n.* Storm Cloud (wife of the god Yuku, Rain)
    ~ omte *iv.* thunder
    ~ ruutia *iv.* thunder
    ~ ve'oktia *n.* lightening
    ~ ve'okte *iv.* be lightening out (tongue)
    ~ wiroata saila *n.* a plant *sp.*

yum *adv. var.* of um, there

yuma *iv.* reach a point in time, attain a goal (*pst.* yumuk; yumá'a-,
    yuyyuma); Kaveta au ~suk. No one has attained it. Kia ne
    Yevuku Yolemta wikoli ne yo ~takai... ka ne huni into ne inia
    ániat ne na ne welamsisimne (s). Yevuku Yoleme's bow over-
    powered me... never again will I, on this world, be walking
    around. In noki ka au ~'ane. May my words not reach her/him
    (in speaking of the deceased).

yumá'a- *comb.* of yuuma$_2$, capable

yuma'i *n.* complete or right amount; Vempo ~k a makak. They gave the
    right amount.

183

ka ~ *n.* freak (mentally disabled or physically deformed)
yuma'isi(a) *adv.* completely, entirely; Aapo yuma'isia lionokak. S/he
    prayed completely.
yumhoe *iv.* rest (~-, yumhohhoe)
yumhoek *iv.* be rested (*pst.* ~an, *fut.* yumhoene)
yumhoene *exp.* come take a rest, take a load off your feet
yumhoiria *n.* relief
yumia *iv.* be exhausted (~-, yuyumia; *s.* yumila; *cf.* lotte); tekilpo ~,
    exhausted from working
yumila *iv.* be exhausted (*s.*; = yumia); vuiti ~, exhausted from running (*s.*)
yumvaekai *iv.* tire one's self (no tenses other than *pres.* usual)
yuu *interj.* look
Yuuma$_1$ *n.* Yuma, Quechan
yuuma$_2$ *iv., tv.* 1. *iv.* capable (of carrying, holding up) 2. *tv.* overcome,
    overpower (~-, yumá'a-, yuyuma)
    ka au ~ *iv.* be agile
yuume *iv.* get tired (yum-, yuyume)
yuutu in: ka ~ *iv.* be persistent
yuuya *adj.* antique, old-fashioned; shabby
yuva(li) *iv.* wash one's self, bathe (*s.*; = uva)
yuyuma'isi *adv.* completely, totally
yuyyuma *rdp.* of yuma, reach a point

ENGLISH-YOEME DICTIONARY

A

a lot *adv.* ama vutti (desire greatly), ousi (with much energy), tokta, tu'isi, unna (excessive amount), yuin (amount)

abalone *n.* veeko

abandon *tv.* sutoha

abandoned *adj.* hima'ari

abate *iv.* soute (swelling)

ability *n.* moreakame (have psychic ~)

about *iv.* naawe (move ~)

abundance *n.* yu'uni

able *iv.* aawe

able *iv.* aawe, waatimachi (~ to remember); *adv.* aa (can, be able)

about *adv.* aet (concerning the topic of), havesake (~ to do), inaeko (~ this time), naa (around, here and there), yet (about/concerning a person); *postp.* -t, -met (~ the topic of) Aapo vihtammet nooka. S/he is talking about the movies. tomit nooka, talking about money

about to *suf.* -vae, -vao; *suf.* -nama (go about doing); *adv.* ave, havesaka

above *postp.* vepasu

abroad *iv.* mekkaikut weama (be ~)

absent *adv.* kaave; *iv.* ve'e

absolutely *adv.* ama vutti (entirely)

absorb *tv.* namya (mentally)

abstain *iv.* hioria

abundance *n.* yu'uni

acacia *n.* hohohna, hu'upa keka'ala (catclaw acacia)

accelerate *iv.* uttea weye

accent *n.* noki uttewa (stress), hachin nooka (way of speaking)

accept *tv.* maveta

acceptance *n.* waatiawa

accepted *adj.* valiaroa (in accord with convention)

accident *n.* nau tahte (kaarom nau tahte, auto ~); *iv.* ka tu'isi au yeu siika (come out badly)

accompany *tv.* kompanyaroa, voo toha (~ a short distance)

accomplish *tv.* yuma (with *refl. obj.*)

accomplishment *n.* chupa'i, ya'ari

according to *postp.* a hiapo amani, nokapo amani (nokapo amani Davidta, according to David)

account, give an *tv.* teuwa

account of, on *postp.* vetchi'ivo

accurately *tv.* tu'i teuwa (tell ~), luturiata teuwa (tell the truth)

accuse *tv.* kulparoa, na'ateo
ache *iv.* wante
achieve *tv.* chupak (attained goal)
achievement *n.* chupa'awame (act of doing), chupa'i (completion of goal)
acknowledge *tv.* teuwa
acorn *n.* kusim
acquainted *iv.* tuisi eu weche (be ~); *tv.* ta'a
acquire *tv.* nu'e
acrobat *n.* maomeo, maromeo, ro'aro'akteme
acrobatics *iv.* marooma (do ~)
across *adv.* wasala (with static predicates), wam (with predicates
        of motion)
act *iv.* aane; *tv.* weiya; *suf.* (~ as)
action *n.* anwame (deed)
activity *iv.* weye (be going on, be ~)
actually *conj.* o'oven ta (really)
adapt *tv.* sauwa (make use of)
adaptation *n.* sauwawame
add *tv.* ama kiima
addition *adv.* ama navuhtia (in ~ to); *n.* nau kimawame
additional *adj.* navuhti; Vempo ~ mamni peesom waata. They need five
        additional dollars.
address *n.* domisilio
adequate *adv.* tu'isi; Vempo ka ~ nawa yechalatukan. They didn't have an
        adequate plan.
adjective *n.* adhetivo
adjust *iv.* hoiwa (get used to; Ringonokiu ~, get used to English; u
        yoemtau ~, get used to that person); *tv.* tu'ute
administration *n.* nesaweme
admire *tv.* tuu eiya
admiration *n.* tuu eiyawame
admission *n.* hiawame (acknowledgement), kivachame (act of allowing to
        enter), kivachawame (one who is admitted)
admit *iv.* kavaeka hunen hia (acknowledge as true); *tv.* kivacha (allow
        to enter)
adobe *n.* saami (brick); *tv.* sami hoa (make ~)
adopt *tv.* nu'e (child), sauwa (new idea or practice; *d.o.* in English is *obj.*
        of *postp.* -u)
adore *tv.* tu'ule
adult *n.* yo'owe
advance *adv.* lauti (early); *iv.* chewasu ha'amu (in skills); *tv.* k'imu (attack)
advanced *tv.* tu'isi hita ta'a (know well)
advantage *adv.* ama, amani; kaita ama anne, there is no advantage
adverb *n.* advervio
advertisement *n.* komersial
advice *n.* konseho, noktehwa; *tv.* nok hikkaila (heed ~)

advise *tv.* konseharoa
advocate *tv.* nokria
affair *n.* newosio (matter, concern, business), yeusikame (event)
affectionate *n.* tu'uliwame
affirm *tv.* teuwa, hewite
afraid *adj.* mahai; *iv.* mahaika (be ~)
after *adv.* ae amapo, natcha'aka (one ~ another)
afternoon *adv.* kupteo (late ~)
again *adv.* intuchia, huchi(a), huchi senu (one more time); ka huni
        (never ~)
against *postp.* vehe'eri
agave *n.* kuu'u, huya kuu'u (wild ~), wah kuu'u (cultivated ~)
age *exp.* ___ vewit weye (be same age; *ex.* ne vewit weye, same age
        as me)
ago *adv.* vehako (a while ~), vinwatuko (a long time ~)
agony *iv.* tiukove (be in ~)
agree *tv.* nau ea
agreeable *iv.* hootu
ahead *adv.* aepat, vach'a (~ of), vansea; *postp.* -pat
ahead, go *interj.* vanseka
airplane *n.* wiikit, eroplano
algae *n.* numerokoa
alike *iv.* nana'ana (be ~)
alive *iv.* hiapsa
all *pn.* si'ime, si'imem; chiktia
all in all *adv.* nat welisia
all over *adv.* si'imkut (from all directions), si'imekuttana (in all
        directions), si'imekunvicha (towards all directions)
alley *n.* kayehon
allow *tv.* hewiteria
allow for *adv.* ka vaeka
almost *interj.* have; *adv.* ave, avesu, avesula,vatte, avetuko, avetuk(o)
        (~ time for)
alone *n.* apelai
along *postp.* -tana, -vétana, vewichi (~ side of); *suf.* -ma (go ~ doing)
aloud *adv.* kusisia
alphabet *n.* hiohtei
already *adv.* tevei, veha, haivu; *suf.* -la
also *adv.* kechia, ket
altar *n.* altaria
Altar Guild *n.* Kiyohteim, Kiyohtei Yo'owe (head), Kiyohtei (member)
alternate *tv.* remoa
although *conj.* o'oven
altogether *adv.* malokai, si'imenawi
always *adv.* hiva, hubwuni
amaranth *n.* wee'e

ambassador *n.* noktotohame
amenable *iv.* hootu
amiable *adj.* tu hiapsek
amount *pn.* yuma'i (right ~); *n.* veleki (*obj.* ~ka); *iv.* kaitapo tawane
    (~ to nothing)
ammunition *n.* huiwa
amusing *adj.* musa'aule
ancient *iv.* winwatu (be ~)
and *conj.* into
angel *n.* anheles, anhelito (little ~)
anger *n.* kuhteerim, omtiwame, kuhtewame (act of being angry)
angler *n.* vo'areo
Anglo *n.* Riingo
angry *adj.* o'omtila (already ~); *iv.* omte, kuhtea, omtiwame (get ~); *tv.*
    o'omtitua (make ~)
anguish *n.* hiokot aneme
anguished *iv.* hiokot aane
animal *n.* yoawa (*gen.*)
anise *n.* anisim
ankles *n.* tero'okim
anniversary *n.* wasuktia yumak, lutupahko (death ~), taewai yo'oriwa
    (birthday)
announce *tv.* yee tehwa, publikaroa
announcement *n.* yee tehwawame
announcer *n.* yee tetehwame
annoy *tv.* haiti eetua, suateatua
annoyed *iv.* suatea (be ~; suati + ea), kuhteiya (be very ~)
annoying *iv.* haitiachisi maachi
annually *adv.* chikti wasuktiapo
another *pn.* ta'abwi, seenu; *adv.* senu wéeme (in ~ vein)
answer *n.* yopnawame; *tv.* yopna
antique *adj.* yuuya
ants *n.* eeye (red ~), eesukim (sugar ~), mochomo (drive\r, leaf-cutter ~),
    hoovo'e (orange-red ~)
anus *n.* chomim
anxiety *n.* suati eewame
anxious *adj.* chumumutea
any *pn.* waáte (re: humans); ka + [verb] (*ex.* empo ka tomek? don't you
    have any money?)
any way *adv.* hakku'uvotana
anyhow *adv.* hachin huni(')
anyone *pn.* have huni('i)
anything *pn.* hita huni('i)
anywhere *adv.* hakhuni, hakun huni('i)
Apache *n.* Hapa'achi; *adj.* Haapat
apart *adj.* naikim tei (taken ~); *iv.* sookte (fall ~); *tv.* kookta (pull ~)

apartment *n.* hoaram
apex *n.* hikachi
apologize *iv.* au hiokoe
apology *n.* emo hiokoewame
apostle *n.* apohtolo
apparent *adj.* hunakiachi
apparently *adv.* hunakiasachi hivatua
appeal *n.* tu'isi yecha'awame (request); *tv.* au a yecha (earnest request)
appeal to *iv.* weche; *tv.* tu'isi tu'ule
appear *iv.* maachi(often with adverbs of manner), yeu machia (come into vision, appear in a vision)
applaud *tv.* mam tohte
apple *n.* mansaana
application *n.* ehkuela hiosia (school), tekil hiosia (work)
apply *tv.* hiosiam tapunia (written request), venta (spread a layer), a hiap-simak tekipanoa (work hard; hoa may substitute for tekipanoa)
appoint *tv.* yeu pua
appointed *iv.* yeu puawa (be ~), ya'awa (be ~)
appointment *n.* taewa yecha'ari (date); *iv.* [noun] + katek (*ex.* kovanaopo katek, have the appointment as governor)
appraise *tv.* vehe'ewata yecha
appraisal *n.* vehe'ewa yecha'awame
appreciate *tv.* tu'ure, vaisae
apprentice *n.* mahtawame
approach *iv.* heela ansime, aavo rukte
apricot *n.* avrekooki
April *n.* Avril
arch *n.* sawan, arko
arching *adv.* tonna
area *n.* pa'aria (open), bwia (region)
argue *iv.* voe
arm *n.* koomim, komia (chair)
army *n.* sontaom
armpit *n.* seekam
around *adv.* bwikola, chikola, naa, kowila (circumference), konila (motion); *iv.* aane, anwa (be ~)
arrange *tv.* nau a yecha (in a particular order), tu'ute (set in order), ánia (help, provide opportunity)
arrangement *n.* yecha'ala (order, plan)
arrest *tv.* bwise
arrested *iv.* bwihwa (be ~)
arrive *iv.* yepsa (*sg.*), yaha (*pl.*)
arrogant *iv.* au hitale (be ~)
arrow *n.* huiwa, vaaka huiwa (cane ~), chumuria (~ notch)
arrowhead *n.* vika
arroyo *n.* hakia

art *n.* arte
artery *n.* ohvo wi'im
article *n.* artikulo
artist *n.* hihyokame
as *postp.* vena, venasi(a); *postp.* -levena; *conj.* -ka, -kai (~, while); *suf.* -kai
    (~ a result)
as well as *conj.* into
as far as *adv.* [pronoun]-mak kaachin (*ex.* neemak kaachin, as far as I am
    concerned)
as if *interj.* hitasu; *adv.* tuata venasia, maisi
as long as *adv.* ketun
as soon as *adv.* -k (*ex.* Hose yepsak ne siime, I'm going as soon as Joe
    arrives)
ascend *iv.* ha'amu
Ash Wednesday *n.* Naposauwa
ashamed *iv.* tiiwe
aside *adv.* sekkatana (to one side)
ashes *n.* naposa
ask *tv.* temai; *iv.* takease (~ favor)
ask about *tv.* nattemai
ask for *tv.* a'awa, nattemai, netane; *dv.* netanria
asking *n.* nattemaiwame
asleep *iv.* koche (be sleeping), kilimaichia (limb)
aspirin *n.* pahtiam
ass *n.* vuuru (animal)
assemble *iv.* mochakte, nau yaha; *tv.* nau toha
assert *tv.* lutu'uriatia
assess *tv.* vehe'ewata yecha
assets *n.* tomi
assembly *n.* hunta
assist *tv.* ánia
assistance *n.* ániawame, servisio
assistant *n.* yee a'aniame
associate *n.* emo a'aniame (mutual helpers), nau cha'akame (associate
    together); *tv.* nau am tamachia (connect ideas)
association *n.* sosiedadim
assume *tv.* hunuen eiya
assumption *n.* hunuen yee eiyame (a may substitute for yee)
assure *tv.* au mimika
astonish *tv.* womta
astonished *iv.* womte (be ~)
astonishment *n.* womtiwame
astray *tv.* naiyote (lead ~)
at *postp.* -po-, -chi
at any rate *adv.* in a hu'uneiyapo
at ease *iv.* yantela (be relaxed)

at first *adv.* chea vat
at hand *adv.* haivu a ayuk
at last *adv.* ultimopo, ahta ke
at least *adv.* ta vea, hiva
at once *adv.* lauti, sepi; *iv.* senu wechia (all at once)
athlete *n.* atleta
atmosphere *n.* heeka
attack *tv.* kiimu, aet a chaya, nau a chaya
attain *tv.* yuma (goal or point; with *refl. obj.*)
attempt *tv.* hiovila
attend *iv.* aane (be present), kakkavetu (not ~); *tv.* hikaha (pay
    attention to)
attention *n.* hikaiwame
attentive *tv.* hita mamatte
attitude *iv.* tu'isi yevicha (have a good ~), haana yevicha (have a
    bad attitude)
attract *tv.* yee wiike (~ a crowd)
attracted to *tv.* kopte
attraction *n.* yee wiikime
attractive *n.* hita wiikime; *iv.* tu'isi machi (be ~)
audience *pn.* hookame, vichame
August *n.* Awohto
aunt *n.* tia (*gen.*), chi'ila (mother's older sister), mamai (younger
    paternal), haaka (older paternal)
author *n.* hihiohteme
authority *n.* ya'ura (person or right to act), hita ta'ame (expert)
authorize *n.* hewiteria
automobile *n.* kaaro, maakina
autumn *n.* otongo
avail *adv.* o'oven (to no ~)
available *iv.* ama aane (be ~)
avenge *tv.* notta
avenue *n.* bwe'u voo'o
average *adj.* nanancha tutu'i (*pl.*; of equal value)
avoid *tv.* wohanria (dodge), nanale (~ meeting), tovuivuite, nanahria
await *tv.* vovicha
awake *adj.* vusa'ala
awaken *iv.* vusa
away *iv.* mekka siime (go ~; *pl.* mekka saka)
away, cat's *exp.* vasou wetla (while the cat's away, the mice will play)
aweful *adj.* hunera
awesome *adj.* vutti
axe *n.* tepuam
ay! *interj.* a'e (*fem.*)
Aztec *n.* Ahteeka

B

baby *n.* aso'ola
babysitter *n.* uhu'ureo
Bacatete Mountains *n.* Vaka Tetteve
bachelor *n.* apelai (especially an old ~)
back *n.* hoo'o (body), huvaria (lower); *adv.* atala (on ~), huchi (huchi Arizona vicha, back to Arizona), kuarto amawi (at the ~ of the room), kova amapo (~ of his head)
back off *interj.* mekka'e; *iv.* amae yehte (back from doing)
back out *iv.* amai yehte
back up *tv.* amae weetua (vehicle)
backbone *n.* hoo ota
backwards *adv.* amae, amau vicha (towards ~)
Bacum *n.* Vahkom
bad *iv.* ka tu'i
bad omen *n.* techoe
badge *n.* choki
badger *n.* huuri
badly *adj.* ka amma'ali
bag *n.* mochila (knapsack), tare'ekam
baggage *n.* hianira
bake *tv.* bwasa
baker *n.* panaleo
baking pan asafaata
bald *adj.* viichi; *iv.* lovola kovak, kova viichi (be ~); *iv.* chon weche (get ~)
ball *n.* katom (shinny ~), pelootam (for sports)
balloon *n.* bomba
bamboo *n.* vakau
banana *n.* platano
band *n.* hiponreom (musical group)
band together *iv.* nau cha'atu
bandage *n.* hisumia, suma'ariam, suma'i; *tv.* suma
bandit *n.* etbwareo
bandoleer *n.* kananam
bang *tv.* poona; *iv.* ruutia
banging *adv.* tinti
bank *n.* mayoa (shore), vanko (money)
bankrupt *adj.* kottila
baptism *n.* vatowawame
bar *n.* kantina (tavern)
barber *n.* hisikareo
bare *adj.* viichi
barefoot *iv.* ka voochak (be ~)
bark *n.* vea (tree); *iv.* voe, chu chae, haiti chae (of dogs)
barley *n.* seva

barracks *n.* waaria, kuartel
barrel *n.* variil
barrel cactus *n.* ono'e
barricade *tv.* patta
barrio *n.* vaario
base *n.* beis (baseball); *postp.* vetuku
baseball *n.* pelootam
baseball team *n.* peloteam
basement *n.* suteranio
bashful *iv.* tiiwe (be ~)
bashfulness *n.* tiura
basic *n.* vat weeme (fundamental, ~ thing, element)
basket *n.* waari
basketball *n.* wari pelootam
bat$_1$ *n.* sochik (animal)
bat$_2$ *n.* bet (baseball)
bathe *iv.* uva; *tv.* uvva
bathed *iv.* uva'ala
bathroom *n.* ehkusao; *iv.* huyaute (go to the ~ outside)
bathtub *n.* behtab
battery *n.* vateria
battle *n.* nassuawa, nahsuawa
bay *n.* vahia
be *iv.* aane
beach *n.* vawe mayoa
beak *n.* piiko
beam *n.* hoo ota (main ~), tachiria (light)
beans *n.* muunim , ehootem (green), heseim (brown tepary), siali
     muunim (green), se'elaim (white tepary), mun ro'ovoim
     (cooked), mun vakim (cooked), mun chihtim (mashed)
bear *n.* hooso (animal)
bearable *iv.* pasaroa machi
beard *n.* chao voam
beast *n.* animalim
beat *tv.* poona, popona, hipona (drum); koova (win)
beautiful ; tu'ulisi (animates); *iv.* uhyoi (inanimates; *var.* uhyooli)
beautifully *adv.* uhyoisi(a)
beauty *n.* tutu'uli
because *conj.* bwe'ituk, poke, veasu; *ptc.* su
become *suf.* -tu
bed *n.* kaama; *iv.* kochi'isek (go to ~; *sg.*), kokotvok (go to ~; *pl.*), hipeteka
     (make ~)
bedbugs *n.* chinchim
bedecked *adj.* sewatuari (with flowers)
bedroom *n.* kuarto
bedtime *n.* kokot oora

bee *n.* muumu, nahi (sweat bee), viko (bumblebee)
beetle *n.* bwita maival (dung)
before *conj.* ke; *adv.* vachia (in position)
beg *iv.* nettane
beg for *tv.* netane
beggar *n.* hoomo; *iv.* homotu (be a ~)
begin *tv.* naate; *suf.* -taite
beginner *n.* hu'ubwa nanateme
beginning *adv.* naateeka (in/since the ~), vatnaataka(i) (in the ~)
behave *iv.* yantia, amma'ali aane (~ properly)
behaved *adj.* yantiachi
behind *adv.* amawi, amapo; *postp.* veas(i), aet cha'aku
belch *iv.* e'ete
Belem *n.* Veenem
belief *n.* sualwame
believable *adv.* sualsi
believe *tv.* suale
belittle *tv.* hunneiya
bell *n.* kampaani, koyoolim (jingle ~s)
bell flower *n.* kampani sewa
belong *iv.* ama weye (go in a certain place)
below *adv.* ko'om(i)
belt *n.* wikosa
bench *n.* vanko
bend *n..* voo'o tottepo (in road); *iv.* po'okte; *tv.* kowikte, chovikukta
bend down *iv.* kom po'okte
beneath *postp.* vetukuni
benefit *n.* yee an'ame; *tv.* yee an'a
bent *adj.* chakkui
bent over *adv.* po'ola
bereaved *adj.* himucha'a
berry *n.* taaka
beside *postp.* ae cha'akaku, naachi, -tana, veas(i), vétana
best *adv.* chea
bet *n.* ha'ate; *tv.* ha'ate
betray *tv.* vehe'e, hina'atoa (tell on, snitch)
better *iv.* yuin ea (feel ~), tuttu'ira (get ~)
between *postp.* vétana; *adv.* nau nasuk (in~)
beverage *n.* hihi'iwame
bewitch *tv.* sivowame
beyond *adv.* navuhtia, wam vicha
Bible *n.* Santo Livrom
biceps *n.* mam kavam
bicycle *n.* visikleeta
bier *n.* urnia; *cf.* tapehtim
big *adj.* bwe'u, bou (*sg.*), bweere (*pl.*), yoyo'otuk (*pl.*)

Big Dipper *n.* Kaarom
big-nosed *n.* yeka'ara
bill *n.* hiosia tomi (money), lei hiosia (legislation), piiko (beak), wikikriawame (debt); *tv.* kopaaroa
billiards *n.* puul
billow *iv.* cha'asime
billy goat *n.* chiva'ato
binoculars *n.* lairavistam
biome *n.* vaa yoawam (aquatic)
bird *n.* wiikit (*gen.*)
bird of paradise *n.* taabwiko (plant)
birth *n.* asoawame (act of giving ~)
birth certificate *n.* akto nasimiento
birth control ka a'asoawame
birthday *n.* taewai yo'oriwa
birthplace *n.* yoemtukapo (with yeu)
bit, a little *adv.* iliikim
bitch *n.* chu hamut
bite *tv.* ke'e, huuha (insect)
bite to eat *exp.* hibwane (have a bite to eat)
bits and pieces *adv.* haamola
bitter *adj.* chiivu
black *adj.* chukui, chukuli, chukuri
black widow spider *n.* chukui huvahe
blackbird *n.* chana, hiak chana (large ~)
blackboard *n.* pisaroon
blade *n.* kuchi'im
bladder *n.* si'ika
blame *tv.* kulparoa; *cf.* ta'abwikut
bland *iv.* ka kia
blank *iv.* kaita ama hippue
blanket *n.* piisam, toosam (baby ~)
blare *iv.* vaaho'oti (be blaring)
blaze *iv.* kohakte, rupakte
bleed *iv.* ohvo woote
bless *tv.* te'ochia, tevat te'ochia (~ ceremonial area), bwánia (make a vow for someone else)
blessing *n.* te'ochiawame, te'ochia
blended *adj.* kurai (mixed)
blind *adj.* lipti, ripti
blink *iv.* kupikupikte, tutucha, repikte
blister *n.* vooyo, vahiya, *iv.* voyola, vooyo (from abrasion)
bloated *adj.* chuyula, puhtia; *iv.* chuuyu
block *tv.* patta
blond *iv.* sawaik kovak (be ~)
blood *n.* ohvo

blood vessel *n.* ohvo wikia
bloodshed *iv.* ohwo wo'ote (be ~)
blossom *n.* seewa; *iv.* tomte, sewa tomte
blotched *iv.* nasonti
blouse *n.* vepa supem, supem
blow *iv.* chom watte (nose), kuuse (wind instrument), hihiutua (wind
    instrument), heeka (wind), puhta (expell air from mouth)
blow away *tv.* puhta
blow up *tv.* pehta
blue *adj.* tewei (dark), toloko (light)
blunder *iv.* ama vutti hiovek (be very mistaken)
blunt *adj.* ka bwaawi (not sharp)
blush *iv.* sikisi ayuk
boa *n.* kurues
board *n.* tavla (wood), yoemra nau cha'akame (committee); *tv.* ha'amu
    (get on boat, plane), kuartota nu'e (rent room)
boast *iv.* veewati hia, au uttia ka nooka
boat *n.* kanoa
boatman *n.* kanoareo
bobbing *iv.* va'apo cha'asime (be ~)
bob head *adv.* naa kouvate
bobby pin *n.* vavepiinim
body *n.* taka
bog *n.* vaata yehtepo
boil$_1$ *iv.* pohte; *tv.* pohta, vaake (food)
boil$_2$ *n.* vooyo, vahiya
boiled *adj.* vaaki
boisterously *adv.* vahooti
bold *iv.* ka tiiwe, au oule
bolt *n.* yuku hima'i (of lightening), tornio (with nut)
bomb *n.* bombam; *tv.* bombiaroa
bone *n.* ota, wituam (charred ~s)
bony ota ausu'uli
book *n.* livrom
booming *adv.* kumti
bopping *adv.* muliliti (gait)
border *n.* linea
bore *iv.* vohokta (hole)
bored *iv.* rohikte, ichakte (get ~)
boring *adj.* ichaktiachi, rohiktiachi
born *iv.* yeu yoemtu, yoemtu
borrow *tv.* reuwa
bosom *n.* kocho'i
boss *n.* teeko; *tv.* sawe
bossy *n.* si nesawe'a (be ~)
both *pn.* nanancha, nawit; *adv.* woikatana (on/along both sides)

bother *tv.* suate vicha, haiti eetua
bothersome *adj.* haitiachi; *iv.* haitiachisi maachi
bottle *n.* votea, vaa nuu'u (water ~)
bottom *postp.* vétuku (on the ~)
bought *adj.* haivinuri
boulder *n.* bwe'uteta
bounce *iv.* tohakte
boundary *n.* linia, lindero
bow$_1$ *iv.* musukte (head)
bow$_2$ *n.* kuta wiko'i (weapon)
bow guard *n.* hato'i
bowed *adv.* muhsu (head ~)
bowl *n.* vatatana (mixing ~)
box *n.* kaaha
boy *n.* ili o'ou
boyfriend *n.* novio
bracelet *n.* mapoa
brag *iv.* veewati hia
braid *iv.* bwahsuma, bwahsuma'i
brains *n.* o'oream
branch *n.* nassaka'aria (tree)
brand *n.* tepohti; *tv.* tepohtia
branding iron *n.* tepohti
brassiere *n.* pip kuttiria
brave *iv.* au oule, bwe'um hiapsek (be ~)
Brazil wood *n.* huchahko
bread *n.* paanim, paanim pa'asek (raisin bread); *iv.* pan hoa (make ~)
bread pudding *n.* kapirotaaram
break *iv.* kotte, karakte (bone), hamte (brittle things), matchu (day); *tv.*
    kotta, hamta (brittle things), riuta (bone)
break down *iv.* nasontu, *tv.* nasonte
breakfast *n.* ketwo hi'ibwame
breast *n.* kocho'i, tawi (chest), pipim (breasts)
breath *n.* hiavihtei; *iv.* tenhaawa (see ~ in the cold)
breathe *iv.* hiavihte, hasohte (~ hard)
breechclout *n.* bwahim
bribe *n.* mordida
brick *n.* laakria, laakrio
bride *n.* hupvawame
bridge *n.* puentes
bright *adj.* kalasolai, velohko
brilliant *adj.* kalasolai
brim *adv.* patala (to the ~)
bring *tv.* nu'upa, kivacha (*sg. obj.*), kiima (*pl. obj.*)
bring up *tv.* vicha eteho (bring up a topic; *d.o.* = *obj.* of vicha)
brink *iv.* kaitapo tawava (be on the ~ of disaster)

bristling *adv.* sanvera, sankira
broad *adj.* bweeka; *adv.* machiako (in ~ daylight)
broken *adj.* chamti, hamti(a), hamtila, kotti(l)a
bronc *iv.* tamahtvaawa (ride a bucking ~)
brook *n.* seke'eka
broom *n.* hichikia
broth *n.* va'awa, mun va'awa (bean ~)
brother *n.* avachi (older; *fem.*), sai (older; *masc.*), wai (younger; *fem.*),
     saila (younger; *masc.*)
brought *adj.* toiri
brow *n.* kumsakam
brown *adj.* husai, husali, husari; *tv.* husaite
brownish *adj.* husama
bruise *n.* ohvo yehtela; *iv.* ko'okosi aula; *tv.* au ko'okosi yaak
brush *n.* broocha
buck *iv.* tamahte; *tv.* tamahtitua (make ~)
bucket *n.* valle
bucking *iv.* tamahtvaawa (ride a ~ horse)
bud *iv.* tomte (flowers), siakikichiite (leaves)
bug *n.* yoeria (insect)
build *tv.* kaate (~ house), naaya (~ fire), hekkate (~ a ramada), koate (~ fence)
building *n.* kari
bulb *n.* vot—n (plant), fooko (light ~)
bull *n.* tooro
bullet *n.* vaala
bullsnake *n.* ala'amai
bully *iv.* au ia (be a ~)
bumblebee *n.* viko, kukusa (Sonoran)
bump *iv.* tahte
bump into *tv.* tahta
bunch *iv.* ivakte
bunches *adv.* nattepola (in ~)
bundle *n.* hisumia (*gen.*), tesia (grass or reeds tied together)
bundled *adj.* hisumai
bureau *n.* koomora (chest of drawers)
burial *n.* hima'awa
buried *adj.* ma'ari
burn *iv.* veete, bwatana (food); *tv.* taya, bwatania (food)
burned *adj.* taya'i; *iv.* veetia, taha (get ~)
burp *iv.* e'ete; *tv.* eetitua (make ~)
burro *n.* vuuru
burst *iv.* pehte
bury *iv.* hima'a, hima'awa; *tv.* ma'a
bus *n.* baas
bush *n.* huya, ouwo
bushed *iv.* sutti kochok (be ~)

bushy *adv.* sanvera, sankira
business *n.* newosio
business, have a *iv.* newosiok
business, none of my *exp.* nepo kaita ama newoisiol, inepo kaita ama
      tu tu'ute
busy *adj.* ovisi; *iv.* ovisaane
busy-body *n. iv.* kucha'arata aman susuta (be a ~)
but *conj.* ala, o'oven, tahu'u, ta
but now *conj.* ta vesa
butcher *n.* wakas chuktireo; *iv.* peute; *tv.* peuta
butt *n.* choove
butt in *tv.* suatam vicha
butter *n.* mantekia
butterfly *n.* vaisevo'i
buttocks *n.* chove
button *n.* votoon
buy *tv.* hinu
buyer *n.* hihinume; *cf.* nunu'eme
buzz *iv.* vi'itia, kuutia (insects)
buzzard *n.* satema (*gen.*), tekoe (white-headed), wiiru (turkey)
by *postp.* ae nachi (see also "beside"), ai (~ means of; *cf.* "with"), -po (*ex.*
      vetanapo wam siika, pass by the window)
by mistake *adv.* hioveka
by one's self *adv.* aapola
by sight *tv.* vit ta'a (know by sight)
by surprise *adv.* sehchuktia
by the *postp.* -po (*ex.* orapo, by the hour; taeawpo, by the day; metpo, by
      the month; wasuktiapo, by the year)
bystander *n.* vitchume

C

cabbage *n.* repooyo
cabin *n.* kari
cache *n.* e'eriari
cackle *tv.* kotkottia (chicken)
cactus *n.* aaki (organpipe, pitahaya), chikul hu'i (pincushion), choa
      (cholla), echo (cardon), museo (senita), naavo (prickly pear),
      nakkaim (Santa Cruz prickly pear), noono (night-blooming
      cereus), ono'e (barrel), sauwo (saguaro), sevi (jumping cholla),
      siina (old man), tosa navo (Indian fig)
cactus wren *n.* vaewaakas
cage *n.* haula
caiman *n.* kama
cake *iv.* raukte; *n.* keekim (dessert)

calendar *n.* almanaake
calf *n.* veseo (animal), wok chava'i (body)
call *tv.* chae
callus *n.* kaayo
calm *adj.* yantela; *iv.* yanti maachi, yantela aane (be ~; weather, person)
camel *n.* kameeyo
camera *n.* kaamara
camp *n.* kampo; *iv.* huyapo to'e
can$_1$ *n.* ohelata (food)
can$_2$ *adv.* aa (be able), chea (can't; see chea)
canal *n.* kanal
can't be *interj.* kaivala
canary *n.* kanario
canceled *iv.* ka ya vawa (be ~)
cancer *n.* kensur
candelabra *n.* kantileom
candidly *adv.* lutula
candle *n.* kanteela
candy *n.* kakawa, luusem
cane *n.* saawi, vaaka (reeds), sana (sugar), voonia (walking stick)
canned goods *n.* ohelata
cannot *iv.* ka aawe
canopy *n.* hekam
canteen *n.* vaa nuu'u
canvas *n.* loonam
canyon *n.* kau kovi'iku
cap *n.* woora
capable *iv.* yeeka, yuuma (~ of carrying, holding up)
cape *n.* kaapam
captain *n.* kapetai
captive *n.* bwisiwame
captivity *iv.* bwisiwa (be in ~)
capture *n.* bwihwa; *tv.* peesote
captured *adj.* bwihri; *iv.* bwihwa
car *n.* kareeta, maakina
car port *n.* karota kechawa'apo
caracara *n.* choawe
carcass *n.* taka
cardinal *n.* wichalakas (bird)
cardon *n.* echo (cactus), echo taka (~ fruit)
cardboard box *n.* kartoon
cards *n.* na'ipisim; *tv.* yewa (play ~)
care *n.* uhu'ume (re: children, elderly); *tv.* nake (~ for, about)
care for *iv.* sánake; *tv.* eiya, nake; ka yee tu'ure (not care for anyone)
carefree *adj.* yantela
careful *iv.* au sua (be ~)

career *n.* voohoria
careful *iv.* au sua
careless *iv.* ka au sua (be ~)
caretaker *n.* susuame
caring *n.* yee nakwame
carpenter *n.* kapinteo
carpet *n.* karpeeta
carress *tv.* emo yeewa
carried *iv.* toiwa (be ~)
carrot *n.* sanooria
carry *iv.* wihhu'ute, *iv.* aakte (on head); *tv.* pu'ate, keve'ete (in mouth), a'ate (on head), puanama (person), weiya (*pl. obj.*), toha (*sg. obj.*), tovo'ote (with hands)
carry out *tv.* weiya
cartoon *n.* kartuunim
carve *tv.* siiva (wood)
cash *n.* tomi
cast *tv.* hissa
castle *n.* kahtiiyo
castor bean *n.* kevenia (plant), kevenia vachia (seed)
castrate *tv.* kaponte
castrated *adj.* kapontei
cat *n.* miisi
cataracts *n.* namuwam (eyes); *exp.* vaa'am kom weche (be waterfalls)
catclaw acacia *n.* hu'upa keka'ala
catch *tv.* bwise
catch up *tv.* hahame
caterpillar *n.* bwiiwi
cat's away *exp.* vasou wetla (while the cat's away, the mice will play)
cattle *n.* wakasim
cause *suf.* -tua
cautious *iv.* hiline (be ~), au sua (be ~)
cautiously *adv.* leuleuti
Cavalry Society *n.* Kavayom, Kavayo (member)
cave *n.* teeso
cavity *n.* tam moera (tooth)
caw *iv.* kaakaatia
cedar *n.* tahkali
ceiling *n.* techo
cellar *n.* suteranio
cement *n.* semento
cemetery *n.* hihima'awa'apo, sementeeria
cent *n.* sentaavo
center *n.* nasukria
centipede *n.* masiwe
cereal *n.* aveena

ceremony *n.* pahko, kopanpahko (daytime ~)
cereus *n.* noono (nightblooming ~ cactus)
certain *pn.* seenu (~ person or thing); *iv.* tu'i machi
certainly *interj.*, *adv.* tua
chain *n.* karenam
chair *n.* siiya
chalk *n.* tiisa
chamomile *n.* si'iya
chance *n.* 1. chansa 2. kulupti wéeme (something that happens)
change *n.* tomi nakuliam (money); *iv.* koakte (course), hiapsi kuakte (of
      heart, of mind), ka hunen ea (~ one's mind); *tv.* nakulia (~
      money, exchange), kuakta (convert)
Chapayekas *n.* Hurasim
chapped *adj.* sisi'ibwala; *iv.* sisi'ibwa
chapter *n.* kapitulo
characterized *suf.* -ra (~ by)
charcoal *n.* maatum
charge *tv.* kiimu (attack), kopaaroa (money)
charged with *iv.* kulparoawa (be ~ a crime)
chase *tv.* hahase
chat *iv.* eteho
cheap *iv.* ka vehe'e
check *n.* cheeki (bank draft); *tv.* hiiwe (sample), chekiaroa (correct)
check over *tv.* vicha
cheeks *n.* hopem
cheer up *exp.* siok yoene
cheese *n.* keesum
cherish *tv.* yosi eiya
cherished *n.* naiyoli, nakwame
chest *n.* kocho'i (body), tawi (body), koomora (~ of drawers), petakia
      (trunk)
chew *iv.* hiko'a, ko'a, kuume
chewed *adj* ko'ori
chick *n.* ili totoi
chickpeas *n.* yoi muunim
chicken *n.* totoi
chicken house *n.* totoi kari
chief *n.* ya'ut
chigger *n.* chinchim (insect)
child *n.* ili uusi, uusi yo'owe (older ~), asoa (female or male; *fem.*), uusi
      (male; *masc.*), maala (female; *masc.*); *iv.* yoemiak (have a ~)
childbirth *n.* usi yeu yoemtu
childhood *n.* usituwame
childishly *adv.* no'ochiamsa; *iv.* no'ochia (act ~)
children *n.* yoemiarim, usira (as a group)
chile *n.* ko'oko'i

chilly *iv.* seve
chiltepin *n.* hua ko'oko'im
chimney *n.* chiminea
chin *n.* chao
chin up *exp.* siok yoene (keep your chin up, cheer up)
chinaberry *n.* piocha
Chinese *n., adj.* Chiino
chips *n.* chutiam
chirping *adv.* piopiokti; *iv.* piupiuti
chocolate *n.* chokolaate
choke *iv.* hu'ukte, *iv.* hukte (on liquids), *iv.* tatte (on solids); *tv.* hu'uktia
cholla *n.* choa, sevi (jumping ~)
choose *tv.* pua
chop *iv.* hima'ako (wood)
Christ *n.* Krihto
Christian *n.* Vato'i
Christendom *n.* pala vato'ora
Christmas *n.* Navilan, Nochi Weena, Krihmem
Christmas Eve *n.* Tu'i Tukaria
Christmas, Merry *exp.* Noche Weena
Christmas presents *n.* Krihmem
chugging *adv.* sutsutti
church *n.* teopo
cicada *n.* mate
cinnamon *n.* kanela
circle *n.* koelai
circus *n.* sirko
citizen *n.* hoome
city *n.* bwe'u ho'ara
clams *n.* aulim
clairvoyant *iv.* navuhti vicha (be ~)
clan *n.* wawaira
clanging *adv.* tinti
clap *iv.* mam tohte
clash *iv.* nau tahte
class *n.* klaase (economic rank; *ex.* vat klaase, first class; sewundo klaase, second class), grado (level), kuarto (in school; hita kuartopo empo weye? what class are you in?)
claw *n.* sutum
clay *n.* vaavu
clean *adj.* tu'ute; *iv.* ka haitimachi aane
cleansed *iv.* vasua (by soaking)
clear *adj.* maachi (focused), kalahko (transparent), namamachi (transparent), navuhti (transparent), tu'i (understandable); *iv.* taa yeu katek (weather); *tv.* maohte (land), kalahkoa (make)
clearing *n.* pa'aria (open area)

clerk *n.* hiohteme
clever *adj.* suak
client *n.* maachante
cliff *n.* kau siiva, siiva
climb up *iv.* ha'amu
clip-clop *adv.* kumkumti
cloak *n.* kaapam
clock *n.* lelo
clod *n.* tesua
close$_1$ *tv.* eta; *iv.* kepe (eyes)
close$_2$ *adv.* heela (near); *iv.* aavo rukte (get ~)
closed *adj.* patti
closer *adj.* rukti
closet *n.* ropeo
clothes *n.* taho'o(ri)
clothes pin *n.* chaapa
clothing *n.* taho'o(ri), atte'a
cloud *n.* naamu
cloud over *iv.* namulopte
clouded *adj.* namulopti
cloudy *adj.* naamuk; *iv.* naamutu (get)
clover *n.* tevoli
clown *n.* payaaso
clown around *iv.* haana aane
club *n.* hivevia (~ for shinny or other game), karoote (weapon)
clumsy *iv.* kaita vetchi'ivo tu'i
clunking *adv.* kumti
clustering *n.* motcha kaate
clusters *adv.* mochala (in ~s)
coal *n.* tetamatum
coals *n.* ouvam
coarsely *tv.* tuuse (grind ~)
coast$_1$ *n.* vaawe mayoa
coast$_2$ *iv.* cha'asime
coat *n.* chaketonim
cob *n.* nao
cobweb *n.* vitosa
cockroach *n.* kukarocha
cocoon *n.* yoeria hoara
coconut *n.* kooko
Cocopa *n.* Kukupa
Cocorit *n.* Ko'oko'im
coffee *n.* kafe, kape
coffee pot *n.* kafeteera
coffin *n.* tauna
coil *tv.* vi'ita

coiled *adj.* lo'alai

coin *n.* tomin

cold *n.* kataro (disease), severia (disease, or ~ weather); *adj.* seve; *iv.* sevele (feel), sevea (get)

collar *n.* kueyo

collect *iv.* cha'atu (clouds); *tv.* nau toha

college *n.* kolehio

collide *iv.* nau tahte

Colonia Militar *n.* Kolonia Militar

color *n.* koloorim

colored *adj.* yokak

colorless *iv.* ka kolorek (be ~)

colt *n.* kavai aso'ola, ili kava'i

comadre *n.* komae

comal *n.* wako'i

comb *n.* cha'apara (chicken's), peina (for hair); *tv.* chike (hair)

combed *adj.* chichikla

combine *tv.* nau chaya

combination *n.* nau cha'akame

come *iv.* yepsa (*pl.* yaha)

come onto *tv.* ka yee yo'ore (sexually, to someone unwilling)

come out *iv.* yeu siime

come up *iv.* yeu weye (sun, moon)

comet *n.* choki hiisa

comfortable *adj.* yantela

command *n.* nesau; *tv.* nesawe, sawe; *suf.* -sae

commander *n.* nesaweme

commandment *n.* nesawi

comment *tv.* monte (only with *neg.*)

commercial *n.* komersial

committee *n.* yoemra nau cha'akame

common *n.* hiva yu vitwame

common, in *iv.* nana'ana (*ex.* vempo vatte ~, they have a lot in common/are about the same)

Communion, Holy *n.* Miisam bwa'e (take Holy Communion)

community *n.* pueplo, ho'ara

community house *n.* komunila

compadre *n.* kompae

companion *n.* hoiwai

compare *tv.* woi vehewata hu'uneiyavae (want to know two values)

company *n.* kompania (business), hoarapo aneme (guests)

comparable *adj.* nana'ana (*ex.* vame karim nana'ana, these houses are the same), hiva ... vena (*ex.* i tomin hiva u vena, this coin is equivalent that one)

compassion *n.* hiokole, hiokoliwame; *tv.* eiya, nake (have ~ on); *tv.* kaita ea (have no ~)

compassionate *n.* yee nakwame
complain *iv.* nok omte (~ about), veewatia (whine)
complete *iv.* chupia, hichupa; *tv.* chupa, emo kovavae
completed *iv.* chupia, chupe, lu'ute
completely *adv.* yuyuma'isi, si'imek
completion *adv.* chupi'iseka (coming into ~)
complex *adj.* oviachi
complicated *adj.* oviachi
comprehension *n.* mammattewame
Compuertas *n.* Kompuertam
computer *n.* komputadora, kempiuter
conceal *tv.* ehso
conceited *iv.* au tu'ure, au hitale
concentrate *iv.* kovahamte (think)
concerned *iv.* suatea; *adj.* yantela (un~)
conclude *tv.* nok ansu (orally), hiohtei ansu
concrete *n.* semento (cement)
condemned *n.* yoem chupia
condition *exp.* haisa maachi? (what ~ ?; the answer is with an *adj.* or *adv.*
    that describes the condition + maachi)
conduct *tv.* weiya
conductor *n.* konlotor
cone *n.* wok tuaka (pine), pikokame (~-shaped); *adj.* koelai
conference *n.* nau yaiwa'apo
confess *iv.* pesekte
confession *n.* pesektiwame
confetti *n.* sewa chukti
confident *adj.* yante'ela
confirm *iv.* muhte
confirmation *n.* muhti
confirmed *iv.* muhtila
confuse *tv.* hiopta (cause on to make a mistake); *dv.* au a ta'arutua (cause
    to be mentally ~d)
confused *iv.* ka hu'uneiya (be ~)
confusing *iv.* ka hu'unakiachi (be ~)
connect *iv.* nau cha'ata
connection *n.* nau cha'atuwame
conquer *tv.* yoo yuuma
conscious *iv.* hu'uneiya (be ~)
consciousness *n.* hu'uneiyawame
consensus *adv.* nanau hia
consider *tv.* vat a mammate
considerable *iv.* yee yo'ore
considerate *iv.* yee yo'ore (be ~)
console *tv.* alle'eetua
constantly *adv.* hubwuni, hiva yu

constipated *adj.* bwita pattila, pottila
constipation *iv.* potte (have)
consult *dv.* konsehota hariwa
consume *tv.* lu'utia
contain *tv.* hippue; *iv.* aayuk (*ex.* soto'opo vaa'am aayuk, there is water in
    the pot)
contemporary *n.* ian katriam
contemptible *adj.* kuhtiachi
content *adj.* allea; *iv.* allete'ea (become ~)
continue *tv.* hiva a hoone
continuously *adv.* hiva yu, piesa(po)
contract *iv.* kitokte
contradict *tv.* nokvehe'e
control *tv.* sawe
controlled *iv.* mampo weche (be in someone else's ~)
convalesce *iv.* ineete
convenient *iv.* ka oviachisi aayuk
conversation *n.* etehowame
convert *tv.* kuakta
convicted *iv.* aet vo'otek
convince *tv.* elevenasia a eetua
cook *n.* hivoleo, kosineo; *iv.* hivoa, bwase; *tv.* bwasa
cooked *adj.* bwasi
cookies *n.* gayeetam
cool *adj.* vaali; *iv.* sipe (get); *tv.* sipa, valiria
cool off *exp.* vali yoene (come cool off)
coolness *n.* vaali
cooperative *iv.* hootu
copper *n.* kovre
copy *n.* koopia; *tv.* mamato (imitate), alevenak yaa (duplicate)
coral bean *n.* chirikote (tree *sp.*)
coral snake *n.* sikkucha'a
coral vine *n.* masa'asai
Corasepe *n.* Koasepe
cord *n.* wikia
corn *n.* avae (fresh), heoko vachi (large-eared), avia (on cob), vachi (seed)
corn ear *n.* sita (young)
corn husk *n.* sanava
corncob *n.* nao
corner *n.* ehkiina (street ~); kovi, kovi'iku, kovi'iria (interior); *adv.*
    chaka'aku (in the ~)
cornsilk *n.* avai choonim
corporal *n.* kaavo
corporation *n.* kompania
corpulent *iv.* tekwak
corral *n.* kora, koa

correct *adj.* tu'i; *n.* witti; *tv.* tu'ute
corrected *n.* witti
correction *n.* witti
corrupt *adj.* naiyotela; *tv.* naiyote
corset *n.* kuttiria
cost *n.* vehe'ewa, vehe'eria; *iv.* vehe'eria
costly *iv.* vehe'e (be ~)
cot *n.* tarima
cotton *n.* chiinim; chin sooka, perennial ~
cottontail *n.* taavu
cottonwood *n.* avaso
cottonwood root *n.* avah nawa
couch *n.* soofa
cougar *n.* ousei
cough *iv.* tase, haaka watte (~ up phlegm)
cough up *iv.* haaka watte
could *exp.* 1. aa + [reduplicated verb]-n (used to be able to; *ex.* ne aa
    vuivuiten, I could run) 2. *adv.* humak (might be the case that; *ex.*
    humak aman aane, might be over there) 3. [verb$_1$]-k, ... [verb$_2$]-
    'ean (providing that; *ex.* ne tomek aman wee'ean, if I had the
    money I could go)
council *n.* ya'ura
counsel *n.* noktehwa; *tv.* tu'i nokta yee maaka
count *iv.* hinaikia, valiaroa (in sports); *tv.* naikia
count on *iv.* tua aet ea (on = aet)
count up *tv.* tomita nau yecha
counted *adj.* hinaikiari
counter *n.* meesa
country *n.* bwiara (territory), nasion (state)
couple *n.* chupiarim (married), nau chupwame (man and woman)
courageous *iv.* oule, bwe'um hiapsek (be ~)
court *n.* koorte
cousin *n.* wawai, prima (female), primo (male)
cousins *n.* wawaira
cover *n.* patpattame; *tv.* hintoa, patta, hine (use as a ~)
covered *adj.* patti, roptihinek (with cloth), lomti (with tarp, blanket)
covered up *iv.* hinte
covet *tv.* savatua, sava
cow *n.* waakas
coward *n.* nawia
cowbird *n.* poute'ela
cowboy *n.* vake'o, kavayeo, kapyeo
cowhide *n.* waka vea
cowlick *n.* pu'ilai (in hair)
coyote *n.* wo'i
Coyote Society *n.* Wiko'i Ya'ura

crab *n.* achakari, haiva

crack *n.* peche'eria; *adv.* peche'eku (in a ~); *iv.* revekte, *iv.* harahte (skin); *tv.* etahte

cracked *n.* etahtia ~ thing)

crackling *adv.* tosisitia

cramp *n.* utte'am

crane *n.* ko'obwabwa'i

cranky *adj.* huena

crash *tv.* chokaroa

crawl *iv.* sunsunte, waka'anama, waka'ate; *iv.* kikichiite aane (feel something crawling up pants, sleeve)

crazy *iv.* ka suak

creak *iv.* kuchichi'itia

cream *n.* kreema

create *iv.* hu'unakte

creation *n.* hu'unaktei

Creator *n.* Yee Hunaktekame

creature *n.* chupiari, hu'unakteim

creditor *n.* wikiriawame

creek *n.* sene'eka (brook)

creosote *n.* kovanao

crest *n.* hiisa (bird, headgear), kau vepa mayoa (mountain ridge)

crib *n.* maaka

cricket *n.* kiichul

crime *n.* leita vehe'e (commit a ~)

criminal *n.* leita vehe'eme

crippled *adj.* lo'i

crisis *n.* ka tu'isi weye (be in a ~)

crisscrossing *adv.* sapala

criticize *iv.* aet nooka; *tv.* kulparoa

crooked *adj.* chakkui, tonnai

crops *n.* hichupak

cross *n.* kus, kus yo'owe (village ~); *iv.* kuhte (self), ama wam siime (traverse)

cross-shaped *adv.* kusaroapo

crow *n.* kooni

crowd *n.* huevena yoemra ama anwa (there is a ~)

crown *n.* koona (object), choam (of head)

cruciform *adv.* kusaroapo

cruel *adj.* hue'ena; *iv.* i'a (with au)

crumble *tv.* kohakta, chokinakta, mohakte, revekta

crumbled *adj.* revektia

crumbling *iv.* mohte, revekte

crumpled *adj.* patalai

crush *tv.* chovikukta, kamta, pitta

crust *n.* vetcho'oria

crutches *n.* mule'etom (with weama)
cry *n.* chachaeri; *iv.* bwaana
crybaby *n.* bwani
crying *n.* bwanwame
cucumber *n.* pepiino
cuddle *tv.* ivakta
cultivate *tv.* kultivaroa
culture *n.* weyeme
cup *n.* koopa, taasa
cupboard *n.* almario
cure *tv.* hitto
cured *iv.* hittowa (become)
curer *n.* hitevi
curious *n.* hita tuttu'ule; *iv.* ta'apea (be ~)
curly *iv.* chinota kovak (have ~ hair)
current *n.* ian weeme (be happening now)
current *n.* koriente (water)
curse *tv.* aetua, siivo; *n.* yee sivowame
curtain *n.* kortiinam
curved *adv.* tonna
curving *adj.* owilai
cushion *n.* muteka
cuss out *tv.* a'aetua
custody *iv.* eta'i (be in ~)
custom *n.* weyeme
customs *n.* aduana (at border)
customer *n.* maachante
cut *n.* chuktia; *adj.* chukti; *iv.* chukte, hisika (hair), chapte (with scissors),
    apat kivake; *tv.* petta, sika (hair), kopelachukta (into short
    pieces), chukta (with saw, knife), chapta (with scissors)
cut it out *interj.* épale (to child)

D

dad *n.* papa
dagger *n.* kuchi'im
daily *adv.* chikti ta'apo
daily grind *iv.* kiavea hiapsa (be locked to the daily grind)
dairy *n.* lecheria
dam *n.* tapoon
damage *tv.* siivo
damaged nasontela
damp *adj.* komonla
dance *n.* yi'iwa (event), Soonim (~ tune), yoi yi'iwa (Mexican), vaile
    (social events), yi'iwame (act of dancing); *iv.* ye'e, yi'iria (~ for);
    tv. yi'itua (cause to ~)

dancer *n.* yeye'eme, *n.* yi'ireo
dandelion *n.* ko'orai
dangerous *adj.* hilinwachi
dangerously *iv.* sulwachi aane (act ~)
daring *iv.* ka tiiwe
dark *adj.* kut tenei, kut horoi (interior), kutko (color), kutvene; *adv.*
    kutwo, kutvea, kutwatwatte, ka machiku (in the dark); *iv.* ka
    mamachi (be ~)
date$_1$ *n.* laatiko (fruit)
date$_2$ *n.* taewai (day)
datura *n.* tebwi
daughter *n.* naaka (*fem.*), maara (*masc.*)
daughter-in-law *n.* havorai
dawn *n.* alva, machi'itana; *adv.* machiauvicha (towards ~); matchuk
    (at ~); maukaapo (before ~); maukaroapo (before ~)
day *n.* machiria, taewai; semanapo taewaim, days of the week
daylight *n.* taewali; *adv.* machiako (in broad ~)
dead *adj.* mukila; *n.* kokoarim (~ people)
deaf *n.* nakapit
death *n.* kokowame, Wakila (Father Time, death personified)
debt *n.* wikiriawame
debtor *n.* wikiriame
decay *iv.* mooye
decease *iv.* luute
deceased *adj.* mukila; *ptc.* tuka'u
deceive *tv.* vehe'e, vaita'a
December *n.* Disiembre
decide *tv.* aman wéevaeka ea
declaration *n.* testamento
decline *iv.* au hima'ala (let one's self go)
decorate *tv.* sewatua (with flowers)
decorated *adj.* sewatuari (with flowers)
decrease *iv.* kom cha'atu
deed *n.* anwame (act)
deep *adv.* mekka ko'omi
deer *n.* maaso, tua maaso (whitetail), soute'ela (magical), maiso (old),
    sevis maso (mule)
Deer Dancer *n.* maso ye'eme
Deer head *n.* maso kova
Deer Singers *n.* maso bwikame
deer skin *n.* mahvea
defecate *n.* bwita
defend *dv.* nokria (verbally)
defend self *iv.* au ania (~ self verbally); *tv.* au nokria (verbally)
defenseless *iv.* ka aa au ánis
deformed *iv.* ka tua yuma'i (body), lovola mamak (~ hand);
    cf. hunchbacked

211

delayed *adv.* vinwatuk
deliberately *adv.* hunakteka
delicate *adj.* wilohko
delicious *adj.* kia
deliver *tv.* nu'upa, hittoha, a'asoaatua (child)
delivery person *n.* hihittohame
delouse *tv.* eteme
deluded *iv.* kaitapo taawala (be ~)
demolish *tv.* wiuta
den *n.* teeso
dentist *n.* tam lotoor
dentures *n.* pohtisom
depend on *iv.* aet ea (on = aet)
dependable *iv.* aet eetu, aet eewachi
depot *n.* liipo
deport *tv.* yeu toha (*sg. obj.*; *pl. obj.* yeu weiya)
depress *tv.* yotta (button on machine)
descendent *n.* vasiula
describe *dv.* tu'isi a teuwa ... haisi machi
desert *n.* pocho'oria
desert broom *n.* heeko
desert hackberry *n.* kunwo
desirable *iv.* veuti machi, veutiachisi maachi, koptiachi
desire *n.* valepo, waatiawa; *tv.* ukkule, waata, kopte (attracted to)
desperately *adv.* ama vutti (desire greatly)
despise *tv.* haita, yee omta
destitute *adj.* poove
destroy *tv.* tehale
detest *tv.* kuhteiya, omta
develop *iv.* yeu chuchupe
devil *n.* yaplo
Devil, the *n.* Vevehe'eri
devil's claw *n.* tamko'okochi
devotion *n.* muhti
dew *n.* vaeweche
dewy *adj.* vahewechia
diamond *n.* diamente
diaper *n.* bwahim
diarrhea *n.* voohtia; *iv.* voohte (have ~)
die *iv.* tiukove, muuke (*sg.*), koko (*pl.*)
die off *n.* kokoriawa (re: groups)
different 1. use ka, not + same 2. ta'abwi (other) 3. ta'abwisi (odd)
different, be *iv.* ka nanancha (be not the same), tabwisi machi (be ~, odd)
difficult *adj.* oviachi
dig *iv.* hi'ibwehe, hibwehe; *tv.* bwehe
digging stick *n.* wi'ika
dilapidated *adj.* moyok

dime *n.* dies sentavo
dip *tv.* susuta
dipper *n.* bweha('i)
direct₁ *adj.* lu'ula
direct₂ *tv.* vicha
directly *adv.* navuhti
directions *adv.* si'imekunvicha (in/to all ~), si'imekuttana (from all ~)
director *n.* nesaweme, vichame, kova
dirt *n.* bwia, poote (powdery), sata (red ~)
dirty *iv.* haiti maachi, haitauya'ala (~ self); *tv.* haitauhoa
disappear *iv.* kaavetuk, kaitatu, kakkavetu (without trace)
disappointed *iv.* ka alleaka taawa
disciple *n.* disipulo
discoloration *n.* mechawa (facial)
discuss *tv.* eteho (*ex.* Vempo o'outa etehok. They discussed the man.)
discussion *n.* hiitewa
disreputable *iv.* ka yo'ori machi
disease *n.* ko'okoa, sivori (from witchcraft), veerok (lip), keekam (skin),
          hiosia, huva'asam (venereal)
disembowel *tv.* sia bwakta
disgrace *n.* tiurame; *iv.* tiurampo taawa (be in ~)
disentangle *tv.* tomta
disgusted *iv.* haita (be ~ by)
disgusting *adj.* haitiachi
dish *n.* puato
dishonest *n.* yee vaitatta'a (~ person)
disk rattle *n.* sena'asom
dislike *tv.* kuhteiya, omta
dismount *iv.* kom chepte
disoriented *iv.* chiktula, chiktu (become)
dispatch *tv.* vittua
disrespectful *adj.* hantiachi, ka yee yo'ore
distintegrating *iv.* mohte
distribute *dv.* naa toha
district *n.* distriito (area), vaario (town)
disturb *tv.* suate vicha
ditch *n.* akia, seekia
dive *iv.* piiki
diverge *iv.* koakte
divide *tv.* naikimte
divided *adj.* naikimtei
division *n.* naikim tewame (arithmetic)
divorce *tv.* hima
dizzy *iv.* naamumuke, naamuke (*sg.*), naakoa (*pl.*); *tv.* naamucha (make)
do *tv.* hoa, yaa, aane; *dv.* hohootua (make someone ~), hooria (~ for
        someone); *adv.* véa (used for emphasis); *exp.* hituni hoa (~ as one
        pleases)

do for *dv.* hohoria
doctor *n.* yee hihittome
dodge *tv.* wohana, wohanria
dog *n.* chuu'u
doll *n.* moono
dollar *n.* peeso
dolphin *n.* huhteme
don't *conj.* kat
done *adj.* yaati
donkey *n.* vuuru
door *n.* pueta
dough *n.* kittim
dove *n.* ommo'okoli (Inca), wokkoi (mourning), kuuku (white-winged)
down$_1$ *n.* voam (feathers)
down$_2$ *adv.* ko'om(i), ko'omisu (~ here); *adj.* tekri (laid ~); *iv.* kom weche
    (go ~ in price), souate (of swelling)
downriver *adv.* vaanam
downtown *n.* sentro
downward *adv.* ko'om(i), kom vicha
doze off *iv.* yeete
dozen *n.* loseena
drab *adj.* ka kolorek (colorless)
drag *tv.* wiksime
dragging *adv.* haroroti(a) wiksime (~ one's feet)
dragonfly *n.* vaikumareewi
draw *iv.* witte
dreadful *adj.* hantiachi; *iv.* ka pasaroa machi
dream *n.* tenkuim; *iv.* tenku
dreamer *n.* tettenkume
dregs *n.* vasea
dress *n.* supem; *iv.* wokte (~ self); *tv.* a'ana (~ someone), supetua, woktua
dried *n.* wacha'i
dried up *iv.* chowia
drill *n.* hita wohowohoktame; *tv.* wohokta
drink *n.* hihi'iwame; *tv.* he'e, pomta (take a ~), kamukta (take a ~);
    tv. pomtitua (give someone a ~, but not of water), vahi'itua
    (give someone water to ~)
drink of water *exp.* vaa yoene (come get a drink of water, quench
    your thirst)
drip *iv.* chakte
dripping *adv.* polopolohti
drive *tv.* maniharoa (vehicle), naama (herd), weamtua (vehicle),
    weetua (vehicle)
driver *n.* maniheo, weweamtuame
drizzle *iv.* silolote, sio yuke
drooling *iv.* chichek
drooping *adv.* wi'ira

drop₁ *n.* chaktia
drop₂ *tv.* tatave
drown *iv.* ropte
drowsiness *n.* yeetem
drug *n.* hittoa
drug store *n.* votiika, hitto'ata nennekiwa'apo
drum *n.* kuvahe, tampa, vaa kuvahe (water ~)
drummer *n.* kuvaeleo; tampaleo (fife-and-drum player)
drunk *n.* naamukia, sankora; *iv.* naamuke (be ~; *pl.* naakoa);
      tv. naamucha (make ~)
drunks *n.* naakoriam
dry *tv.* waacha, wakia
dry out *iv.* waake
dry up *iv.* choowe
duck₁ *iv.* po'ola cha'atu
duck₂ *n.* paato (bird), vetayeka (bird), vakoni (bird)
duckling *n.* ili pato
dull *adj.* ka viohko (not sparkling), ichaktiachi (boring); *tv.* bwawi
      yotohta (make ~)
dumb *n.* ka nokame (unable to speak)
dune *n.* see pa'aria
durable *adj.* namaka
dusk *adv.* heohomteo (at ~), kutsa'iteo (at ~); *iv.* kusa'ite (get to be dusk)
dust *n.* to'ochia; *tv.* take, tatake
dust devil *n.* teekuku
dusted *adj.* tataki
dusty *adj.* toochivei, toorovoi
duty *n.* tekil, tekia
dwell *iv.* ho'ak

E

each *pn.* chikti
each other *pn.* emo
ear *n.* nakam
ear hole *n.* naka woho'oria
early *adv.* lauti; *iv.* maukaroa (get up ~)
earn *tv.* koova, tomi yo'o
earring *n.* reepam
ears, behind *adv.* nakatavaku (in the area behind the ears)
earth *n.* bwia, ania
earthquake *iv.* ania au yoa, ania vuite
east *adv.* taa'ata yeu weye vetana, taiwo
Easter *n.* Aleluya
easy (simple) *adj.* ka oviachi (not difficult), *iv.* hioria (take it ~)
eat *tv.* bwa'e, hi'ibwa

eat, something to *exp.* hibwane (come have a bite to eat)
eaves *n.* séve'i, cha'aparia (overhang)
echo *n.* kukupapa
eclipse *iv.* maala mecha muuke (be a lunar~), taa'a muuke (be a solar ~)
edge *n.* mayoa
edible *adj.* abwa'atu
egg *n.* kavam, totoi kava (chicken); *iv.* kakava (lay ~s)
eight *num.* wohnaiki
eight times *adv.* wohnaikisia
eighteen *num.* wohmamni ama wohnaiki
eighty num naiki taka
elbow *n.* techom
elder *n.* yo'owe
elderberry *n.* sauko
elders *n.* yo'ora, yo'owam, yoyo'ora (collectively)
electricity *n.* tahi, elektrisita
element *n.* vat weeme (fundamental)
elephant *n.* elefante
elevator *n.* eleveitor
eleven *num.* wohmamni ama senu
elf owl *n.* wichik
else *pn.* hitaven (something ~)
embarrasing *adj.* tiusi (with the verb aane)
embarrassment *n.* tiura
embarrassed *iv.* tittiwe (easily)
embers *n.* ouvam
embrace *tv.* ivakta, iva'achaka
embroider *iv.* sea hi'ika
embroidery *n.* sea hikwame
emergency *n.* 1. unna ko'okoe (health) 2. hiita siika (mishap)
empty *adj.* hune'ela
enchanted *adj.* yo
enchilada *n.* enchiladam
end *iv.* ansuwa; *tv.* suvina
endorse *tv.* nokria
enduring *adj.* ka lulu'uteme
enemy *n.* vehe'eri, vevehe'eri
energetic *n.* pappewame; *iv.* pappea
engine *n.* motoor
engineer *n.* trenta weweamtuame (railroad)
English *n.* Ringo noki (language); *iv.* Ringo noka (speak ~)
enjoy *adv.* tu'ulemcha (~ing)
enlarge *tv.* bwe'uria
enough *n.* soparoa
enter *iv.* kivake (*sg.*), kiimu (*pl.*)
enthusiastic *iv.* hoopea, pappea, tekipanoapea

entire *pn.* si'ime, pala
entirely *adv.* si'imek, ama vutti
entrance *n.* kimuria
envelope *n.* soovre
envious *iv.* envidiak (be ~)
envy *iv.* koptiwame
epidemic *n.* ko'okoa
equal *pn.* nanancha (see also "same")
equally *adv.* nanawichi
equipment *n.* trahte
equivalent *adj.* nana'ana (*ex.* vame karim nana'ana, theose houses are the same), hiva ... vena (*ex.* ime livrom hiva ume livrom vena, these books are like those books)
erase *tv.* tuucha, tucha'aria
erect *adj.* tenela; *tv.* kecha
escape *iv.* yeu vuite (*pl.* yeu tenne)
esophagus *n.* bwa'amtakomweamapo
establish *tv.* naate, yaa
esteem *tv.* utte'esea
eternal *adj.* ka lulu'uteme; *iv.* ka nuklak
eternal life *n.* yo hiapsiwame
evaluate *tv.* vat a mammate
even *adv.* chiktia
even so *conj.* taakialia
even though *conj.* chiktia, hain, kausi, kiali, o'oven, -taka
evening *adv.* kupteo (towards, in); *iv.* kupte (be ~)
event *n.* yeusikame (public ~)
eventually *adv.* haksaweka(i)
ever *adv.* ka chansan
every *pn.* chikti
everyone *pn.* chiktia, si'ime, si'imem
everything *pn.* si'imem
everywhere *n.* si'imekut
evil eye *n.* puhtuari
exactly *adv.* hiva naeni, tuttuti
exaggerate *iv.* ama vuttia
examine *tv.* vicha, vitchu
exceed *tv.* yeu ve'e
except *conj.* e'e, ta
exciting *iv.* tu'isi allea machi
excrement *n.* bwita
exchange *n.*, *tv.* nakulia
excuse me *exp.* ta chuvala ne hiokoe
execute *tv.* 1. weiya (carry out) 2. chaya'ana (by hanging), moina (by firing squad)
exhausted *iv.* yumia

exist *iv.* aane (be), kia hiapsa (merely ~, lead a boring life)
exit *n.* yeu sasakawa'apo (freeway), yeu kakatwa'apo (passage); *iv.* yeu
    siime (*pl.* saka)
expect *tv.* erawen
expense *n.* vehe'ewa
expensive *iv.* vehe'e, vehe'ebwan (too)
experience *tv.* pasaroa
expert *n.* hita ta'ame
explain *dv.* tehwa
explode *iv.* pehte, ruutia; *tv.* pehta
extra *n.* yeu ve'ekame (~ one)
extract *tv.* yeu wike
extracted *adj.* bwaktai
eye *n.* puusi, *iv.* puhte/remte (open ~s), kepe/kepikte (close ~s)
eyebrow *n.* kumsakan
eyelashes *n.* puse'eve'im
eyelid *n.* puhvea

F

face *n.* puhva
face to face *adv.* nau vicha
facing *adv.* puhvaka
fact *n.* ta'ewame (what is known), tua (certain thing)
factory *n.* chumti hita hohowa'apo
fade *iv.* tohte; *tv.* tohta (make)
faded *adj.* tohtia
faint *iv.* kupitomte, taamu
fair *adj.* weero (light-complected), *iv.* tu'isi aane (be ~), tu'isi yeyewe
    (play ~)
fall *iv.* yohte, weche (*sg.*), watte (*pl.*)
fall apart *iv.* rererevekti weche
fall down *iv.* kom wechise
fallen *adj.* kom wechila (~ down), sapa wechia (snow); *iv.* wechia
falling *adv.* hamhamti
false teeth *n.* pohtisom
family *n.* yoemia, wawaira (extended ~)
famous *adj.* ta'ewak; *n.* ta'ewame (~ person); *iv.* ta'ewa
fan avaniike; *iv.* hihha'aria, tapicha (fire)
far *adv.* mekka, hakun vennikut (~ away), meka'atana (from ~ away), wai
    ve'emu (that ~)
far, too *adv.* mekka hela (a little too far)
far side *adv.* wanna'avotana
far away *adv.* mekka vicha
Fariseo *n.* Fariseo (member), Fariseom (Society)
farmer *n.* etleo

fart *n.* huham; *iv.* huha
fast *adj.* chumti(a): *adv.* ute, uttea
fast *n.* hiowane (not eat); *iv.* hioria (not eat)
fat *n.* seevo; *adj.* awi; *iv.* a'awia (get)
father *n.* achai, hapchi *(fem.)*, achaiwai (as family head); *tv.* uuse
father-in-law *n.* ase'ebwa
fatigued *iv.* sutti kochok (be ~), yuume (get)
fatten *tv.* awiria
fattening *iv.* yee a'awiria
faucet *n.* yaave
fault *n.* kulpa
favorite *adv.* chea
fawn *n.* malichi, malit
fearless *tv.* kaveta hatteiya
feather *n.* voa *(gen.)*
February *n.* Fevreo
feed *tv.* hi'ibwatua(spoonfeed), hiapsitua (give sustenance), a'avose
        (visitors)
feel *iv.* ine'a, -re (have opinion); *tv.* ea, ine'etua (make ~); *exp.* haiseakai
        (how are you ~ing?); *exp.* kikichiite aane (~ something crawling
        up pants, sleeve)
female *adj.* hamuchia
fence *n.* kora; *iv.* korate
fertile *iv.* u'use (man), a'asoa (woman)
fever *n.* taewechia; *iv.* taiweche (have)
few *pn.* haleki
fiber *n.* kavavoa
fickle *iv.* ka yoem eiya maachi (be ~)
fidget *iv.* nayeehte
field *n.* waasa
field hand *n.* wahreo
fierce *adj.* sunwachi
fifteen *num.* wohmamni ama mamni
fifty *num.* woi taka ama wohmamni
fifty cents *n.* naiki tomi
fig *n.* chuuna (cultivated)
fight *tv.* nassua
fighter *n.* nahsuareo, nanahsuame
fighting *n.* nassuawame
file *n.* liimam (tool)
fill *tv.* tapunia; *iv.* hovo hi'ibwak (eat one's ~)
film *n.* vihtam (movies)
filter *tv.* kolaroa
filtered *adj.* kolaroari
filth *n.* techuniam
filthy *iv.* haiti maachi, techuniak
finally *adv.* ultimopo

find *tv.* tea
fine *adj.* tu'i (quality), hochi (granular)
finger *n.* mampusiam
finger, little *n.* ili mam pusiam
finger, middle *n.* nasuk mam pusiam
fingernail *n.* mam pusia sutum
finish *tv.* chupa, ansu (~ up)
finish up *iv.* suvina, yaate, ansuwa (be finishing up)
finished *iv.* lu'ute
fire *n.* tahi, naya'i (already built); *iv.* hitta (make, set)
fire engine *n.* bombo
firecrackers *n.* triikim
firefly *n.* kuupis
fireman *n.* tahita tutuchame
fireplace *n.* chiminea
first *n.* ke'esam(i); *adv.* vat; *interj.* vach'a (go ~)
fiscal *n.* pihkan
fish *n.* kuchu; *iv.* kuchusua (with net); *tv.* vo'a
fisherman *n.* kuchuleo (with net), vo'areo (with line)
fist *iv.* lovola mamak (have one's hand in a ~); *tv.* mam kitoktia (make ~)
fit *iv.* kia (into), ama weye (go in a certain place)
fitness *n.* allewame
five *num.* mamni
five times *adv.* mamnisia
fix *tv.* tu'ute
fixed *adj.* tu'utei
flabby *adj.* cholapelai
flag *n.* vanteam
flag-bearer *n.* alpes
flame *n.* tahi, rupaktiam (~s)
flap *iv.* masa vaite (wings)
flashlight *n.* fooko, vateria
flat *adj.* vetala(i), verai (small items); sumia (tire)
flattened *adj.* patalai
flatter *tv.* vava'atoa
flavor *iv.* yuin tekwak (have a strong ~)
flea *n.* ete, teput, kuurum (sand), chu ete (dog ~)
flesh *n.* tekwa
flexible *iv.* tottatu, tottotte
float *iv.* vo'osime (*sg.*), hapsaka (*pl.*); *iv.* chasisime (~ in breeze)
flood *iv.* vaa'a viakte
flooded *iv.* vaa yepsak (be ~)
floor *n.* piiso
flotsam *n.* vaseka
flounder *n.* tahkaim kuchu, yavarai
flour *n.* ainam, tuusi

flow *iv.* vaa weye
flower *n.* seewa, chunahkam (mesquite); *iv.* sewa tomte, seate (make ~s)
fluently *adv.* tuttuti
flute *n.* kusia
flute player *n.* kusiareo
flutter *iv.* vaite
fly *iv.* ne'e, cha'asime (~ing along)
fly *n.* sevo'i (insect), teeka sevo'i (horse ~)
foam *n.* somo'ochia
fog *n.* vahewa
foggy *iv.* vae weche (be ~), vae wetvae (get ~)
fold *tv.* totta
folded *adj.* tottila, chapa'a; *adv.* lapala; *iv.* totte (arms, legs), chapala
    mamak (have hands ~)
follow *iv.* nat cha'aka weye (*sg.*), nat cha'aka kaáte (*pl.*); hahase (~ a road)
fondle *tv.* emo yeewa
food *n.* bwa'ame
foolishly, act *iv.* sulwachi aane
foot *n.* wooki (body), piiye (measure)
football *n.* Ringo himari
footprint *n.* wokla
for *postp.* -po (~ a certain amount), vetchi'ivo (~ the benefit of, ~ the pur-
    pose of)
foreign *exp.* ka im + [adjective, adverb, OR verb]
foreigner *n.* ka im ho'akam
forever *adv.* hiva vetchi'ivo
fork *n.* tatakalim (~, any ~ed item)
forked *n.* tatakalim
forcefully *adv.* sutta'a
forehead *n.* kovameheria, mehe'eria
foreman *n.* mooroma
forget *tv.* kopta, aawas kopte, veaskopte; koove (leave behind)
forgive *tv.* hiokoe
forgiveness *iv.* au hiokoe (ask ~)
fork *n.* teneror
forked takalai
form *n.* ya'ane, haisa a machiaka'apo
formerly *adv.* ka nappat
fort *n.* kuartel
forty *num.* woi taka
found *adj.* teula; *iv.* teak (be ~); *tv.* naate, yaa (establish)
foundation *n.* fundasión, ya'ane
four *num.* naiki
four times *adv.* naikisia
four ways *adv.* naikiwe (in four ways)
fourteen *num.* wohmamni ama naiki

fox *n.* kawis, mata'e (kit)
fracture *iv.* riute; *tv.* riuta
fractured *adj.* riutia
frail *adj.* wakira
Frances *n.* Pasihka
frank *adv.* lutula
Frank *n.* Pasihko
freak *iv.* ka yuma'i (not formed right)
free *adj.* liokis (no cost), vasou wattila (be ~ to do as one likes); *iv.* kaita
    hoa (not doing anything)
free-loading *iv.* kaitapo an'a (be ~)
free-standing *adj.* tennei
freeze *iv.* hu'uwasu
fresh *adj.* vaali
freshness *n.* vaali
fret *iv.* ka tu'isi ea
Friday *n.* Vienes
fried *adj.* kisaroari
friend *n.* halla'i; *iv.* halla'ek (have a ~), halla'i bwise (make ~s)
friendly *adj.* tu hiapsek
frighten *tv.* womta, mahautua
frightened *adj.* womtila; *iv.* womte, mammahe (easily)
frightened of *tv.* suumeiya
frightening *adj.* mamaiwachi
frightful *adv.* sanvara
fringe *n.* seve'im
frog *n.* kuareepa
from *postp.* vétana, -po, -tana, -u (in transactions); *adv.* hiva yu
    (~ then on)
front *postp.* aepat, -pat (in front of)
frown *iv.* chokinaik puhvaka a vitchu
frozen *adj.* sapa wechia
fruit *n.* taaka, kakawa; *iv.* si'ita (set ~)
fruit tree *n.* huya tatakame
fry *tv.* kisaroa
frying pan *n.* saarten
fugitive *n.* vuitilame
fulfill *iv.* hichupa; *tv.* chupa (vow)
full *adj.* hovoi, tapuni; *iv.* hovoa (get), tapuna (get; liquid, particulate
    matter)
full-blooded Yoeme *n.* tua Hiaki
fun *iv.* alletua (have); *tv.* hunniawa (make ~ of)
fundamental *n.* vat weeme (basic thing)
funnel *n.* emvuudo
funny *adj.* musa'ala; *iv.* musala maachi; *tv.* musa'aule (consider ~)
fur *n.* voam

furious *iv.* tu'isi omte (be ~)
furniture *n.* muevlem
furry *adj.* voa rovoi
furthermore *conj.* navuhti vicha
future *adv.* vichau vicha (in the ~)
fuzz *n.* voam
fuzzy *adj.* voa rovoi

G

gain *tv.* koova
gall bladder *n.* chivu si'ika
gallon *n.* galoon
gamble *tv.* ha'ate
gambler *n.* hahateme
game *n.* yeuwame
garage *n.* garaachi (repairs), karota kechawa'apo (parking)
garlic *n.* aasos
gasp *iv.* hiavihmumuke
gather *iv.* mochakte; *tv.* nau toha, kowikta (into skein)
gathering *n.* hunta (meeting), voolo (social)
gear *n.* trahte
gelatinous *adj.* heloko
generations *n.* tomti kateme (future ~)
generous *iv.* ka au hiokoe
gentle *adj.* manso
gesture *adv.* naa mamma
get *iv.* nu'u (go to ~); *tv.* nu'e; *suf.* -se (go get; *pl.* -vo), -vaawa (get ready)
get away from *tv.* wohanria
get down *iv.* kom chepte
get together *i.* nau toha (with *refl.*)
get well *iv.* tuttu'iria
ghost *n.* muukia
gibberish *n.* veewa
gift *n.* makri, miiki
gigantic *adj.* unna bwe'u
giggle *iv.* ili aache
Gila monster *n.* sakkau
girdle *n.* kuttiria
girl *n.* nana (little), *n.* ili hamut, uusi hamut (preteen), *n.* (young) veeme
girlfriend *n.* novia
give *dv.* maka (with expectation of return), miika (permanently)
giver *n.* mimika
glare at *tv.* omteka a vitchu ("at" = *d.o.*)
glass *n.* vaaso (drinking)

glasses *n.* leentim, antihom (*Son.*)

glide *iv.* cha'asime

globular *adj.* lovola(i)

Gloria *n.* Savala Looria

glory *n.* looria

gloves *n.* wantem

glow *iv.* veete

glue *n.* koola; *tv.* chu'akta

glued *adj.* chu'aktila, *iv.* chu'akte

glutton *n.* tevai mukiari (*pl.* tevai kokoarim)

gnat *n.* wetepo'i

gnaw *tv.* kuume

go *iv.* weye (*sg.*), kaáte (*pl.*), konte (~ around), -ma (~ along doing), -nama (~ about doing), -se (~ get; *pl.* -vo), -sisime (~ along doing; *pl.* -sasaka); *tv.* yaa (~ according to plan)

go ahead *interj.* hava, vachia, vanseka

go away *interj.* simise'e (*sg.*), saka'avo'em (*pl.*); *iv.* siime (*pl.* -saka)

go out *iv.* tuuke (fire, light)

goat *n.* chiiva

goat herder *n.* chivam susuame

God *n.* Itom Achai, Lios, Ya'uchiwa (the Lord), Lios Achai O'ola (God the Old Father)

God willing *exp.* Diohta ela'apo

godchild *n.* vato'o asoa (*fem.*; said of boy or girl)

goddaughter *n.* vato'o maara (*masc.*; *fem.* uses vato'o asoa)

godfather *n.* vato'o achai (*masc.*), vato'o hapchi (*fem.*)

godmother *n.* vato'o ae (*fem.*, *masc.*)

godparents *n.* vato'o yo'owam

godson *n.* vato'o uusi (*masc.*; *fem.* uses vato'o asoa)

going *exp.* pues ne wéevae (I'll be ~)

gold *n.* ooro

goldfish *n.* karpa

gone *adj.* simla

good *adj.* tu'i

good for *postp.* vetchi'ivo

good for nothing *iv.* kaita vetchi'ivo tu'i (be ~)

goodbye *exp.* Lios emak weye

good-hearted *adj.* tu'i hiapsek

goodness *n.* tu'uwa

goodnight *exp.* alleaka yeu matchune

gooey *iv.* choachoakte

goof off *iv.* hana aane

gopher *n.* tevos

gospel *n.* evanheelio

gossip *n.* yet nokwame (the ~ itself), nonnokame (person who ~s); *iv.* yet nooka; *tv.* na'ateo, nonnoka (~ about) gourd *n.* visa'e, bweha'i (half ~), teta'ahao (wild, coyote)

government *n.* govierno, nesaweme, ya'uram

governor *n.* kovanao

grab *tv.* nunu'e

grace *n.* tachiria

gradually *adv.* halekisia

grains *n.* amoe (cooked)

gram *n.* gramo

grammar *n.* noki hoowame

grandchild *n.* amu (daughter's child; *fem.*), apala (daughter's child; *masc.*), hakara (son's child; *fem.*), havoli (son's child; *masc.*)

grandfather *n.* apa (maternal), havoi (paternal; *aff.* havoli)

grandmother *n.* asu (maternal), haaka (paternal)

grape *n.* uuva

grapefruit *n.* toronha

grapevine *n.* uva wiroa

grasp *tv.* bwisi

grass *n.* vaso

grasshopper *n.* woo'ochi, yoo woo'ochi (large)

grateful *iv.* nukisia, vaisae

gratitude *n.* vaisaewame

grave *n.* hima'aripo

gravel *n.* tetam, tutukam

gray *adj.* tosa; *iv.* tosa'a kovak (have ~ hair)

graze *tv.* hi'ibwatua

greasy *adj.* ochoko

great grandfather *n.* hamuli

great grandmother *n.* namuli

greedy *n.* tevai mukiari (~ person; *pl.* tevai kokoarim); *iv.* au hiokoe

green *adj.* siali, siarí

greenish *adj.* siasaalai

greens *n.* hi'u, mamyam, vakoe

greet *tv.* tevote, tevotua

greetings *exp.* aman ne tevote em yevihnewi (I send my ~)

grill *n.* hihsova, wako'i

grimace *iv.* kinakte

grime *n.* techuniam, wok techuniam (foot ~)

grin *iv.* aache

grind *iv.* saktuse; *tv.* hota (finely), mohta (pulverize), tuuse (coarsely)

groan *iv.* te'ine

groom *n.* kunawaituvaeme, kunavawame

groomed *adj.* chichikla (combed)

groove *n.* raaya

ground *adj.* tuusi, tutusi

group *adv.* mocha'ala (in a ~), momochala (in groups)

grove *n.* saniloa, sania

grow *iv.* siwe (plants)
grow out of *iv.* yeu chuchupe
growl *iv.* omte
growl *iv.* ruutia (stomach)
grubby *iv.* techuniak
grudge *iv.* kuhti maachi (hold a ~)
grumpy *iv.* ili omte
Guadalupe *n.* Waluupe
guamuchil *n.* mako'ochini
Guarajio *n.* Warahio
guard *tv.* sua
guasima *n.* aiya (tree)
Guaymas *n.* Wa'emam
guaymuchil *n.* mako'ochini (tree *sp.*)
guess *tv.* tinaaroa
guest *n.* itou aneme
guide *tv.* weiya
guilty *iv.* kulpak (be ~)
guilty,be found *iv.* aet vo'otek
guitar *n.* kitara
guitarist *n.* kitareo
gull *n.* vatosai
gullet *n.* vuuchi
gulp *iv.* pomte
gum *n.* chikitam (chewing), chu'ukam (resin)
gun *n.* tahi wiko'i
guts *n.* to'ona
Gypsy *n.* ungara

H

habit *n.* avi'itom (clothing; *syn.* santo supem), tiri'isia (behavior)
hackberry *n.* kunwo
had *suf.* -suk (perfect tense)
hail *n.* teeham
hair *n.* voam (body), chinota kovak (curly), choonim (head), seekavoam
    (underarm); *iv.* sanveta kovak (have unkempt ~); *tv.* chonim
    vutta (let down), tosa'a kovak (have gray ~)
hairy *adj.* voa rovoi, voara
half *adj.* no'asi (~ full, in ~); *adv.* kopela (in ~), nasuk amani (in ~)
hall *n.* haal (passageway), komunila (assembly house)
halo *n.* mecha kari (moon), tachiria (of saint)
ham *n.* kowi waakas
hammer *n.* martiom
hammock *n.* maaka

hand *n.* mam, mamam (~s); *adv.* mamammea, by hand
handful *n.* machuktia
handkerchief *n.* paayum
handle *n.* bwisiria, votoon (door, furniture); *tv.* aet mamma (with hand),
 vicha (oversee)
handshake *iv.* mam tevote
handsome *adj.* tutu'uli
handy *iv.* ka oviachisi aayuk
hang *tv.* chaya, yoemta chaya (execute)
hang out *iv.* anwa (be around), hitcha'ala (laundry); *tv.* hitcha (laundry)
hanging *iv.* cha'aka
happen *iv.* siime (with yeu), hivatune (will ~)
happen to *iv.* ian weeme
happy *adj.* allea; *iv.* allete'ea (get ~)
harbor *n.* puerto
hard *adj.* oviachi (not easy); *adj.* namaka, ousi (physically ~)
hard-headed *adj.* turuik kovak
harm *tv.* nasonte, siivo
harmful *iv.* ka tu'i
harp *n.* aapa
harpist *n.* aapaleo
harpoon *n.* sopoi
harsh *adj.* vutti; *iv.* ama vutti machi (be ~)
harvest *n.* hichupak, etta; *iv.* hichupa; *tv.* tovokta
has-been *iv.* kaitapo tawasuk (be a ~)
hat *n.* move'i
hate *tv.* kuhteiya, yee omta
hateful *iv.* kuhtea
have *tv.* hippue, atte'ak; *suf.* (-ek) (to nouns; -suk, perfect tense)
hawk *n.* taawe (*gen.*)
hay *n.* paakam, vahu'uri; huya wakia (dry ~, straw)
he *pn.* aapo
head *n.* kova, moa (grass, grain), kovanao (of society)
head cloth *n.* movektia
headache *iv.* kova wante (have a ~)
headdress *n.* choomo, movektiam
headlights puusim (of car)
head-on *adv.* navuhti
heal *iv.* yoore
health *n.* allewame
heap *n.* mo'ola
heaps *n.* motcha; *adv.* monti (in ~)
hear *tv.* hikka
hearing aid *n.* yee hihikkaituame
heart *n.* hiapsi
hearts *n.* hiapsim (cards)

heat *n.* tataria; *iv.* ohvora (be inn ~), tatai (be in ~)

heathen *iv.* kaita suale

heatstroke *iv.* tatai mukuk (have ~)

heaven *n.* looria, teeka

heavy *adj.* vette

heed *tv.* nok hikkaila (~ advice)

heel *n.* pempe'im

Hell *n.* Ka Maachikun

help *tv.* ánia

hemorrhoids *iv.* huvariapo ko'okoe (have ~)

hen *n.* totoi hamuchia

her *pn.* a, apo'ik

hebalist *n.* hittuareo

herd *tv.* naama

here *interj.* hiva; *adv.* im, a'ava (near speaker), a'avo (over ~), inim(i) (right ~), iniminsu (over ~; in songs, iyiminsu), ko'omisu (down ~), vina (over ~), yet (~ and there)

hereabouts *adv.* imcha

Hemrosillo *n.* Pessio

heritage *n.* erensia

herself *pn.* au, emo

hex *n.* yee sivowame

hey! *interj.* hepa, omme (*masc.*)

hiccups *n.* he'oktiam; *iv.* he'okte (have ~)

hidden *adj.* eusila

hide$_1$ *tv.* ehso, *iv.* euse (~ self), eusi katek (~ out; *pl.* eusi hooka), eusise (go to ~)

hide$_2$ *n.* vea

hideout *n.* e"eusiwa'apo

high *adv.* cho'ola(i) (too ~)

hike *iv.* huyapo weama (*pl.* huyapo rehte)

hill *n.* chopoi

hilly *n.* chopo'oria

him *pn.* a

himself *pn.* au

hips *n.* wepe'im

hire *tv.* takea

his *pn.* a

Hispanic *n.*, *adj.* 1. *n.* Yoori 2. *adj.* Yoi

hiss *iv.* siotia

history *n.* hakwo siikame

hit *tv.* chochona, hiveva, veeva; *tv.* tahta (impact)

hive *n.* mumukari (bee); *cf.* maiko

hoarse *adj.* sokiktula; *iv.* na'ove, sokiktu; *iv.* sokiktu (get ~)

hobo *n.* traampa

hoe *n.* asaroonim; *tv.* hina

hog *n.* koowi, tevai mukiari (person who takes something even though others may need; *pl.* tevai kokoarim); *tv.* chumte (~ food)

hold *tv.* bwisi; machu'unama (~ while moving), machu'uweyek (~ while standing), tekiak (~ a job)

hold it! *interj.* vachu

hole *n.* wooho'oria; *iv.* wohokte; *tv.* wohokta

hollow *adj.* hotolai

hollowed out *adj.* bwaktai

Holy Saturday *n.* Looria

Holy Spirit *n.* Ehpirito Santo

Holy Week *n.* Bwetaewaim

home *n.* ho'ara; *adv.* ho'arapo (at ~); *iv.* ho'apo katek (be at ~)

homeland *n.* bwiara

homeless *iv.* ka ho'akame

hometown *n.* ho'ara

homosexual *n.* seve (male or female)

honest *iv.* sualsi maachi

honey *n.* mumum, mielim

honk *iv.* kuuse (car)

hood *n.* yeka (of car)

hoof *n.* sutum, wooki

hook *n.* vo'arim (fishing)

hop *iv.* chepte

horn *n.* aawam

horned *n.* awakame (any ~ thing)

horned toad *n.* motcho'okoli

horrible *adj.* sunwachi

horse *n.* kava'i

horseback *n.* kakava'ekame (on ~)

hose *n.* siiya

hospital *n.* ospitaal

host *n.* miisam (for mass)

hostage *n.* etbwaim

hot *adj.* yosi, ko'oko (spicy); *iv.* tatai, yossia (get ~), tatale (feel ~ from weather), ko'oko'itu (get ~ from chiles); ouvatu (get ~; coals)

hot-headed *n.* eiyachume (~ person)

hotel *n.* hoteel

hour *n.* oora

house *n.* kari

household *n.* ho'ara

housewife *n.* huviawai

hover *iv.* cha'aka, koowe, kowema (be ~ing)

how *adv.* hachini, haisa, keche; *interj.* alasu (~ nice); *exp.* haisempane (~ are you?)

how big *adv.* haivetchi

how come *adv.* maasu

how many *adv.* haiki
how well *adv.* haisamaisi
however *adv.* san, ta
huddled *adv.* saiyula
hug *tv.* ivakta
huge *adj.* unna bwe'u
Huirivis *n.* Wiivisim
hum *iv.* kuutia (insects)
human *n.* yoeme
humanity *n.* yoemra
humbly *adv.* polovesi(a)
hummingbird *n.* semalulukut
hump *n.* lochi
humped *adj.* lovola(i)
hunchback *n.* lochi
hunchbacked *iv.* lovola hoo'ok, rovou hoo'ok
hundred *num.* mamni taka
hungover *adj.* ka bwasi
hungry *adj.* tevauri; *iv.* tevaure (feel ~), tettevaure (get ~)
hunt *tv.* aamu
hunter *n.* amureo, masoleo (deer ~)
hunting *iv.* amuse (go ~)
hurricane *n.* chuvahko
hurry *adv.* vaamse (in a ~); *iv.* vamse; *tv.* vamihtua; *interj.* vanseka, noolia
    (~ up)
hurt *iv.* wante; *tv.* ko'okosa hoa
husband *n.* kunawai (in general), kuuna (woman speaking of her ~)
husky *n.* awilovolai
hut *n.* sankoa kari
hymn *n.* alavansam

I

I *pn.* inepo, ne
I see *interj.* alavea
ice *n.* sapam
ice-cream *n.* sapam
icey *adj.* sapak
icicle *n.* sapam
idea *n.* eewame
idle *iv.* kaita hoa (be ~)
if *conj.* ala; *suf.* -k(o)
ignite *tv.* taya
ignore *iv.* ka au vitchu (*d.o.* = au)
iguana *n.* kuta wikui

illness *n.* ko'okoa
imagine *tv.* ea
imagination *iv.* kiavea hiapsa (have no ~)
imitate *tv.* mamato
immediately *adv.* lauti, sep(i)
immovable *iv.* ka ruktatu
impatient *iv.* ka vovicha (be ~)
implore *tv.* maate
impolite *iv.* kaveta yo'ore
important *iv.* aman [noun]-po cha'aka
impossible *iv.* ka ho'otu, ka ya'atu
improperly *adj.* háana, ka amma'ali
improve *iv.* tuttu'ira
impure *iv.* haiti maachi
in *postp.* -po
in front of *postp.* -pat
incarcerate *tv.* eta'ana
incense *n.* kopaalim; *tv.* santom hi'ibwa
inch *n.* pulgada
incomplete *iv.* ka chupia
inconsiderate *iv.* a eau hoa (be ~)
increase *iv.* ha'amuria
incredible *adj.* vutti
indeed *adv.* huna'ala
indigestion *n.* pottila; *iv.* potte (have ~)
indigo *n.* chiihu
indoors *adv.* karipo waiwa
inept *iv.* kaita vetchi'ivo tu'i
infant *n.* aso'ola
infantile *iv.* no'ochia
infantry *n.* woklem
infected *iv.* viika, ripte (eyes ~)
inform *iv.* hina'atua (tattle); *tv.* na'atua (tattle)
inhabitant *n.* hoome, ho'akame
inhale *tv.* hakta
inject *tv.* inchetaroa
injection *n.* chaatim
injure *tv.* ko'okosa hoa
ink *n.* tiinta
innocent *iv.* kaita hu'uneiya
inquire *tv.* nattemai (about = *d.o.*)
insect *n.* yoeria (*gen.*)
insert *tv.* kiima, tutta
inserted *adj.* tuttala
inside *adv.* karipo waiwa (~ of a house)
inside of *postp.* waiwa

instruct *iv.* aet mammatte (*d.o.* = aet)
insult *tv.* hana hiuwa
intelligent *n.* moreakame; *iv.* kova suawak (be ~)
intelligentsia *n.* susuakame
intend *tv.* -roka
intended for *postp.* vetchi'ivo
intentionally *adj.* hunaktekai
interesting *adj.* uhyoi
interpret *iv.* ___nokiu vicha yecha
interrupt *tv.* suatam vicha
intersecting *adv.* sapala
intestines *n.* siam
intoxicate *tv.* naamuke (*sg. obj.*), naakoa (*pl. obj.*)
invisible *iv.* ka mamachi
invite *tv.* nehunwa (formally), nunu (informally)
invited *iv.* nunuwa
iron *n.* sisiwooki (metal), plancham (for clothes); *tv.* plancharoa
ironwood *n.* ehea
irrigate *tv.* vaane, suati eetua
irrigator *n.* vanreo
irritating *adv.* suati
irritating *adj.* suatiachi; *iv.* suatiachisi maachi
island *n.* isla
it *pn.* a
itch *iv.* elesikile
itchy *adj.* elesiiki
its *pn.* a

J

jacal *n.* techoa kari
jacket *n.* chake'etam
jackrabbit *n.* paaros
jaguar *n.* yóoko
jail *n.* karsel; *tv.* eta'ana
January *n.* Enero
jar *n.* tinaaha, va'achia
jaundice *n.* sawaria
javelina *n.* hua koowi, pocho'oku koowi
jaw *n.* tavawasa'i
jealous *adj.* na'ivuki; *iv.* na'ivuke; *tv.* koptiwame (be ~ of)
jeans *n.* me'gliiyam
jelly *n.* sito'im
jerky *n.* waka wacha'i
Jesus Christ *n.* Hesu Krihto

Jew *n.* Hurio
jimson weed *n.* tebwi, toloachi
jingling *iv.* rii'itia
job *n.* tekil; *iv.* teakiak (hold a ~)
jog *iv.* vuivuite
jogger *n.* vuivuiteme
join *tv.* nau chaya (fasten), amemak cha'atu (a group)
joint *n.* tonua
jojoba *n.* hohoova
joke *n.* vaitiuwame; *tv.* vaitia
Judas *n.* Huuras
juice *n.* va'awa
July *n.* Hulio
jump *iv.* chepte
jump over *tv.* chepta, tuvukta; Aapo kanalta ~k. He jumped over
      the canal.
junction *n.* hinanke
June *n.* Hunio
just *adv.* hiva, kia, hubwa hiva (~ recently), wepu'ulai (~ one)
just so *adv.* kia veha

K

kangaroo rat *n.* vacha'e
keep *tv.* hippue
kettle *n.* soto'i
key *n.* yaavem
kick *tv.* temu
kick out *tv.* veeva
kid *n.* asoa (child), ili chiva (goat)
kidneys *n.* sikupuriam
kill (*sg. obj.*) *tv.* me'a (*sg. obj.*), sua (*pl. obj.*)
killdeer *n.* tuivit (bird)
killer *n.* yee sussuame
kilogram *n.* kilogramo
kilometer *n.* kilometro
kin *n.* wawaim
kind$_1$ *adj.* tu'i hiapsek (*var.* tu hiapsek)
kind$_2$ *suf.* -taka (what ~ of)
kindergarten *n.* kinder
kindling *n.* chuutiam
king *n.* rei
kiss *iv.* nat tente, tetente, vesiito
kitchen *n.* kosina
kite *n.* papalote

kitten *n.* miisi aso'ola, ili misi
knapsack *n.* mochila
knead *iv.* kitte
knee *n.* tonom
kneel *iv.* tonommea wek (with legs upright); *adv.* chunula (~ing while
  sitting on one's legs)
knife *n.* kuchi'im, nava'asom (pocket ~)
knob *n.* bwisiria (handle), tekuriam (on antler), votoon (door ~)
knock *tv.* poona
knock down *tv.* tave, tatave, ko'omamaya (with rock)
knot *n.* nuudo; *tv.* wikiata suma (tie a ~)
know *tv.* ta'a, hu'uneiya, mammatte (~ well); *interj.* heitu (I don't ~)
know how *tv.* ta'a
knowing *n.* hu'unewame
knowledge *n.* hita ta'awame (that which is learned), hu'uneiyawame (that
  which is known), teuwawame (what is told)
knowledgeable *iv.* hu'unea
known *adj.* hu'uneiyawari; *n.* ta'ewame
knuckle *n.* mam pusiam tottote'epo

L

laboratory *n.* lavatorio
lace *n.* enkaahe
lacking *iv.* ve'e
ladder *n.* ehkaleam
ladle *n.* kuta wisa'e
lady *n.* naaka (in address)
laid *adj.* tekri
lake *n.* vahkom
lamb *n.* bwala aso'ola
lamb's quarters *n.* choali, kapa
lame *adj.* lo'i
lamp *n.* lampa, lampara
land *n.* bwia, nasion
language *n.* nooki
lantern *n.* linteena
lard *n.* manteeka
large *adj.* bwe'u (*sg.*), bweere (*pl.*)
lariat *n.* reata
lark *n.* maavis, vavi cho'ola
laryngitis *iv.* nauve
larynx *n.* kusia
Las Guasimas *n.* Waasimam
lasso *tv.* cho'ila

lasting *adj.* ka nuklak

last *adv.* iniavu (~ year); *adj.* ultimo (in position or turn)

lasting *adj.* ka lulu'uteme

late *iv.* kupte (be ~ evening); *adv.* kupteo

later *adv.* chukula

lather *n.* somo'ochia; *iv.* sasavua

laugh *n.* ache'a (one who ~s a lot); *iv.* aache; *tv.* atbwa (~ at)

laughter *n.* atwame

laundry *n.* taho haiti machiwame (clothes), hihipaksiawa'apo (place)

law *n.* lei

lawyer *n.* avogáo

lay *tv.* teeka (~ across)

lay down *tv.* to'a

layered i. nat to'oka

laziness *iv.* oove wechia

lazy *adj.* ove'a; *iv.* oove, ouva (feel ~), oove weeche (get ~)

lazy person *n.* ove'era, ove'a

lead *tv.* weiya

leader *n.* ya'ut; *iv.* yo ya'awa (become a ~)

leadership *n.* ya'uchiwa

leaf *n.* sawa; *iv.* siakikichiite (~ out)

leak *iv.* hiikia, chakte (faucet), vaawe (roof)

lean *adj.* wakila

leaning *iv.* cha'aka, chakkai, tavilai

leap *iv.* tuvukte

leap over *tv.* tuvukta

learn *n.* tatta'a, namya (absorb knowledge)

leather *n.* vakeeta

leave *tv.* sutoha, hima (behind), himo'ote (~ in another's care), simtua
(make; *sg. obj.*), saka'atua (make; *pl. obj.*); *tv.* koove, taawa
(~ unintentionally)

leave off (*sg. obj.*) *tv.* to'osiime, to'osaka (*pl. obj.*)

leave out *tv.* yeu'aveve'a (exclude), yewa'ave'ene (for convenience)

left *adv.* mikko'otana (on the ~), ayatana (~ turn)

left over *iv.* ve'e

left-handed *adj.* mikkoi

legend *n.* etehoi, kia etehoi

leg *n.* wokim; *adv.* sutta (~s extended), metela (~s crossed), ekka
(~s open; *var.* ekala)

lemon *n.* liimon

lend *tv.* reuwa

Lent *n.* Waehma

Lenten Society *n.* Kohtumre Ya'ura

let *interj.* ela'apo(su)

let me *interj.* ateka

let's *interj.* antevu (~ go), chumtia (~ go)

lethargic *iv.* ka pappea
letter *n.* karta (writing), letra (alphabet)
lettuce *n.* lechuuwa
level *postp.* vewit (same)
lever *n.* bwisiria
liar *n.* anoki'ichi
library *n.* biblioteeka
license *n.* lisensia; *tv.* lisensiaria
lick *tv.* te'ebwa
lid *n.* pattiria, patpattame, taparea (of pot)
lie *n.* anoki'ichia (falsehood)
lie down *iv.* vo'oka (*sg.*), to'oka (*pl.*)
lieutenant *n.* teniente
life *n.* hiapsiwame, voohoria; *n.* hiva vetchi'ivo hiapsiwame, yu
    hiapsiwame (eternal ~) lift *tv.* pu'akta, soita, pa'akta (with lever),
    topakta (with wedge)
light *n.* machiria, kaila (pre-dawn), tachiria (fire), weero (~ complected
    one); *iv.* tahek (have ~s on); *tv.* naaya (fire)
light bulb *n.* fooko
lighted *adj.* maachi
lightning *n.* yuku ve'oktia (flash), yuku hima'i (~ strike or bolt); *iv.* yuku
    ve'okte, ve'ove'okte
like *postp.* vena, venasi(a) (similar); *adv.* inen(i) (~ this), hunaen (~ that),
    hunulevena (~ that), nian (~ this)
like *tv.* kiale, tu'ule, tuttu'ule (prefer)
likewise *adv.* hunalensu
lima bean *n.* tosai munim
limberbush *n.* sapo
lime *n.* liima (fruit), kaal (mineral)
limping *adv.* ro'iro'ikti
line *n.* witti, linia; *tv.* witta (make a ~)
lion *n.* ousei (mountain ~, African ~)
lip(s) *n.* tenveria, aasa (of pot)
listen *tv.* hikka
listless *iv.* ka pappea
litany *n.* letania
liter *n.* litro
literate *iv.* hiosia ta'a
litter *n.* 1. antas (vehicle) 2. sankoa wo'oti
little *adj.* ili, ilitchi
little by little *adv.* halekisia
live *iv.* ho'ak
liver *n.* heemam
liver spots *n.* mechawa
livestock *iv.* vukek
lizard *n.* wikui

load *n.* pu'akti; *tv.* pu'akte
loaf *n.* paanim
loan *tv.* reuwa; *dv.* maka
lobster *n.* kochimai
lock *n.* gannao, lakim
lock up *tv.* eta'ana
logger *n.* kuta chuktireo
loincloth *n.* bwahim
lonely *iv.* rohikte, sioka
long *adj.* teeve; *adv.* haleppan(i) (so ~), tevesi (a long way), vinwa
    (~ ago), vinwatuk (for too ~), vinwatuko (~ ago), wai ve'emu
    (that ~, that far)
longer *adv.* yuin chuvva (in a while ~)
look *iv.* vicha; *interj.* yuu, =ma
look at *tv.* vitchu
look for *tv.* hariwa, haiwa
look good *iv.* ala maachi
look good on *tv.* uttia
look out for *tv.* hiiwe
look over *tv.* vicha, vitchu
loose *iv.* vutte (become), sookte (come), alilite (teeth, pole); *adj.* aliliti
    (teeth, pole), vaalai (hinges, joint)
loosen *tv.* vaahta, vutta
lope *iv.* laplapti weye
lord *n.* senyoor
Lord's Prayer *n.* Itom Achai
lose *iv.* kovawa (competition, fight); *tv.* ta'aru (object)
lost *adj.* au ta'arula; *iv.* ta'aru (get)
lot *adv.* ousi, unna (a ~); *n.* loot (land)
loud *adj.* kusi
loudly *adv.* kusim, kusisi(a), vahooti, yamyamti
louse *n.* ete
love *tv.* eiya, nake, tu'ule
loveable *adj.* a tu'ulitu
loved one *n.* nakwame
low *adj.* vetuk
lowlife *n.* sankora (trashy person)
luck *n.* suerte
lucky *adj.* suertek; *tv.* tinaaroa (be ~ with; with = *d.o.*)
lunch (box) *n.* lonchi (box ~), nuu'u (sack ~)
lungs *n.* hemaha'achim
lying down *iv.* vo'ote (*sg.*), to'ote (*pl.*)
lynx *n.* bwahilovon
lyrics *n.* bwika noki

M

machete *n.* mache'etam
machine *n.* maakina
macho *n.* o'ou au ouleme
made *adj.* ya'ari, ya'awak
maestro *n.* maehto, malehto (lay priest); *n.* maehto yo'owe, yoo maehto
    (head ~)
magician *n.* mahikeo
magnetic stone *n.* chukui teta
maguey *n.* kuu'u
maid, old *n.* apelai
maiden *n.* naaka
mail *n.* kartam
main *n.* prinsipaal (~ person or thing)
make *tv.* aane, hoa, yaa; *suf.* -te, -tia
make up *n.* paro hoo'o (one who can easily ~)
male *n.* o'ouwia
malign *tv.* hunniawa
mallow *n.* heoko kuta (plant)
man *n.* o'ou, hu'ubwa yo'otume (young)
manage *tv.* vicha
management *n.* nesaweme
mange *n.* keekam
mangrove *n.* paseo
mangy *adj.* keka'a
manifest *iv.* yeu chuchupe
mano *n.* tutuha, tuusa
Manuel *n.* Manwe
many *pn.* huevena, vuu'u; *adv.* ka haiki (not ~), huevenasi (~ times)
map *n.* mapa
March *n.* Marso
mare *n.* kava'i hamuchia
margarine *n.* mantekia
Maricopa *n.* Marikoopa
mark *n.* seyo (insignia); *tv.* markaroa
market *n.* merkao
married *iv.* kuunak (be ~; of a woman), huuvek (be ~, of a man);
    chupe (get ~), huhupwa (get ~, of a man), kukunawa (get ~,
    of a woman)
married man *n.* huvekame
married woman *n.* kunakame
marry *iv.* huuve (of a man), kuuna (of a woman)
marsh *n.* vaata yehtepo
Mary *n.* Itom Ae (St. Mary)
mash *iv.* chihte; *tv.* chihta, poona

mashed *adj.* chihti

masher *n.* chihchihtame

mask *n.* choomo (helmet), mahkara (pascola), naka'a(ra) (with large ears); mechawa (pregnancy mask)

mason *n.* alvanyi

mass *n.* miisa; *tv.* miisam teuwa (say mass), misa vicha (hear), misa hoa (say), misate (say ~)

massage *tv.* bwiha, sovaroa

master tekowai (of servants or animals)

mat *n.* hipetam; *iv.* hipette (make ~s)

Matachin *n.* Matachinim (society), Matachini (member), malinchi (apprentice member), monaha (leaders), yoo monaha (head dancer)

matavenado (spider) *n.* kovatarau

match$_1$ *n.* pohporo

match$_2$ *iv.* nana'ana (be alike)

matron *n.* yoo hamut

matter *n.* newosio (affair, business)

matter, what's the *exp.* haisempaula?

matting *n.* tapehtim

mature *adj.* momoi; *iv.* yo'otu

Maundy Thursday *n.* Yo'otui Hahawa (day before Good Friday)

max, to the *adv.* sutti

May *n.* Maayo

may *adv.* humak (may possibly; *ex.* humak wéene, may go), tu'isi (be allowed to; tu'isi yeune, allowed to play)

mayate *n.* maival (beetle)

maybe *adv.* ha'ani, hivatua, humaku'u, hunak hu'uni, kun

maybe so *adv.* humaksan

Mayo *n.* Maayo; *adj.* Mao; *n.* Mao noki (~ language); *iv.* Mao noka (speak ~)

Mayo country *n.* Maayom

maypole *n.* roppo'otiam

me *pn.* ne

meal *n.* saktusi, tuusi (flour)

mean *adj.* hue'ena (cruel); *n.* ka vato'i (~ person)

measles *n.* sarampionim

measure (length) *n.* ve'emu; *tv.* tamachia

meat *n.* tekwa, waakas, hihsovai (barbecued), waka wacha'i (dried), wakapoponi (shredded)

medicine *n.* hittoa

medium *adv.* amma'ali (*ex.* amma'ali siari, medium green)

meet *tv.* nanke; *iv.* hinanke

meeting *n.* etehowa (for a purpose), hinanke (chance meeting)

melody *n.* bwika hiawa

melon *n.* minai

melt *iv.* kahho'ote; *tv.* kahho'ota

memory *n.* memooria, tu'ik memoriakame (one with a good ~)

mend *tv.* hi'ika, na'awacha'abwa, tu'ute

merchant *n.* nenenkame

mesh *n.* alambre soolai

mesquite *n.* hu'upa; hu'upa taakam (~ beans)

mess *n.* haitim

mess around *iv.* haiti aane

messenger *n.* noktohame, hiosia totohame, wok koreo

messy *iv.* haitaula, nasontela, sanchivei

metal *n.* sisiwooki

metate *n.* mata

meteorite *n.* suawaka

meter *n.* metro

method *n.* weiyame

Mexican *n.* 1. *n.* Yoori 2. *adj.* Yoi

Mexico *n.* Mehiko

mezcal *n.* kuu'u

mice will play *exp.* vasou wetla (while the cat's away, the mice will play)

midden *n.* sankoa monti

middle *n.* nasukria; *adv.* nasuk(u) (in the ~)

midnight *adv.* nasuk tuka'apo (at ~)

midwife *n.* yee a'asoatuame, parteera

might *adv.* humak (may possibly; *ex.* humak wéene, may go)

might as well *interj.* vansea

mile *n.* miiya

milk *n.* hipi'ikim, kauwam (mother's ~), wakahipi'ikim (cow's ~)

Milky Way *n.* Napowisa'im

mill *n.* muina

millipede *n.* eye'ekoe

mind, change *iv.* ka hunen ea, amae yehte

mind wreaking *adv.* kovahamti

mine *n.* miina (minerals), *iv.* onawatte (~ salt), tetata yeu wiike (ore, minerals)

miner *n.* mineo

mint *n.* yervawena

mirror *n.* ehpeeko

misbehave *iv.* haana/suati aane

miscarriage *iv.* tomaheklek (have a ~)

miserable *iv.* hiokot ea (feel ~)

misinform *tv.* vaita'a

miss *tv.* neeka (in aim), to'osiime (transportation), havoi (~ out on food)
    miss *tv.* rohikte (person, place); *iv.* ho'arau wáate (be homesick)

missing *iv.* ve'e (be ~)

mist *n.* vahewa, vaiweche

mistake *tv.* hiove (make a ~)

mistaken *adj.* hiovek
mistletoe *n.* chichiham
mistreat *tv.* hiokot hoa
mistrust *tv.* ka yoem eiya
mix *tv.* bwaata, kuuta
mixed *adj.* kurai (blended, stirred), ka nanaumachi (variety of items)
mixture *n.* nau kutti
moan *iv.* te'ine
mockingbird *n.* neo'okai
model *n.* plaano
moist *adj.* va'ari
moisten *tv.* komonia
molars *n.* tampa'im
moldy *iv.* voak, voatu (get)
mole *n.* lunar (on body)
molest *tv.* ka yee yo'ore
molt *iv.* voa weche
mom *n.* ma
moment chuvala vetchi'ivo, for a moment
momentarily *adv.* chuvala, chuvva
Monday *n.* Lunes
money *n.* tomi; tomin (coin); siari tomi, hiosia tomi (paper ~)
monkey *n.* chango (AZ), moono (*Son.*)
monsoon *n.* tevuhlia yuku
monsoon season *n.* tevuhlia
monster *n.* chupiari
month *n.* meecha
monthly *adv.* chikti mechapo
mooch *tv.* netane, nettane
moon *n.* meecha
Moor Society *n.* Morom
more *adv.* chea
more and more *adv.* che'ewasu
more then *postp.* vepa
moreover *conj.* che'ewa
Mormon tea *n.* maso kuta (plant *sp.*)
morning *n.* ketwo, yoko ketwo (tomorrow ~), tuuka ketwo (yesterday ~)
morning star *n.* bwe'u choki
mosquito *n.* woo'o
moth *n.* paloma, mariposa
mother *n.* ae, maala
mother-in-law *n.* aseka
mother-of-pearl *n.* veeko
motor *n.* motoor
mountain *n.* kawim
mountain range *n.* kawi vo'okame

mountain sheep *n.* ove'eso
mounted *n.* kakava'ekame
mourning *n.* luutu
mouse *n.* chikul
mouth *n.* teeni
mouthpiece *n.* taparia (flute)
movable *iv.* aa ruktatu (able to move)
move *iv.* hoa'ate, nahiveva (side to side), omot rukte (residence), nayeehte
    (fidget); *tv.* rukta
movies *n.* vihtam
much *pn.* huevena; *adv.* chea, huevena, ousi, veeki, yuin(i); *adv.* nuki
    (so ~); *adv.* tokti, tu'isi, unna (too ~)
mucus *n.* haakam; *iv.* choomek (have ~)
mud *n.* techoa
mule *n.* muula, muura
multiplication *n.* yo'oturiawame (arithmetic)
multiply *iv.* vu'uria
mumble *iv.* hanna nooka (murmur bad things), momo'oti nooka (for dis-
    cretion)
mumps *n.* moe'esom
murmur *iv.* momotia
muscle *n.* tekwa
museum *n.* museo
mushroom *n.* kavai siisi
music *n.* musikom
musician *n.* musiko
must *adv.* ka vaekai
mustache *n.* himsim
mustard *n.* mohtasa
mute *iv.* ka nooka
my *pn.* in
myth *n.* etehoi, kia etehoi

N

nail *n.* sutum (toe, finger), laavos (metal); *tv.* laavohtua
naked *adj.* viichi, topechei
name *n.* teakame, team, uhteam (last ~), vato'o teak (first ~); *tv.* teatua;
    apo haisa teak? (what's her/his ~?)
named *iv.* teak (first name), uhteak (be surnamed)
nape *n.* vi'am (of neck)
narrow *adj.* ilikkani, na'ulai (hall or passage), witalai (thin strip)
nation *n.* nasion
native *n.* hoome
naughty *iv.* ka yantiachi

nauseated *iv.* eutea
Navajoa *n.* Navahoa
navel *n.* siiku
near *adv.* heela, ka mekka, -napo, naapo
neck *n.* kutana
neckerchief *n.* paayum
necklace *n.* kookam (*gen.*), charkiam (of intertwined strands),
        hopo'orosim (pascola, deer dancer)
necktie *n.* paayum
need *adv.* ka vaeka (allow for); *tv.* nesitaroa
needle *n.* hi'ikiam
needy *iv.* hiokot ea
negligent *iv.* kaita nake (be ~)
neighbor *n.* vesiino, heela ho'akame
neighborhood *n.* ho'ara
nephew *n.* asowaara
nervous *adj.* chumumutea; *iv.* tirisiak (have ~ habit), heka'ula
        (have a ~ tick)
nest *n.* maiko (bee or wasp ~), toosa (bird's ~)
net *n.* wite'i
never *adv.* kaivu; ka huni (~ again)
new *adj.* vemela (innovative), vemelasi (position, situation); *iv.* weemta
        (recent)
New Pascua *n.* Vemela Pahkua
New Year *n.* Vemela Wasuktiawi
New Year, Happy *exp.* alleaka te au yumak Vemela Wasuktiawi
news *tv.* yee eteoria (relate ~)
newspaper *n.* perioriko
newt *n.* poowim
next *adv.* huchi(a), yokoriapo (~ day); *iv.* navuhtia weye (happen ~)
next to *postp.* naachi, naapo, vewichi, vewit
nice *iv.* tu hiapsek (be ~)
nickel *n.* mamni sentaavo (coin)
nickname *n.* omtiteam
nicknamed *iv.* omtiteak (be ~)
night *n.* tukaria; *adv.* kamachiako, tuka'ariapo (at ~, during the ~),
        tutukaviako (last ~)
nightblooming cereus *n.* noono
nightfall *adv.* tukariau
nightmare *n.* ka tu'i tenkuim
nightly *adv.* chikti tukapo
nine *num.* vatani
nineteen *num.* wohmamni ama vatani
ninety *num.* naiki taka ama wohmamni
nipples *n.* pip aso'ola
nit *n.* natchi'ika

nixtamal *n.* napo vaki
no one *pn.* kaave
no sense *iv.* haania (make ~ ~)
noise *n.* haitiuwame, hiawi, kuusi; *n.* kayayati, vahotiuwa (background)
noisy *adv.* vaaho'oti, kemkemti (noisily)
none *pn.* kaita
nonetheless *adv.* o'oven
nonsense *n.* veewa; *iv.* veewatia (talk ~; with hia)
noon *iv.* lu'ula katek
normal *adj.* nanancha tutu'i (of equal value)
north *adv.* hikau vicha (to the ~)
nose *n.* yeka, yeka pohna (bloody); *iv.* vaa chomek (have a runny ~)
nosey *n.* hita tuttu'ule, hu'uneiya vaane
nostrils *n.* yeka woho'oriam
not *adv.* ka
not at all *adv.* kachansan
noted *adj.* ta'ewak
nothing *pn.* kaachin, kaita; *iv.* kaitapo taawak (be left with ~)
notice *n.* koreom (posted ~); *tv.* mammatte, tatta'a
notify *tv.* yee tehwa
November *n.* Noviemre
novena *n.* noveena
now *adv.* ian, ian ala (right now), ian lautipo (right ~), ian tahti (up to ~);
    interj. ala (well ~)
now, but *conj.* ta vesa
nowhere *adv.* kaakun(i)
nude *adj.* topechei, viichi
numb *adj.* si'ibwia
number *n.* numero
nurse *n.* nersi; *iv.* che'e; *tv.* chi'itua
nut *n.* taaka (food), tuerka (with bolt)

O

O'odham *n.* Hua Yoeme
oak *n.* koowi veyotam (black of emory ~), kusi ouwo (~ tree)
oar *n.* reemam
oats *n.* aveena
obey *tv.* hikkaha
object *tv.* ka tu'ure
objection *n.* ka tu'uriwame
obligated *adj.* bwaniari (by vow)
oboe *n.* chirimia
Obregon *n.* Kahe'eme
obscure *n.* aawas (~ view)

observe *tv.* vitchu
observation *n.* vitchuwame
obstruct *tv.* patta
obvious *adj.* hu'unakiachi
occasional *n.* kulupti wéeme (something that happens ~)
occasionally *adv.* kulupti (also indicated by secondary reduplication; see
    Appendix A)
occupied with *tv.* vo'o hoa
occur *iv.* yeu siime
ocean *n.* vaawe; *iv.* sisia (smell like the ~)
ocotillo *n.* mureo
October *n.* Oktuvre
octopus *n.* vaa huvahe
odd *adj.* ta'abwisi
oddly *iv.* haana aane, hachin aane (act ~)
of *postp.* -po (from a particular substance; *ex.* kutapo, wooden)
of course *interj.* na'aka
off *adv.* weama (be ~ the premises)
offensive *adj.* eoktiachisi
offer *suf.* -roka
office *n.* ofesiina
offspring *n.* yoemiawam
oil aseite
okay *interj.* na'aka; *exp.* kaachin maachi (no problem)
old *n.* o'ola (person, animal); *adj.* yoo (animate), moera (inanimates),
    yo'otui (people); *iv.* mooye (get)
old age *iv.* yoo chupa (live to ripe ~ ~)
old man *n.* o'ola
old man cactus *n.* siina
Old Pascua *n.* Pahkua
old person *n.* yotuli
old woman *n.* hamyo'ola
oldtimer *iv.* yoyo'otukan
oleander *n.* laureel
olive *n.* asei tuuna
olive oil *n.* aseite
olla *n.* va'achia (clay water pot)
omen *n.* techoe (bad ~)
on *postp.* aechi, aet, -t/-chi; *iv.* tahek (have lights or electricity ~)
on its side *adv.* chakala
on top *adv.* hikat
on top of *postp.* vepa
once *adv.* sehtul(ia), wepulsi (one repetition); senu we'epo (at ~); *cf.*
    sepia, sepsu)
once in a while *n.* kulupti wéeme (something that occurs once in a while)
once upon a time *adv.* chea vatnateaki

one *num.* seenu, wepul, wepu'ulai (*cf.* -me, -kame, -wame, -mta); iiket (this ~), waaket (that ~)

onion *n.* sevora

onlooker *n.* vitchime

only *pn.* kia, hiva, we'epulai

oof *interj.* uppala

Opata *n.* Opata

open *adj.* etapoi, vohtila (bag); *adv.* mamachiasia (in the ~), mamachikun (right out in the ~), sekola (with arms~); *iv.* puhte, remte ~ eyes); wa'akte (~ mouth); *tv.* etapo

opportunity *n.* chansa

oppose *tv.* ka tu'ure

opposition *tv.* ka tu'urikame

or *conj.* o

orange *n.* na'aso; *adj.* naranhao (in color)

orator *n.* e'etehome

order *n.* nesau (command), yecha'ala (arrangement); *tv.* nesawe, sawe; *suf.* -sae

ordinary *adj.* nanancha tutu'i (of equal value); *n.* hiva yu vitwame (usual thing or person)

organpipe cactus *n.* aaki; aki taaka (fruit)

orphan *n.* leepe

other *pn.* senu, ta'abwi; *adv.* senu wéeme (in ~ words), waitana, wana'avo (on the ~ side)

others *pn.* waate

otter *n.* matupari

ounce *n.* onsa

our *pn.* itom

out *adv.* yea'a

out and about *iv.* weama (be ~)

out there *adv.* wait

outset *adv.* chea vatnateka (at the very ~)

outside *adv.* omola, pa'akun(i), yeewi (towards ~)

outwards *adv.* yeu, yewim(a)

oven *n.* hoona

over *postp.* vevepa; *adv.* amae (~ there), aman(i) (~ there), aman vicha (towards ~ there), haareki (over and over), harekisia (over and over again), hunam(a) (~ there; farther than amani), iniminsu (~ here), wannavo (along/from ~ there)

overcast *adj.* namulopti

overfeed *tv.* potta

overhead *postp.* vepasu

overheat *iv.* tatai

overpower *tv.* yoo yuuma, seariak (~ by thought, feeling)

oversee *n.* vicha

overseer *n.* vichame

overturn *tv.* movekta
owe *dv.* wikiria
owl *n.* muu'u (*gen.*), bwawis (barn), bwia mu'u (burrowing), wichik (elf)
own *tv.* atte'ak, hippue, vuke (animal); *adv.* ta'apo (in one's ~ words)
owner *n.* atteakame
ox *n.* voes
oyster *n.* kooyo

P

pace *iv.* nahkuakte
pacify *tv.* yantitua
pack *iv.* hikima (clothes); *n.* pu'akti
package *n.* hisumia; *tv.* hisuma
paddle *n.* reemam; *iv.* rema wiike
pagan ka vato'i
paid *iv.* soota (be ~); *adj.* vehe'etuari
pail *n.* valle
pain *n.* wantia, ko'okoe; *iv.* ko'okole (be in ~)
painful *adj.* ko'oko; *iv.* hiokot maachi
paint *n.* pintura; *tv.* yoka
pair *n.* emo waik (they are a ~; ref: shoes, socks, partners)
palate *n.* kaapa'i
palm$_1$ *n.* mam vetaria (of hand); *adv.* mam veta'aku (in one's ~)
palm$_2$ *n.* hovei (tree *sp.*), laatiko (date ~), tako (tree *sp.*)
Palm Sunday *n.* Ramos, San Ramos, Tako'ouwa
paloverde *n.* cho'i, nawi'o (white), vaka'apo (Mexican)
pampered *iv.* nakwa
pan *n.* vandeha, saarten (frying ~)
panhandle *iv.* nettane
panic *iv.* mahiwa
pant *iv.* chumti hiavihte
pants *n.* saweam
paper *n.* hiosia
paper money *n.* hiosia tomi
parallel *adj.* sekala
paralyzed *iv.* paraliista
paraphernalia *n.* trahte
parched corn *n.* saakim
pardon *tv.* hiokoe
pardon me *exp.* nee hiokoe, ta chuvala ne hiokoe
park *n.* parke
park *tv.* parkiaroa (**AZ**), ehtsionaroa (*Son.*)
parking lot *n.* parkiaroawa'apo
parrot *n.* tavelo

parsley *n.* pawis (wild)
participate *tv.* tutta
pascola *n.* pahko'ola, yoo pahko'ola (head ~)
Pascua *n.* Pahkua
pass *tv.* pasaroa (exam), bwise (hand to)
pass away *iv.* lu'ute
pass out *iv.* taamu
passenger *n.* pasaheo
past *adv.* sikamtachi, simla, hakwosa iat tiempo (in the ~)
paste *tv.* chu'akta
pasted *iv.* chu'akte
pastry *n.* pahteelim
pasturage *n.* vahu'uri
patch *iv.* hicha'abwa; *tv.* nawa'acha'abwa, cha'abwa
path *n.* ili voo'o
pathetic *iv.* hiokot maachi
patient *n.* ko'okoeme (sick person); *iv.* si vovicha (be ~)
patio *n.* tevat, tevachia
patio cross *n.* rama kus
paw *n.* mamam, wooki
pawn *tv.* peenta
pawned *n.* peenti (~ item)
pay *tv.* vehe'etua
peace *n.* yantelwame; *tv.* yantelwame yaa (make ~)
peaceful *adj.* kopalai; *iv.* yanti maachi
peach *n.* ruenasim, rurahno
peacock *n.* paavo
peak *n.* pu'ilai (mountain)
peanut *n.* kakawaate
pear *n.* peera
peas *n.* peonasim, yoi munim (black-eyed)
pebble *n.* ili teta
peccary *n.* hua kowi, pocho'oku kowi
peek *iv.* yeu hiiwe, etbwa vitcha
peel *tv.* vesuma
pelican *n.* tenwe
pencil *n.* laapis
penis *n.* hu'i
penetrate *tv.* suuta
penny *n.* peeni, sentaavo
people *n.* Yoemem; *suf.* -taim
pepper *n.* ko'oko'i (chile), pimientam (black)
perfect *adj.* tua tu'i; *iv.* tua tu'i
perhaps *adv.* humaku'u
period *iv.* ohvora (have one's ~)
permit *tv.* hewiteria

perpetual *iv.* ka nuklak
person *n.* yoeme
perspiration *n.* tatavuhtia
peso *n.* peeso
pet *n.* vuki
pharmacy *n.* votiika
phlegm *n.* choomim, haakam
Phoenix *n.* Finika
phonograph *n.* fonoora
photograph *n.* retraato
physician *n.* lotoor, yee hihittome
piano *n.* piano
pick$_1$ *tv.* pua (choose, ~ crops)
pick$_2$ *n.* piikom (tool)
pick up *tv.* hahau, pu'akta, tovokta (with hand)
picnic *iv.* kopana
picture *n.* yoka'i
pie *n.* pahteelim
piece *n.* levelai, revei
piecemeal *adv.* reverevekti
pierced *adj.* wohoktila
pig *n.* koowi
pigeon *n.* paloma
pile *n.* mo'ola, motcha (~s); *tv.* monto; *adv.* mocha'ala (in a ~), monti
(in ~s)
pillow *n.* muteka
pilot *n.* ninnituame
Pima *n.* Piima
pimples *n.* kuchuwam (facial)
pin *n.* affiler (safety), hi'ikia kovalam (sewing ~), vavepiinim
(bobby ~ for hair)
pinch *tv.* kitta
pincushion cactus *n.* chikul hu'i
pine *n.* woko (tree)
pink *adj.* sikhewei, koloroosa, amma'ali siki
pinkeye *iv.* ripte (have)
pinole *n.* saktusi
pinto bean *n.* yooko munim
pipe piipa (tobacco), tuuva (plumbing)
pistol *n.* pihtoola
pit *n.* váchia (of fruit)
pit house *n.* huuki
pitahaya *n.* aaki, aki taaka (fruit)
pitch *n.* chu'ukum (resin)
pitched *adj.* chapa'a
pitcher *n.* piichel (liquid)

pitiful *iv.* hiokot maachi, hiokotwachi
pitifully *adv.* hiokot
pity *tv., n.* hiokole
place *suf.* -wa'apo (~ where)
placenta *n.* asoakari
plague *n.* ko'okoa
plain *adj.* hunera (not attractive)
plan *n.* hu'unaktei (planned thing), yecha'ala (arrangement); *tv.* tehwa
plane *tv.* vekta
planet *n.* tabwi ania
planned *adj.* hu'unaktei
plant *n.* eechi, huya; *tv.* eecha
planted *iv.* eechi
plaster *tv.* chitonia
plastered *adj.* chitoniari
plastic *adj.* sololoi
plate *n.* puato
play *iv.* yeewe, peloota (ball), kuuse (flute), hipona (drum or music in
 general); *tv.* poona (instrument, radio, phonograph), yeewa
 (game, cards), hiruke (musical rasp)
play with *tv.* yeewa
player *n.* yeuleo
plaza *n.* pa'aria
please *iv.* vasou wattila (do as one ~s); *exp.* nee hiokoe; *exp.* hituni hoa
 (do as one ~s), a eau hoa (be inconsiderate)
Pleiades *n.* Vahtekoim
plenty *n.* yu'uni
pliers *n.* tena'asam
plenty *n.* yu'uni (abundance)
plop *adv.* pokti
plough *n.* arau
plow *iv.* moite; *tv.* moita
pluck *tv.* pona
plug *n.* tapoon
plump *iv.* yuin tekwak
plunking *adv.* pokti
pocket *n.* volsa
pockmarked *adj.* soso'oki
poem *n.* nok bwikam
poet *n.* nok bwibwikame
point *iv.* hikkubwa (~ at; at = -u)
points *n.* puntam (automobile)
poison *n.* pahti, hoyo; *tv.* pahtitua
poisoned *iv.* hoyok
poisonous *iv.* hoyok
poke *iv.* hissoa; *tv.* soa

pole *n.* kuta
police *n.* polesiam
police officer *n.* polesia (AZ), hurisial (*Son.*)
police station *n.* waaria
polite *tv.* yee yo'ore (respect others)
pomegranate *n.* kannao
pond *n.* vahkom
ponder *iv.* kia pensaroa (think about)
ponytail *n.* chavulai
pool *n.* puul (billiards)
poor *adj.* poloove, poove
poorly *adv.* polovesi(a)
pop *n.* sooda (beverage)
popcorn *n.* saakim, sea vachi
popping *adv.* tomtomtia
popular *iv.* ta'ewa
porcupine *n.* wichakame
porpoise *n.* huhteme
port *n.* puerto
portions *adv.* illikim (in small ~)
posole *n.* posoim
possess *tv.* hippue
post office *n.* koreo
pot *n.* soto'i, kafeteera (coffee)
pot-bellied *adj.* topa'a
potable *adj.* ahi'itu
Potam *n.* Potam
potato *n.* paapa, papachihtim (mashed ~s)
pottery *tv.* soto'ote (make)
pound *n.* livra
pount *tv.* poona
pour (*pl. obj.*) *tv.* to'a (requires *pl. obj.*), vava'atoa (liquid)
powder *n.* mohtiari
powdered *adj.* mohti
power *n.* ya'ura, utte'a, utte'awa
practice *tv.* kiavea
praise *n.* tuwa'apo nokwame; *tv.* tuwa'apo nooka
pray *iv.* lionoka, liohbwania
prayer *n.* lionoki
preach *iv.* hinavaka; *tv.* hinavakamta ya'a
precipice *n.* siiva
precisely *adv.* tuttuti
predict *tv.* erawen
prefer *tv.*. kiale, chea tu'ure
preferable *adv.* humak
pregnant *iv.* asoavae (be ~)

prejudiced *iv.* ka yee tu'ure
premises *iv.* weama (be off the ~)
premonition *iv.* huiwa (have a ~)
prepare *tv.* lihtaroa
preschool *n.* kinder
presoak *tv.* vavasua
press *tv.* yotta, pitta
pressing together *adv.* chapala
pressed *adj.* yotti
presume *tv.* hunuen eiya
pretend *iv.* kia valichiapo
pretty *adj.* tutu'uli
price *n.* vehe'ewa
prick *iv.* hihsoa, *tv.* soa
pricked *adj.* soari
prickly pear *n.* naavo (*gen.*), tosai navu (Indian fig), nakkaim (Santa
        Cruz); navo sito'im (~ jelly)
pride *n.* uttiawame
priest *n.* paare
primary *n.* prinsipaal
primrose *n.* tatchi'ina
prison *n.* karsel
prisoner *n.* peeso; *iv.* peesotu (be a ~); *tv.* peeste (take ~)
probably *adv.* humaku'u
probation *iv.* suawa (be on ~)
problem, no *exp.* kaachin maachi
proceed *tv.* yaa (with plan); *iv.* vichau vicha weye (go forward)
process *iv.* kaminaroa (do a religious procession)
procession *n.* kontiwa(me), hinankiwa; konti (circular)
procurer *n.* nunu'eme
producer *n.* yaakame
project *n.* proyekto
promiscuous *adj.* hantiachi; *n.* kuta hu'i (of a male)
promise *iv.* au bwánia; *tv.* bwánia (vow for someone else)
prone *adv.* petala
properly *adv.* amma'ali
property *n.* atte'ari (moveable), solaar (land)
prostitute *n.* antuari
protect *tv.* sua
protection *n.* suawame
proud of *tv.* uttia
prudent *iv.* hiline
prune *n.* silweela
pry *tv.* kookta
psychic *n.* moreakame (one with ~ powers)
publish *tv.* publikaroa

pudding *n.* vannai, kapirotaaram (bread ~)
puff *iv.* puchi yena (cigarette)
pull *tv.* wiike
pull out *tv.* yeu wike
pull up *tv.* popona
pulverize *tv.* mohta
pulverized *adj.* mohti
puma *n.* ousei
pump *n.* pompa; *tv.* pomiaroa
pun *n.* nokita kuaktala
punch *tv.* chona, wohokta (hole)
puncture *tv.* wohokta
punctured *adj.* wohoktila
punish *tv.* kahtikaroa, hiokot hoa
pupil *n.* puh aso'ola (eye)
puppy *n.* chuu'u aso'ola, ili chu'u
pure *adj.* ausu'uli; *iv.* ka haitimachi
purify *iv.* au bwasa (self)
purple *adj.* morao
purpose *n.* tekia; *adv.* hunakteka (on ~); *postp.* vetchi'ivo (for the ~ of)
purse *adv.* kamula (lips); *n.* portinera
pus *n.* va'awa
push *tv.* yu'a, yu'uria
push aside *tv.* yeu a poota
pustule *n.* taakam
put *tv.* mana, aakte (~ on head to carry), yecha (*sg. obj.*), hoa (*pl. obj.*)
put away *tv.* e'eria
put on *iv.* supete (dress, shirt), kovate (dress, skirt), wokte (clothing
    below waist), kokte (necklace), mawokte (shoes and socks),
    ko'ate (skirt)
put out (fire) *tv.* tuucha
put together *tv.* nau chaya
putrid *adj.* vikala
pyromaniac *n.* hita tattaame

Q

quail *n.* suva'u, suva'i
quarter *n.* woi tomi (coin), vaario (district)
quarrel *iv.* voe (argue), nau emo nok nassua (fight verbally)
queen *n.* reina
queen's wreath *n.* masa'asai (plant)
quench *iv.* va'ayole (thirst; *var.* vaayole)
question *n.* nattemaiwame
quick *adj.* chumti(a)

quickly *adv.* sepia, chumti
quiet *adj.* kopalai, yanti; *iv.* ka wotte (taciturn)
quiet down *tv.* yantitua
quilt *n.* kolcham
quit *adv.* ka into (for good); *iv.* ya'atek (momentarily)
quite *adv.* si, tu'isi
quiver *n.* huiwa to'oria

R

rabbit *n.* taavu (cottontail), paaros (jackrabbit)
rabid *n.* naamukia
raccoon *n.* choparao
race *tv.* hinko'ola
racer *n.* hihinkolame (runner)
radio *n.* raadio
ragweed *n.* chi'ichivo
Rahum *n.* Raahum
rail *n.* trake
railroad tren traakem
rain *n.* yuku; *iv.* yuke
rainbow *n.* kurues
raindrop *n.* yuku chaktia
rainy season *n.* tevuhlia
raise *iv.* yo'oturia (child); *tv.* uhu'u (children), vuke (animals), kultivaroa
          (plants)
raisin *n.* pa'asi
ram *n.* ove'eso (sheep)
ramada *n.* hekka, rama
ranch *n.* rancho
rancher *n.* rancheo
range *n.* kawi vo'okame (mountain)
rape *tv.* ka yee yo'ore, violaroa
rapid *adj.* chumti(a)
rash *n.* huttiam, sihoniam; *iv.* vata sutte (have a ~ in crotch); *tv.* hutta
          (give a ~)
rasp *n.* hirukiam (musical)
rat *n.* tori
rattle *n.* ayam (musical), tenevoim (cocoon ~s), sena'asom (disk ~), wahi
          (Matachin)
rattlesnake *n.* aakame, awa'ala (sidewinder)
raven *n.* sanku'ukuchi
raw *adj.* siali, ka bwasi
ray *n.* taa himsim
reach *adv.* mekhikachi (out of ~); *iv.* yuuma (point in time)

read *tv.* hiosia nooka
ready *adj.* lihto; *interj.* veha (~?); *suf.* -vaawa (get ~)
realize *tv.* hune'eiya
really *adv.* hunueni, ka tea, tua; *conj.* o'oven ta; *interj.* tua
rear end *n.* chove (of car)
reason *adv.* hulentuko, huntuk (for that ~)
receive *tv.* maveta, nu'upa
recently *adv.* hubwa heela, hubwiva (just ~)
recognition *n.* tatta'awa
recognizable *adj.* ta'ewachi
recognize *n.* tatta'a
record *tv.* hiohte (in writing), gravaroa (on tape)
red *adj.* siki; *iv.* sikisi (become ~)
red racer *n.* siktavut
redden *tv.* sikisa hoa, sikite
reed *n.* vaaka
refrigerator *n.* yeleo
regards *exp.* aman ne tevote em yevihnewi (give them my ~)
region *n.* bwia
relate *dv.* tehwa (tell); *tv.* yee eteoria (news)
related to *iv.* weri (with -mak)
relatives *n.* weweri
relaxed *cf.* yantelwame
relaxing *adv.* kopan
relay runner *n.* wok koreo
release *tv.* sutoha
reliable *iv.* yoem eiya maachi (be ~)
relic *n.* relikia
relief *n.* yumhoiria
relish *tv.* kiale
remain *iv.* taawa
remainder *n.* ve'ekame
remember *iv.* waate; *interj.* katin (~...), kati'ikun (don't you ~?)
remind *tv.* wawatitua
renew *tv.* vemelate
renovate *tv.* vemelate
rent *tv.* rentaroa
repair *tv.* tu'ute
repaired *adj.* tu'utei
repay *tv.* vehe'etua, notta (~ a favor or take revenge)
repeat *tv.* huchi aane (action), huchi teuwa (say again)
repetitiously *adv.* piesapo
reply *n.* yopnawame; *tv.* yopna
request *n.* uhbwani (ceremonial); *tv.* uhbwana (ceremonial)
require *adv.* ka vaeka (allow for)
rescue *tv.* hinne'u

rescued *adj.* hinneori
resentful *iv.* kuhti maachi
reserve *n.* e'eriari; *tv.* ve'a
reside *iv.* ho'ak
resin *n.* chu'ukum
respect *tv.* yo'ore; *n.* yee yo'oriwame
respectable *adj.* yo'ori
respected *n.* yo'oriwame (~ person), *iv.* yo'oriwa (be ~)
respectful *iv.* yee yo'ore (be ~)
respectfully *adv.* yee yo'orimaisia
respond *iv.* tu'isi eu weche (~ to medication)
rest *iv.* yumhoe
rest, take a *exp.* yumhoene (come take a rest)
rested *iv.* yumhoek
restaurant *n.* restaurante
restrictions *n.* hiowa (Holy Week)
resuscitate *tv.* hiavihtetua
retarded *iv.* ka tua yuma'i
return *iv.* notte, wechise
revenge *tv.* notta (take ~)
revive *tv.* hiavihtetua
reversed *adj.* kuaktala
revolve *iv.* kuvikuvikte
rheumatism *n.* riuma
rhythm *n.* bwika hiawa
rib *n.* sana'im
ribbon *n.* lihtonia, sekawam (of Matachin crown)
rice *n.* aro'osim
ride *iv.* aa kava'e (can ~ a horse), atamahtvaawa (~ a bronco), weye
    (vehicle)
right *n.* ya'ura; *adj.* tu'i (correct); *adv.* ian ala (~ now), mamachikun
    (~ out in the open), vatan (at/on the ~), vatan vétana (along/from
    the ~), vatan vicha (toward the ~)
right away *adv.* sepia
rim *n.* maikuchi (drum ~)
rind *n.* vea
ring *n.* anilio (finger), moso'okia (~ stand for carrying pots on head)
ring *tv.* hiutua
rinse *tv.* rauta
ripe *adj.* bwasi, momoi; *iv.* bwase (get)
ripening *adj.* momoik
river *n.* vatwe
road *n.* voo'o
roadrunner *n.* taruk
roar *iv.* ruutia (train, rain, thunder, sea; natural phenomena)
roast *tv.* sova, tohta, waawa (in coals)

robe *n.* tunikam (ceremonial)
rock₁ *n.* teta
rock₂ *iv.* nayeehte, ro'akte; *tv.* yoa
rocket *n.* kuete
rodeo *n.* tamahtiwa
roll over *iv.* viakte
roll up *tv.* hiite, ro'akta, viakta, vechehta (pants, sleeves)
rolled up *adj.* temula
rolling *iv.* viaktisime (be ~)
roof *n.* vepa, kova (of car)
roofing tile *n.* teeham
room *n.* kuarto; *iv.* aayuk (be ~)
rooster *n.* totoi o'owia
root *n.* nawa
rope *n.* wikia; *tv.* hichoila
rosary *n.* kuusim
rose *n.* roosa
rot *iv.* mohte, mooye, viika
rotten *adj.* vikala
rotting *adj.* moyok
rough *n.* rurumui (ground); *adj.* sosoko (surface)
round *adj.* kowilai, tekolai
round trip *iv.* yeu bwelta
rounded *adj.* lovola(i), rovoi
rounds *n.* vitchime (one making the ~s visiting)
row *adv.* hepelam (in a ~)
row *iv.* rema wiike
rub *tv.* ruuse, sovaroa, wike
rubber *n.* uuli
rude *iv.* kaveta yo'ore, ka yee yo'ore
rue *n.* ruura
rug *n.* hipetam
ruin *tv.* nasonte
ruined *iv.* nasonti
rule *n.* nesawi; *tv.* nesawe
rumor *n.* kia nooki
run *iv.* vuite (*sg.*), tenne (*pl.*); *iv.* totenne (~ away); *tv.* tovuivuite (~ away
    from; from = *d.o.*)
rung *n.* aet chepitiawame (ladder)
running along *exp.* pues ne wéevae (well, I'll be ~)
runt *n.* kome'a
rust *iv.* poposiwe
rusted *adj.* moyok
rustling *adv.* siosioti (with hia)
rusty *adj.* poposiula

S

sack *n.* tare'ekam, voosa
sacred *iv.* yo'oriwa (be ~)
sacristan *n.* tamahti, teopo kovanao
sad *adj.* rohiktiachi, sioka; *iv.* rohikte, sisioka (get ~); *tv.* sioktua (make ~)
saddle *n.* siila; *tv.* silate
safe *adj.* hinneori
safety pin *n.* affiler
sagging *adj.* tanna(i)
saguaro *n.* sauwo
saguaro skeleton *n.* akwo
sail *n.* veelam; *tv.* va'apo weye
saint *n.* saanto
saints *n.* santora (coll.)
salad *n.* ensalada
salamander *n.* hipuyesa'alim, poowim, pusiyesa'ala, wa'itopit
sale *iv.* nenenkiwa (be for ~)
saliva *n.* chichi
salt *n.* oona; *tv.* ontua
salt water *n.* vacho'oko
salty *adj.* cho'oko; *iv.* chotcho'okoe (get); *tv.* cho'okote (make ~) same *n.*
    a'aatene, nana'ana, nanancha; *adj.* hiva vena (*cf.* huna), nareki
    (amount), naarechi, vetchi (size); *adv.* venak, nanancha (age),
    nareempani (length), hiva vena'aku (at the ~ place); *postp.* vewit
    (at the ~ level); *tv.* nana'ate (make the ~)
sand *n.* see'e
sand dune *n.* se'eparia
sandals *n.* vera'a voocham
sandy area *n.* se'eparia
satiated *iv.* hovoa
Saturday *n.* Savala
Saturday, Holy *n.* Savala Looria
sausage *n.* chorriso
save *tv.* hinne'u, ve'a, yeu'ave'a; *tv.* nu'ute (food); *dv.* nu'uteria (~ for
    someone)
save up *tv.* e'eria
saved *adj.* hinneori; *iv.* hinneuwa
savings *n.* e'eriari
saw *n.* seruuchom (tool)
say *iv.* tauhia
say yes *tv.* hewite
scabies *n.* chinchim
scale *n.* kuchukuupe (fish), valansa (for weighing)
scaley *adj.* sosoko
scalp fetish *n.* choonim

scandal *iv.* kia nooki
scar *n.* kuucho
scare *tv.* mahautua, womta
scared *iv.* mahe, mammahe
scary *adj.* mamaiwachi
scatter *iv.* naikimte (*pl. subj.*); *tv.* hissa (by throwing)
schedule *n.* oraario; *tv.* orarioroa
school *n.* ehkuela
scissors *n.* chaptiam
scorpion *n.* maachil
Scottsdale *n.* Eskatel
scowl *iv.* chokinaik puhvaka a vitchu
scowling *iv.* omtemta puhvak (be ~)
scrape *iv.* vekte; *tv.* vekta, chahe (~ bark)
scraped *adj.* vekti, kesiktila (abrasion)
scratch *tv.* chi'ike, hechihtia, suke, wo'oke
scream *iv.* chae
scree *n.* tutukam
screw *tv.* kuvia
screwed *iv.* kuviari
screwing *tv.* kuvvi'ita
scripture *n.* noklutu'uria
scrub *tv.* ruuse
sea *n.* vaawe
sea gull *n.* vatosai
sea lion *n.* vaa loovo
seal *n.* seyo (insignia), vaa loovo (animal)
search *tv.* haiwa
seat *n.* siiyam (car ~s), vankom (car ~s); *tv.* yehtetua
secret *n.* ka teuwawame (untold), ka hu'uneiyawame (unknown)
secretary *n.* hiohteme
secretly *adv.* eusi, ka kusisi
see *tv.* vicha
seed *n.* vachia, echimu (for planting)
seed head *n.* mo'a
seem *adj.* maachi
seemingly *adv.* maisi
seen *iv.* mamachi (be ~)
segment *n.* tonua
seize *tv.* nunu'e
select *tv.* pua (with yeu)
self *adv.* apela (by ~)
self identify *iv.* au ___le (*ex.* au ringole, consider one's self to be Anglo)
sell *tv.* nenka
seller *n.* nenenkame
send *tv.* vittua

senile *iv.* ka suak
sense *n.* sentirom (perception); *iv.* ine'a; *tv.* huiwa (premonition)
sense, common *iv.* suawak (have common sense)
sense, make no *iv.* hania
sensitive *iv.* tam pipisa (be ~, of teeth), tam piisak (have ~ teeth)
separate *iv.* wo'ota (couple)
separated *adj.* hima'ari (couple), naikimtei (things)
September *n.* Septiemre
sergeant *n.* sarhento
Seri *n.* Seeri
sermon *n.* hinavakawame, sermonia
serve *tv.* miika (food, beverage)
set *iv.* sita (fruit); *tv.* mana, taya (~ fire to); *dv.* mana'aria (~ down
    for someone)
set aside *tv.* nu'ute (food)
seven *num.* wovusani
seven times *adv.* wovusanisia
seventeen *num.* wohmamni ama wovusani
seventy *num.* vahi taka ama wohmamni
sew *tv.* hi'ika
sewing machine *n.* hik maakina (*syn.* maakina)
sewn *adj.* hi'ikri
sex *tv.* emo tu'ule (have ~)
shade *n.* hekka
shadow *n.* hekka
shake *tv.* kouria, yooa (with rope)
shake hands *iv.* mam tevote
shall *suf.* -ne (future tense)
shallow *adj.* ka mekka ko'omi
shape *n.* haisa a machiaka'apo, ya'ane
shampoo *n.* champu
share *tv.* nau a saawa
shark *n.* tamekame
sharp *adj.* bwawi
sharpen *tv.* bwawite
sharpened *n.* bwawia, bwawiteri
shave *tv.* vekta
shaved *adj.* vekti
shawl *n.* hiniam
sheep *n.* bwala (domestic), ove'eso (mountain ~)
sheepherder *n.* bwalam susuame, bwalareo
sheer *adj.* to'ochorai
sheet *n.* savana (bedding), lamina (metal)
shell *n.* vea, kovea (oyster), aulivea (clam); *iv.* hichiwe; *tv.* chiiwe
shield *iv.* tapekonariina (eyes)
shift *tv.* omola (piles)

shine *iv.* tahek
shining *adj.* velohko
shinny *n.* taahivevia
shiny *adj.* viohko
ship *n.* varko
shirt *n.* kamisoolam, supem
shiver *iv.* piitau yoa, au yoa
shoes *n.* voocham
shoot *tv.* muhe, putte
shop *n.* tienda
shore *n.* vawe mayoa
short *adj.* ilippani, kome'ela (person), molonko (person), poochi, pochilai
(string, rope)
shot$_1$ *adj.* muhiri
shot$_2$ *n.* chaatim (injection)
should *adv.* ean
shoulder *n.* henom
shove in *tv.* suuta
shovel *n.* paalam
show *tv.* vittua, voo'ota tehwa (~ the way)
shower *n.* vanyo (for bathing); *iv.* yuke (rain)
shrewd *adj.* suak
shrimp *n.* vaa koochim
shrink *iv.* nau siika
shuffle *iv.* siksiktia
shut *adj.* eta'i (closed); *tv.* eta
shy *adj.* tiwe'era; *iv.* tiiwe
shyness *n.* tiura
sick *n.* ko'okoeme (~ person); *iv.* ko'okoe
sickle *n.* hoosom
sickness *n.* ko'okoa, wantia, womtia (from fright)
side *adv.* omochi (at the wrong ~), iivo (on this ~), iatana (from this ~),
wana'avo (on the other ~), wana (from the ~), haku'uvotana
(from which ~), wanna'avotana (on the far ~)
side by side *adv.* hepela, lopola; *iv.* nahiveva (move side by side)
sideways *adv.* chakaka'ati, *adj.* chakalai, *iv.* chakukte (go ~)
sift *tv.* sa'ina
sign$_1$ *n.* techoe (bad omen)
sign$_2$ *tv.* firmaroa
signature *n.* firma
silhouette *n.* kut tenei
silhouetted *adv.* kutvea
silver *n.* teokita
silverfish *n.* kuliichi
similar *adv.* nanau
simple *adj.* ka oviachi

since *conj.* veasu (because); *adv.* naateka (since the beginning)
sinew *n.* tate
sin *n.* ka amma'ali anwame
since *adv.* ketun(ia)
sing *iv.* bwiika
singer *n.* bwikleo, koparia (woman hymn ~; kantoora)
Singer Society *n.* Kopariam
single *pn.* wepu'ulai; *adj.* apelai (not married)
sink *iv.* ropte (in water or liquid), suume, wo'okte (in dirt, mud, sand), suume (pool, tide, water in reservoir)
sink in *iv.* kovate, tutte
sinner *n.* pekadoor
sip *tv.* chipta, yatta
sissy *n.* nawi wo chume'a
sister (older; *fem.*) *n.* ako (older; *fem.*), wai (younger; *fem.*)
sister-in-law *n.* machi'ira
sistrum *n.* sena'asom (disk rattle)
sit down *iv.* yeesa (*sg.*), hooye (*pl.*)
sitting *iv.* katek (*sg.*), hoote (*pl.*); *cf.* ekala, ekka
situated *iv.* katek, manek (massive object or liquid)
six *num.* vusani
six times *adv.* vusanisia
sixteen *num.* wohmamni ama vusani
sixty *num.* vahi taka
size *adj.* veletchi; *adj.* naarechi, vetchi (same ~); *adv.* inia vetchi (this)
skeleton *n.* kalavera, ota
skillet *n.* saarten
skin *n.* vea; *tv.* vea yecha, vesuma
skin and bones *exp.* empo kia ota ausu'uli (you're nothing but skins and bones)
skinny *adj.* choora; *n.* wiiko (~ person); *iv.* wakila, ka tekwak (have little flesh), wakiltu (get ~)
skirt *n.* ko'arim; *iv.* ko'ate (put on), ko'arek (wear)
skunk *n.* hupa
sky *n.* teeka
slander *tv.* hana hiuwa
slash *n.* hivevia
slaughter *n.* suawame
slave *n.* vuki
sleep *iv.* koche (*sg.*), kokoche (*pl.*)
sleeper *n.* kokkocheme
sleepy *iv.* kotpea, kotpet'ea (get ~)
sleepyhead *n.* koche'a, koche'ela
slender *adj.* lo'alai, owilai, vahwiolai, wilohko
slice *tv.* revekta
sliced *adv.* kopela

slide *n.* kom susuluwa'apo (playground); *iv.* suulu
slightly *adv.* heelai
slingshot *n.* wicha'arakim
slip *iv.* chitohte
slippery *adj.* chitahko
slow *adv.* ka uttea (not rapid); *iv.* ka tua suak (stupid)
slowly *adv.* lautia (vehicle), leueluti (animal, person)
smacking *adv.* toktokta
small *adj.* ili, ilitchi; ilikkani (~ area)
smallpox *n.* tomtiam; *iv.* tomte (have)
smart *adj.* suak
smash *tv.* chovikukta, pitta
smear *tv.* venta
smell *tv.* huhu'ubwa, hukta
smile *iv.* aache; *n.* atwame
smoke *n.* bwich'a; *iv.* bwich'ata hoa (be smoking); *tv.* yena (tobacco)
smoker *n.* yeyename
smoky *iv.* bwiichi
smooth *adj.* bwalko, chitahko; *tv.* bwalkote
snake *n.* vaakot (*gen.*), sikkucha'a (coral), siktavut (red racer), wiroavakot
       (vine), aakame (rattlesnake), awa'ala (sidewinder)
snapping *adv.* haitowikti
snare *n.* wite'i
sneak *adv.* solti
sneeze *iv.* ha'achihte
sniff *tv.* huhu'ubwa
snitch *iv.* hina'atua, na'ateo; *tv.* yeabwise, na'atua
snobby *iv.* haana maachi, havele
snore *iv.* ho'otia
snoring *adv.* hooti
snow *n.* sapam; *iv.* sapa weche
so *interj.* ela'apo (~?), ala'akun (~ it is), o'ovek (yes, it is ~); *adj.* nuki
       (~ long); *adv.* haleppani (~ long), hunuen (thus, therefore), ket
       (also), nukisia (to a great extent), ve'ekik (~ much)
so, it's *exp.* ka tea
soak *tv.* vaasu
soap *n.* saavum; *tv.* sasavutua
soapy *iv.* sasavua (get)
soccer *n.* Yoi himari
society *n.* kohtumre (religious), sosiedadim (secular)
socks *n.* karsetiinim
soft *adj.* bwalko
soften *tv.* bwalkote, hota
soil *n.* bwia; *tv.* haitauhoa
sold *adj.* hinuri
soldier *n.* sontao

sole *n.* wok hiapsa, wok veta'i
solicitation *n.* limohna (ceremonial)
some *pn.* waáte (re: humans)
somehow *adv.* hachin huni'i
someone *num.* seenu; ta'abwi (~ else; *cf.* ta'abwikut)
something *pn.* hitaven (~ else)
sometime *adv.* hakweeka, hale'evu
sometimes *adv.* amak(o)
somewhere else *adv.* omot, hakhuni
son *n.* ou asoa (*fem.*), uusi (*masc.*)
son-in-law *n.* mo'one(wai)
songs *n.* bwiikam (*var.* bwikam), limohnaim (devotional), alavansam
        (hymns)
soot *n.* bwitchovia
soothe *tv.* yantitua
sorcerer *n.* yee nanasonteme, yee sisivome
sore *n.* sa'awa, keekam); *iv.* kutana kutte (have ~ throat)
soul *n.* hiapsi
sound *n.* hiawi; *iv.* hia, hiawa, hiusaka; *tv.* tiitua, hihiutua (musical
        instrument)
soup *n.* va'awa; mun va'awa, *n.* bean soup
soupy *iv.* unna va'ak (be ~)
sour *iv.* cho'oko
south *adv.* kom vicha (to the ~)
spade *n.* paalam (tool)
Spanish *n.* Yoi Noki (language)
spank *tv.* vemmucha, vepsu, toktokta veva
spark *n.* chihpa
sparkling *adv.* viohkosi
sparrow *n.* mo'el
sparsely *adv.* lilihti
spasm *n.* pahmo
speak *iv.* eteho
speaker *n.* e'etehome (person)
spear *n.* laansam
spectator *n.* vichame
speech *n.* etehoi
speed *iv.* uttea weye
spend *tv.* gahtaroa (money), wiuta (money)
spherical *adj.* lovola(i)
spider *n.* huvahe (*gen.*), vaa huvahe (water ~)
spill *tv., iv.* wo'ota
spilled *adj.* vohtek, wo'oti; *iv.* wo'ote
spinach *n.* wah hi'u
spindle *n.* taravia
spirit *n.* hiapsi

spit *iv.* chitwatte
splash *n.* chihakti; *iv.* chihakte; *tv.* chihakta, chihaktia (cause to)
splinters *n.* wicha
split *iv.* chamte, samte (cane); *tv.* chamta, samta (cane)
split ends *n.* choni kottila, sea choni
spoil *iv.* nasonte, viika
spoiled *adj.* vikala
sponsor *n.* pahkome, pahko yo'owe (ceremonial)
spoon *n.* kucha'ara
spoonfeed *tv.* hi'ibwatua
sprain *iv.* silikte (ankle)
spray *tv.* puhta
spread *adj.* chivehti; ; *iv.* chivehte; *tv.* chivehta, venta, mantekiatua
        (butter)
spring *n.* sene'eka, vaa puusim (water)
sprinkle *iv.* vaa si'ite (liquid), (particulate matter); *tv.* vaa si'ita (liquid),
        wihta (particulate matter)
sprout *n.* vasiula; *iv.* siwe, vasiwe
spur *n.* tepua (of a chicken); *tv.* temtia
spy *n.* etbwa yee vichame; *tv.* etbwa vicha
squash *n.* kama (*gen.*), aya'awi, kiakama (variety with a throat), selwaka;
        tv. pehtivuite
squashed *adj.* chihti
squatting *iv.* chumula katek, muhsu katek
squeak *iv.* kuchichi'itia
squeeze *iv.* hipi'ike; *tv.* pipi'ike
squint *iv.* kinakte (with au)
squirrel *n.* teku, malon (ground)
staff *n.* kovanao kuta (ceremonial)
stagger *iv.* naname
stain *iv.* yokte; *tv.* yokta
stained *adj.* yokti, yokok; *iv.* yoki
stairs *n.* ehklalonim
stake *n.* ehtaka
stamp *n.* ehtampia; *tv.* ehtampiaroa
stand up *iv.* kikte (*sg.*), hapte (*pl.*); *tv.* haha'abwa (*pl. obj.*)
standing up *iv.* weyek (*sg.*), ha'abwek (*pl.*)
star *n.* choki
stare at *tv.* hana vitchu
start *tv.* naate; *adv.* naateka (from the ~), chea vatnateka (from the
        very ~)
startle *tv.* womta
starving *iv.* tevaimuuke (*sg.*), tevaikoko (*pl.*)
statement *n.* testamento
station *n.* estasion (train, bus), liipo (depot), waaria (police ~)
statue *n.* moono

stay *iv.* taawa
stay up *iv.* velaaroa
steak *n.* waakas
steal *tv.* etbwa
steal from *dv.* etbwaria
stealthily *adv.* ka kusisi, solti
steam *n.* haawa; *iv.* hawassate
steer *n.* toro kapontei (animal); *tv.* wéetua (vehicle)
steering wheel *n.* ruera
stem *n.* ota
step *n.* wokti (act), cheptiawame (on stairs); *iv.* chepte; *tv.* wokita hoa
    (take a)
step down *iv.* kom chepte
step over *tv.* wa'akta
stepdaughter *n.* waim maara
stepfather *n.* waim achai
stepmother *n.* waim ae, waim maala
steps ehklalonim (stairs)
stepson *n.* waim uusi
sterile *iv.* ka u'use (of a man), ka a'asoa (of a woman); *n.* muula
stew *n.* waka vaki (meat and vegetable), posoim (hominy), tiiko posoim
    (wheat stew), mun posoim (bean stew)
stick *n.* hivevia (shinny, golf club)), kuta, voonia (walking), karoote
    (weapon); *iv.* ve'okte
stickers *iv.* sooso (get)
sticky *iv.* choachoakte (be ~)
still *adj.* kopalai; *iv.* yanti maachi; *adv.* haivu, kette, ketun(ia)
stimulus *n.* eetuame
sting *tv.* huuha
stinger *n.* chumim
stingy *n.* au hiokoe
stink *iv.* huuva, viika huva
stinkbug *n.* huvachinai
stir *iv.* rukte (move); *tv.* bwaata, kuuta, kuuria (not food)
stockings *n.* meriam
stocky *iv.* yuin tekwak (be ~)
stolen *iv.* etbwawa
stolen *n.* etbwaim (~ thing)
stomach *n.* toma
stomachache *iv.* tompo wante (have a ~)
stone *n.* teta, váchia (of fruit)
stool *n.* aet hohowame (bathroom)
stoop *iv.* kom po'okte
stooping *adj.* po'ola cha'aka
stop *tv.* kecha, yaatitua; *dv.* yatitua (make ~)
stop it *interj.* épale (to child)

stop up *tv.* kecha, patte
stopped *adj.* yaatituari
stopper *n.* tapoon (sink, tub, jug)
store *n.* tienda; *tv.* ve'a (reserve)
story *n.* etehoi
storyteller *n.* eteoreo, e'etehome
stove *n.* ehtuufa
straddling *adj.* bwakala
straight *adj.* lu'ula
straight ahead *adv.. n.* witti
straighten out *iv.* rutukte
strain *tv.* kolaroa
strained *adj.* kolaroari
strange *adj.* ta'abwisi
straw *n.* huya wakia (hay)
stream *n.* seke'eka (creek)
strength *n.* utte'a
stretch *iv.* semte; *tv.* semta, sutte (legs, arms)
stretch out *tv.* veakta
strewn *adj.* wo'oti
strike *iv.* yuku hima (lightning); *tv.* hiveva, veeva
string *n.* wikia (*gen.* or musical), kuera (musical)
stroll *iv.* kia weama
strong *adj.* ousi; *adv.* namakasia (mentally, physically); *iv.* utte'ak, yuin
      tekwak (in flavor)
strongly *adv.* uttea, utte'esia
stubborn *iv.* ka hootu, ka yuutu
stuck *adj.* chu'aktila, chu'ala; *iv.* chuu'a (get), suuta (be)
stuck together *adj.* nat chu'aktila, nat cha'aka
stuck up *iv.* haana maachi
student *n.* mahtawame
stuff one's self *iv.* chumte (self); *tv.* potta (with food)
stumble *iv.* te'ite, wetchime
stump *n.* kuta naawa (tree)
stupid *iv.* ka tua suak
sturdy *adj.* ousi
stutter *iv.* ne'otula
stutterer *n.* nee'o
sty *n.* chi'imu (in eye)
suburb *n.* vaario
submerge *iv.* ropte
submergible *iv.* ropropte
subside *iv.* kom cha'atu (pain)
subtraction *n.* uurawame (arithmetic)
suck *tv.* chuune; *tv.* piine (suck out)
sudden *adv.* seechuktia (all of the ~)

suddenly *adv.* sehchukti(a), senu wechiapo
suds *iv.* sasavua (make ~)
suffer *iv.* hiokot aane, wantaroa; *tv.* eetua (make ~)
suffocate *iv.* heeka lu'ute
sugar *n.* asuka, sankakam (brown)
sugarcane *n.* sana
suicide *tv.* au me'a (commit)
suit *n.* suut
suitcase *n.* veliis
sum *n.* hinaikiawakame
summarize *tv.* nok ansu (orally), hiote ansu (in writing)
summer *n.* tasaria, tataria
sun *n.* taa'a
sunburnt *adj.* taa bwasi
Sunday *n.* Lomiinko
sunflower *n.* taa'ata vitchu
sunlight taa machiria
sunstroke *iv.* soliaroa (have ~)
sung *adj.* bwiiki
sunk *adj.* roptila (in water), tuttila (in the ground)
sunlight *n.* taa himsim, taa tachiria
sunstroke *adj.* taa mukia; *iv.* soliaroa (get or have~)
supervisor *n.* nesaweme, teeko
supposed to *adv.* tea
surname *n.* uhteam
surrender *tv.* au nenka
surround *iv.* konte; *tv.* konta
survey *tv.* tamachia (land)
swallow *n.* kutapapache'a (bird)
swallow *tv.* wi'ukta
swamp *n.* vaata yehtepo
swarthy ama vutti chukuli (be ~)
swear *tv.* aetua (curse)
sweat *n.* tatavuhtia; *iv.* tatavuhte
sweat bee *n.* nahi
sweep *iv.* hichike
sweet *adj.* kaka, win huva (smelling); *iv.* kakae, kakkai (get)
sweetly *adv.* winhuvasi (smelling ~)
sweeten *tv.* asukatua
sweets *n.* kakawa, luuse
swell *iv.* vaha
swelling *n.* vaiya
swiftly *adv.* sunsunti
swig *iv.* pomte
swim *iv.* vahume
swing *n.* kulumpio (playground); *iv.* koowe, kakalo; *tv.* kouria

swollen *iv.* vahiya
sword *n.* ehpam
sympathy *tv.*, *n.* hiokole
sympathy, our deepest *exp.* ian lautipo te enchi(m) hiokole
symbol *n.* seyo (insignia, mark)
system *n.* sisteema

T

table *n.* meesa; *cf.* tapehtim
tablecloth *n.* mantelim
taciturn *iv.* ka wotte
tack *n.* tachuela (metal)
tadpole *n.* sivo'oli
tail *n.* bwasia
tail end *n.* bwasia
taillights *n.* luusim (of car)
take *tv.* toha (*sg. obj.*), weiya (*pl. obj.*)
take apart *tv.* wi'okta
take away *tv.* u'a, nuksiime (*sg. obj.*), nuksaka (*pl. obj.*); *dv.* uura
take care of *tv.* sua, uhu'u (children)
take down *tv.* vaahta
take off *iv.* yeu wokte (garments below waist); *tv.* watta (clothes)
take out *tv.* bwakta, *tv.* yeatoha, (*sg. obj.*; yewamtoha *pl. obj.*), toiwa (from
    a group; deport)
take over *tv.* noita, hinneola, tovokta
taken *adj.* u'ari; *iv.* toiwa (be ~)
tale *n.* etehoi
talk *iv.* eteho, nooka, nokwa (be ~ed about)
Talking Tree *n.* Kuta Nokame
tall *adj.* choora, tevesi, teeve
tallow *n.* seevo
tamales *n.* nohim, mun nohim (bean), ; avai nohim (green corn);
    tv. noha (make)
tame *adj.* manso
tan *tv.* bwalkote, tomta
tangled *adj.* kurula; *iv.* kuuru
tank *n.* tanki
tape *n.* tepim (recording)
Tarahumara *n.* Tarumaara
tarantula *n.* maisooka
task *n.* tekipanoame
tassel *n.* moa (corn)
taste *tv.* hiiwe (sample)
tasteless *iv.* ka kia

tattle *iv.* hina'atoa, na'ateo; *tv.* na'atua
taught *adj.* mahti
tax *n.* taksim
tea *n.* tee
teach *iv.* mahtitekipanoa; *tv.* mahta
teacher *n.* yee mahmahtame
teaching *n.* ye mahtawame
tear *iv.* siute; *tv.* siuta
tear apart *tv.* mohakte
tears *n.* oppoam
tease *tv.* haana hiuwa, hunniawa
teaspoon *n.* ili kucha'ara
teeth, false *n.* pohtisom
telephone *n.* telefon
television *n.* televisión
tell *dv.* tehwa
tell on *iv.* hina'atua, na'ateo; *tv.* na'atua
temper *n.* eiyachume (person with bad ~)
tempt *tv.* naiyote
ten *num.* wohmamni
ten times *adv.* wohmamnisia
tendon *n.* tate
Tenebrae *n.* Tiniepla
tent *n.* karpa
tepary bean *n.* se'elaim
terminate *tv.* suvina
termite *n.* kuta ete, polia
terrible *adj.* hunera
testicles *n.* kavam
tether *tv.* chaya
thank *tv.* liobwania
Thank God *exp.* Liohta vaisaene
thankfulness *n.* vaisaewame
thanks *n.* Liohbwana (formal)
that *pn.* hu, u, wa, wai; *adv.* hunaen (like ~), hunulevena (like ~), wa
        veeki (~ much), wai ve'emu (~ far, ~ long)
that's the way s/he is *exp.* tevei eak
their *pn.* am
them *pn.* am, vempo'im
themselves *pn.* emo; *adv.* vempola (by ~)
then *adv.* hunako (and ~), hunaksan, véa (used for emphasis); *adv.* hiva
        yu (from ~ on)
there *adv.* ama, aman(i), um, wa'am(i), amawam (through); *adv.* vina
        (toward)
there is/are *iv.* a'ayu
thermos *n.* vaa nuu'u

these *pn.* ime
they *pn.* vempo
thick *adj.* turui
thief *n.* e'etbwame
thigh *n.* macham
thin *adj.* lo'alai, tapsiolai, wilohko, witalai (~ strip); *iv.* unna wa'ak
(be ~, watery)
thing *n.* hita
think *tv.* ea (feel like, intend to do), machia (entertain ideas), pensaroa
(intend to do)
think of *iv.* waate
think over *tv.* vat a mammate
thirst *iv.* va'ayole (quench ~)
thirsty *iv.* vai muuke (*sg.*), vai koko (*pl.*), vai mukne (get ~; *pl.* vai kokone)
thirteen *num.* wohmamni ama vahi
thirty *num.* senu taka ama wohmamni
this *pn.* i, ia; *adv.* ia veeki (~ much), inen(i) (like ~), iat (on ~), inilen
(~ way), ilempo (~ way), iae (with ~)
thistle *n.* wichakame
thorn *n.* wicha
thoroughly *adv.* tuttuti
those *pn.* ume
thought *n.* éewame (idea)
thoughtful *iv.* che'ewale
thoughts *n.* eerim
thousand *num.* miil
thread *n.* wii'i
three *num.* vahi
three times *adv.* vahisia
three ways *adv.* vahiwe (in three ways)
throat *n.* kutana; *iv.* kutana kutte (have sore ~)
throw *tv.* himma, hissa
throw away *tv.* yeu wo'ota
throw out *iv.* wo'ota
throw up *tv.* pota (dirt)
thumb *n.* bwe'u mam pusiam
thudding *adv.* havohavoti, havohti, kumkumti, yotohti, pompomti
thunder *iv.* yuku omte, yuku ruutia
thunderbolt *n.* senteiya
thundering *adv.* ru'uru'uti; *iv.* ru'uru'utia
thunderstorm *n.* yuku heka
Thursday *n.* Hueves
thus *adv.* hunen, huni, hunuen, unen
tick *n.* tema'i (insect)
ticket *n.* tiket, voleeto (*Son.*)
tickle *tv.* chikipona

tie *tv.* suma
tie up *tv.* hisuma
tied up *adj.* hisumai
tiger *n.* tigre
tight *adj.* kuttia; *iv.* kutte (get)
tighten *tv.* kutta
tightened *adj.* kutti
tile *n.* teehma (clay roofing ~)
till *conj.* tahtia
time *n.* tiempo, etwa (planting ~); *adv.* hiva yu (all the ~), senu wechiapo (in no ~ at all), vinwa (for a long ~), huchi senu (one more ~), vinwatuko (a long ~ ago), huevenasi (many ~s), avetuko (almost ~ for); *exp.* haikimsia (what ~ is it?)
tin can *n.* ohelaata
tip *n.* punta
tiptoe *adv.* chelechele'eti
tire *n.* yantam (vehicle)
tire *iv.* yumvaekai (self); *tv.* lottia
tired *adj.* lottila; *iv.* lotte (be ~), lotlotte (get ~)
tired of *iv.* o"ouva
tires *n.* voocham (of car)
tiresome *adj.* lottiachi
title *n.* teakame
to *postp.* au, vicha
toad *n.* voovok (Colorado River)
toast *tv.* tohtaroa, *tv.* saake (grain)
tobacco *n.* viiva, makucha (native), Hiak vivam (Yoeme)
toe *n.* wok pusiam
toenail *n.* wok sutum
together *adv.* nau, nausu, nawi
Tohono O'odham *n.* Hua Yoeme
toilet *n.* ehkusao
tomato *n.* tomaate
tomb *n.* tauna
tomorrow *adv.* y—oko, matchuko (day after ~), yokosu (~ evening), yoko ketwo (~ morning)
tongue *n.* nini
tonight *adv.* ian tukapo
tonsils *n.* moe'esom
too *adv.* unna
too long *adv.* vinwatuk (time)
too much *adv.* kaitu'una, tokti
tooth *n.* tami
toothbrush *n.* sepio
toothless *iv.* ka tamek
top *n.* hikachi (apex), pattiria (lid); *postp.* hikattana (on ~)

Torim *n.* Torim
torn *adj.* siuti(la)
tornado *n.* namu vakot
tortilla *n.* tahkaim; *iv.* tahkae (make ~s)
tortoise *n.* mochik, kau mochik (mountain)
torture *adv.* ko'okosi
toss *tv.* hissa
total *n.* hinaikiawakame; *tv.* tomita nau yecha, numerom nau yecha
touch *tv.* bwibwise, chimta, mamma, tahta, mamte (with hand)
tough *adj.* namaka
tour *iv.* pasiyaloa
toward *postp.* au, vicha
towel *n.* toeyam
town *n.* bwe'u hoara
toy *n.* huweetem
track *n.* wokla; *tv.* wokte
tractor *n.* traktor
trade *n.*, *tv.* nakulia
trail *n.* wok voo'o
train *n.* tren
traitor *n.* tooko yoi, yee vehe'eme
tramp *n.* traampa
transparent *adj.* namamachi, navuhti
transport *tv.* hittoha, pu'ate
trap *n.* trampa; *tv.* wite'eria (by netting)
trash *n.* sankoa, sankoawo'oti (~ scattered about)
trash heap *n.* sankoa monti
travel *tv.* vo'o hoa
tread *iv.* woktesime
tree *n.* huya, ouwo
tremble *tv.* bwalwotta (make)
trench *n.* akia
treasure *n.* tesooro
trial *iv.* yeu toiwa (be on ~)
tribe *n.* trivu
trick *tv.* vaita'a
trickling *adv.* silili'iti
trickster *n.* yee vaitatta'a
Trinity *n.* Tiniran
trip *n.* voo hóowame; *iv.* te'ite; *iv.* watakte (prepare for)
troops *n.* wokleom
trot *iv.* laplapti
trousers *n.* saweam
truck *n.* trooke
trucker *n.* hihittohame
trumpet *n.* trompeta

trunk *n.* kuta naawa (tree), ota (tree), petaka (chest), trank (automobile)

trust *n.* sualwachi; *tv.* yoem eiya

truth *n.* lutu'uria

try *tv.* hiovila

try on *tv.* ama hiove, hiovila

try out *tv.* hiovila (machine, vehicle, appliance)

tub *n.* tiina

tube *n.* tuuva

Tucson *n.* Tuson

Tuesday *n.* Maates

tuft *n.* mo'a (seed head)

tumble *iv.* ro'akte

tumbleweed *n.* mo'oko, huya ro'akteme

tune *n.* soonim, kaminaroa sonim (processional); *iv.* kutte

tuning *n.* kusaroa, kuttiwame, partiyo (normal), kampania (after
          midnight)

turkey *n.* chiiwi, koovo'e

turn *n.* masatana (right); *iv.* bwelta (revolve); *tv.* kuakta, kuuria, kowia
          (crank, handle), kuvia (screw in)

turn around *iv.* tatawiilo

turn off *tv.* kecha (machine), tuucha (electricity, light), tuuke (lights,
          electricity)

turn on *tv.* taya (lights, electricity), naatetua (machine)

turn upside down *tv.* movekta

turned *adj.* kuaktala; *iv.* kuviari

turned over *iv.* veakti

turtle *n.* mahau (freshwater), moosen (sea), wa'ivil (small ~ *sp.*)

tweezers *n.* piinsam

twelve *num.* wohmamni ama woi

twenty *num.* senu taka

twice *adv.* woisia, woosa

twig *n.* huya vakulia

twinkle *iv.* kalalipapati aane

twinkling *iv.* kulalipapati (with aane)

twins *n.* wo'olim, wo'orim

twist *iv.* vi'ite, ravikte (ankle); *tv.* chovikukta, kuvia, vi'ita

twisted *adj.* chakkui, vi'iti (wound around)

two *num.* woi

U

ugly *adj.* hunera

umbilical cord *n.* siiku

umbrella *n.* sombriya

unable *iv.* ka aawe, ka yeeka (to move)

unbearable *iv.* ka pasaroa machi

uncaring *iv.* ka yee nake, a eau hoa, ka yee tu'ure

uncle *n.* tio (*gen.*), sama'i (older paternal), mamai (younger paternal), kumui (older maternal), taata (younger maternal), haavi (oldest maternal)

uncomfortable *iv.* suatea

unconvinced *tv.* ka'ayu'e

uncooked *adj.* ka bwasi

uncover *tv.* hinepo

under *adv.* ko'om(i); *postp.* vetuku

underground *n.* bwiata vétuku

undershirt *n.* kamisetam

understand *tv.* hikka

understanding *n.* mammattewame

underwater *adv.* vaa vétuku

underwear *n.* tosa'a saweam, wahu supem, waiwa supem, choorim (men's)

undesirable *adv.* haiti

undo *tv.* vahta

undress *iv.* supeyecha, bwai yecha

uneasy *adj.* suatea

unemployed *iv.* ka tekipanoa

unending *iv.* ka nuklak

uneven *adj.* horoi, ka nanawichi, rumui; *adv.* ka nareempani (in length)

unexpected *n.* kulupti wéeme (something that is ~)

unexpectedly *adv.* kulupti weye

unfamiliar *n.* chiktula (~ place); *iv.* ka hunakiachi (be ~)

ungrateful *iv.* kaita vaesae

unhappy *adj.* ka allea

unhealthy adj ko'oko'era

unheard of hakun vennikut (in ~ places)

unhurried *iv.* ka vamvamse

uniformly *adv.* nana'anasi (in the same way)

United States *n.* Riingo Bwia

unity *n.* nau eewame

universe *n.* pala ania

university *n.* universita

unkempt *adv.* sanchina

unkind *iv.* au i'a

unknown *iv.* ka ta'ewak (be ~)

unlock *tv.* yavemmea etapo

unlucky *adj.* ka suertek

unmarried *iv.* ka chupia, ka huvek (man), ka kunak (woman)

unnatural *n.* chupiari (~ person or animal)

unobtainable *iv.* ka nu'utu

unopenable *tv.* ka'ayu'e

unpaid *iv.* ka vehetuari
unreliable *iv.* ka yoem eiya maachi (be ~)
unroll *iv.* veakte; *tv.* veakta, wi'okta
unsociable *adj.* kuhtiachi
unsteady *iv.* ka yanti maachi
untie *tv.* vutta, woita
untied *adj.* vutti; *iv.* vutte (get)
until *conj.* ahta, tahti(a)
untold *n.* ka teuwawame
unused *adj.* ka sauwari
unusual *iv.* hachin maachi
unveil *tv.* hinepo
uphill *adv.* hikau vicha
upright *adj.* tenela
upriver *adv.* taiwo
uproot *iv.* nawa kookta, nawapona
upset *iv.* ka allea (be unhappy); *tv.* movekta
upside down *adj.* movekti; *adv.* movela
upset *iv.* omte
upside-down *adv.* atula
urinate *iv.* siise
urine *n.* siisi; *iv.* sishuva (smell like ~)
urinary *iv.* sihpattila (have ~ trouble)
us *pn.* itom
use *n.* sauwawame; *tv.* sauwa
use up *tv.* lu'uta, tehale; lu'utaria *dv.* use up someone else's resources
used *n.* moeram (~ items); *adj.* sauwari
used to *iv.* hoiwala, hoiwa (get ~ ~)
useful *adj.* tu'i'ean
useless *iv.* kaita vetchi'ivo tu'i
usual *adv.* ka nappat (as ~); *n.* hohowame (customary), hiva yu vitwame
        (common thing or person)
usually *adv.* (indicated by reduplication of verb; see Appendix A)

V

vacation *n.* vakasión
vaccine *n.* vakuuna
vacillate *iv.* amae yeehte (change mind often; *pl.* amae hohote)
vagina *n.* chumim
vague *iv.* ka hunakiachi
vale of tears *n.* bwan bwia
valley *n.* vaaye
valuable *iv.* vehe'e (be ~)
valve *n.* varvula

vanish *iv.* kakkavetu (~ without trace)
vapor *n.* haawa
variety *iv.* ka nanau maachi, ka nanau aane
varnish *n.* varnis; *tv.* varnistua
vegetable *n.* siari bwa'ame, verduura
vehicle *n.* kaaro, maakina
veil *n.* veelom
vein *n.* ohvo wikia; *adv.* senu wéeme (in another vein)
venom *n.* hoyo
verdant *iv.* sialapti
very *adv.* si, tu'isi
vespers *n.* vihpa
veternarian *n.* yoamwa lootor
Vicam *n.* Vikam
victor *n.* yo'okame
videotape *n.* vidiotepim
view *n.* vitwame
village *n.* ho'ara, pueplo
village cross *n.* kus yo'owe
vine *n.* wiroa
vinorama *n.* kuka (tree)
violate *tv.* ka yee yo'ore (sexually)
violin *n.* laaven
violinist *n.* laveleo
Virgin Mary *n.* Itom Ae
visit *iv.* noite, yeu bwalte; *tv.* yee eteoria (relate news, chat)
visitor *n.* a'avo aneme, noitekame, itou aneme, hoarapo aneme
voice *n.* nokhiawai
volcano *n.* tahikawi
vomit *iv.* visata
vomit *n.* visachia
vow *n.* manda; *iv.* bwania (make), hichupa (fulfill)
vulture *n.* wiiru (turkey), tekoe (white-headed)

W

wag *tv.* kouria
wagon *n.* kareeta
waist *n.* wikosa
wait for *tv.* vovicha
wake *n.* mukila velaroawa, mukila pahko (of child or unmarried person), usi mukila pahko (child's)
wake up *iv.*, *tv.* vusa
walk *iv.* weama, weye (*sg.*); *iv.* kaate, rehte (*pl.*)
walker *n.* andarera (for elderly)

wall *n.* sapti
wallet *n.* viyateera
wand *n.* palma (Matachin)
wander *iv.* sisime (mind)
want *tv.* nake
want *n.* waatiawa; *tv.* waata, waatia
war *n.* nassua, nahsuawa
warm *adj.* suka, sukkai; *iv.* sukawe; *tv.* sukaria
warm up *tv.* yosia
warm yourself *exp.* suka yoene (come in and warm yourself)
warmth *n.* sukawa
warn *tv.* a tehwa
warning *n.* a tehwak
warp *iv.* tante
warped *adj.* tonalai
warrior *n.* nahsuareo
wart *n.* teru'usia
wash *iv.* hipaksia (clothes), vahu'urina (face), vahima (hands), uva (self);
      tv. vaksia
wash *n.* hakia (gully)
wasp *n.* viicha
waste *tv.* am hoa; *interj.* veuti (what a ~)
wasteful *iv.* kaita veutia (be ~)
watch *n.* lelo (wrist)
watch over *tv.* sua
watched *iv.* suawa (be ~)
water *n.* vaa'am; *tv.* vaane (plants), vahi'itua (animals)
water, drink of *exp.* vaa yoene (here, have a drink of water)
water drum *n.* vaa kuvahe
water lily *n.* kapo sewa
waterfall *exp.* vaa'am kom weche
watermelon *n.* sakovai, sakvai
waterspout *n.* namu vakot (marine tornado)
wattles *n.* vu'uchi
wave$_1$ *iv.* hihha'aria (hand); *tv.* kouria, wiuta
wave$_2$ *n.* mareha
wax *n.* bwania
way *adv.* haana (in some ~), ileni(a) (this ~), hunulevena (that ~), tevesi
      (a long way)
way, I'll be on my *exp.* abwe pues ne wéevae
way, that's the *exp.* tevei eak (that's the way s/he is)
we *pn.* itepo, te
weak *n.* nawia (person); *iv.* bwalkimula, nawitu, wakila, ka utte'ak (not
      strong); bwalwotte (feel); ka huuva (odor); ka yeeka (unable to
      move); *tv.* bwalwotta (make)
weaken *tv.* nawite

wear *iv.* kookak (necklace), ko'arek (skirt), -sime (jewelry; *ex.* mapoasime, go wearing a bracelet), supek (shirt, blouse, dress)

wear down *iv.* nasontu

wear out *iv.* mooye

weariness *n.* lottia

weather *n.* tiempo; *iv.* an'a haisa maachi (~ be a certain way)

weave *tv.* hihoa

web *n.* witosa, huvae toosa (spider)

wedding *n.* vooda

wedge *tv.* topakta

Wednesday *n.* Miokoles

week *n.* semaana; semanapo taewaim, days of the week

weekly *adv.* chikti semanapo

weep *iv.* oppoa

weigh *tv.* pesaroa

weight *n.* vettea

weld *tv.* sisivokta nau chu'akta

well$_1$ *interj.* abwe, ala, huntuko, pues

well$_2$ *adv.* alleaka (health); *iv.* hioria, ineete, tu'uria (get)

well$_3$ *n.* pooso (water)

west *adv.* taa'ata kom weche vetana, vaanam

well-behaved *iv.* yanti maachi

wet *adj.* komonla, va'ari; *iv.* komona; *tv.* komonia

wetback *n.* mohao, ho'opo vaari

what *pn.* hita; *interj.* hitaa

whatever 1. *pn.* hita 2. *exp.* (uses a subordinate clause with -o) 3. *adv.* hachin huni (~ it takes)

what if *adv.* hitasu, su

wheat *n.* tiikom

wheel *n.* ruera, voocham (of car)

wheelbarrow *n.* karuucha

wheelchair *n.* siiya rueratame

wheezing *iv.* hokte

when *adv.* hakwo, intok(o)

whenever *adv.* hakwo huni'i

where *adv.* haksa, hakun(i), hakunsa, haksiani, haku'uvo (from ~), hawvicha (~ to)

whether *conj.* (use clause with *conj.* si, if)

which *pn.* haveta, hita

which way *adv.* hausa

while *adv.* chuvala vetchi'ivo (for a while), chuvvalatuko, hu'ubwa, into, hu'ubwasu (in a ~), kulupti weme (once in a ~), yuin chuvva (in a little while longer)

whinje *iv.* veewatia

whip *tv.* vemmucha, vepsu

whiskers *n.* chao voam

whisper *iv.* saasaati noka
whistle *n.* kusia; *iv.* vikue, viute
white *adj.* tosai, tosali, tosari
whiten *tv.* tosaite
whitewash *tv.* tosaite, tosaisa yoka
whitish *adj.* tohsaalai
who *pn.* have
whoever *pm.* have huni'i
wholly *adv.* si'imek
whooping cough *n.* hoktia
whore *n.* antuari
why *adv.* haisaka(i); *conj.* maachea (so ~), huntuksan (that is ~),
    kiali'ikun (that is ~); *interj.* hulen, hunensu (that's ~)
why not *adv.* haisia'ani
why, that is *conj.* hunuensan
wick *n.* meecha (candle)
wicked *adj.* hue'ena
wide *adj.* bwebbweka
widely *adv.* bwekasia
widen *tv.* bwekate
widow *n.* hokoptui
widower *n.* hokoptui
wife *n.* huuvi (man speaking of his), huviwai (in general)
wild *adj.* ka manso (animals), huya (plants); *iv.* hunerasi anwa (be
    uncontrollable)
wild cat *n.* hua miisi
wildflower *n.* kampo sewa (*gen.*)
wilderness *n.* pocho'oku
will -ne (suffix of future tense), *adv.* véa (used for emphasis)
willow *n.* wata (*gen.*), vachomo (seep)
wilt *iv.* choowe
win *tv.* koova, yo'o
win for *dv.* yo'oria
wind *n.* heeka
wind *iv.* totte; *tv.* kuuria
wind around *tv.* vi'ita
windmill *n.* papolote
window *n.* ventaana
windpipe *n.* kusia
windshield *n.* ventaana
windshield wipers *n.* ventanam tutu'uteme
wine *n.* viino, vachi vino (corn ~)
wing *n.* masa
wink *iv.* puusim tutucha
winter *n.* severia, sevemecham (~ months)
wipe *tv.* heota

wiper *n.* ventanam tutu'uteme (windshield ~s)
wisdom *iv.* moreak (have ~, be wise)
witch *n.* yee sisivome
with *postp.* ai (by means of)
withered *adj.* wakila; *iv.* chowia
witness *n.* vitchume
wolf *n.* loovo
woman *n.* hamut, hamyo'ola (old), veeme (young)
womanizer *n.* hamutreo
womb *n.* matriis
wonder *n.* womtiwame; *adv.* clitic =sa (~ if); *iv.* kia pensaroa (ponder,
    think about)
wonderful *iv.* uhyoisi maachi
wondrous *adj.* vutti
won't *interj.* kate
wood *n.* kuta; *iv.* ke'ewe (get)
woodcutter *n.* kutareo, kuta chuktireo
woodpecker *n.* cholloi
wood seller *n.* kutareo
wool *n.* bwaravoa, kavavoa
word *n.* nooki; *adv.* senu wéeme (in other ~s)
work *n.* tekil, seewa (ceremonial), tekipanoawame (act of ~king); *iv.*, *tv.*
    tekipanoa
worker *n.* tekipanoareo
world *n.* an'a
worm *n.* bw'chia
worn out *n.* moera (inanimates)
worry *iv.* ka tu'isi ea
worse *adj.* chea ka tu'isi
worship *n.* muhti; *iv.* muhte
worst *adj.* chea ka tu'iakan
worth *iv.*, *n.* veheria
worthless *iv.* kaita vetchi'ivo tu'i
would *suf.* -'ean (with clause with si, if)
wound *n.* kuchi suaripo (knife ~), muuripo (shot ~), susukipo (scratch ~);
    tv. ko'okosi a hoa
woven *adj.* hiho'ori
wrap *tv.* hisuma, vihta
wrapped *adj.* hisumai
wren *n.* mo'el, vaewaakas (cactus)
wring *tv.* piike, hipi'ike, pipi'ike
wrinkled *adj.* chookinai, choori
wrist *n.* mamam tottotte'epo
write *tv.* hiohte
writer *n.* hiohteme
writing *n.* hiohtei

wrong *iv.* aula; *n.* ta'abwi (~ one)
wrong, nothing is *exp.* kaachin maachi
wrong, what's *exp.* haisempaula

Y

Y-shaped *adj.* takalai
Yaqui River *n.* Hiak Vatwe
yard *n.* pa'aria, teevat (area)
yawn *iv.* wa'akte
year *n.* wasuktia; *adv.* iniavu (last ~); *iv.* wasukte (become a ~)
yearly *adv.* chikti wasuktiapo
years, for *adv.* wasuwasukteka
yeast *n.* revarua
yell *iv.* chae
yellow *adj.* sawai; *tv.* sawaite (make ~)
yelp *iv.* ya'e'etia
yes *interj.* heewi
yesterday *adv.* tuuka, vat tuuka (day before), tuuka ketwo (morning)
yet *adv.* kee (not ~)
Yoeme *n.* Hiaki, Yoem noki (language); *iv.* Yoem noka (speak)
Yoeme Country *n.* Hiakim
Yoeme River *n.* Hiak Vatwe
yoke *n.* sawaika kavampo ankame (egg), wihhu'utiria (for animals)
you *pn.* empo (*sg.*; *sg. obj.* enchi), em (*pl.*; *pl. obj.*)
young *n.* nuhmeela (~ man), naaka (~ woman), uusira (youth, ~ people)
your *pn.* emo
yourself *pn.* emo
youth *n.* nuhmeela (young man; *syn.* hu'ubwa yo'otu), naaka (young
        woman; *syn.* veeme), uusira (young people)
Yuma *n.* Yuuma

Z

zero *pn.* kaita
zipper *n.* siper
zonked *iv.* sutti kochok (be ~)
zoo *n.* yoawata hippwa'apo

APPENDIX A: YOEME ALPHABET AND SPELLING

The Alphabet and Alphabetical Order

Letter	Yoeme Key Word	English
'	o'ou (man)	oh-oh
a	am (them)	father
bw	bwa'ame (food)	subway
ch	choki (star)	search
e	eta (close)	met
h	hinu (buy)	hat
i	ili (small)	machine
k	kari (house)	ski
l	lelo (clock)	let
m	maaso (deer)	make
n	nohim (tamales)	no
o	ota (bone)	wrote
p	pahko (ceremony)	spin
r	rumui (uneven)	room
s	siki (red)	so
t	tenku (dream)	stay
u	tu'i (good)	suit
v	vaa'am (water)	very
w	woi (two)	way
y	yeka (nose)	yes

The following letters are also found in loanwords borrowed from Spanish and English: **b**, **d**, **f**, **g**. These letter follow their usual order in the alphabet.

Note that the glottal stop (written as an apostrophe /'/) is the first letter of the alphabet. This means that the word **aa** "can/able" comes after **a'e** "well", and the **ae** "mother" come after **aa**.

The consonants sound approximately as in the English examples above. Note, however, that the puff of air after English /p/, /t/, and /k/ (as in p<u>ut</u>, <u>t</u>a<u>ke</u>, and <u>k</u>i<u>tchen</u>) is absent when Yoeme /p/, /t/ and /k/ are made. Note that /l/ and /r/ in Yoeme may have symbolic values: /l/ is used to give a positive or affectionate sense, while 'r' may occur in the same word to give a derogative sense (for example, **chukuli** "black" and **chukuri** "black"). Only the consonants /bw/ and /'/ will cause a speaker of Spanish or English much trouble; a little practice will readily take care of any difficulty.

a'e	*interj.*	ay, well
aa	*adv.*	can, be able
ae	n.	mother

283

Note that long vowels (spelled as two vowels as in **aa** "can") come after the short vowels (**a** "her/him/it" precedes **aa** "can").

Sound Symbolism With /l/ and /r/

The consonants /r/ and /l/ are in a symbolic relationship (**sound symbolic**). The same word may have either /r/ or /l/ is variant forms.

chukuli   black (*aff.*)
chukuri   black (*derog.*)

Both of these words mean "black": **chukuli** means "black" but also means that the speaker has an affectionate feeling about the item being described as black; the abbreviation *aff.* stands for "affectionate." The form **chukuri** means "black," but indicates that the speaker has a derogative feeling about the item described; the abbreviation is *derog.*

The noun suffix -**reo** (-**leo**), meaning "one who does," is a frequent item where one encounters this sound symbolism. Another is the word **tu'ure** (**tu'ule**) which means "to like." The words for the colors are another frequent place where this sound symbolism is used. One suffix that always has /l/ is the suffix that makes names familiar, -**lai** (see "Nouns" in Appendix C).

Sound Symbolism With /w/ and /g/

The borrowed consonant /g/ may be substituted for the native consonant /w/. This is particularly frequent in Sonora; it gives the feeling of "sounding more Mexican."

Goi go'i go'olim gokim go'oke.

Two coyote twins are scratching (their) legs.

In this tongue twister, the initial consonant is /w/ in ordinary speech.

Woi wo'i wo'olim wokim wo'oke.

Note that the /l/ (affectionate) is used in the word **wo'olim** ("twins") instead of the form with /r/.

Vowels

The vowels sound much as they do in Spanish. Yoeme vowels may be either short or long in duration. The long vowels are simply written with a double vowel.

a	her/him/it
aa	can, be able
hekam	canopy
heeka	wind
vika	arrowhead
viika	rot
kova	head
koova	win
huha	pass gas
huuha	bite, sting

As you can see, the difference between a long and short vowel can make a difference in meaning. It is therefore important to pay attention to vowel length when writing, reading or speaking Yoeme.

Length and Shortening

A long vowel in the first member of a compound shortens, although long vowels in the second member of compounds remain.

choonim	head hair
chonim vutta	let down one's hair
wooki	foot, toe
wok sutum	toenail

In two-syllable words used as the first members of compounds, the second vowel drops. Note, too, that when this happens, /w/ becomes /u/.

kawi	mountain
kau mochik	mountain tortoise
kau siiva	cliff

Both members of a compound receive stress, and so they are written as separate words.

Consonants can also be long in Yoeme. This always occurs in the middle of the word.

hita	something
hitta	set fire to
véeva	chase out
vevva	usually chases out

Because many verbs can double their second consonant (as in the second example above), every Yoeme consonant may occur double.

Diphthongs

Yoeme may also have combinations of vowels. Such combinations are called diphthongs. Every possible combination occur in native Yoeme words except /uo/.

ae	mother
ainam	flour
nao	corn cob
au	herself/himself
ean	should
heitu	I don't know
neo'okai	mockingbird
euse	hide one's self
hiapsi	heart, soul
piesapo	over and over
hiokot	pitifully
riute	be fractured
voa	fur
voe	bark (dog)
rovoi	round headed
ousei	mountain lion
pua	to pick crops
hunuen	thus
yuin	a lot, much
uo	(lacking)

The combination /ie/ is rare.

Reduplication

Verbs and adjectives in Yoeme double (reduplicate) all or part of their first syllable. The most common pattern, called primary reduplication, is to copy the first consonant and vowel of the word at the front of the word. Primary reduplication of a verb indicates habitual action ("usually").

If the first vowel is long, the copy vowel is short.

vaane	irrigate
vavane	usually irrigates
vusa	awaken
vuvusa	usually awakens

If there is a consonant cluster in the middle of the word, then the copy will retain a long vowel. If the first vowel is not long, the second consonant is copied.

vaahte	loosen
vaavahte	usually loosens
vamse	hurry
vamvamse	usually hurries
chepta	jump over
chepchepta	usually jumps over
patta	cover
patpatta	usually covers

Note that if the middle consonant is long, it counts as a consonant cluster. Primary reduplication of verbs indicates habitual action.

If the verb begins with a vowel, the reduplication will begin with a short vowel.

eta	shuts
e'eta	usually shuts
amuse	go hunting
a'amu	usually hunts
eecha	plants
e'echa	usually plants
ivakta	hug someone
i'ivakta	usually hugs

| ontua | salt it |
| o'ontua | usually salts |

| uuse | father a child |
| u'use | usually fathers a child |

When there is a diphthong, the first vowel only copies.

| hia | sounds |
| hihia | usually sounds |

| wiúta | tear it down |
| wiwiúta | usually tears down |

| suale | believe |
| susuale | usually believe |

Sometimes the diphthong is repeated.

| wíuta | wave it |
| wíuwiuta | usually waves it |

| siute | be torn |
| siusiute | be usually torn |

There are three groups of verbs in Yoeme that have special reduplicated forms. The first of these drops a final syllable -ya in the reduplicated form. These verbs are mostly transitive.

| chaya | tether it |
| chatcha | usually tethers |

| ko'omamaya | knock it down |
| ko'omamama | usually knocks it down |

| maya | toss it, hurl it |
| mama | usually tosses |

If the verb contains the thematic suffix -k- (which always occurs with another suffix, usually -ta or -te), everything before the -k- is copied in the reduplication.

| chokinakta | smash |
| chokinakinakta | usually smashes |

| kohakte | revolve |
| kohakohakte | usually revolves |

tuvukte	leap
tuvutuvukte	usually leaps
chu'akta	glue it
chu'achu'akte	usually glues it
musukte	bow one's head
musumusukte	usually bows head

The third group of verbs with unusual reduplicated forms doubles the first vowel in the copied syllable. These verbs may be either transitive or intransitive.

wokte	put on pants
wookte	usually puts on pants
wo'ote	be spilled, strewn
woowo'ote	usually be spilled
vahte	loosen it
vaavahta	usually loosens it

Compare the first example above with the verb **wokte** 'track one/it', which has the reduplicated form **wokwokte**.

Secondary Reduplication

The second consonant of verbs may also be doubled; this is called secondary reduplication.

bwiika	sing
bwibbwika	sing from time to time
teéka	lay it across
tetteka	in the process of laying across
vahume	swim
vavvahuma	swim occasionally
wohana	dodge it
wohanna	dodging it
yena	smoke (tobacco)
yeyyena	have an occasional smoke

Secondary reduplication either has a distributive meaning ('from time to time'), as in the first example, or a progressive meaning ('in the process of doing'), as in the second. Note that if there is a long vowel in unreduplicated form of a word, that it does not appear in the secondary reduplication, suggesting a constraint on length. In the last pair of examples above, note that the second consonant is doubled, not the first; this occurs sporadically.

Reduplications With Adjectives

With adjectives, primary reduplication indicates plural.

teeve	tall
teteve	tall (*pl.*)

Not all adjectives have a plural form, and some of them have irregular plural forms (**bwe'u** "big" has the plural **bweere**, for example).

Stress and Homophones

In Yoeme, stress is normally on the first long vowel of a word. If there is no long vowel, it is on the first short vowel.

yuma	reach a point in time
yuuma	to overpower

Note that if there is a long vowel, that stress is normally on the second vowel of the long vowel. This pattern also occurs in loanwords.

maákina	car (*Spanish* <u>maquina</u>)
kaáro	car (English <u>car</u>)

tooro	bull (*Sp.* <u>toro</u>)
peloota	to play ball (*Sp.* <u>pelota</u>)
baás	bus (Eng. <u>bus</u>)

Note that the normal stress on long vowels occurs in loanwords from both English and Spanish.

There are several pairs of words that have a long vowels with a difference of stress on long vowels, diphthongs and short vowels. The following list is complete.

ánia	to help
anía	world
bwánia	to pray
bwanía	wax
bwíchia	worm
bwichía	smoke
hávoi	miss out on
havói	uncle
húvahe	spider
huváhe	tree species
káate	to build
kaáte	to travel
kíimu	to attack
kiímu	to enter
pópona	be beating
popóna	uproot
téeka	sky
teéka	lay it across
váchia	seed
vachía	go ahead
véa	then
veá	skin
véeva	chase out
veéva	to hit
wáate	thick
waáte	some
wíuta	wave
wiúta	tear down, demolish
yóoko	spotted
yoóko	tomorrow

There are very few of these pairs in Yoeme, and native speakers are not aware of them until they are pointed out. They have arisen in Yoeme due to varying historical factors. It necessary to distinguish between these words by writing an accent mark for the stress, as in Spanish **si** "yes" and **si** "if". It is not necessary, however, to mark stress in the rest of Yoeme words. The word with the first accent mark precedes the other; for example, **ánia** "world" comes before **anía** "help."

In Yoeme, there are also homophones (words that sound exactly alike, but have different meanings and historical origins).

kia_1	only, just
kia_2	delicious
kia_3	fit into
$kama_1$	squash
$kama_2$	cayman (reptile)

Most languages have a few homophones, and these are usually indicated in a dictionary by putting small numbers (subscripts) below each main entry.

The following is a near exhaustive list of the homonyms in Yoeme.

ae	of him/her/it
ae	mother
ai	with (by means of)
ai	wow!
au	toward him/her/it
au	by one's self
awi	fat, obese
awi	to her/him/it
bwan	indeed
bwan	weeping
ea	of you (singular)
ea	think
hiva	here!
hiva	only, just
hiva	always
hoa	do, make
hoa	place them

huiwa	sense a premonition
huiwa	arrow
kia	only, just
kia	delicious
kia	fit into
kiale	prefer
kiale	you just
kovanao	governor
kovanao	pomegranite
kusi	loud
kusi	acorns (combining form)
kusim	acorns
kusim	loudly
ma	let's
ma	mom
maala	mother
maala	daughter (male speaker)
Maayo	May
Maayo	Mayo
-me	one who
-me	de-
o	oh, yes
o	or
peeso	prisoner
peeso	dollar
-po	in, at
-po	un-
si	very
si	if
siiva	carve
siiva	cliff

sita	young
sita	sprinkle it
sua	kill them
sua	care for
-te	cause
-te	intransitive suffix
tea	quotative particle
tea	find it
=tia	variant of quotative particle
-tia	adverb suffix
-tia	cause
tia	aunt
-vae	want to
vae	by means of water
vai	three (combining form)
vai	water (combining form)
vai	swell (combining form)
vai	fresh, cool (combining form)
-vat	water (combining form)
vat	foremost
vesa	okay for now
vesa	already
vicha	toward
vicha	see it
vittua	show
vittua	send
-wa	passive suffix
-wa	possessive suffix
wai	younger sibling (female speaker)
wai	that
wee-	go, walk (combining form)
wee	amaranth (combining form)

wokte	track it
wokte	put on pants
yuuma	capable
Yuuma	Yuma Indian

The synonyms of Yoeme involve both native and borrowed elements.

Combining Forms

There are several things that also may influence spelling in Yoeme. One of these is the existence of combining forms, which are the forms of words to which suffixes are added, or which are used in compounds. Many verbs have special combining forms, and a few nouns do as well.

kawi	mountain
kau mochik	mountain tortoise
yoeme	person
Yoem Nooki	Yoeme language
paanim	bread
pan hoa	make bread
panreo	baker

These examples show the three major characteristics of combining forms: (a) if the first vowel is long, it shortens (a diphthong doesn't shorten); (b) the last vowel (and any following consonants) drop(s); (c) the consonant w̲ may change to -u̲ (as in the first example).

If the word has a glottal stop and a repeat of the first vowel, the glottal and the final vowel drop, and the long vowel is shortened.

| chuu'u | dog |
| chu aso'ola | puppy |

The word *vaa'am* ("water") is an exception; its usual combining form is *vaa* (as in *vaa loovo*, "sea lion").

A final /s/ will change to /h/ in the combining form.

maaso	deer
mahta vitchu	looking at the deer
baas	bus
bahta vitchu	looking at the bus

This type of combining form is only used with nouns when they form objective forms (see the section on "Nouns" in Appendix B).

Verbs have special types of combining forms; see below.

Special Verb Forms

There are four classes of verbs, with the grouping based on the shape of the combining form of the verb. The first group uses the basic ("look up") form of the verb. The second group has a long vowel in the combining form (with stress shifting to the first vowel of the long vowel of the combining form). The third group shifts the stress and copies the vowel. The fourth group shortens the base form, and retains stress on the first vowel. In the following examples, stress is marked on the base form, the combining form, and finally the combining form with the future suffix (-ne) added.

tá'a	know
tá'a-	
tá'a-ne	will know
hívóa	cook
hivóo-	
hivóo-ne	will cook
chupa	finish
chupá'a-	
chupá'a-ne	will finish
vicha	see
vít-	
vít-ne	will see

All suffixes except for the past suffix -k are added to the combining form. In the dictionary, the combining form is listed for every verb in parentheses after the definition, and then the reduplication (if any) is given.

With many intransitive verbs, the combining form ends in -i.

mahe	be scared
mahi-ne	will be scared
lu'ute	be used up
lu'uti-ne	will be used up

There is a small group of verbs whose combining forms change both vowels of the base form to /i/.

ne'e	to fly
ni'i-ne	will fly
ne'e-ka	flew
ye'e to	dance
yi'i-ne	will dance
ye'e-ka	danced

Notice that the vowel in these verbs in the base form is always /e/, and that the second syllable of the base form is a glottal stop and a repetition of the first vowel. These verbs always form their past tense with -ka instead of -ki.

APPENDIX B: YOEME SENTENCE STRUCTURE

The following sketch of the structure of Yoeme is not intended to be complete. It covers the main points, and lists irregular forms. A definitive grammar of Yoeme remains to be written. Technical terms that describe grammar are set in **bold**; their meanings may be found in any standard English dictionary.

The Simple Sentence

Consider the following sentence.

> I am looking at the house.

The Yoeme equivalent is as follows.

Inepo	kari-ta	vitchu.
I	house	looking at

The literal equivalent in English of the Yoeme sentence is "I (am) (the) house looking at", where "the" and "am" are understood.

Notice that the usual word order in the Yoeme simple sentence is SOV (**S**ubject + **O**bject + **V**erb). This contrasts with English, where the basic word order is SVO (Subject + Verb + Object).

Nouns: Subject, Object, and Plural

Words that stand for entities are called **nouns**.

In Yoeme sentences, there may be a do-er (called the **subject**) and a do-ee called the **object**), and an action word (called the **verb**). In Yoeme, nouns have the ending *-t* if they are used as an object. Also, in Yoeme, the object comes before the verb.

> Aapo karit hinuk.   S/he sold the house.

In the sentence above, the **direct object** is *kari* ("house"); the object marker *-t* has been added to it.

If a noun ends in /t/, the form of the object marker is *-ta*.

> Aapo hamutta tu'ule.   He likes the woman.

The common nouns that end in /t/ are given below.

The following nouns have irregular object forms.

kari	house
kaata	(objective)
maaso	deer
mahta	(objective)
baas	bus
bahta	(objective)

There are not many irregular objective forms for nouns in Yoeme.

When nouns are **plural** (more than one), they add the suffix -*m* if they end in a vowel, and they add the suffix -*im* if they end in a consonant.

uusi	child
uusim	children
maaso	deer
maasom	deer
tekil	job
tekilim	jobs
hamut	woman
hamuchim	women

If the final letter of a noun is t̲, it changes to c̲h̲ before the suffix -*im* is added; such nouns commonly include the following.

hamut	woman
teput	flea
vaakot	snake
wiikit	bird

Some nouns always appear in the plural, even if they are singular in meaning: *paanim*, bread; *vaa'am*, water; *choonim*, head hair; *saweam*, pants.

When a plural noun is used as an object in a sentence, it does not add -*ta*. Only the suffix -*(i)m* is used.

Hamut karita vitchu.	The woman is looking at the house.
Hamut karim vitchu.	The woman is looking at the houses.

It is not possible to say * *Hamut karimta vitchu* for "the woman sees the houses." (A star before a sentence means that it would not be correct from the point of view of a native speaker.)

Personal Pronouns

A word that can stand in place of a noun is called a **pronoun**. Consider the following sentence.

Inepo	enchi	vitchu.
I	you	looking at

This means "I am looking at you" in English. In Yoeme, pronouns have forms used as subjects, and forms used as objects (like English *I* and *me*).

inepo, ne	I
nee	me
empo	you (singular)
enchi	you
aapo	he, she, it
a	him, her, it
itepo, te	we
itom	us
em	you (plural)
enchim	you
vempo	they
am	them

It is also possible to indicate "I" and "we" by putting **ne** ("I") or **te** ("we") after the first word in the sentence.

Enchi ne vitchu.	I'm looking at you.
Enchi te vitchu.	We're looking at you.

These are called **subject clitics**, and there are no clitic forms of the other persons.

Demonstrative Pronouns

In all human languages, there are equivalents of "this" and "that", "these" and "those". In Yoeme, the following are the equivalents.

	Subject	Object
this	ii	ika
these	ime	ime
that	u, nu, hunu	uka
those	ume	ume
that yonder	wa	waka
those yonder	wame	wame

These words are used a lot in Yoeme; learn them by putting them on a flash card and drilling them often.

Reflexive Pronouns

In order to express the idea of "self," the following special set of object personal pronouns are used.

ino	myself
emo	yourself
au	herself/himself
ito	ourselves
emo	yourselves
emo	themselves

Inepo ino chuktak.	I cut myself.
Empo emo chuktak.	You cut yourself.
Aapo au chuktak.	S/he cut herself/himself.
Itepo ito chuktak.	We cut ourselves.
Em emo chuktak.	You cut yourselves.
Vempo emo chuktak.	They cut themselves.

The pronoun **emo** is can mean three different things; the subject pronoun disambiguates the intended meaning.

Indirect Objects

In Yoeme, as in English, one of the objects may indicate the goal or recipient of an action. This kind of object in called an **indirect object**.

U o'ou tomit hamutta maka.
The man is giving the woman money.

302

In this example, the **object** that is affected by the action of "giving is the money (**tomit**; the direct object). The recipient of the action of giving is the woman (**hamutta**, the indirect object).

Tense: Present, Past, Future

In English, the suffixed -*ed* is used to indicate that something happened in the past. In Yoeme, the suffix -*k* is used to mark **past tense** (past time).

U o'ou bwa'amta nu'upak.   The man brought food.

The words *shall* and *will* are used to indicate that something happened in the future in English. In Yoeme, the suffix -*ne* is used to mark **future tense** (future time).

U o'ou bwa'amta nu'upane.   The man will bring food.

For some verbs, the suffixes **-k** "past" and **-ne** "future" are added to the basic (present tense) form. For nearly all verbs, the basic form of the verb is used as the form that takes the past tense suffix **-k**.

Past Tense

For most verbs, the suffix **-k** is added to the basic (present tense) form of the verb. The suffix **-kan** is a past tense marker (with adjectives and nouns used as predicate; *var.* -**kan**, -**akan**, -**ekan**, -**ikan**; the allomorph -**kan** is used with adjectives that end in a diphtong, -**akan** to adjectives ending in **i**, -**ekan** to adjectives ending in o **and** u;, -**ikan** to adjectives ending in **a**); contrasts with -**tukan** to indicate change when attached to nouns, and sometimes with adjectives to indicate change of state; *cf.* -**k**, -**tukan** **chookinaikan**, was wrinkled; **hamtiakan**, was broken; **horoikan**, was bumpy/uneven; **kalasolaikan**, was bright; **kiakan**, was sweet; **hatiachiakan**, was enormous; **hochiakan**, was fine; **ilikkaniakan**, was narrow; **kusiakan**, was sweet; **chihtahkoekan**, was slippery; **chiivuekan**, was bitter; **chookoekan**, was salty; **helokoekan**, was gelatinous; **ko'okoekan**, was hot; **kakaikan**, was sweet; **koloroosaikan**, was pink; **Tuuka u plantano ket sialikan; ian u sawai.** Yesterday the banana was still green; now it's yellow. **David lotortukan.** David became a doctor. **David lotorkan.** David was a doctor. **David usitakai ka yantiachiakan.** When David was a boy, he was not well behaved. (*var.* **David usitakai ka yantiachitukan.**) **Aapo aman ma'aritukan.** S/he was buried there (but no longer is). **Aapo aman ma'arikan.** S/he was buried there (and the body still is there). There are three other tenses that may be used in Yoeme.

-n	past progressive ("was verbing")
-suk	perfect ("have/had verbed")
-sula	past habitual

hi'ibwa	is eating
hi'ibwan	was eating
hi'ibwak	ate
hi'ibwasuk	has eaten, had eaten
hi'ibwasula	have finished eating

These past progressive and simple past are added to the basic (look-up) form of the verb. The perfect and past habitual—like the future—are added to the combining form (which may be identical to the basic form; see "Special Verb Forms" in Appendix A). In the case of the verb **hi'ibwa**, the combining form is the same as the present (look-up) form, the form listed as the main entry in the dictionary.

Note that the basic verb form itself has not only a present tense meaning, but a **progressive** one as well.

The past habitual is not encountered frequently.

Inepo huyapo weamsula. I have often wandered in the woods.

The following list of verbs, because of their meaning, have only the **-n** "past progressive" past tense.

cha'aka	be hanging
chikipona	tickle one
chona	punch one
ea	think
eo'otea	be nauseated
he'okte	have the hiccups
hiavihte	breathe
hooka	sit down (plural)
ko'okoe	be sick
mamma	touch
oove	be lazy
ouva	be difficult to do
sevele	feel cold
ta'ewa	be popular
take	dust it
tase	cough
te'ine	moan
to'oka	be lying down (plural)
tu'ure	like it/one
vavasua	soak laundry
vo'oka	be lying down (singular)

| weye | go/walk |
| yoa | shake/rock it |

The following verbs all end in -**k**, which means "having." They take -**an** as their past tense marker.

atte'ak	own it (**atte'akan**)
chichek	drool (**chichekan**)
ho'ak	live, dwell (**ho'akan**)
ko'arek	wear a skirt (**ko'arekan**)
manek	be situated (**manekan**)
tahek	shine (**tahekan**)
teak	be named (**teakan**)

Some verbs have irregular past forms. There are two basic groups. One group adds -**ka** as the past tense marker.

bwa'e	eat (**bwa'aka**)
he'e	drink (**he'eka**)
ke'e	bite (**ke'eka**)
ne'e	fly (**ne'eka**)
nu'e	get it (**nu'uka**)
ye'e	dance (**ye'eka**)

Another group adds -**k**, but changes the second vowel of the basic verb form.

Verb	Past	Gloss
chupe	chupuk	get/find it
koche	kochok	sleep
muhe	muhuk	shoot it
muuke	muukuk	die (singular)
suke	susukuk	scratch one's self
sumia	sumuk	go flat
suume	suumuk	sink (of water)
tuuke	tuukuk	go out (fire)
yuke	ukuk	rain
yuma	yumuk	reach (a point)

Another group of verbs have a variety of irregular past tense forms.

Verb	Past	Gloss
aane	auka	be/do
aane	aayuk	be/do
aawe	a'ayuk	be able

Verb	Past	Gloss
huuva	huuvakan	stink
sabwa'ania	sa'abwaniak	re-injure one
saka	sahak	go out (plural)
siime	siika	go out (singular)
sokituk	sokitula	be temporarily hoarse
weche	wetchuk	fall down

Future Tense

The future tense may also be used to indicate a situation or event which is hypothetical, or to mark a universal truth.

Kuta va'aritaka kaiva veetine.	The stick is wet and won't burn.
Aa ne cheptene.	I can jump.

Verb Combining Forms

Some verbs have special forms to which all suffixes are added, except for the past tense marker -k (which is almost always added to the basic form). These forms are called **combining forms**.

bwa'e	eat
bwa'a-	eat (combining form)
he'e	drink
hi'i-	drink (combining form)

A very few verbs have irregular past tense forms (fewer than twenty). These must be learned as they occur. For example, the past tense forms of the two verbs above are: **bwa'aka** and **he'eka**.

There are four classes of verbs in Yoeme. This grouping is based on the shape of the combining form. The first group uses the basic ("look up") form of the verb as the combining form. The second group has a long vowel in the combining form (with stress shifting to the first vowel of the long vowel of the combining form). The third group shifts the stress and copies the vowel. The fourth group shortens the basic form, and retains stress on the first vowel.

In the following examples, stress is marked on the basic form, the combining forms, and finally in examples of the combining form with the future suffix.

306

tá'a	know
tá'a-	
tá'a-ne	will know
hivoa	cook
hivóo-	
hivóo-ne	will cook
chupa	finish
chupá'a-	
chupá'a-ne	will finish
vicha	see
vit-	
vit-ne	will see

All suffixes except for the past suffix -k are added to the combining form.

With many **intransitive** verbs (verbs that don't have an object; two common examples are "go" and "come"), the combining form ends in -i.

mahe	be scared
mahi-ne	will be scared
lu'ute	be used up
lu'uti-ne	will be used up

There is a small group of verbs whose combining forms change both vowels of the basic form to the letter i, except for the past tense.

ne'e	to fly
ni'i-ne	will fly
ne'e-ka	flew
ye'e to	dance
yi'i-ne	will dance
ye'e-ka	danced

Notice that the vowel of the basic forms of these verbs is always *e*.

Habitual (Reduplicated) Verbs

Verbs in Yoeme can double (**reduplicate**) all or part of their first syllables. The most common way is to copy the first consonant and vowel of the word at the front of the word. If the first vowel is long, the copied vowel is

307

short, and the long vowel is also shortened. These reduplicated verbs mean "usually", and are called the **habitual** verbs forms.

See the appropriate section in Appendix A for details about reduplication in verbs.

Reduplicated Verbs With a Progressive Meaning

Some reduplicated verb forms have a progressive or stative meaning rather than a habitual meaning. The following list is intended as exhaustive.

alilite	be loose
chochona	be hitting someone
hippue	be having, owning
huhu'ubwa	be sniffing
huhupwa	be getting married (man)
kakae	be sweet
kukunwa	be getting married (woman)
mamachi	be seen, appear
mamaka	have one's hands on
momotia	be murmuring
mumuhe	be shooting
nunu'e	be grabbing
pipi'ike	be wringing
poposiwe	be rusting
-sasaka	go along doing (plural)
sasavua	get sudsy
-sisime	go along doing (singular)
sosoko	be rough/scaly
susukuk	scratched
tata	be hot
tutucha	close one's eyes, blink

Adjectives in Simple Sentences

In every language, there are words that describe conditions, such as "new", "hot" and "red". These descriptive words are called **adjectives**. Like nouns in Yoeme, adjectives have plural forms. These are usually made by doubling the first consonant and vowel of the singular form (with any long vowels shortening).

Singular	Plural	Gloss
tu'i	tutu'i	good
moera	momoera	old
va'ari	vava'ari	wet
wakia	wawakia	dry

Some adjective plurals follow this rule, but have a different ending than the singular.

Singular	Plural	Gloss
yoo	yoyo'owe	enchanted
seve	sesevea	cold

Some adjective plurals double the first vowel, or else double the second consonant as part of the reduplication. These may also have additional letters at the end. The following list is intended as exhaustive.

Singular	Plural	Gloss
bwe'u	bweere	big
kia	kikkia	delicious
vemela	veemela	new
ilitchi	illichi	small
tata	tattae	hot
teeve	tetteve	tall, long

There is a variant form of **bwe'u** "big", **bou**; its objective form is irregular (**bo'uk**).

The most common way of using adjectives in Yoeme is in place of a verb, at the end of a sentence. For past tense, one of these suffixes is added to the adjective: -**kan**, -**akan**, -**ekan**, or -**ikan**. For future tense, -*ne* is added.

Tuuka u platano sawaikan.	Yesterday the banana was yellow.
Ian u platano ket sawai.	Now it is still yellow.
Yoóko u platano ka sawaine.	Tomorrow the banana will not be yellow.
Yoóko chukuitune.	Tomorrow it will be black.

In some instances, the past or future forms of adjectives are irregular.

heka'ula, having a nervous tick
heka'une, will be having a nervous tick

chihti, smashed
chihritukan, was smashed

The use of -**tukan** for the past tense of adjectives indicates a change in a condition or state that was true in the past.

U o'ou aman ma'arikan.	The man is buried there.
U o'ou aman ma'aritukan.	The man was buried there.

The second sentence means not only "the man was buried there," but also implies "but no longer is."

Irregular tense forms of adjectives are noted in the dictionary.

If a noun ends in -m, but is singular in meaning (example: livrom, "book" or "books"), an adjective will make the meaning clear.

Ume livrom ka bwe'u.	This book is not big.
Ume livrom ka bweere.	These books are big.

It is the adjective that indicates if singular or plural is intended in these cases.

Indefinite Pronouns: "Who/Someone" and "What/Something"

In all languages, there is an equivalent of "who" and "what." In Yoeme, the word for "who" is **have**, and "what" is **hita**.

Have aman weyek?	Who is standing there?
Have sakvaita bwa'aka?	Who ate the watermelon?
Empo haveta vitchu?	Who are you looking at?
Aapo haveta tomita miikak?	Who did s/he give the money to?
Hitasa mesapo katek?	What is on the table?
Hitasa hunu?	What is s/he buying?
Hitasempo hinuk?	What did you buy?
Aapo hitaa enchi makne?	What will s/he give you?

As in other languages, Yoeme also has an equivalent of "someone" and "something." The Yoeme equivalent for "someone" is **senu**, and the equivalent for "something" is **hita**.

Senu aman weye.	Someone is standing there.
Senu minaita bwa'aka.	Someone ate the melon.
Empo senuk vitchu.	S/he sees someone.
Aapo senuk tomita mikne.	S/he will give money to someone.
Hita mesat katek.	Something is on the table.
Empo hita hinuk.	You bought something.
Aapo hita enchi mikne.	S/he will give you something.

You will come across these words frequently.

No Verb "to be"

In Yoeme, there is no equivalent of the English word "to be."

Joseph is a Deer singer.

The Yoeme equivalent of this sentence is the following.

Hose Maso bwikreo.

U o'ou Maso bwikreo.

The second sentence means "the man is a Deer Singer."
To make this kind of identifying sentence in Yoeme, a second noun or noun phrase is used in place of a verb.
In order to show tense, the suffix -**tu** is used before -**ne** "future" or -**kan** "past" is added.

U uusi bwikreo.	The boy is a singer.
U uusi bwikreotune.	The boy will be a singer.
U uusi bwikreotukan.	The boy was a singer.

Note that this is similar to when an adjective is used in place of a verb (see "Adjective," above).

Expressing Ownership

In Yoeme, there is a way of saying "whose." The word one uses is **haveta**.

Haveta kari?	Whose house is it?
In kari.	My house.
Em kari.	Your house.
A kariwa.	Her/his house.
Itom kari.	Out house.
Enchim kari.	Your house.
Vem kari.	Their house.

When the owner is third person singular (**a**, her/his/its), the suffix -**wa$_2$** must be added to the noun.
The "owned" noun may be plural.

Haveta laapisim?	Whose pencil is it?

In laapisim.	My pencil.
Em laapisim.	Your pencil.
A laapisiwam.	Her/his pencil.
Itom laapisim.	Our pencil.
Enchim laapisim.	Your pencil.
Vem laapisim.	Their pencil.

If the owned noun is one of those that ends in -**m** whether or not it is singular or plural (examples: **livrom**, **vaa'am**), there is no way of telling where the owned noun is singular or plural.

It is also possible to use a second noun as the owner of the possessed noun. The owner is placed before the owned noun, and the owner noun has the objective suffix -**ta**.

U hamutta kari vemela.	The woman's car is new.
Itom kari ventaanam hamtila.	Our house's windows are broken.
Ne in maalata kari vitchuvae.	I want to see my daughter's house.
Empo uka yoemta maakina hinune?	Are you going to buy that person's car?

It is possible to use an adjective before a owned noun.

| Aapo vemela maakinata hippue. | S/he has a new car. |
| Aapo vemelak maakinak. | S/he has a new car. |

The first sentence means "s/he has a new car", and the second one means "s/he has a new car" as well. In the second sentence, the verb **hippue** has been dropped and the verb suffix -**k** "have" substituted. The object marking (marked in the first sentence by -**ta**) shifts to the adjective (the object marker for adjectives is -*k*; do not confuse this with the verb suffix -**k**, "have").

Negative Marking With "not"

In order to make a sentence negative, the word **ka** "not" is put in front of the object or the verb of a simple sentence.

| U o'ou hamutta vitchu. | The man is looking at the woman. |
| U o'ou ka hamutta vitchu. | It is not the woman the man is looking at. |

U o'ou hamutta ka vitchu.   The man is not looking at the woman.

It is also possible to put the word for "not" in front of other parts of the sentence.

Making Commands

In all languages, there are ways of giving commands. In Yoeme, commands may be shown by special suffixes.

Hita teuwa'e.   Say something (singular).

Hita teuwa'em.   Say something (plural).

The suffix -'e is added to a verb for a singular command, and the suffix -'em is added for a plural command. Both are given falling intonation. It is also possible to simply use falling intonation without the suffixes.

Hita teuwa.   Say something.

Negative commands are made by putting the word **kat** in front of a sentence.

Kat hunuen aane.   Don't be bad.

Kat televisionta vivitchu.   Don't watch TV all the time.

There are two particles that may be put at the beginning of a sentence to make negative commands.

Kate pahtelim hi'ibwa.   Don't eat the pie.

Katem pahtelim hi'ibwa.   Don't eat the pie.

Kate is used to make a negative command to a singular person addressed; **katem** is the plural.

One may also make suggestions in Yoeme. The word **ante** or **te** is used where English would you "let's."

Ante pueplowi.	Let's go to town.
Perioriokota te hinune.	Let's buy a newspaper.
Ante vihtammewi.	Let's go to the movies.
Hita te bwa'ean.	Let's get something to eat.

Question Formation

In order to ask a question in Yoeme, the word **haisa** is put at the beginning of a sentence.

U o'ou hamutta vitchu.   The man is looking at the woman.

Haisa u o'ou hamutta vitchu?   Is the man looking at the woman?

It is also possible to use a rising intonation to indicate a question without **haisa**.

U o'ou hamutta vitchu?   Is the man looking at the woman?

There is a short form of the question marker: **=sa**, a clitic that attaches to nouns or pronouns.

I hitasa?   What is this?

Haiki kuchumsa?   How many fish are there?

Em maala su hoa'po katek?   Is your mother at home?

The clitic **=su** may be used with the question marker **haisa**.

**Emesu haisa aane - kave   Is everyone well at your house?
ko'okoe?**

It is possible to form an alternative question by putting the tag **heewi** after a statement.

Empo sakvait tu'ule, heewi?   You like watermelon, don't you?

The clitic **=su** may be used in three ways to form questions. If it is put after the subject or object, it makes a question that means "is it really the case that".

Em maala=su ho'apo katek?   Is you mother in fact at home?

Apo sakvaita=su tu'ule?   Does s/he really like watermelon?

If **=su** is added to a verb, it means "what if?"

Apo sakvait tu'ule=su?   What if s/he like watermelon?

314

Used with a single noun, =**su** means "where?"

David=su?   Where is David?

Used with a single pronoun, =**su** means "what about?"

Vempo su?   And them (what about them)?

All four uses of =**su** to make questions requires that question intonation be used.

It is also possible to ask questions with "who" and "what" (see section on indefinites above).

APPENDIX C: YOEME WORD STRUCTURE

In Yoeme, there are many suffixes that are used to form new words. In some cases, doubling a part of the word (**reduplication**) is used to modify the basic meaning of a word. This appendix surveys the formation of new words (**derivation**) from roots.

For the way words are used in sentences, see Appendix B.

The following **parts of speech** are commented on in this section.

> nouns
> pronouns
> adjectives
> numerals
> verbs
> adverbs
> postpositions
> conjunctions
> particles

Note that Yoeme has **postpositions** instead of prepositions.

Nouns

For the way nouns are used in sentences, see "The Simple Sentence" and "Nouns" in Appendix B.

Yoeme has several suffixes that derive (make) new nouns from other nouns or from other words.

-**lai** suffix added to English names

> **Tivilai**, Stevey
> **Temilai**, Tammy

-**ra** OR -'**a**, "characterized by" (derives nouns from nouns and verbs; a noun this suffix is added to may reduplicate the last vowel; the -r- may be dropped)

> **tiura**, shyness (from **tiiwe**, be shy))
> **kova'ara**, big-headed (from **kova**, head)
>
> **ache'a**, one who laughs a lot (from **aache**, laugh)
> **ete'a**, one with head lice (from **etem**, louse)

-reo OR **-leo**, agentive

> **tekiapanoareo**, worker
> **kuchureo**, fisherman
> **masoreo**, hunter
> **amureo**, hunter
> **hivoleo**, cook
> **ahpareo**, harpist
> **etleo**, farmer
> **panareo**, baker

-ria$_2$ OR **-ia**, "quality of" (forms nouns from adjectives or nouns)

> **severia**, coldness (**seve**, cold)
> **o'owia**, masculinity (**o'ou**, man)

-taim, "the people of ___"

> **Hose intok Huantaim**, Joe and John's people

-taka 1. what kind of (with **hita**) 2. even though

> **hita kuta~**, what kind of wood is it?
> **Yoem~ huni, ka yoem noka**. Even though Yoeme, s/he can't
> speak it.

-wa'apo, "the place where" (usually attaches to a reduplicated verb)

> **hi'ibwawa'apo**, eating place
> **e"eusiwa'apo**, hideout/hiding place
> **kokkowa'apo**, sleeping place
> **hita bwabwasawa'apo**, eating place

Pronouns

The suffixes here all have to do with the formation of **case** forms of pronouns. The most general of these is **-k**; its use is shown above in Appendix B in the sections on "Personal Pronouns" and "Demonstratives." The suffix -'**ik** is a form of **-k** found only with one word.

The suffix **-e** is noteworthy in that it represents a possessive case that comes from an older stage of the language. It is found not only in the singular personal possessive marker, but also in their use with **postpositions**.

-e₂

1. possessive case marker (on demonstratives)
2. with person markers used with **amapo** 'behind' and **vichapo** 'in front of (no motion')

> **ne**, of me
> **ee**, of you
> **ae**, of her/him/it

The plural forms are irregular: **itom, enchim, vempo'im**, the objective forms serving this function).

U hamut ae amapo katek.   The woman is sitting behind her/him.

There is another old case marker that is used for objective case on demonstratives and personal pronouns. This is the suffix **-a**, which is an old Uto-Aztecan case ending. The set of personal pronouns are as follows.

> **nea**, me
> **ea**, you
> **ae**, her/him/it
> **itoa**, us
> **emoa**, you
> **amea**, them

These are used with certain verbs such as **ichakte**, be bored with; **rohikte**, be tired of; **tiiwe**, be ashamed of.

On demonstratives, the objective marker **-a** is added before a postposition may be added to the demonstrative.

> **inia**, this (objective form)

> **Inepo iniau nooka.**
> I talked with this person.

> **Itepo iniamak sahak.**
> We went with this person.

The other cases suffixes for pronouns are **-k**, the general marker of objective case for pronouns and adjectives, and the variant form **-'ik** which is found only in the word **aapo'ik**, "her/him/it."

Adjectives

The general objective case marker for adjectives is **-k**; there is a variant form (**-kan**) used when the adjective is used instead of a verb. For alternate forms of **-kan**, refer to the dictionary entry. For examples and more information, see the section on "Adjectives" in Appendix B.

Adjectives may often be used in place of a noun. For example, "big" can be used as if it were a noun ("the big one"); see the section on "Possession" in Appendix B for examples of this.

There are two distinct adjective suffixes that are spelled the same way. One is added to verbs to make adjectives, while the other is the general adjective marker (and occurs on roots that are already adjectives).

-la$_1$, "already done" (added to verbs; may be used freely)

> **tekipnaoala**, already worked
> **vitla**, already seen
> **nokla**, already has spoken
> **ovewehila**, has gotten lazy

This suffix may be used in sentences as well as to make new words.

> **Haivu ne hamutta ~.**   I have already seen the woman.

The other suffix is found on many basic adjectives; it often has the **resultative -i**, which may be dropped in ordinary speech.

-la$_2$, adjective marker (the i- may be dropped in rapid speech

> **koelai**, round
> **lottila**, tired

On some adjectives, such as **lottila**, the **-i** never appears.
The suffix **-le** may indicate "have the quality of."

> **o'ou**, man
> **oule**, be brave/brave

This suffix has the basic meaning of "consider to be."
Another suffix, **-tula**, means "be amiss", "be wrong."

> **chiktula**, disoriented
> **etetula**, infested with head lice
> **no'otula**, stuttering

This does not appear to be a productive suffix.

A suffix called the **resultative** is added to verbs to produce adjectives. It translates as a past or completed verb in English. There are several forms of this suffix, each of which has a different way of being added.

-**ri** is added to the combining form of a verb

> **ya'ari**, made

-**i** replaces the final vowel of a verb, or is added after a glottal stop

> **hovoa**, get satiated becomes **hovoi**, full
> **hiapsa**, be alive becomes **hiapsi**, life
> **bwasa**, cook it becomes **bwasa'i**, food
> **nenka**, sell becomes **nenki**, thing sold

-**ia** replaces the final vowel of a verb

> **hokte**, cough becomes **hoktia**, whooping cough
> **weche**, fall becomes **wechia**, fallen

There is also another form of the resultative, -**ti**, which is discussed below in the section on verbs.

Numerals

Numerals add the general adverb marker -**sia** or -**we** to produce adverbs.

	Number of Times	Number of Places
woi, two	**woisia**	**woiwe**
vahi, three	**vahisia**	**vahiwe**
naiki, four	**naikisia**	**naikiwe**

These are productive for the lower numerals. For "once," see the English-Yoeme index.

With the lower numerals, one may reduplicate the first syllable to produce the pattern "one by one."

wewepulaika	one by one
wowoika	two by two
vavahika	three by three
nanaikika	four by four
mamamnika	five by five
vuvusanika	six by six

The suffix -**ka** is added.

The following ordinals are the only ones in common use.

ke'esam	first
sewundo	second

Verbs

The primary reduplication of verbs indicates a usual or habitual action. The secondary reduplication of verbs indicates an occasional action. Both types are discussed in Appendix A.

Verbs may have special combining stems. These are also discussed in Appendix A.

Suppletive Verbs

The word **suppletive** refers to a pair of verbs; one verb is used for singular, and one verb is used for plural. There are **stance** (having to do with bodily position), intransitive, and transitive suppletive verb pairs.

Stance Suppletive Verbs

For each stance verb in Yoeme, there is an active and nonactive pair.

vo'oka	be lying down (*sg. subj.*)
to'oka	be lying down (*pl. subj.*)
vo'ote	lie down (*sg. subj.*)
to'ote	lie down (*pl. subj.*)
weyek	be standing up (*sg. subj.*)
ha'abwek	be standing up (*pl. subj.*)
kikte	stand up (*sg. subj.*)
hapte	stand up (*pl. subj.*)
yehte	be sitting down (*sg. subj.*)
hoote	be sitting down (*pl. subj.*)
katek	sit down (*sg. subj.*)
hooka	sit down (*pl. subj.*)

The singular form is used when there is a singular subject: **inepo vo'oka**, I am lying down. The plural verb is used with a plural subject: **itepo to'oka**, we are lying down.

The verb **yeesa** is used instead of **hoote** for the plural verb of "sit down" only in commands.

em hoote	you (*pl.*) are sitting down
yeesa'em	sit down (*pl.*)

This is the only instance; the other stance verbs do not have special command forms.

There are a pair of verbs related to **vo'ote** and **to'ote** ("lie down").

vo'e	spend the night/sleep over (*sg.*)
to'e	spend the night/sleep over (*pl.*
Hakunsa empo vo'e?	Where did you spend the night?
Hakunsa eme to'e?	Where did you sleep last night?

Both verbs have an inherent sense of past tense; the progressive past marker -**n** may be added, but the sentence still means the same thing: **Empo ama vo'en**? Did you sleep over there?

Intransitive Suppletive Verbs

Most intransitive suppletive pairs of verbs have to do with locomotion.

weye	go/walk (*sg. subj.*)
kaáte	go/walk (*pl. subj.*)
vuite	run (*sg. subj.*)
tenne	run (*pl. subj.*)
yepsa	arrive (*sg. subj.*)
yaha	arrive (*pl. subj.*)
kivake	enter (*sg. subj.*)
kiimu	enter (*pl. subj.*)
siime	go/exit/leave (*sg. subj.*)
saka	go/exit/leave (*pl. subj.*)

The other intransitive pairs have fairly common meanings.

weche	fall (*sg. subj.*)
watte	fall (*pl. subj.*)
muuke	die (*sg. subj.*)
koko	die (*pl. subj.*)

"die" Suppletive Verbs

In Yoeme, there is a residue of verbs that use the "die" suppletive pair as the second member of verb-verb compounds. These pairs refer to bodily sensations and emotional states.

vai muuke	be thirsty (*sg. subj.*)
vai koko	be thirsty (*pl. subj.*)
tevai muuke	be starving (*sg. subj.*)
tevai koko	be starving (*pl. subj.*)
naamuke	get drunk/dizzy (*sg. subj.*)
naakoa	get drunk/dizzy (*pl. subj.*)
hiavihmumuke	gasp/be short of breath (*sg. subj.*)
hiavihkoko	gasp/be short of breath (*pl. subj.*)

This subset of intransitive suppletive verbs is small, but fairly frequent.

Transitive Suppletive Verbs

Number in transitive suppletive verbs refers to the object. If the direct object is singular, the singular verb is used. If the direct object is plural, the plural form is used.

yecha	put it
hoa	put them
tovokta	pick it up
hahau	pick them up
toha	carry it
weiya	carry them
kivacha	bring it
kiima	bring them

324

me'a	kill it
sua	kill them

Although the singular forms above are translated with "it" as the object, the singular object can be a living, just as the plural object can be "we" or "you (*pl.*)."

Ume Seerim o'outa me'a.	The Seris killed the man.

Verb Prefixes

Like most Uto-Aztecan languages, Yoeme has few prefixes. An important exception are verb prefixes indicating a generalized object. These include **ne-** ("people") and **te-** ("things"); in Yoeme, both of these appear as relics in only a handful of words.

netane	*tv.* ask for (*cf.* Piman **taani**, ask for)
nesawe	*tv.* command (*cf.* Yoeme **sawe**, order)

tehale	*tv.* use up, finish up
tevote	*tv.* greet

To the latter pair may perhaps be added: **temai**, *tv.* ask.

In place of these general object suffixes, Yoeme (and is close Cahitan relatives, Mayo and Cáhita—as well as the related Opata and Eudeve) uses the prefix **hi-** (from **hita**, something).

poona	*tv.* bong, knock
hipona	*iv.* beat a drum

nanke	*tv.* meet
hinanke	*n.* meeting

chupa	*tv.* finish it
hichupa	*iv.* be finishing up

ma'a	*tv.* bury it/her/him
hima'a	*iv.* be burying

As may be seen, the prefix **hi-** makes transitive verbs intransitive.

Verb Suffixes

Verb suffixes in Yoeme are abundant. For description of the suffixes that indicate how a verb is used in a sentence, see Appendix B, as well as "Passives" in Appendix D.

The suffixes discussed here are **derivational**; they create new verbs from other verbs or from nouns or adjectives.

The first group of suffixes are added to nouns to make new verbs. All three suffixes are productive. The first has two forms. The suffix **-(e)k** "have" drops when the future suffix is added.

-ek, have (added to nouns, replacing final vowel; *pst.* **-ekan**, *fut.* **-ne**)

    karek, have a house (*pst.* **karekan**, *fut.* **karine**)

-k, have (added to nouns; more frequent)

    Apo si uhyoik maso kovak.   He has a beautiful Deer head.

It is also possible to use verbs that mean "have:" **attea'k** and **hippue**. Another suffix, **-tu**, is used in three ways.

1. become
    yoemtu, become a person

2. act as
    ya'uttu, act as a leader

3. be characterized by
    etetu, beginning to have head lice
    ettetu, one who always has head lice

The **-tu** is also used to use nouns and adjectives in place of verbs; see the appropriate sections in Appendix B ("Adjectives," "No Verb to be"). Verbs ending in **-tu** do not change in any way to form a combining form (the same form is used).

The suffix **-te$_1$** ("causative") is added to nouns; verbs derived with this suffix do not vary their shape when other suffixes are added). Verbs ending in **-tu** do not form special combining forms. The suffix has two distinct senses.

1. make
    kari, house
    káate, build

káatene, will build
so'to'i, olla
soto'ote, make pottery
soto'otesuk, has made pottery

2. wear
ko'arim, skirt
ko'a(ri)te, put on a skirt

supem, shirt/blouse
supete, put on a shirt/blouse

For "wear," one uses the suffix -**(e)k**, "have."

ko'arek, be wearing a skirt
supek, be wearing a shirt/blouse lovate

In Yoeme, many verbs have forms that end in /a/, /e/, and /i/. These forms of verbs are common. The forms that end in /a/ are transitive (taking a direct object), the forms end in /e/ are intransitive, and the forms in /i/ are resultative.

kuakta	turn it
kuakte	turn around
kuakti	turned

There are many such instances in the language. The suffix -**ti** is related to the resultative suffixes discussed under "Adjectives" above.

Many of these verbs have -**k** as an intermediate (and meaningless) suffix, as may be seen in the example above. Sometimes the /k/ has softened to an /h/.

-**k**, thematic verb suffix (used with -**ta** transitive, and -**te** intransitive; verbs with this suffix double the two syllables before -**k**- in reduplication;

chokinakta, smash it
chokinakinakta, usually smash it

kohakte, revolve
kohakohakte, usually revolve

The verbs in -**(k)ta** do not change to form combining forms; the verbs in -**(k)te** change the suffix to -**(k)ti**.

Beside the productive -**ta**, -**te**$_2$, and -**ti** (discussed below), there is a rarer -**te**$_3$ which appears in a handful of transitive verbs.

nasonte, ruin it
nawite, weaken someone
nu'ute, set food aside

There are three suffixes that create transitive verbs. One of them is rare (**-ya**), and one is limited to Spanish loanwords (**-oa**).

-oa marks transitive verbs borrowed from Spanish

tekipanoa, work
pasároa, pass/happen

-ya, transitive verb marker (lost in reduplication)

chaya, tether/hang it
chatcha, usually tethers it

ko'omamaya, knock it down
ko'omamama, usually knocks down

The third suffix, **-tua** ("causative"), means "make" or "force." It is added to intransitive and transitive verbs to make new transitive verbs.

koche *iv.* be sleeping
kottua *tv.* put to sleep

hi'ibwa *tv.* eat it
hi'ibwatua *dv.* force feed, make one eat

The suffix **-tua** does not change to form a combining form; the suffixes are added after **-tua**.

There is a suffix called applicative that makes a transitive verb from intransitives; the form of the suffix used for this is **-ia**. The suffix, in the form **-ria**, may be applied to transitive verbs to produce **ditransitive** verbs (ones that take both a **direct object** and an **indirect object**).

tapuna, get full
tapunia, fill it
tapuniaria, fill it for someone

eecha, plant it
etria, plant for someone

Another form of the applicative suffix is **-tia**, which is added to verbs that end in **-te$_2$**.

328

mohte, be rotting
mohtia, cause to disintegrate

pohte, be boiling
pohtia, boil it for someone

Verbs derived with this suffix (**-ia**, **-ria**, **-tia**) do not vary their shape when other suffixes are added.

There are also two rare suffixes which have to do with undoing an action.

-me₂, de-

    eteme, delouse

-po₂, un-

    hinepo, uncover/unveil (**hine**, use it as a cover)
    etapo, open it (**eta**, close it)

Both of these suffixes, like all suffixes having transitive value, do not vary or change when other suffixes are added; there are no special combining forms.

Adverbs

There is a general adverb suffix in Yoeme which corresponds to **-ly** of English. This is **-si(a)** which changes adjectives into adverbs. the final /a/ may be dropped in everyday speech.

    bwe'u, big
    bwe'usi, (immensely)

Tu'isi bwe'usi pahkowak.   It was a grand religious celebration.

A few adverbs end in **-tia**.

    laautia, slowly
    lautia, immediately

The final /a/ may be dropped in speech.

The focus marker =**su** ("really did") on adverbs (especially adverbs of location intensifies the adverb.

che'ewasu, more and more
nausu, really together
komsu, downward

The verb suffix -o ("while/as") is used to derive adverbs of time.

kupteo, in the evening (kupte, be late)
ketwo, in the morning (ketun, still —> ketu- —> ketw-)

The basic adverbs of time are root words: ian, now; tuuka, yesterday,; yo—ko, tomorrow, etc.
The following suffixes create adverbs of place from nouns.

-ku, locative

> pocho'oku, in the wilderness
> kovi'iku, in the corner

-kuni, towards, in the direction of

> pocho'okuni, towards the wilderness
> hakuni, to where
> pa'akuni, toward outside

-napo, near

> karitanapo, near the house
> huyatanapo, near the wilderness

These suffixes do not occur with personal markers, as with postpositions (see immediately below). Note that -napo requires the objective case, so it had an origin as a postposition.

There are also adverb forms of the numerals; see the section on "Numerals" above in this appendix. Note also that nouns used with postpositions have an adverb-like meaning.

Postpositions

In Yoeme, there are postpositions instead of prepositions. This means that they go after the noun the modify; instead of "at (the) house" as in English, one says "(the) house at" in Yoeme.

There are some postpositions that are added directly to nouns as suffixes. There are called **primary postpositions**. There are also a second set of postpositions that are independent words that follow a noun or

330

pronoun (which will be in objective case, or in the case of certain pronoun forms, in a rare possessive case). These are called **secondary postpositions**.

Primary Postpositions

The postpositions that can be added directly to nouns AND pronouns are the following. Some of them have plural forms (that go with plural nouns or pronouns), and some of them have forms that are used only in response. Not every primary postposition has a plural or response form.

-t, 1. on 2. about a certain topic 3. in a period of time (*var.* **-chi** is used in response)

net, on me
et, on you
aet, on her/him/it
itot, on us
emot, on you
amet, on them

kava'it, on horseback

Hunio mechat, in the month of June

Woi livrom mesat hooka.
There are two books on the table.

Apo tomit nooka.
S/he's talking about money.

vo'ochi, on the road (in response to "where?")

Apo vihtammet nooka.
S/he's talking about the movie.

The variant **-chi** is also used with person markers (**nechi**, **echi**, **achi**, **itochi**, **emochi**, **vempo'im mechi**) in response to "where?" The suffix **-met** is the plural form of **-t**, on/about; it is used with plural nouns or pronouns.

To express "with" (by means of"), there are two suffixes; one is singular and one is plural.

-e₁, with/by means of (instrumental; singular)
-mea, with/by means of (used with plurals)

kutae, with a stick

wokimmea weye, go by means of the feet/legs

-mak, with/in the company of (comitatve;, with nouns requires objective case; variant **-make** used in response

> **nemak**, with me
> **emak**, with you
> **aamak**, with her/him/it
> **itomak**, with us
> **enchimmak**, with you
> **amemak**,with them

Huantamak siika.	S/he went with John.
A: Aapo havetamak siika?	**B: Huantamake.**
A: Who did s/he go with?	B: With John.

-pat, in front of, ahead of (with motion)

> **inepat**, ahead of me
> **eepat**, ahead of you
> **aapat**, ahead of her/him/it
> **itopat**, ahead of us
> **emopat**, ahead of you
> **amepat**, ahead of them

Aapo inepat weyen.
S/he was walking ahead of me.

The postposition **-po$_1$** has five distinct uses.

1. in, at
2. from
3. for (an amount)
4. may be used to form a relative clause (the subject of which is in possessive case)
5. from, of a particular substance

> **karipo**, in/at the house

> **Mumum woho'oriapo yeu sakak.**
> Bees came pouring out of the hole.

Aapo kava'ita miil peesopo hinuk.
He bought a horse for a thousand pesos.

Ne ka hu'uneiya haisa em hiapo.
I don't know what you are saying.

U kuta wiko'i kunwopo yaritukan.
The bow was made of desert hackberry.

The personal forms of this postposition (**inepo**, **empo**, etc.) are now used as the subject pronouns.

-tana 1. from 2. alongside of

> **netana**, alongside me
> **eetana**, alongside you
> **aetana**, alongside her/him/it
> **itotana**, alongside of us
> **emotana**, alongside you
> **ametana**, alongside them
>
> **karipo**, from the house/alongside of the house
>
> **iatana**, from/alongside this
>
> **waitana**, from alongside that (*cf.* **vétana**)

The **-u** is a postposition with two distinct uses.

(*var.* **-wi**; when used with nouns, the objective case is required; paradigm: **neu**, **eu**, **au**, **itou**, **emou**, **ameu**);

1. to, toward

> **Aapo hamuttau weamak.**
> S/he walked toward the woman.
>
> **U o'ou kava'it tekileu weweama.**
> The man rides a horse to work.

2. from, when referring to transactions

> **Maria paanim Lupitau hinuk.**
> Mary bought bread from Lupe.
>
> **Aapo kava'ita Hosetau mil peesapo hinuk.**
> He bought the horse from Joe for a thousand dollars.

The variant **-wi** is used in responses.

> **A: Uusim hakunsa sahak?**   **B: Vatwewi.**
> A: Where did the children go?   B: To the river.

Secondary Postpositions

Secondary postpositions are postpositions that do not attach directly to a noun or pronoun. Instead, they follow a noun or personal pronoun in the objective case.

> **karita vena**   like (the) house
>
> **ne vena**   like me
> **e vena**   like you
> **ae vena**   like her/him
> **ito vena**   like us
> **enchim vena**   like you
> **vempo'im vena**   like them

If a secondary postposition follows a demonstrative pronoun, the demonstrative pronoun has the object marker **-a**.

> **ia vena**   like this

Here is a list of the secondary postpositions that follow a noun or pronoun in the objective case.

> **veasi**   behind, after
> **vehe'e**   against
> **vena**   like, as, similar to
> **vepa**   above, on top of
> **vétana**   1. along
>   2. from
> **vetchi'ivo**   1. for, on behalf of
>   2. because of
> **vétuku**   under, below
> **vewit**   next to
> **vichapo**   in front of (moving; *cf.* **-pat**)

There is one secondary postposition that follows pronouns in the possessive case; if a noun follows, it is in the objective case because nouns do not have a special possessive case.

karita amapo	behind the house
in amapo	behind/after me
em amapo	behind/after you
a amapo	behind/after him/her
itom amapo	behind/after us
enchim amapo	behind/after you
vem amapo	behind/after them
i amapo	behind/after this

Another secondary postposition requires that the preceding noun or pronoun have the primary postposition -**u** "to."

karitau vicha	towards the house
neu vicha	towards me
eu vicha	towards you
au vicha	towards her/him
itou vicha	towards us
emou vicha	towards you
ameu vicha	towards them
iau vicha	towards this

APPENDIX D: SENTENCE COMPLEXITY

In Yoeme **sentence complexity** means using a different word order other the SOV (Subject + Object + Verb), or having more than one subject object, or verb. It also refers to combining sentences, or putting one sentence in another sentence.

Related to such complexity is **focus** placed on a single part of a sentence, a topic to which we will turn first.

Focus

The term **focus** refers to focusing attention on a single part of the sentence. In Yoeme, this may be done with a single marker, or by **backing** (putting a subject, object, or adverb) at the back of the sentence. Verbs are not moved in Yoeme.

The focus markers are usually put after the sentence part they mark. The two exceptions are **ka** ("not" discussed under "Negation" in Appendix B), and the intensive markers ("very").

The **intensive** marker **tu'isi** (and its short form **si**) are put in front of the word they intensify.

U parke tu'isi vasok.	The park has lots of grass.
U uusi tui'isi au sua.	The child is very cautious.
Tu'isi bwe'usia pahkowak.	It was very much a ceremony.
Hunera si neu etowa.	They were telling me ugly stories.

The adverb **tua** ("truly") may be put at the beginning of a sentence to focus on the truth of the entire sentence.

Tua ne lotte.	I'm truly exhausted.
Tua ka tu'iakan ta vesa ian tu'i.	It wasn't going too well, but now it's okay.

This may be applied to impersonal situations (as in the last example) or personal situation (as in the first).

The **delimiting** markers =**san** ("however") and =**to** (a"and so") are put after the sentence part they delimit. Both of them point out exceptions.

Ne kaita yuumak in chu'u=san hi'ibwak.
I got nothing, but my dog did eat.

Enchim=to ka ha'avosek?
And so they didn't pay you?

Itom=to ka vehe'etuak.
And us he didn't pay.

The =**san** is a more general marker; =**to** (from **into**, and) appears to be used only with the negative marker and attached to a sentence part that is plural.

The clitic =**su** ("really did") may be attached to adverbs, pronouns, and nouns, especially in song language).

Itom to'osiika, isu yoyo an'a (s.).
It left us, **this** enchanted world.

San Huan San Pasihkota wiko'ita su kottak.
St. John **did** break St. Francis' bow.

Notteka toloko bwiapo komsu siika (s.).
Returning, you **did** go down in the light blue earth.

The **quotative** clitic =**tea** (or its variant =**tia**)is used in direct and indirect quotes.

Vempo ha'ani a'avo katetea.
They say that they are coming.

Backing

Backing usually occurs in Yoeme with the secondary postposition **vetchi'ivo** ("for") to indicate reason or purpose.

Katin sauko seewam tu'isi tu'i taiwechiata vetchi'ivo.
Recall that elderberry flowers are good for fever.

Another common backing construction indicates "whether or not."

Ka ne hu'uneiya si aman katne o no.
I don't know if they're going over there or not.

This is a Hispanic construction, using **si** ("if") ... **o no** ("or not"). It is possible to use simply the **o** ("or") to indicate an alternative; however, the alternative is also backed.

Empo ian haivu simvae o chukula?
Do you want to go now or later.

Passive

The passive suffix -wa$_1$ (future passive -na) may be added to intransitive and transitive verbs to derive intransitives

> **mahtawa**, is being taught
> **mahtawak**, was being taught
> **mahtana**, will be being taught

> **U em uusi chea nuvuhti mahtawa.**
> You child is being taught even more.

> **U uusi tuuka ki'iwak.**
> The child was bitten yesterday.

In English, the passive often has a "by" phrase. In the last example above, it is not possible to mention the **agent** that did the biting (such as "by a dog"). Instead, after saying **uusi tuuka ki'iwak** ("the child was bitten yesterday"), the speaker could add **chu a ke'eka** ("a dog bit her/him").

The passive may also indicate "there is/are" when added to nouns.

> **Tusoneu pahkowa.**
> There is a ceremony in Tucson.

This impersonal use underscores the lack of mentioning an agent in Yoeme passive constructions.

Conjoining

Parts of sentences may be linked (**conjoined**) with the Yoeme equivalents of "and, "or," and "but." This may be by means of conjunctions (separate words) or by means of verb suffixes.

Conjoining With Simple Conjunctions

The most common conjunction in Yoeme is the native word **into** ("and"). It is used in two distinct ways. In the first pattern, two sentences are joined by simply putting them next to each other; the second subject has **into** after it.

Senu huena, senu into tu hiapsek.
One is bad, and one has a good heart (of twins).

In achai bwiikak, in sai into yi'ika.
My father sang, and my older brother danced.

In the second pattern, a second object or verb is added to a simple sentence with **into** being added first.

Apo na'asom hinuka into plaatanom.
She bought oranges and bananas.

Apo ka tua hihi'ibwa into ka hehe'e.
S/he won't eat or drink.

It is also possible to join two nouns or adjectives together.

Em miisi chukuli into tosali.
Your cat is black and white.

Apo paanim into munim bwa'e.
She's eating bread and beans.

In achai Yoi, in ae into Yoeme.
My father is Mexican, and my mother Yoeme.

The other native conjunction is **ta** ("but"). This word is used to join two simple sentences.

Haivu te kat'ean ta hamut ketun lotte.
We should be going but the lady is still tired.

Apo pa'aku ousi tekipanoa ta senu into ove'a.
He is outside working up a storm but the other one is lazy bones.

There is a way of indicating alternatives ("but"). This is with the borrowed word **o**.

In huuvi tahkaene o ne paanim hinune.
My wife will make tortillas or I'll buy bread.

Inepo bwikpea o yi'ipea.
I feel like singing or dancing.

Peo aman wéene o Huan ama wéene.
Peter or John are going over there.

Conjoining With Suffixes

It is also possible in Yoeme to join two sentences with the suffixes.

-ka(i)   1. as, while'
         2. as soon as

-o   1. when
     2. if

Examples of **-ka(i)** follow.

Huyapote nas kaátekai vavu soto'im te teak.
While walking around in the desert, we found pottery.

Kaita hoaka ho'arapo katek.
He is at home doing nothing.

Apo hi'ibwasuka sep kochok.
Having eaten, he immediately fell asleep.

Inepo aman yepsaka sep ne hita bwa'aka.
When I arrived, I had something to eat.

**Ayamansu seewailo, imsu yo sewa tevat tevatchiapo vivichaka
weyeka** (*s.*).
Over there in the flowered, here in the flowered patio, as (you) are
looking, (you) are walking around.

The subjects of simple sentences conjoined by **-kai** may be the same of different; if different, the subject in the sentence to which **-kai** is attached is in the objective case. Also, the final /i/ of the suffix may drop.
It is possible to shift the order of the two sentences.

Apo unna tekipanoaka lottila.
He worked so hard he got tired.

Apo lottila unna tekipanoalatakai.
He worked so hard he is tired.

Ata vehe'etuaneaki bwe'ituk apo ousi tekipanoa.
We will pay him because he is working hard.

Apo ousi tekipanoa bwe'ituk ata vehe'etuavaeka tua.
Because of his working hard, we will pay him.

In the reverse sentence (the second above), the second verb has been made a noun (**tekipanoa-la**, having worked) and is in the objective case; another translation is "having worked hard, he became tired." This use may also translate "in the capacity of"

Hose ko'okoe wechek ketun ya'uttakai.
Joseph became sick while still being a leader.

The process of making adverb into a noun is called **nominalization**, and is discussed below as the last topic in this appendix.
Here are examples of **-o**.

Hunera si neu eteowao u usi ne tahtaka ne chaechaetuak.
They were telling me ugly stories when the child touched me and made me scream.

Inepo tiikom echako, che'a huni tomi'ean.
If I had wheat, I would have more money.

This suffix may also be used idiomatically to mean "whatever you want."

Em ya'avaeo ya'ane.
Do whatever you want.

It is also possible to reverse sentences joined with **-o**.

O'outa aman yepsako itepo sahak.
When the man arrived, we left.

Itepo sahak o'outa aman yepsako.
We left when the man arrived.

The subject of the sentence with **-o** is in objective case.
The clitic **=su** may be used in two ways to conjoin two simple sentences. One way means "as/while."

Aapo hi'ibwaka=su tattek.
As s/he was eating, s/he choked.

Tua vempo hi'ibwavaawau=su aapo yepsak.
As they were about to eat, s/he arrived.

In this usage, **=su** must follow the suffix **-ka(i)** ("as/while") in its form as -**ka**. The other usage means "because."

Aapo=su ka hikkahaka woho'oriapo kom wechek.
It is because s/he did not listen that they fell into the hole.

In this pattern, **=su** is attached to the subject.

Conjoining With Conjunctions

By **conjunctions**, we mean conjunctions (separate words) that conjoin, but a large than one syllable (in distinction to **simple conjunctions** which are monosyllabic).

hunak(o), then

> **Aapo koreo noitek hunak into tiendau noitek.**
> She went to the post office, and then to the store.

bwe'ituk, because

> **Apo hiva yu mo'voek bwe'ituk lovola kovak.**
> He always wears a hat because he is bald.

kiali'ikun, so (that)

> **Im tu'isi tata kiali'ikun vempo sahak.**
> It's hot here so they left.

o'oven, even though/although

> **Ne tomeka o'oven ta ne ka aman siika.**
> Although I have the money, I didn't go there.

hain ... huni('i), even though

> **Apo vinota hihinu hain a vehe'ak huni'i.**
> S/he buys wine, even though it's expensive.

> **Aapo hain ko'okoeka huni aman siika.**
> Even though he was sick, he went anyway.

Complementation

The term **complementation** refers to the joining together of sentences in such a way as one of them translates in English with the word "to" OR a verb with the suffix -**ing**. Two examples show that the two sentences that are joined may have the same or different subjects: "I wanted to go to town" OR "I wanted him to go to town." In the second English example, the subject is in objective case; this is also the case in Yoeme.

This section is mostly concerned with suffixes that are added to a verb to produce in Yoeme the equivalent of complementation in English. The survey here includes suffixes joining simple sentences with single subjects, suffixes that are **impersonal** (have an indefinite entity as the first subject), and suffixes that join simple sentences with two different subjects.

Complements With Same Subject

The following suffixes have may be grouped together on the basis of locomotion, intent, and beginning.

Locomotion
The following suffixes indicate movement.

-**ma**, go along doing

> **Apo aman hi'ibwama**. He is going along eating.

-**nama**, go about doing (*hab.* -**nanama**; final vowel drops if other suffixes follow)

> **iva'anama**, go about cradling in one's arms
> **iva'anamne**, will cradle in one's arms

> **Vempo iva'ananama**.
> They're always cradling (something) in their arms.

-**se**, go to get (singular subject; plural subject is -**vo**)

> **va'achise**, go to get water
> **vatvo**, go to get water

-**sisime**, go along doing (singular subject; plural subject is - **sasaka**

> **hi'ibwasisime**, go along eating
> **hi'ibwasasaka**, go along while eating

Intent
The following suffixes indicate intent.
-**pea**, usually want to (habitual desiderative)

Ketwo ne hita hi'ibwapea.
In the morning I usually feel like eating.

-**roka**, say that one intends to do something)

Maala paanim hinuroka.
Mother said she wants to buy bread.

Hose aavo kom yevihroka.
Joe wants to come down.

-**vaane**, really want to do

ya'avaane, really want to make

-**vae**, desiderative suffix (variants. -**vale**, -**vali**), "want" or "intend" or "be on the verge of"

Pueplou ne simvae.
I want to go to town.

In mala kapata hi'uvae, a bwasavaeka.
My mother is going to pick lamb's quarters for supper.

Have Maso yi'ivae ian tukapo?
Who is going to dance the Deer tonight?

Apo si he'oktivaen.
She was on the verge of hiccups.

This suffix may also indicate a state of affairs with reference to the weather.

An'a haisa machi? What is the weather like?

An'a ka tu'ivae. The weather looks bad.

Beginning
A single same-subject indicates starting.

-**taite**, begin to (inceptive)

yuktaite, begin to rain

Impersonal Complementation

The following two suffixes can create impersonal complements, where the subject is "it" (understood) in the equivalent English sentence.

-'**ean**, if only

> **Aapo hi'osia ta'a'ean.**
> If only s/he could read.

-**machi**, it would be good if

> **Aapo nokmachi.**
> It would be good if s/he would speak.

Complementation With Two Subjects

The following suffixes link two sentences with different subjects. The second subject is in the objective case.

-'**i'a**, want someone to do something

> **Ne a hinu'i'a.**
> S/he wants me to buy it.

> **Ne a bwa'i'a.**
> S/he wants me to eat it.

> **Hamut o'outa siim'i'a.**
> The woman wants the man to leave.

-**le**, consider to be

> **Ka ne enchi yevihmachile.**
> I didn't think you were going to come.)

-**sae**, order, command

> **Maala Tomasta hi'ibwasae.**
> Mother told Tom to eat.

-**vao**, be about to (singular subject; plural subject -**vaawa**)

> **Ne hachihtivaosu ne vevak.**
> As I was about to sneeze, (s/he) hit me.

Vempo hi'ibwavaewasuko yepsak.
As they are getting ready to eat, he arrived.

It is also possible to make two-subject complements with second verbs that are separate words such as: **hu'uneiya** ("know"), **ea** ("think"), **vicha** ("see"), and others. Complements may be also created with the quotative clitic =**tea** (or its variant =**tia**). For examples of these, please consult the dictionary.

Equivalents of English Modal Verbs

There are several different ways in which to express the modal verbs of English in Yoeme.

The Yoeme equivalent of "can" (be able to) is to use the adverb **aa** with a verb in the present tense.

Aapo ka aa weye.
S/he is unable to walk.

Apo aa Hiaknoka.
S/he can speak Yoeme.

The equivalent of "could" (used to be able to) is to use the habitual (reduplicated) form of a verb with the past progressive tense marker **-n**.

Ne aa vuivuiten.
I could run.

To express "could" (providing that), the suffix **-'ean** is used.

Ne tomek aman wée'ean.
If I had the money, I could go over there.

To express "should" (be obligated to) in Yoeme, the clitic =**su** is used with the suffix **-'ean**.

Empo amansu wée'ean.
You should go there.

Vempo=su aman katne, ta ka hunen ea.
They should go there, but they won't.

Aapo=su nok'ean.
S/he should be the one to speak.

To express "will" or "shall," simply use the future tense marker **-ne**; there are many examples of this in the appendices and in the dictionary.

To express "would" (be the case that), the suffixes **-o** and **-'ean** are used.

> **Apo aman wée'ean tomeko.**
> S/he would go there if they had the money.

To express "may" or "might," the adverb **humak** ("perhaps") is used with the future tense.

> **Vempo aman humak katne.**
> They may/might go there.

To express "must" (need to), the adverb **kavaeka** is used.

> **Kavaeka te pueplou noitine.**
> We must go to town.

Nominalization

The term **nominalization** refers to using a verb in place of a noun. The following are nominalizations in English.

> His working all night really saved the day.

> I am not happy about his working all night.

> The dog that you saw bit the little girl.

> I chased the dog that bit the little girl.

In these sentences, there are gerunds (verbs in -ing) and relative clauses.

In Yoeme, a set of verb suffixes is equivalent to both of these English pattern. The set of suffixes varies according to tense.

-me, the one(s) who, -er

> **ániame**, helper(s)

-kame, the one(s) who (verb)-ed

> **ániakame**, the one(s) who helped
> **tekipanoakame**, the one who worked

348

-neme, the one(s) who will

>**an'aneme**, the one(s) who will help

-wame, ing(s)/one(s) being verbed

>**nu'uwame**, things being procured
>**etbwawame**, stolen thing or things

These nominalizations can all be used as objects. The final /e/ of the basic suffix **-me** is lost when the object marker **-ta** is added.

>**Peo kochemta vusak.**
>Peter woke up the one(s) who were sleeping.

>**Ne chuu'uta voemta hikkahak.**
>I heard a dog barking.

>**Ana hu'une'eiyak waka ama tekpanoamta.**
>I found out the one who works there.

>**Uka chuu'uta nee voemta hikkahak.**
>He heard the dog that was barking at me.

>**Aapo hu'uneiya itom vichakamta.**
>He knows the one who saw us.

>**Ana hu'uneiya uka o'outa aapata ponnemta.**
>I know the man who will play the harp.

>**Aapo vepsuwamta vena.**
>He looks like he's been beaten up.

In these examples, the nominalizations is put after the main sentence if it has a tense marker (**-ka-**, past; **-ne-**, future) or passive marker (**-wa-**), or if there are nouns or pronoun that go with the nominalized verb.

There is another set of suffixes that nominalize verbs that make nominalizations that are always objects and which go in the middle of the sentence. The subject of **-'u** is in the possessive case (for pronouns; objective case for nouns).

-'u, the one which (present)

>**Chuu'u em vicha'u Suzi ti teak.**
>The dog that you're looking at is called Suzi.

Chuu'u yee kekeme em vicha'u Suzi ti teak.
You're looking at Suzi, the dog that bites.

-ka'u, that which (in the past)

>**in bwaka'u**, what I ate
>**in tenkuka'u**, what I dreamed

>**Empo uka karita em hinuka'u tu'ure**.
>You fixed up that house that you bought.

>**U kuta wiko'i u ili o'outa bwe'u wikitat me'aka'u kunwopo yaritukan**.
>The bow that the little boy used to kill the Big Bird was made of desert hackberry.

-ne'u, that which (in the future)

>**Yoko em vitne'u uhyoine**.
>What you will see tomorrow will be beautiful.

-wa'u, that which is (passive)

>**U tukapo vitwa'u yokoriapo etehona**.
>That which is seen at night will be discussed the next morning.

The verb with **-'u** may be used to form relative clauses.

>**Apo hu'uneiya haveeta a vichaka'u**.
>He₁ knows the one who he₁ saw.

>**Apo hu'uneiya haveeta apo'ik vichaka'u**.
>He₁ knows the one who he₂ saw.

>**Aapo hu'unea itom vichaka'u**.
>He knows the one who we saw.

>**Ne ka hu'unea hita em teuwa'u**.
>I don't know what you're saying.

>**Empo hu'unea hita em teuwaka'u**?
>Do you know what you said?

In this usage of **-'u**, the verb with the nominalizing suffix is at the end of the sentence.

It is also possible to make a relative clause with the postposition -**po** ("at, in").

Ne hu'uneiya hita in ya'anepo.
I know what I will do.

The subject of the relative clause is marked as a possessive; **in** ("my") is used as the subject in the second sentence.